Using JavaWorkshop

Que®

Using Java Workshop

Written by Clayton Walnum

Michael Desmond • John Gordon • Gerald Honeycutt
David Johnson • Brady Merkel • Ken Poore • Bob Voss

Using Java Workshop

Library of Congress Catalog No.: 96-09007-4

ISBN: 0-7897-0900-7

98 97 96 3 2 1

Interpretation of the printing code: the rightmost double-digit number is the year of the book's printing; the rightmost single-digit number is the number of the book's printing. For example, a printing code of 96-1 shows that the first printing of the book occurred in 1996.

Screen reproductions in this book were created using Collage Plus from Inner Media, Inc., Hollis, NH.

Credits

PRESIDENT
Roland Elgey

PUBLISHER
Joseph B. Wikert

ACQUISTIONS MANAGER
Cheryl D. Willougby

ACQUISITIONS EDITOR
Stephanie Gould

EDITORIAL SERVICES DIRECTOR
Elizabeth Keaffaber

MANAGING EDITOR
Sandy Doell

DIRECTOR OF MARKETING
Lynn E. Zingraf

PUBLISHING MANAGER
Jim Minatel

PRODUCT DEVELOPMENT SPECIALIST
Benjamin Milstead

PRODUCTION EDITOR
Noelle Gasco

COPY EDITOR
Sydney Jones

ASSISTANT PRODUCT MARKETING MANAGER
Kim Margolius

TECHNICAL EDITOR
Matthew Brown

TECNICAL SPECIALIST
Nadeem Muhammad

ACQUISTIONS COORDINATOR
Jane Brownlow

OPERATIONS COORDINATOR
Patricia J. Brooks

EDITORIAL ASSISTANT
Andrea Duvall

BOOK DESIGNER
Ruth Harvey

COVER DESIGNER
Dan Armstrong

PRODUCTION TEAM
Jason Carr
Bryan Flores
Staci Somers
Kelly Warner

INDEXER
Andrew McDaniel

Composed in *Century Old Style* and *Franklin Gothic* by Que Corporation.

About the Author

Clayton Walnum, who has a degree in Computer Science, has been writing about computers for almost 15 years and has published hundreds of articles in major computer publications. He is also the author of over 25 books, which cover such diverse topics as programming, computer gaming, and application programs. His most recent book is *Windows 95 Game SDK Strategy Guide,* also published by Que. His other titles include the award-winning *Building Windows 95 Applications with Visual Basic* (Que), *3-D Graphics Programming with OpenGL* (Que), *Borland C++ 4.x Tips, Tricks, and Traps* (Que), *Turbo C++ for Rookies* (Que), *Dungeons of Discovery* (Que), *PC Picasso: A Child's Computer Drawing Kit* (Sams), *Powermonger: The Official Strategy Guide* (Prima), *DataMania: A Child's Computer Organizer* (Alpha Kids), *Adventures in Artificial Life* (Que), and *C-manship Complete* (Taylor Ridge Books). Mr. Walnum lives in Connecticut with his wife Lynn and their four children, Christopher, Justin, Stephen, and Caitlynn.

To my wife, Lynn.

We'd Like to Hear from You!

As part of our continuing effort to produce books of the highest possible quality, Que would like to hear your comments. To stay competitive, we really want you, as a computer book reader and user, to let us know what you like or dislike most about this book or other Que products.

You can mail comments, ideas, or suggestions for improving future editions to the address below, or send us a fax at (317) 581-4663. For the online inclined, Macmillan Computer Publishing has a forum on CompuServe (type **GO QUEBOOKS** at any prompt) through which our staff and authors are available for questions and comments. The address of our Internet site is **http://www.mcp.com** (World Wide Web).

In addition to exploring our forum, please feel free to contact me personally to discuss your opinions of this book: I'm **102121,1324** on CompuServe, and I'm **bmilstead@que.mcp.com** on the Internet.

Thanks in advance[md]your comments will help us to continue publishing the best books available on computer topics in today's market.

Ben Milstead
Product Director
Que Corporation
201 W. 103rd Street
Indianapolis, Indiana 46290
USA

Contents at a Glance

Table of Contents

Introduction

The Internet is growing by leaps and bounds. It won't be too long before you'll be able to contact just about anyone online—not only your friends and acquaintances, but also every major company in the country. This incredible growth is the pathway to opportunity. Everybody who's anybody in the world of telecommunications is looking for ways to enhance the Internet's online experience. One company that has scored a big hit on the Internet is Sun Microsystems, which recently released an unusual programming language called Java. Once people got their hands on Java, the Internet was guaranteed to never be the same again.

What's so special about Java? Java enables programmers to create something called applets. Applets are special computer programs that can be included as an element of a Web page. When the user views a Web page containing one of these applets, the machine he's connected to automatically sends the applet to the user and the user's own Java-compatible browser runs the applet. Because applets are transferred in a non-machine-specific form, they can run on any machine that has a Java interpreter.

Using Java, you can do everything from adding simple animation to your Web pages to writing sophisticated computer programs that your Web page's users can use online. Applets that have already been released include games, spreadsheets, graphing programs, animation controllers, simulators, and much, much more. Java is so intriguing and so successful that even major players in the industry, including Netscape and Microsoft, have jumped aboard, providing Java-compatible software for the Internet.

Now that Sun Microsystems has released Java, however, it hasn't sat back and relaxed. New from Sun in the Java series of products is Java Workshop, a sophisticated development shell for the Java Developer's Kit (JDK). A few months ago, in order to write applets, Java developers had to use the command-line tools that came with the JDK. Java Workshop makes using these various tools much easier, by providing a graphical, point-and-click interface. Moreover, Java Workshop adds its own set of tools to the mix, including a full-featured source-code editor and a project manager.

In this book, you'll learn not only how Java applets work on the Internet, but also how to include Java applets in your Web pages. More importantly, you'll learn step-by-step how to write your own applets using Java Workshop. You can write these applets for your own personal use or for general release on the Internet. Imagine the thrill of seeing one of your own Java creations being used on Web pages all over the world! ■

Who This Book Is For

This book is the perfect starting point for anyone who wants to learn about Java. Although it's helpful to have previous programming experience (especially with C or C++), this book includes a complete tutorial on the Java language and how to build applets with Java Workshop. The Java Workshop tools—such as the Portfolio Manager, Project Manager, and Project Tester—that you need to create your own applets are described in detail. Moreover, you'll learn the Java language starting with the basics and working your way toward writing full-featured applets and applications.

Although this book is suitable for programming novices, more experienced programmers will find much of interest here, as well. If you're already familiar with languages such as C and C++, you'll be able to skim over the Java language introduction and dive right into the business of creating applets. Although the Java language is very much like C++, the way it's used is unique. Up until Java, you've never seen anything quite like applets.

To summarize, this book is for both novice and intermediate programmers. Novice programmers will get an introduction to the Java language, whereas more experienced programmers can concentrate on getting the most from the language by quickly learning how to build powerful applets for the Internet. Even expert programmers may find this book to be a useful introduction to the world of Java. To understand this book, however, you should at least be familiar with basic programming constructs such as functions and loops.

Hardware and Software Requirements

The Java language is currently supported on Windows 95, Windows NT, Sun Solaris, Macintosh, and UNIX machines. Parts of this book's content are applicable to any type of computer that can run the Java Developers Kit. However, Java Workshop currently runs only on Windows 95, Windows NT, and Solaris machines. Because Windows 95 will undoubtedly be the operating system under which the greatest majority of Java applets are created, the programs and examples in this book were written for the Windows 95 version of Java Workshop.

The minimum system requirements for Windows 95 or NT users are as follows:

- An IBM-compatible 80486 with at least 16M of memory
- Windows 95 or Windows NT
- A hard drive
- A CD-ROM drive
- A Microsoft-compatible mouse
- 256-color graphics
- A Windows-compatible sound card. (If you don't care about hearing sound files with Java's applets, you don't need a sound card.)

You can get a copy of the Java Developers Kit for their machines from its Microsystems' Web site at **http://www.sun.com**.

Compiling the Programs in This Book

As you work through the examples in this book, you'll learn how to install Java Workshop and compile the example programs that are presented in each chapter. In general, though, you can compile the programs in this book by following the procedures given here.

1. Install Java Workshop on your system, using the default root directory of C:\Java-Workshop. (It would also be useful to have a copy of Netscape Navigator 2.0 installed. You can get a copy of this Java-compatible browser from Netscape's Web site at **http://www.netscape.com**.)
2. Load your system files with SYSEDIT.EXE (you can find SYSEDIT.EXE in your WINDOWS\SYSTEM directory).
3. Go to the AUTOEXEC.BAT window and find the PATH statement. At the end of the PATH statement, add a semicolon followed by the path `C:\Java-Workshop\Jdk\Bin`.
4. Save the changes and restart your machine so the changes take effect.

   Adding the path to your PATH statement ensures that the system can find Java's tools if you should need to use them from a command line.

Finally, you should create a directory called C:\Classes in which you will place the Java files you create throughout this book. To compile and run an applet's Java source-code file, follow these steps:

1. Create a folder called Classes on the root directory of your C: drive. The Classes folder is where you'll store the Java programs you create in this book.
2. Create a folder for the applet inside your Classes folder. This folder, which should have the same name as the applet's class, is where you'll store the files for the applet you're creating in these steps.

For example, if you're creating a folder for an applet class called Applet1, you should create a folder called Applet1 inside your Classes folder.

3. Type the applet's source-code file and save it to the folder you just created. The source-code file always has a .java file extension, although some applets also require sound or graphics files, as well.

   For example, the Applet1 applet will have a source code file called Applet1.java. Check the appropriate chapter's text to discover whether the applet requires additional source-code, graphics, or sound files.

4. Start Java Workshop. You'll see the window shown in figure 0.1.

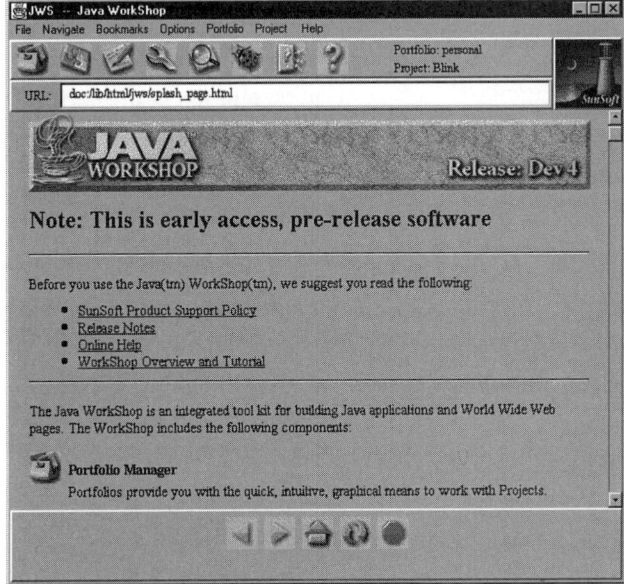

FIG. 0.1
This is Java Workshop when you first run it.

5. If you have already created a portfolio for the book's programs, skip to step 7.

6. Select Portfolio, Create from Java Workshop's menu bar. The Create Portfolio dialog box appears.

7. Type **c:\Classes\Using Java Workshop.psf** into the Portfolio text box, as shown in figure 0.2. Then, click the Create button to create the new portfolio.

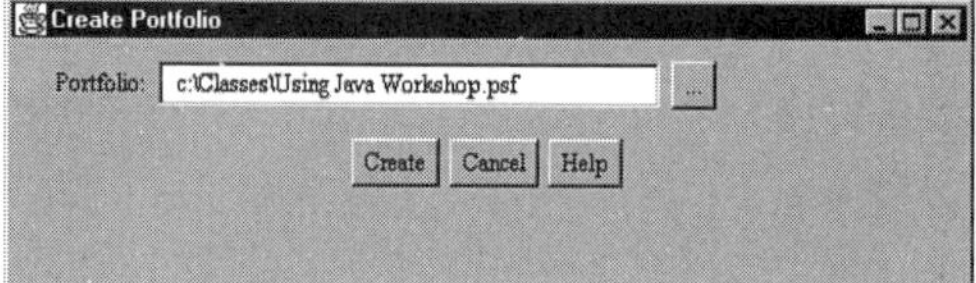

FIG. 0.2 You use the Create Portfolio dialog box to start a new portfolio.

You use portfolios to organize the source-code files that make up your various Java projects. You'll use the Using Java Workshop portfolio to organize all of the programs you'll create in this book.

8. Select Project, Create, Applet from Java Workshop's menu bar. The property sheet for applet projects appears.
9. Type the applet's name into the Name text box. Type **c:\Classes** followed by the applet's folder name into the Source Directory text box.

   For example, if you are creating a project for the **Applet1** applet, you'd type **Applet1** into the Name box and **c:\Classes\Applet1** into the Source Directory box.
10. Click the Yes button for Existing Sources, and click the Add All in Directory button. The applet's source-code files appear in the Sources box.
11. Finally, type the applet's name followed by the file extension **.class** (i.e., Applet1.class) into the Main Class File text box (see fig. 0.3) and click the Apply button. Java Workshop starts the new applet project and opens the text editor.

FIG. 0.3 You use this property sheet to create new projects.

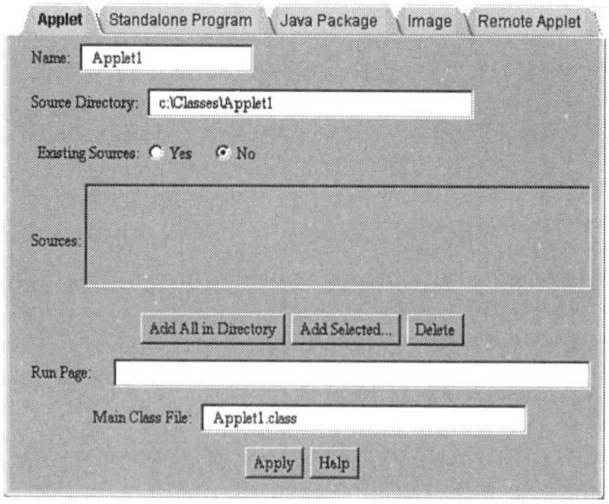

Projects organize the source-code files for each individual program in a portfolio. You can think of a portfolio as a folder that contains all of your Java projects, whereas the projects are similar to subfolders in the portfolio folder.

12. Click the Build Manager button (the one that looks like a wrench) in Java Workshop's main toolbar. Build Manager appears.
13. Click Build Manager's Build button (the first button on Build Manager's toolbar). Build Manager runs the Java compiler, javac, in order to compile your new applet (see fig. 0.4).

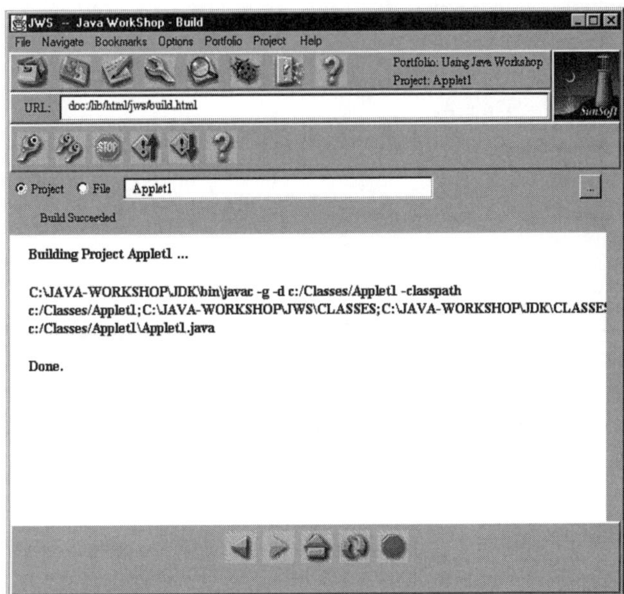

FIG. 0.4
Build Manager runs Java's compiler to compile your applet.

14. Click the Project Tester button (the one that looks like a light switch) on Java Workshop's toolbar to test your new applet.

A Word to the Wise

As every programmer knows, a good program is virtually crash-proof. Error-checking must be done for every action that may fail, and appropriate error messages must be given to the user. Unfortunately, good error checking requires a lot of extra program code. For the programmer working on his next magnum opus, this is all just part of the game. But for an author writing a programming book, this extra code has different implications.

A programming book should present its topics in as clear a manner as possible. This means featuring programs whose source code is not obscured by a lot of details that don't apply directly to the topic at hand. For this reason, the programs in this book do not always employ proper error checking. For example, user input often goes unverified and dynamic construction of objects is assumed to be successful.

In short, if you use any of the code in this book in your own programs, it's up to you to add whatever error-checking may have been left out. Never assume anything in your programs. If you aren't 100 percent sure of your program's state, you must add error checking to ensure that the program doesn't come crashing down on your user. Just because this book's author may have been lax in his error checking (for good reasons), that doesn't let you off the hook.

On into the Wonderful World of Java

If you're still reading this introduction, you're probably convinced that Java is something you really want to learn about. If you're interested in the Internet, that decision is a wise one. (If, on the other hand, you thought this was a book of coffee recipes, return this book to the shelf and leave the store.) At this point, Java is virtually guaranteed its place in Internet history. Want to know why? Turn the page and keep reading.

Clayton Walnum
June 1996

PART I

The Starting Line

CHAPTER 1

Java Overview

Why Java is a powerful language for creating Internet applications.

Java is specially designed to be a secure and full-featured language for creating special programs called applets that can be passed freely from one computer to another as part of an HTML document.

How to install and use the Java Developer's Kit's basic tools.

Although Java Workshop provides a sophisticated interface for the Java Developer's Kit (JDK), the basic Java development tools are easy to use from the DOS command line.

How to use the JDK's sample applets.

The JDK comes with many sample applets that demonstrate some of the things you can do with Java.

How to add applets to HTML documents.

Sun Microsystems created a new HTML tag that you can use in HTML documents to not only load and view applets, but also to pass parameters to applets.

Anyone who's had anything to do with computers in the '90s knows that the Internet is all the rage. The immense growth of this global computer network has not only created a handy way to download files and information but has also sparked major controversies over freedom of speech, copyright law, and computer security. Hardly a day goes by without the Internet making the news.

But not all Internet activity is steeped in controversy. One of the more positive Internet newsmakers has been the release of Java, a computer programming language that enables folks like you and me to create applications that can be used across the Internet without worrying about platform compatibility or network security. The two types of Java applications—applets for use within World Wide Web pages and stand-alone

Java applications—are guaranteed to do more to liven up the World Wide Web than even the most heated controversy.

Java was conceived long before its suitability for the Internet was noted and taken advantage of. You may be surprised to learn that Java was developed for a very different use. In fact, "Java" isn't even the language's original name. In this chapter, you get a quick look at Java's history and learn why Java is an excellent tool for creating Internet applications. ■

The Java Story

Back in 1990, a gentleman by the name of James Gosling was given the task of creating programs to control consumer electronics. Gosling and his team of people at Sun Microsystems started designing their software using C++, the language that most programmers were praising as the next big thing because of its object-oriented nature. Gosling quickly found that C++ was not suitable for the projects he and his team had in mind. They ran into trouble with complicated aspects of C++, such as multiple inheritance of classes and with program bugs, such as memory leaks. Gosling decided that he was going to have to come up with his own, simplified computer language that would avoid all the problems he had with C++.

Although Gosling didn't care for the complexity of languages such as C++, he did like the basic syntax and object-oriented features of the language. So when he sat down to design his new language, he used C++ as its model and stripped away all the features of C++ that made that language difficult to use with his consumer-electronics projects. When Gosling completed his language-design project, he had a new programming language that he named Oak. (The story goes that the name Oak came to Gosling as he gazed out his office window at an oak tree.)

Oak was first used in something called the Green project, wherein the development team attempted to design a control system for use in the home. This control system was to enable the user to manipulate a list of devices all from a hand-held computer called *7 (Star Seven), such as TVs, VCRs, lights, and telephones. The *7 system featured a touch-sensitive screen that the owner used to select and control the devices supported by the control.

NOTE The *7 screen display featured a number of animated figures, of which Duke (now the little guy considered to be the Java mascot) was one. Once you get involved with Java, you're liable to see a lot of Duke, who pops up on the Sun Microsystems Web site (see fig. 1.1), and is featured in some of Sun's sample Java applets. ■

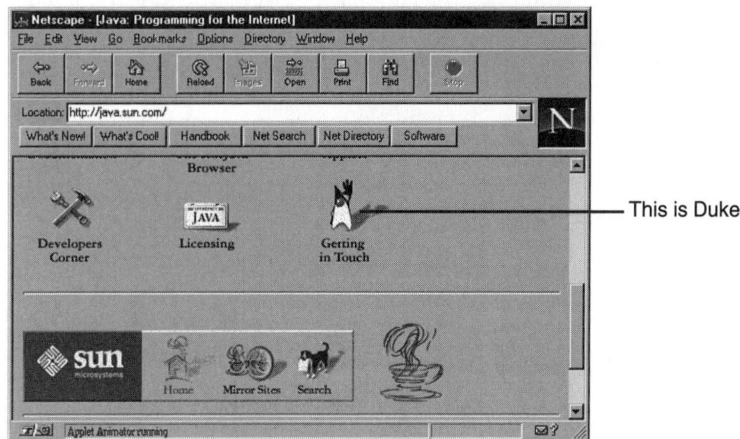

FIG. 1.1
Duke has become the Java mascot.

The next step for Oak was the video-on-demand (VOD) project, in which the language was used as the basis for software that controlled an interactive television system. Although neither *7 nor the VOD project led to actual products, they gave Oak a chance to develop and mature. By the time Sun discovered that the name "Oak" was already claimed and they changed the name to Java, they had a powerful, yet simple, language on their hands.

More importantly, Java was a platform-neutral language, which meant that programs developed with Java could run on any computer system with no changes. This platform independence was attained by using a special format for compiled Java programs. This file format, called byte-code, could be read and executed by any computer system that had a Java interpreter. The Java interpreter, of course, must be written specially for the system on which it is to run.

In 1993, after the World Wide Web had transformed the text-based Internet into a graphics-rich environment, the Java team realized that the language they had developed was perfect for Web programming. The team came up with the concept of Web applets, small programs that could be included in Web pages, and even went so far as to create a complete Web browser (now called HotJava) that demonstrated the language's power.

In the second quarter of 1995, Sun Microsystems officially announced Java. The "new" language was quickly embraced as a powerful tool for developing Internet applications. Netscape Communications, the developer of the popular Netscape Navigator Web browser (see fig. 1.2), added support for Java to its new Netscape Navigator 2.0. Other Internet software developers are sure to follow suit, including Microsoft, whose Internet Explorer 3 (currently in beta) offers Java support. After more than five years of development, Java has found its home.

FIG. 1.2
The new Netscape Navigator 2.0 Web browser is Java compatible.

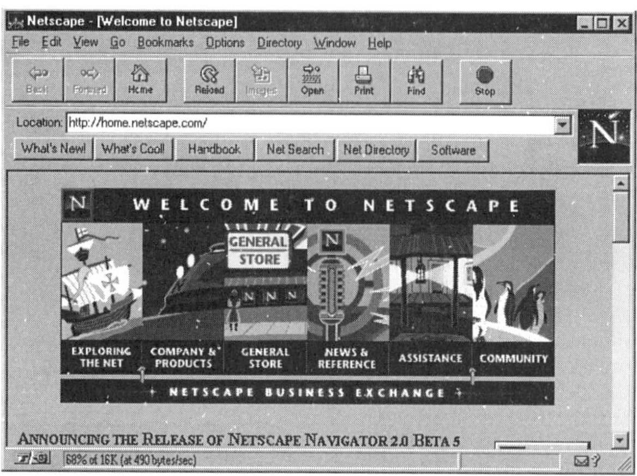

Introducing Java

By now, you may be curious as to why Java is considered such a powerful tool for Internet development projects. You already know that Java is a simplified version of C++. Anyone who has struggled with learning C++ knows that the key word in the previous sentence is "simplified." C++ added so much to the C language that even professional programmers had difficulty making the transition.

According to Sun Microsystems, Java is "simple, object-oriented, statically typed, compiled, architecture neutral, multi-threaded, garbage collected, robust, secure, and extensible." That's a mouthful, and that description of Java probably doesn't help you understand the language much. The following list of Java's attributes, however, should clear out some of the cobwebs:

- *Simple.* Java's developers deliberately left out many of the unnecessary features of other high-level programming languages. For example, Java does not support pointer math, implicit type casting, structures or unions, operator overloading, templates, header files, or multiple inheritance.
- *Object-oriented.* Just like C++, Java uses classes to organize code into logical modules. At runtime, a program creates objects from the classes. Java classes can inherit from other classes, but multiple inheritance, wherein a class inherits methods and fields from more than one class, is not allowed.
- *Statically typed.* All objects used in a program must be declared before they are used. This enables the Java compiler to locate and report type conflicts.
- *Compiled.* Before you can run a program written in the Java language, the program must be compiled by the Java compiler. The compilation results in a "byte-code" file that, while similar to a machine-code file, can be executed under any operating system that has a Java interpreter. This interpreter reads in the byte-code file and translates the byte-code commands into machine-language commands that can be directly executed by the machine that's running the Java program. You could say, then, that Java is both a compiled and interpreted language.
- *Multi-threaded.* Java programs can contain multiple threads of execution, which enable programs to handle several tasks concurrently. For example, a multi-threaded program can render an image on the screen in one thread and continue to accept keyboard input from the user in the main thread. All applications have at least one thread, which represents the program's main path of execution.
- *Garbage collected.* Java programs do their own garbage collection, which means that programs are not required to delete objects that they allocate in memory. This relieves programmers of virtually all memory-management problems.
- *Robust.* Because the Java interpreter checks all system access performed within a program, Java programs cannot crash the system. Instead, when a serious error is discovered, Java programs create an exception. This exception can be captured and managed by the program without any risk of bringing down the system.

- *Secure.* The Java system not only verifies all memory access but also ensures that no viruses are hitching a ride with a running applet. Because pointers are not supported by the Java language, programs cannot gain access to areas of the system for which they have no authorization.
- *Extensible.* Java programs support native methods, which are functions written in another language, usually C++. Support for native methods enables programmers to write functions that may execute faster than the equivalent functions written in Java. Native methods are dynamically linked to the Java program; that is, they are associated with the program at runtime. As the Java language is further refined for speed, native methods will probably become unnecessary.
- *Well-understood.* The Java language is based upon technology that's been developed over many years. For this reason, Java can be quickly and easily understood by anyone who has experience with modern programming languages such as C++.

As you can tell from the preceding list of features, a great deal of thought went into creating a language that is easy to use and provides the most powerful features of a modern language like C++. Thanks to features such as automatic garbage collection, programmers can spend more time developing their programs instead of wasting valuable man-hours hunting for hard-to-find memory-allocation bugs. Features, such as Java's object-oriented nature, and its ability to handle multiple threads of execution, ensure that the language is both up-to-date and powerful.

Java Programs

As I mentioned previously, Java can be used to create two types of programs: applets and stand-alone applications. An applet is simply a part of a Web page, just as an image or a line of text can be. A browser takes care of displaying an image referenced in an HTML document in the same way as a Java-enabled browser locates and runs an applet . When your Java-capable Web browser loads the HTML document, the Java applet is also loaded and executed.

Using applets, you can do everything from adding animated graphics to your Web pages to creating complete games and utilities that can be executed over the Internet. Some applets that have already been created with Java include: Bar Chart, which embeds a configurable bar chart in an HTML document; Crossword Puzzle, which enables users to solve a crossword puzzle on the Web; and LED Sign, which presents a scrolling, computerized message to viewers of the Web page within which the applet is embedded. Figure 1.3 shows a spreadsheet applet running in Netscape Navigator 2.0.

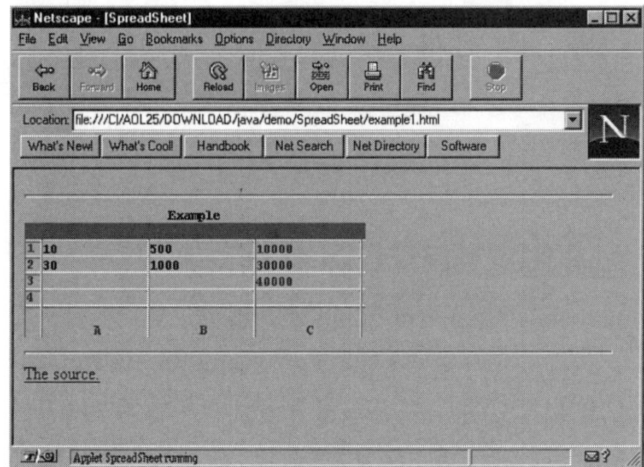

FIG. 1.3
Applets are small programs that are run from within an HTML document.

Although most Java programmers are excited by the ability to create applets, Java can also be used to create stand-alone applications—that is, applications that don't need to be embedded in an HTML document. The most well-known application is the HotJava Web browser itself (see fig. 1.4). This basic browser is completely written in the Java language and shows how Java handles not only normal programming tasks such as looping and evaluating mathematical expressions, but also how it handles the complexities of telecommunications programming.

FIG. 1.4
The HotJava Web browser is written entirely in the Java programming language.

The Java Developer's Kit

Java is actually more than a computer language; it's also a programming environment that includes a complete set of programming tools. These tools include a compiler, an interpreter, a debugger, a disassembler, a profiler, and more. Before Java Workshop was released, to create a Java program, you first had to use a text editor to create the source-code file. (You write the source code, of course, in the Java language.) After you completed the source code, which is always saved with a .java file extension, you compiled the program into its byte-code format, the file for which has the .class file extension. It is the .class file that the interpreter loads and executes. Because the byte-code files are fully portable between operating systems, they can be executed on any system that has a Java interpreter.

NOTE Many of Java's tools require long file names, especially the long extensions .java and .class. Both Windows 95 and Windows NT allow these long file names, even under DOS sessions.

Other tools include the Java debugger, which can help you find programming errors; the Java profiler provides handy information about your program. If you run into a compiled Java program that you'd like to see in source-code form, the Java disassembler does the translation for you. Java also includes a program that creates the files you need in order to take advantage of native methods (functions written in another language, such as C++). There's even a program that can create HTML documents from Java source-code files. Although all the development tools are DOS applications—that is, they don't run under Windows—they provide a complete environment for creating and managing Java projects.

Java Workshop uses these same tools to help you create Java programs. However, Java Workshop provides a graphical interface between you and most of the tools in the Java Developer's Kit. If you're a little confused about how the many Java programs work together, though, don't worry about it. You learn more about the Java tools and Java Workshop as you work through this book. At this point, just be aware that Java provides everything you need to create your own applets and stand-alone applications. In the second part of this book, you start to learn the Java language, and in the third part, you start to use Java Workshop and Java's tools to create your own applets.

Where Is Java?

All this talk about Java doesn't do you much good until you get your own copy of the Java Developer's Kit (JDK). You may also want a copy of HotJava and Netscape Navigator 2.0, so that you can try out the Web pages you create with your Java applets.

If you'd like to be sure you have the latest versions, you can find Java Workshop, HotJava, and the JDK on the Sun Microsystems site, located at **http://www.sun.com**. Once you connect to Sun Microsystems' home page, navigate to the page (follow the developer's links) shown in figure 1.5, which provides access to tons of information about Java and enables you to download the files you need. (Of course, Web pages constantly change. Sun Microsystems' site may have changed significantly by the time you read this.)

If you want to try out a copy of Netscape Navigator 2.0, hop onto the ol' WWW and go to **http://www.netscape.com**, which is Netscape's home page. From there, you can find your way to the page shown in figure 1.6. From this page, you can download the latest version of Netscape Navigator.

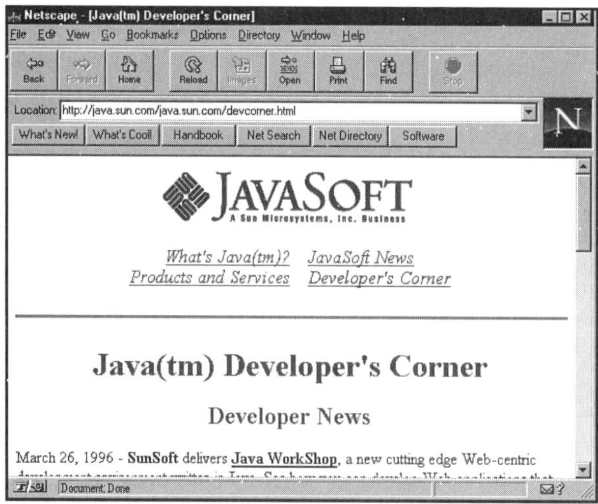

FIG. 1.5
You can download Java tools and documentation from Sun Microsystems' Web pages.

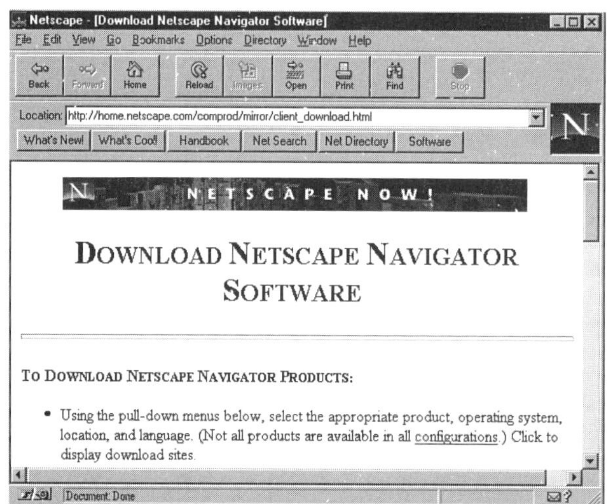

FIG. 1.6
You can get Netscape Navigator 2.0 from Netscape's WWW site.

NOTE You might also want to make your way to **http://www.microsoft.com**, where you can find information about Microsoft's new Web browser, Internet Explorer 3, which features Java support.

Installing HotJava

The HotJava browser is contained in a self-extracting compressed file. After you download the latest version from the Web, you extract HotJava's many files (there's a ton of them!) by double-clicking the file. The extraction program then sets to work, decompressing the files and storing them in a folder named HOTJAVA. Once the files are extracted, you can copy the folder anywhere you like on your hard disk.

When you examine the HOTJAVA folder, you'll see the directory structure shown in figure 1.7. The BIN folder contains the main HotJava application (HOTJAVA.EXE), and many of the Java environment's tools, including the compiler, interpreter, and profiler. The LIB folder contains a number of subfolders that hold documentation (in HTML format) and images needed by HotJava. The CLASSES.ZIP file, which contains all of Java's classes needed to run a Java application, is also located in the LIB folder. Don't forget to look over the COPYRIGHT and README files in the main HOTJAVA folder!

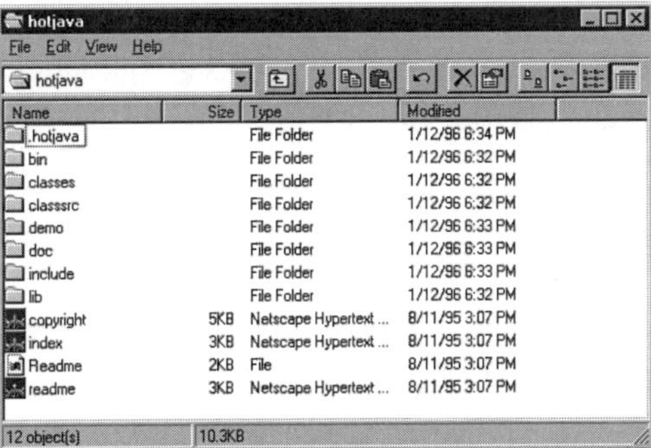

FIG. 1.7
After extraction, the HOTJAVA directory contains all of HotJava's many files.

Installing the JDK

A version of the Java Developer's Kit is automatically installed when you install Java Workshop (which you do in the next chapter). If you want to install the original version of the JDK, this section gets you started.

You can download the latest version of the JDK from the Sun Microsystems' Web site. After you download the JDK from Sun, you install it in exactly the same way you installed the HotJava browser. That is, you double-click the self-extracting compressed file. Figure 1.8 shows the contents of the JAVA folder (at least, the contents at the time of this writing; the development kit may have been revised by the time you read this).

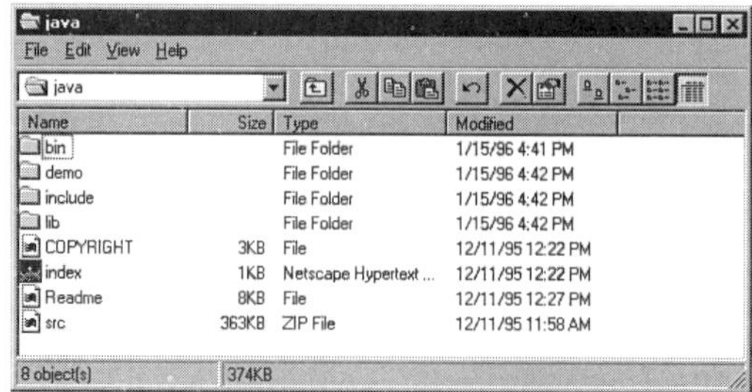

FIG. 1.8
The Java Developer's Kit is located in the JAVA folder after you extract its compressed files.

If you examine the folders that make up the JDK, you see that the BIN folder holds the developer tools, such as the compiler, the interpreter, and the debugger. The DEMO folder contains the many example applets that you can examine to learn more about the Java language and how it's used. In your JAVA folder, you also find a file called SRC.ZIP. This compressed file contains the source code for the classes included with the JDK.

Because you're interested in writing Java applets (you bought this book, after all), you're probably already pretty familiar with using HTML (Hypertext Markup Language) to create Web pages. If not, you should pick up a book on HTML and get some idea of how that scripting language works. Even if you're an HTML expert, though, you may not have seen the HTML extension that Sun Microsystems created in order to support Java applets in Web pages. In the following section, you not only get a chance to see Java applets up and running; you also learn how to add them to your Web pages.

The Sample Java Applets

As you learned earlier in this chapter, the Java Developer's Kit (JDK) includes many sample applets that you can test in your Web pages. (The HotJava browser, too, comes with a few of these sample applets.) If you installed the JDK as described, you're all ready to start experimenting with Java applets. In this section, you get a quick look at some of the applets included with the JDK by using the

Appletviewer tool that also comes with the JDK. In the following sections, you learn to add an applet to a Web page.

The Appletviewer Tool

Later in this book, you learn how to use Java Workshop to run and view applets. However, there's a quick way to get applets up on the screen, and you don't even need a Java-compatible browser to do it, thanks to the Appletviewer tool that comes as part of the JDK. Appletviewer is a Windows application that you run from a DOS command line. Part of the command line is the applet that you want to run. When Appletviewer appears, the applet shows in the viewer's main window.

To run the Appletviewer application, you must have installed the JDK. Bring up an MS-DOS window by selecting the MS-DOS Prompt command from Programs on the Start menu. Then, switch to the folder containing the applet you want to run and type the following command line:

```
C:\JAVA\BIN\APPLETVIEWER DOC.HTML
```

In the above command line, DOC.HTML is the name of an HTML document that contains the tag for the applet you want to see.

Running TicTacToe

Suppose you want to run the TicTacToe demo applet that comes with the JDK. To do this, just execute the following steps:

1. Select the Start/Programs/MS-DOS Prompt command.
2. Change to the directory containing the TicTacToe applet.
3. Type the command line `C:\JAVA\BIN\APPLETVIEWER EXAMPLE1.HTML`.

Now that you have the applet started, try a few games of TicTacToe against the computer. To place an X, click on the square you want. You'll quickly discover that the computer player is as dumb as yogurt. Let's just say that you don't have to be a rocket scientist to win (see fig. 1.9).

FIG. 1.9
Beating this version of Tic-Tac-Toe doesn't require a degree in computer science.

If you want to avoid typing the full path name for Appletviewer every time you run it, type the command **PATH=C:\JAVA\BIN** at the MS-DOS prompt to add Appletviewer's directory to your path. (Of course, if you installed the JDK somewhere else on your hard drive, you have to use a different path in the command.) Then you can run TicTacToe by switching to the TicTacToe directory and simply typing **APPLETVIEWER EXAMPLE1.HTML**. You can also add Appletviewer's path to the PATH statement in your AUTOEXEC.BAT file to avoid typing it in by hand every time you start your system and want to use Appletviewer.

The Animator Applet

Another applet that demonstrates some interesting facets of Java programming is the Animator applet, which not only displays various animation sequences, but also plays sound effects simultaneously. To run the Animator applet, switch to the C:\JAVA\DEMO\ANIMATOR folder and type the command line **APPLETVIEWER EXAMPLE1.HTML**. (The previous command line assumes that you've set your path to the JAVA\BIN directory.) When you do, you see the display shown in figure 1.10. (Yes, it's the ubiquitous Duke, waving at you from his very own applet.)

FIG. 1.10
The Animator applet includes several animation and sound examples, including this one featuring Duke, the Java mascot.

Animator is an example of a configurable applet. That is, by modifying the HTML tag that loads and runs the applet, the user can display his own custom animation sequences and sound effects. You learn about configurable applets in Chapter 10, "Events and Configurable Applets." For now, though, it's enough for you to know that Java is capable of adding both animation sequences and sound effects to your Web pages.

The BarChart Applet

The configurable applet called BarChart is especially useful when you need to graphically display data values in a Web page. To check out BarChart, switch to the JAVA\DEMO\BARCHART folder and type the command line **APPLETVIEWER EXAMPLE1.HTML**. When you do, you see the window shown in figure 1.11.

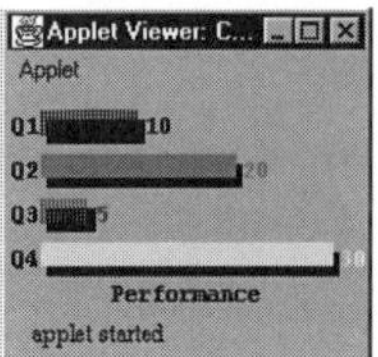

FIG. 1.11 The BarChart applet enables you to create graphs in your Web pages.

Since BarChart is configurable, you can create all sorts of different bar charts in your Web pages just by specifying different parameters in the applet's HTML tag. As you can see, applets can be powerful tools for creating dynamic and useful Web pages.

Other Demo Applets

The DEMO folder contains many sample applets that you can experiment with using Appletviewer. All of the demo applets are run from HTML documents with names like EXAMPLE1.HTML, EXAMPLE2.HTML, and so on. All demo applets have at least the EXAMPLE1.HTML document, while others have additional examples. To run any demo applet, change to the applet's folder and type **APPLETVIEWER EXAMPLE1.HTML** (assuming that you've set your path to the Appletviewer application). Use the DIR command to display the contents of an applet's directory in order to discover whether the applet features additional example HTML files.

Adding Applets to an HTML Document

If you've created Web pages before, you know that you use HTML to create a script for the page. The commands in the script tell a Web browser how to display the Web page. When Sun Microsystems developed Java, they also had to come up with an extension to HTML that would enable Web pages to contain Java applets. That extension is the `<applet>` tag, which Sun Microsystems defines as shown in listing 1.1.

Listing 1.1 LST1_1.TXT: The *<applet>* Tag Definition

```
<applet attributes>
parameters
alternate-content
</applet>
```

In the above tag, the text in normal characters is typed literally. The text shown in italics gets replaced by whatever is appropriate for the applet you're including in the document. As you can see, the `<applet>` tag is similar to other HTML tags, with which you may be familiar. For example, the tag starts with `<applet attributes>` and ends with `</applet>`, which is not unlike the format of other HTML tags. The first and last lines are required. Other lines in the tag are optional.

The first line of the `<applet>` tag contains important information about the tag, including the associated .class file and the applet's width and height. The last line tells the browser that it has reached the end of the tag. You can load and run the TicTacToe applet, for example, with the `<applet>` tag shown in listing 1.2.

Listing 1.2 LST1_2.TXT: A Tag for Loading and Running TicTacToe

```
<applet
    code=TicTacToe.class
    width=120
    height=120>
</applet>
```

In the above example, the code attribute is the name of the .class file for the applet. If you remember, the .class file holds the applet's byte-code representation, which can be run by the Java interpreter. The width and height attributes control the size of the applet.

The TicTacToe tag above is the simplest applet tag you can write. That is, the code, width, and height attributes are all required, as is the final `</applet>` line.

Optional Attributes for Applets

There are several optional attributes you can use with the `<applet>` tag. The first is `codebase`, which specifies the applet's base folder or URL (Uniform Resource Locator). This folder or URL is used in combination with the file specified in the `code` attribute to find the applet's code. In the case of a folder, the `codebase` attribute is relative to the location of the HTML document containing the applet's tag. In listing 1.2, because the `codebase` attribute is missing, the Web browser looks for the applet's files in the same folder as the HTML document. The `<applet>` tag in listing 1.2 looks like listing 1.3 when the `codebase` attribute is used.

Listing 1.3 LST1_3.TXT: Using the *codebase* Attribute

```
<applet
    codebase=tictactoe
    code=TicTacToe.class
    width=120
    height=120>
</applet>
```

The above tag tells the browser that the TicTacToe.class file is located in a folder called TICTACTOE. This folder must be on the same level in the directory tree as the HTML file. That is, if the HTML file is in the folder JAVA\DEMO, then the path for the .class file should be JAVA\DEMO\TICTACTOE\TicTacToe.class. You can also use an URL, such as **http://www.provider.com/my_pages/tictactoe**, for the `codebase` attribute. This causes the applet to be loaded from the specified site.

Other optional attributes you can use with the `<applet>` tag are `alt`, `align`, `name`, `hspace`, and `vspace`. The `alt` attribute enables you to specify text to be displayed by text-only browsers, whereas the `name` attribute gives the applet a symbolic name that's used to reference the applet.

The `align`, `hspace`, and `vspace` attributes all work together to position the applet within the text flow of the HTML document. These attributes work exactly as they do with the `<img>` tag, which is used to display images in Web pages. The `align` attribute can be any one of these values: `left`, `right`, `middle`, `absmiddle`, `bottom`, `absbottom`, `baseline`, `top`, or `texttop`. The `hspace` and `vspace` attributes control the amount of white space around the applet when `align` is set to `left` or `right`.

Listing 1.4 shows the script for a simple Web page using the `<applet>` tag. Figure 1.12 shows Netscape Navigator 2.0 displaying the page.

Listing 1.4 LST1_4.TXT: A Simple HTML Document Using the *<applet>* Tag

```
<title>TicTacToe</title>
<hr>
This is a bunch of text whose sole purpose is to demonstrate
the placement
<applet
    codebase=TicTacToe
    code=TicTacToe.class
    width=120
    height=120
    alt="This is the TicTacToe applet."
    name=TicTacToe
    align=middle>
</applet>
of the TicTacToe applet within the text flow of an HTML document.
<hr>
```

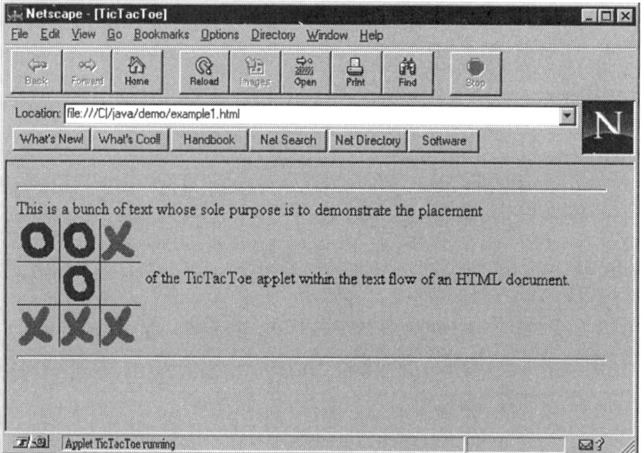

FIG. 1.12
This is the Web page created by listing 1.4.

To load an HTML document into Netscape Navigator 2.0, select the File, Open File command or press Ctrl+O. Then, select the file in the dialog box that appears.

Applet Parameters

As you know, many Java applets are configurable, meaning that the applet user can specify certain values for the applet to use when it starts. A good example is the BarChart applet you saw earlier in this chapter. When you need to specify parameters for an applet, you use the `<param>` tag. The `<param>` tags, one for each parameter you want to set, are placed after the starting `<applet>` tag and before the ending `</applet>` tag. For example, listing 1.5 shows parameters being set for the BarChart applet. Figure 1.13 shows the resultant bar chart. As you can see from the listing, each parameter has two parts, the parameter name and the value to which it should be set.

Listing 1.5 LST1_5.TXT: Using Parameters with Applets

```
<applet
    code="Chart.class"
    width=251
    height=125>
<param name=title value="Sales">
<param name=orientation value="vertical">
<param name=scale value="5">
<param name=columns value="3">
<param name=c1_style value="solid">
<param name=c1 value="10">
<param name=c1_color value="blue">
<param name=c1_label value="Jan">
<param name=c2_style value="solid">
<param name=c2 value="12">
<param name=c2_color value="green">
<param name=c2_label value="Feb">
<param name=c3_style value="solid">
<param name=c3 value="15">
<param name=c3_color value="red">
<param name=c3_label value="Mar">
</applet>
```

Non-Java Browsers

You may wonder what happens when a browser that's not Java-compatible finds an applet in an HTML document. In this case, as is standard behavior for browsers, the non-Java browser simply ignores the tags it doesn't recognize. You may want to provide a more user-friendly response to users who are trying to view your applets with non-Java browsers. You can do this easily by placing alternate content right before the ending `</applet>` tag. Listing 1.6, for example, shows the HTML script for running the TicTacToe applet with alternate content for browsers that don't support Java.

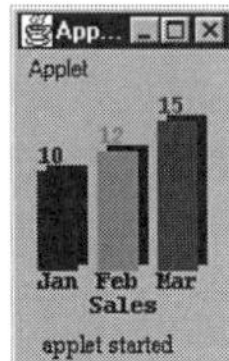

FIG. 1.13 This is the bar chart created by the parameters in listing 1.5.

Listing 1.6 LST1_6.TXT: Supplying Alternate Content for TicTacToe

```
<applet
    code=TicTacToe.class
    width=120
    height=120>
<b>If you had a Java-compatible browser,
you'd be playing TicTacToe right now!</b>
</applet>
```

The alternate content you provide can be comprised of any standard HTML commands and is ignored by Java-compatible browsers. That is, the alternate content appears only in non-Java browsers.

Applets and the Internet

Now that you have some idea of how you can add Java applets to your Web pages, you need to discover how applets are handled on the Internet. After all, it's the applet's ability to hitch a ride on the Information Superhighway that makes it so unique. In fact, applets are really the first step towards making the Internet a true extension of your computer's local storage system. When you view a Web page containing applets, those applets may be coming to you from just about anywhere on the Web—from the office down the street or from a software distributor in Hong Kong. In the following sections, you discover just how this interaction works.

Local and Remote Applets

One of Java's major strengths is that you can use the language to create dynamic content for your Web pages. That is, thanks to Java applets, your Web pages are no longer limited to the tricks you can perform with HTML. Now your Web pages can do just about anything you want them to. All you need to do is write the appropriate applets.

But writing Java applets is only half the story. How your Web page users obtain and run the applets is equally important. It's up to you to not only write the applet (or use someone else's applet), but also to provide users access to the applet. Basically, your Web pages can contain two types of applets, local and remote. In this section, you learn the difference between these applet types, which are named after the location at which they are stored.

A local applet is one that is stored on your own computer system (see fig. 1.14). When your Web page must find a local applet, it doesn't need to retrieve information from the Internet—in fact, your browser doesn't even need to be connected to the Internet at that time. As you can see in listing 1.7, a local applet is specified by a path name and a file name.

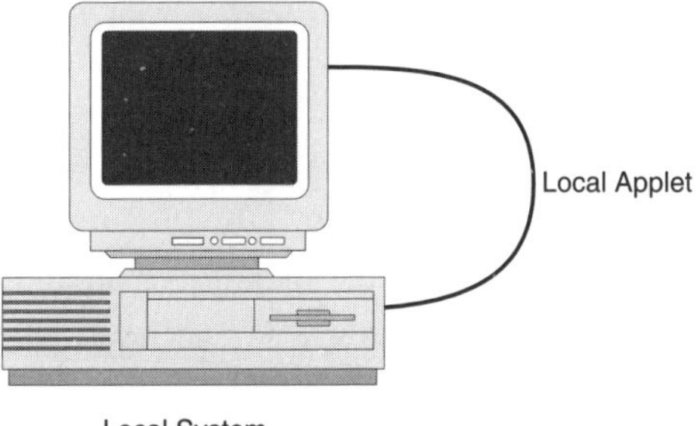

FIG. 1.14
Local applets are stored on and loaded from your computer system.

Listing 1.7 LST1_7.TXT: Specifying a Local Applet

```
<applet
    codebase="tictactoe"
    code="TicTacToe.class"
    width=120
    height=120>
</applet>
```

In listing 1.7, the `codebase` attribute specifies a path name on your system for the local applet, whereas the `code` attribute specifies the name of the byte-code file that contains the applet's code. The path specified in the `codebase` attribute is relative to the folder containing the HTML document that references the applet. (See this chapter's "Optional Attributes for Applets" section for more information.)

A remote applet is one that is located on another computer system (see fig. 1.15). This computer system may be located in the building next door or it may be on the other side of the world—it makes no difference to your Java-compatible browser. No matter where the remote applet is located, it's downloaded onto your computer via the Internet. Your browser must, of course, be connected to the Internet at the time it needs to display the remote applet.

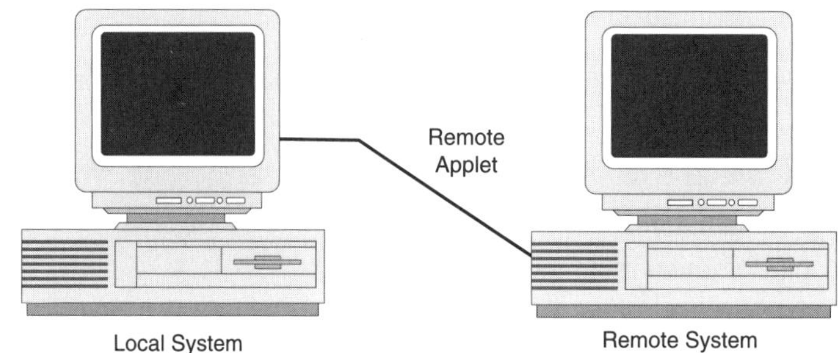

FIG. 1.15
Remote applets are stored on another system and are downloaded onto your computer via the Internet.

To reference a remote applet in your Web page, you must know the applet's URL (where it's located on the Web) and any attributes and parameters that you need to supply in order to display the applet correctly. If you didn't write the applet, you need to find the document that describes the applet's attributes and parameters. This document is usually written by the applet's author. Listing 1.8 shows how to compose an HTML `<applet>` tag that accesses a remote applet.

Listing 1.8 LST1_8.TXT: Specifying a Remote Applet

```
<applet
    codebase="http://www.myconnect.com/applets/"
    code="TicTacToe.class"
    width=120
    height=120>
</applet>
```

The only difference between listing 1.7 and listing 1.8 is the value of the `codebase` attribute. In the first case, `codebase` specifies a local folder, and in the second case, it specifies the URL at which the applet is located.

Clients and Servers

If a required applet is not located on your system, it can be downloaded automatically to your system and then run. To the user, this exchange of applets over the Internet is mostly transparent. All the user knows is that she's looking at a page that contains a game of TicTacToe, an animated image of Duke, or some other Java-based content. In this way, the Internet becomes almost an extension of the user's basic system, sort of a gigantic hard drive that contains a practically infinite number of accessible applets and applications.

Currently, there's a client/server relationship between a browser that wants to display an applet and the system that can supply the applet. The client is a computer that requires services from another system; the server is the computer that provides those services. In the case of a Java applet, the client is the computer that's trying to display an HTML document that contains a reference to an applet. The server is the computer system that uploads the applet to the client, thereby allowing the client to use the applet. In figure 1.15, you could call the local computer the client and the remote computer the server.

The difference between a client and a server quickly begins to get muddy. Since Java browsers can send as well as receive applications, computers constantly switch between being a client and a server. For example, suppose you load up your favorite Java-compatible browser and connect to a Web site. The home page on the Web site contains an animated title, so your system downloads the applet that displays this title. For the time being, your system is the client and the remote system is the server.

Later you decide that you want to search the remote system's public databases for a particular file because you've just written a search application that can do the job for you. Your system transmits the application to the remote computer, where it finds the file you specified. Suddenly, your computer is the server and the remote computer is the client.

This sort of switching between client and server tasks is a step toward making the Internet a huge extension of your computer. That is, more and more, the Internet will seem to be a part of your own local system, rather than a collection of computers located all over the world. You'll be able to access the Internet almost as easily as your own hard drive. In fact, you might not even need a hard drive at all! You can just run applications located somewhere on the Internet and store your data in any number of special storage sites.

Security

You may have heard horror stories about people who have downloaded programs from the Internet only to find, after running the program, that they had infected their system with a virus or otherwise wreaked havoc with their computer. Therefore you may be reluctant to jump on the applet bandwagon. After all, with so many applets flying around the Internet, trouble could rear its ugly head like a demon from a Clive Barker movie.

The truth, however, is that Java applets are a secure way to transmit programs on the Internet. This is because the Java interpreter doesn't allow an applet to run until the interpreter has confirmed that the applet's byte-code has not been corrupted or changed in some way (see fig. 1.16). Moreover, the interpreter determines whether the byte-code representation of the applet sticks to all of Java's rules. For example, a Java applet can never use a pointer to gain access to portions of computer memory for which it shouldn't have access. The bottom line is that, not only are Java applets secure, they are virtually guaranteed not to crash the system.

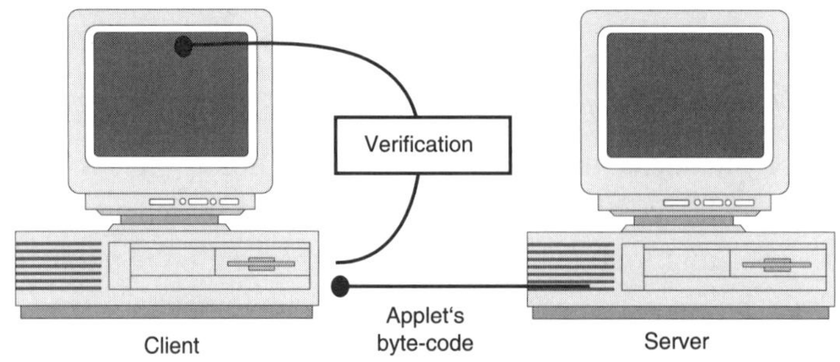

FIG. 1.16
Applets are verified before they run, so they are virtually guaranteed to be safe and secure.

Your Pages on the Web

Since you bought this book to learn how to write applets, you're probably also interested in setting up your own Web pages. (Of course, you may be interested only in creating applets that other people can use. That's okay, too.) To set up your own Java-compatible Web site, you need to create publicly accessible folders on your hard drive. You also should gather all the applets you need so you can store them together in one place on your hard drive. That is, you want your Web pages to contain local applets. The instructions in this section get you started on organizing a public folder.

First, create a folder on your hard drive's root directory. Name this folder something like PUBLIC. Use the PUBLIC folder to contain all of the files that you want to make accessible to Web users who connect to your pages. Inside the PUBLIC folder, create a folder called something like APPLETS.

Now that you have created your folders, copy all the applets you need into the APPLETS folder. The applets' .class files should be in the APPLETS directory, with their support files (such as graphics and sounds), in appropriately named folders within the APPLETS directory. For example, if wanted to use the BouncingHeads applet in one of your pages, you'd copy the contents of the JAVA\DEMO\BOUNCINGHEADS folder to your APPLETS folder. You end up with the directory structure shown in figure 1.17.

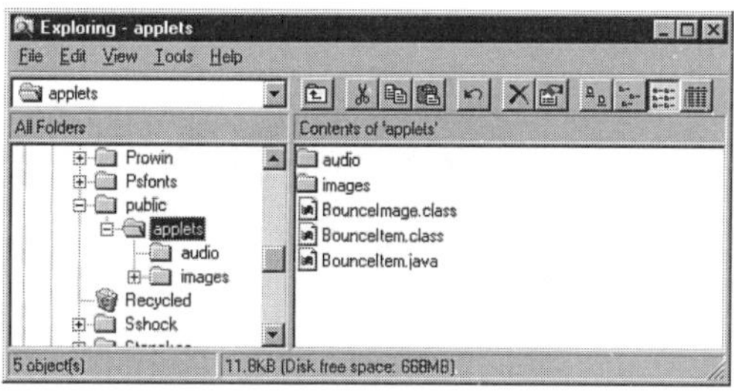

FIG. 1.17
You need to set up your public directories properly.

The next step is to create the HTML files for your pages. When you've written these pages, they should be placed in the PUBLIC folder. Listing 1.9 shows the HTML file for a simple home page that displays the BouncingHeads applet and enables the user to view the applet's source code. The corresponding Web page is shown in figure 1.18. Notice that the user can view the applet's source code by clicking on the link at the bottom of the page. When she does, she sees a window similar to figure 1.19.

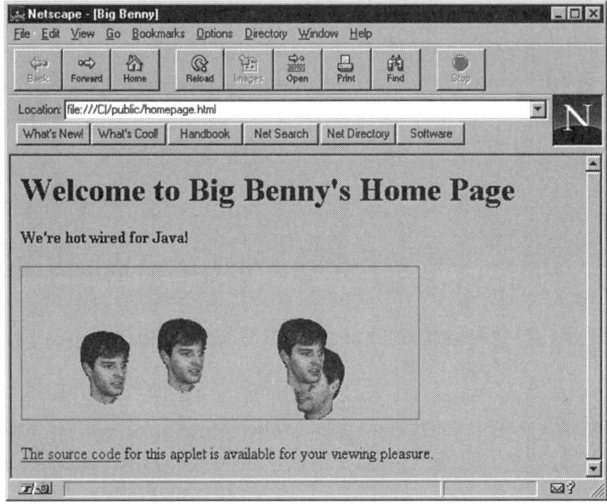

FIG. 1.18
Here's an example of a simple, Java-powered home page.

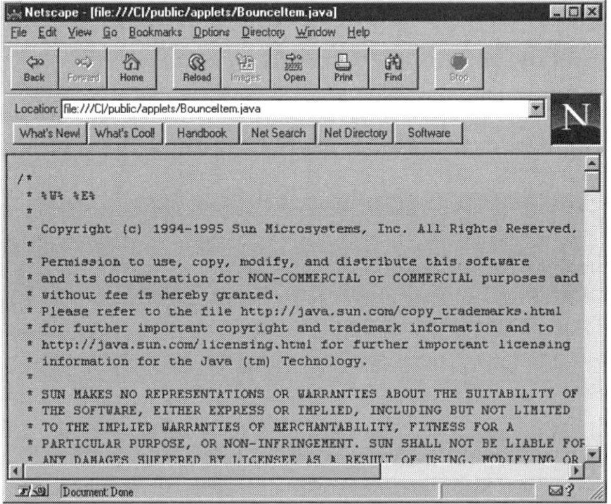

FIG. 1.19
The user can view the applet's source code by clicking the link.

Listing 1.9 LST1_9.TXT: A Home Page That Displays a Java Applet

```
<title>Big Benny</title>
<h1>Welcome to Big Benny's Home Page</h1>
<b>We're hot wired for Java!</b>
<p>
<applet
    codebase="applets"
    code="BounceItem.class"
    width=400
    height=150>
</applet>
<p>
<a href="applets/BounceItem.java">The source code</a>
for this applet is available for your viewing pleasure.
```

NOTE Generally, you do not need to copy Java source code files to your APPLETS folder. Source code is not required to load and run applets.

By placing all the publicly accessible files in one root directory, you can set up your system's security to ensure that the rest of your system is kept safe from prying eyes. Moreover, you know exactly where you need to store any additional files that you may add to your site. Exactly how you create the folders for your Web pages depends on the applets and files you need to use, but the previous example should get you going fairly easily.

NOTE Of course, to create a Web site, you need to be connected to the Internet either directly or through an Internet provider that enables you to set up your own Web pages. If you are currently unable to have your own Web site, you can still set one up on your hard drive and then use your Java-compatible Web browser to load and view your Web pages. Then, when you get your Internet access, you'll be all ready to go. To find more information on setting up your own Web site, crank up your browser and log onto the handy Lycos directory at **http://www.lycos.com**; then fish around under the Computers, Web Publishing & HTML subdirectory.

From Here...

Java just may be the biggest thing to hit the World Wide Web since the Web itself. Java not only provides a way to create secure applications that can be used safely on the Internet, but the language also represents a complete shift in the way people may think about their computers in the future. Because a Java applet can be located anywhere on the Web (and still be executable on your computer), your computer's storage may well expand from its tiny hard drive to include all of the Internet.

Because HTML was designed long before there were Java applets, Sun Microsystems had to create an extension to HTML in order to accommodate applets in Web pages. The extension takes the form of the `<applet>` tag, which enables you to not only provide values for an applet's attributes, but also to include a list of parameters and even offer alternate content for non-Java browsers.

Thanks to a Java-compatible browser's ability to download applets, users who log on to Java-powered Web pages can enjoy the Java experience without even realizing what's going on behind the scenes. This is unlike other types of applications on the Internet, which the user must explicitly download before they can be run.

For additional information, please refer to the following chapters:

- Chapter 2, "Introducing Java Workshop," discusses how Java Workshop simplifies using the Java Developer's Kit.
- Chapter 6, "Applets and Graphics," shows how to create a simple applet and how to display data in the applet's display area.
- Chapter 11, "Images, Sounds, and Communications," tells you how to use applets to communicate over the Internet.
- Chapter 13, "Writing Java Applications," describes how to create stand-alone applications (applications that aren't applets) with Java.

CHAPTER 2

Introducing Java Workshop

How to create and organize projects with Project Manager and Portfolio Manager.

Having Project Manager and Portfolio Manager around is like having digital secretaries that keep your work organized and easy to access.

How to use Build Manager and Project Tester.

With Java Workshop, you can compile and run your applets with a quick click of the mouse using Build Manager and Project Tester.

How to use Source Editor, Source Browser, Debugger, and Visual Java.

Java Workshop features its own full-featured text editor. The Source Browser tool organizes and displays information about the source code you create with the editor. Java Workshop's debugger helps make the troubleshooting process less painful.

How to get and install Java workshop.

You can't use a program until you install it. And you can't install Java Workshop until you download it from the Web.

In the previous chapter, you got a quick introduction to Java and learned what Java can do for you on the Internet. You learned that small Java applications called applets enable you to include programs right in your Web pages. However, if you were going to create your Java applets using only Sun Microsystem's Java Developer's Kit (JDK), you'd have to use a lot of command-line tools, including the Java compiler and interpreter. This usually means starting a DOS session under Windows and entering your command lines, along with appropriate parameters, in the DOS window.

If you're a person who likes the conveniences of running applications under a windowed environment like Windows 95, you may be put off by having to go back to a command-line interface. That's why Sun Microsystems came up with Java Workshop. Java Workshop is like a sophisticated shell application for the JDK, enabling you to create applications from the familiar and easy-to-use Windows environment. Using Java Workshop, you can run most of the JDK's tools with a quick mouse-button click. ■

Java Workshop's Tools

Java Workshop features many tools, some of which act as an interface between you and the JDK, as well as others that are not included in the JDK, such as a text editor and project manager. When used together, these tools comprise a powerful, graphical development environment that makes it easier and more enjoyable to create Java applets (and other Java projects). Java Workshop includes the following eight main tools:

- Project Manager
- Portfolio Manager
- Build Manager
- Project Tester
- Source Editor
- Source Browser
- Debugger
- Visual Java

The sections that follow introduce you to each of these tools.

Project Manager

If you've ever used other Windows development packages, such as Visual C++ or Borland C++, you're already used to the idea of projects. A project is a collection of attributes that define how a program-in-progress is to be handled by the development environment. The attributes managed by a Java project include the names of all the source-code files needed to compile the program, as well as how the program should be compiled and run. In Java Workshop, Project Manager organizes Java programs into projects.

Figure 2.1 shows what Project Manager looks like when you first start a new applet. All of the information you enter into the project dialog box is retained by Project Manager so that Java Workshop can handle the project's details without your intervention. Once you've set up a project, the task of compiling and running a program is as easy as clicking a button.

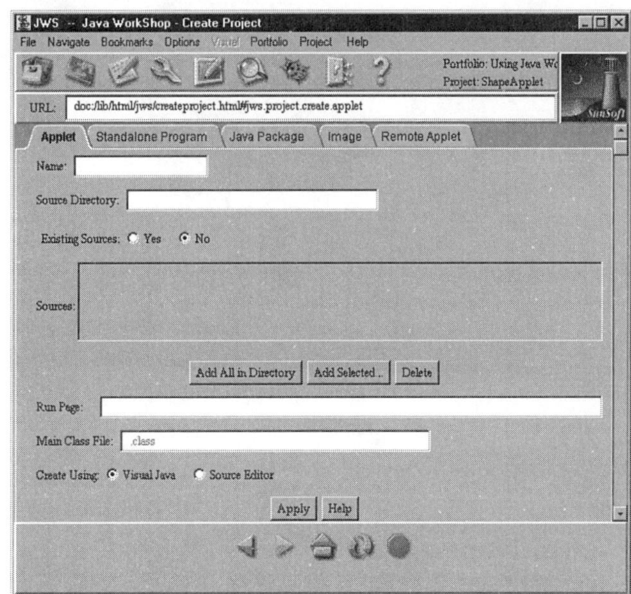

FIG. 2.1
When you create a project, Project Manager stores the information you enter into the dialog box.

Of course, just because Project Manager handles the project's details for you doesn't mean you can't fine-tune things as needed. Java Workshop's Project menu enables you to create, delete, select, run, and copy projects. You can even edit any of the attributes that have been assigned to the current project. Figure 2.2, for example, shows some of the attributes that control how Java Workshop runs an applet. Most of these attributes have default values, but all may be edited by the programmer. As you can see in the figure, Project Manager enables you to edit six different categories of attributes, each category having its own tabbed page in the dialog box.

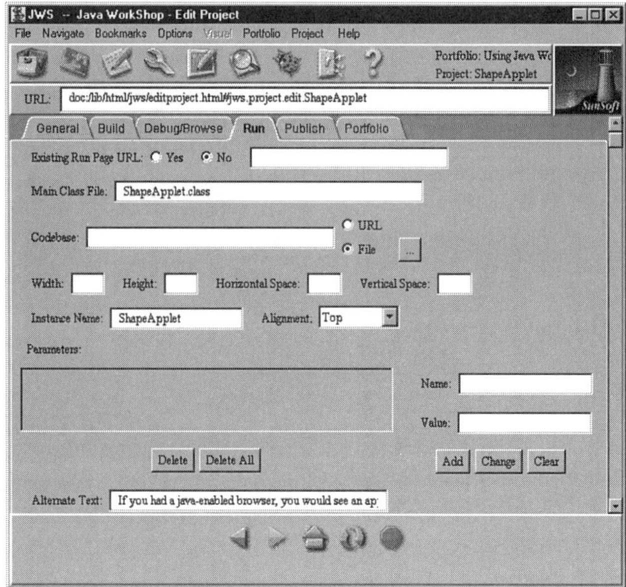

FIG. 2.2
You can edit any of a project's attributes.

PortfolioManager

Once you start working on several different applets, you need a way to organize the projects that represent those applets, so that you can find what you need when you need it. You may even find yourself sharing Java Workshop with other users on a network, each user having his own set of projects on which he's working. Without some way to manage these projects, things can quickly get out of hand.

Enter Portfolio Manager, which organizes projects into a logical group called a portfolio. How you choose to set up a portfolio is up to you. You can, for example, have serious applets in one portfolio and games in another. Or, if several users are using Java Workshop concurrently, you can give each user his own portfolio. If set up properly on a network, you can even prevent unauthorized users from opening portfolios.

Portfolio Manager's main screen is a set of icons, each icon representing one project in the portfolio (see fig. 2.3). Each type of project (i.e., applet, stand-alone application, package, image, or remote applet) gets its own icon, so you can see at a glance not only what projects comprise the portfolio, but also what types of projects they are. Java Workshop's Portfolio menu contains commands that enable you to add, delete, select, or import portfolios.

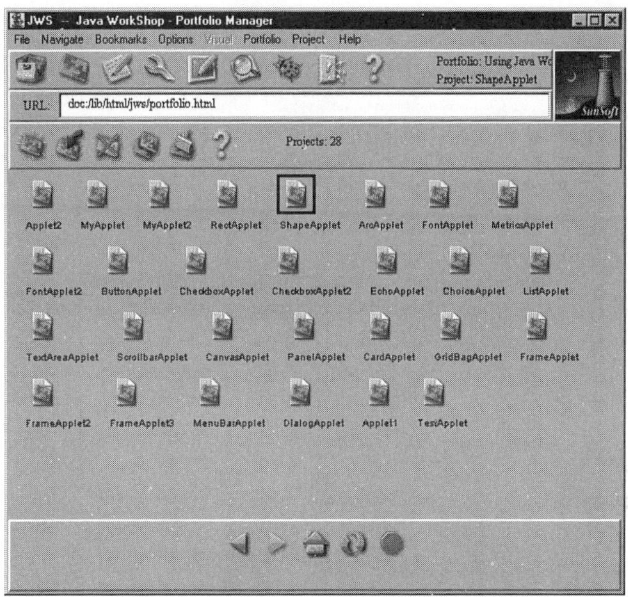

FIG. 2.3
Portfolio Manager organizes projects into logical groups.

Build Manager

At some point in the creation of your applet under Java workshop, you're going to want to compile your source code into the byte-code file that the Java interpreter can understand. This is the task of Build Manager (see fig. 2.4). Using Build Manager, you can compile whole projects or just single files. In the case of a project, Build Manager keeps track of which files are up-to-date and which have to be recompiled, which avoids Java Workshop's having to compile source-code files that haven't changed since the last build.

As you can see in the figure, Build Manager prints messages in its window as it works, keeping you informed of the compilation process. If your source-code contains syntax errors, Build Manager displays the errors in the window too, as shown in figure 2.5. Because Java Workshop's tools are so tightly integrated, you can click on an error in Build Manager's window in order to load the source-code file and automatically locate the offending line of code.

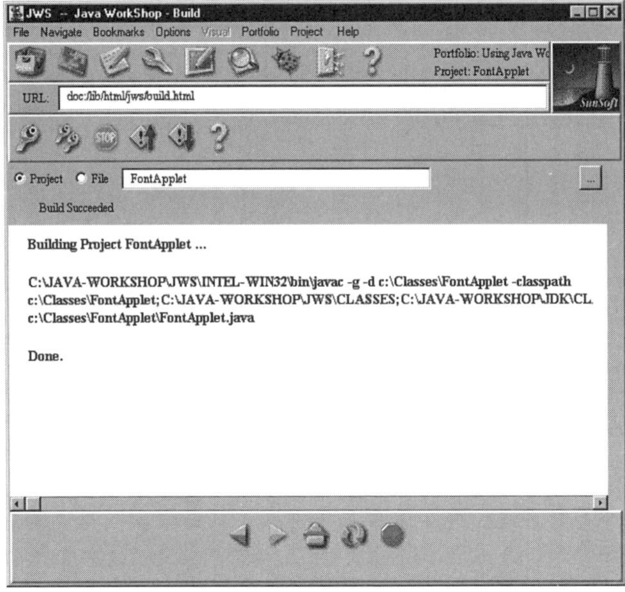

FIG. 2.4
Build Manager compiles your applets.

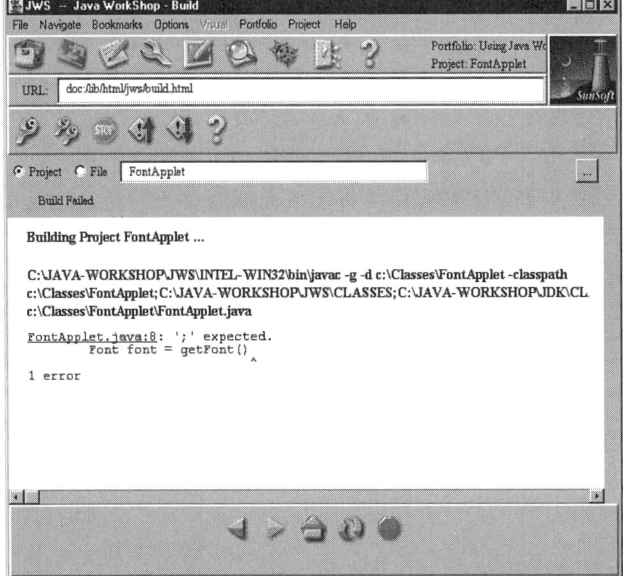

FIG. 2.5
Build Manager also informs you of syntax errors in your source code.

Project Tester

Project Tester is one of the simplest of Java Workshop's tools to use, yet it makes testing your newly compiled applet a breeze. Just click Project Tester's button (the one that looks like a light switch) in Java Workshop's toolbar, and Project Tester creates an HTML document for the applet (if needed) and runs the applet in Java Workshop's window. Figure 2.6, for example, shows Project Tester running one of the applets you'll learn about later in this book. In order to run the applet, Project Tester uses some of the attributes defined for the project by Project Manager. You may recall that you can edit these attributes so that your applet runs exactly as you'd like it to.

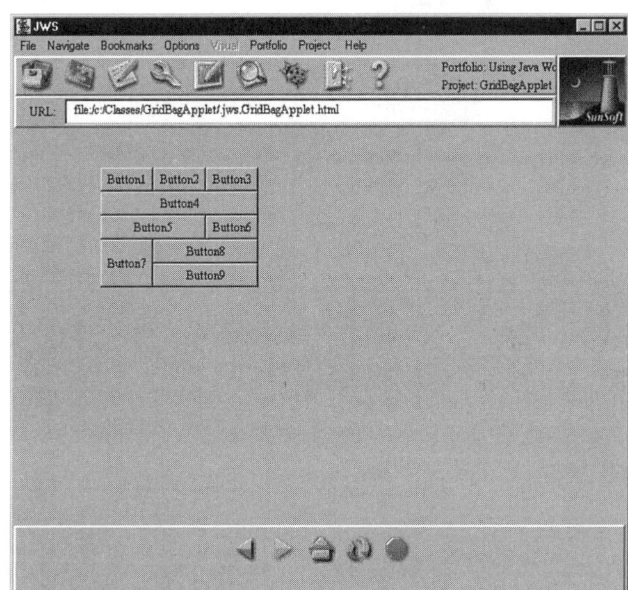

FIG. 2.6
Project Tester runs your applets.

Source Editor

Writing applets would be a tough job without some sort of text editor. Sure, you can use a marking pen to write your code directly on the computer's screen, but saving it to disk is a real trick! Although you can edit your Java source-code files with any text editor capable of saving plain text (ASCII) files, Java Workshop includes its own text editor, called Source Editor. While it's true that Source Editor isn't the greatest editor that ever came down the pike, it is still quite usable and, more importantly, it is closely integrated with the other Java Workshop tools, especially Build Manager and Debugger.

Figure 2.7 shows Source Editor in action. The editor includes a full set of editing commands, including text-block functions like cut and paste. Source Editor's fancy-looking toolbar has icons that enable you to open and save files, locate syntax errors, and control Java's debugger.

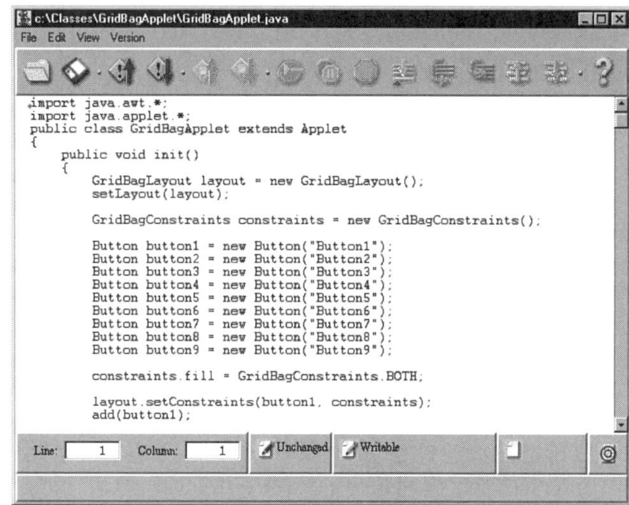

FIG. 2.7
Source Editor is tightly integrated with other Java Workshop tools.

Source Browser

If you have experience with object-oriented programming, you know that sometimes it can be tough to keep track of where your classes come from. Although using techniques like inheritance enables you to write better classes faster, you don't want to spend a lot of time keeping track of your applet's family tree. Java Workshop's Source Browser tool handles this for you, as well as keeping track of which functions are where, so that you can jump to any function almost instantly. You can even search for occurrences of a given text string. No more scanning through long source-code listings!

Figure 2.8 shows Source Browser's class page displaying the applet's inheritance tree. As shown in figure 2.9, Source Browser also creates a list of a class's methods. Just click a method in order to jump to it in Source Editor.

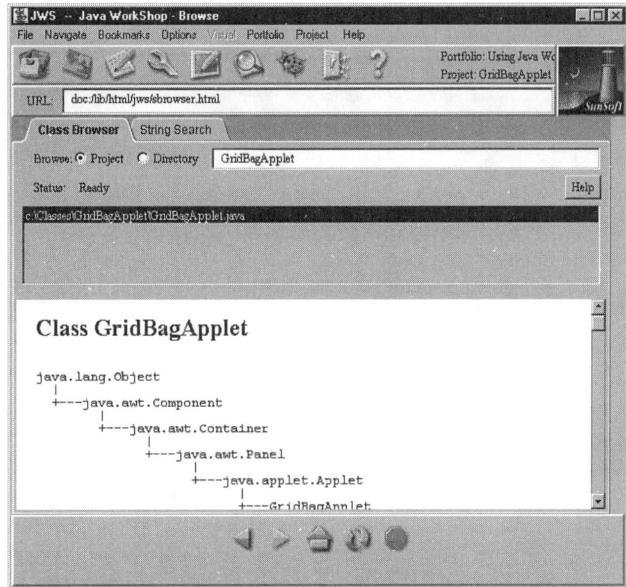

FIG. 2.8
Source Browser can display a class's inheritance tree.

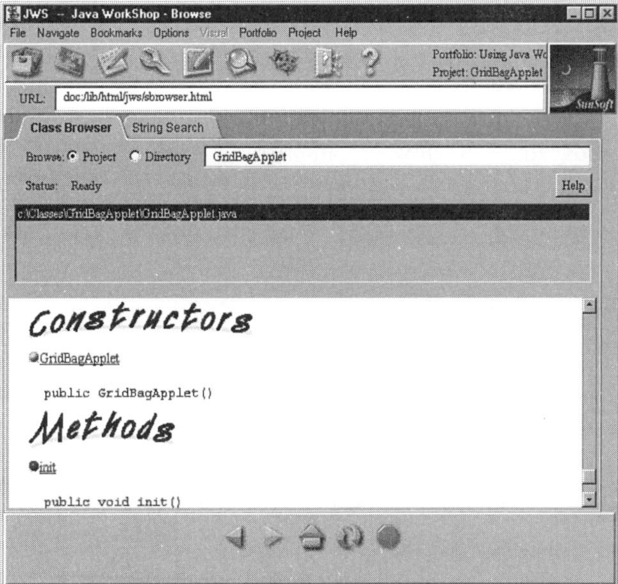

FIG. 2.9
Source Browser can also display a list of a selected class's methods.

Finding occurrences of any text string in your source code is also easy with Source Browser. This particular task is handled by the String Search page, as shown in figure 2.10. After locating each occurrence of a text string, you can click one of the matches displayed in Source Browser's window to jump to the associated line in the source code.

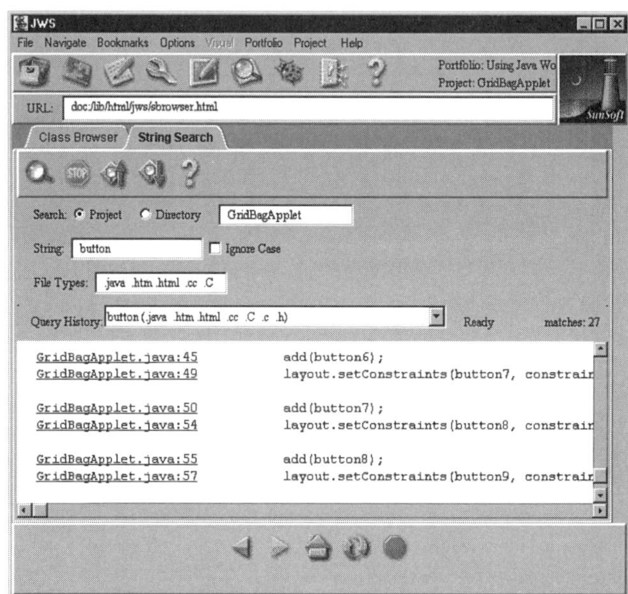

FIG. 2.10
Source Browser does string searches like a pro.

Debugger

As all programmers know, creating even a simple program without introducing a bug or two is nearly impossible. Luckily, programming environments now usually include some sort of program debugger to help the programmer find and fix problems. Java Workshop is no exception, featuring the Debugger tool shown in figure 2.11. As you can see, Debugger's main display includes six pages of information about a currently running applet. Using this information, you can do everything from set breakpoints to trace the execution of threads and evaluate the current values of variables.

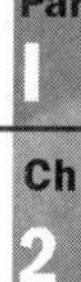

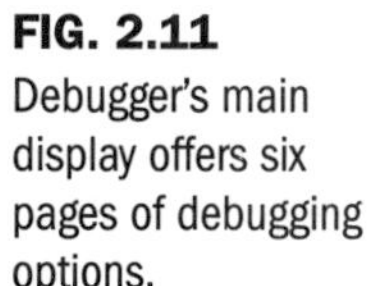

FIG. 2.11
Debugger's main display offers six pages of debugging options.

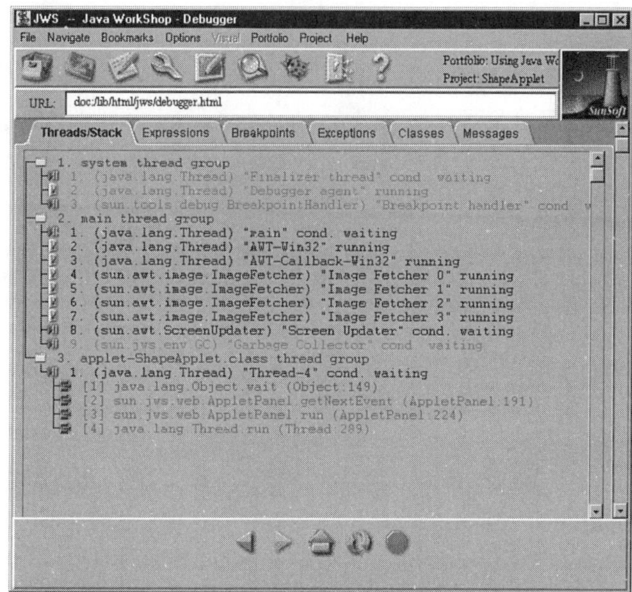

When you run Debugger, Java Workshop also loads Source Editor with the current project's source code and runs a special debugging browser in which the applet is executed. During a debugging session, Source Editor's debugging toolbar is fully active (see fig. 2.12), enabling you to single-step through a program, set breakpoints, step over or into blocks of code, and more.

FIG. 2.12
Source Editor is closely linked to Debugger.

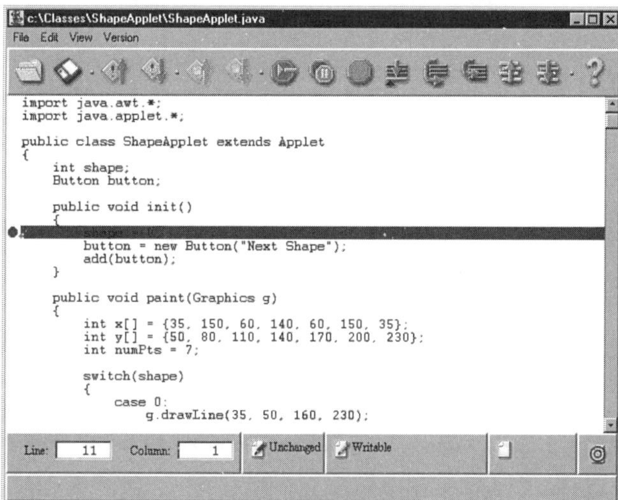

Visual Java

Visual Java not only enables you to design your applet's interface before you start programming, it also creates the starting source code for the applet when your design is done. Then, you need only customize the source code to make the interface perform as you like.

You start off your design using the layout frame window to create a grid of cells that will contain your applet's various components, such as buttons and text boxes (see fig. 2.13). You then use Visual Java's toolbox to add components to the grid and create your applet's interface (see fig. 2.14). Finally, you tell Visual Java to generate the source-code for the interface you've created.

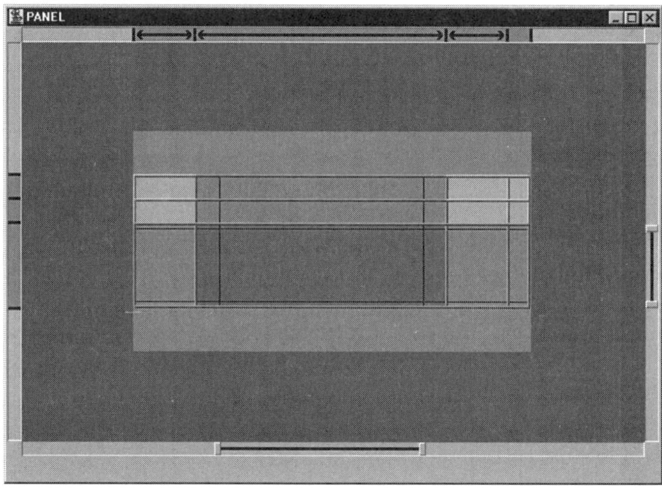

FIG. 2.13
First you create a grid of cells.

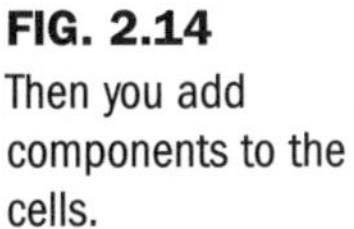

FIG. 2.14
Then you add components to the cells.

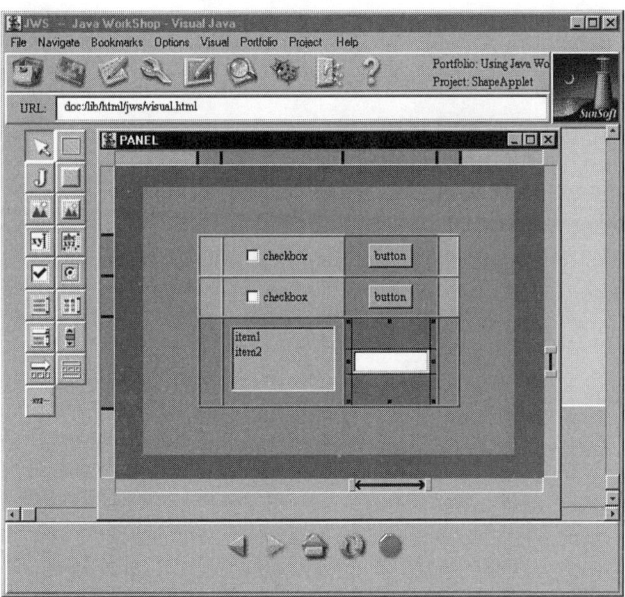

Installing Java Workshop

Now that you know something about Java Workshop's tools, you'd probably like to see them firsthand. But, before you can use Java Workshop, of course, you have to install it on your computer. The first step is to hop onto the World Wide Web, go to **http://java.sun.com**, and download your copy of Java Workshop. When you log on to the site, follow the developer links to Java Workshop.

After you download Java Workshop, you'll have a file called SETUPWS.EXE on your disk. Double-click this file to start the installation process. After some setup, you'll see the screen shown in figure 2.15. Just follow the instructions in each of the Setup Wizard's dialog boxes and you'll end up with a folder called Java-Workshop on your hard disk. This folder contains your copy of Java Workshop. Under Windows 95, the installation program will also add Java Workshop to your Start menu.

FIG. 2.15
This is Java Workshop's installation program.

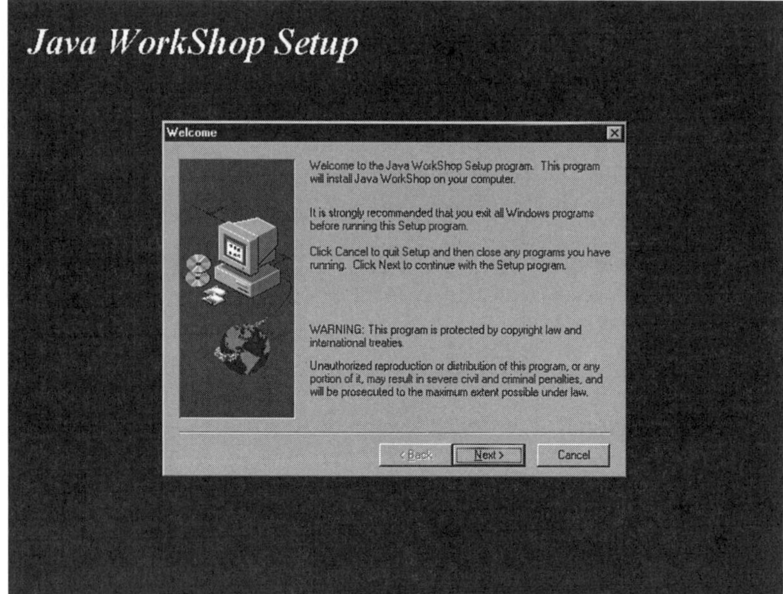

From Here...

This chapter has been only a brief introduction to the tools that make up Java Workshop. In the rest of this book, you'll learn how to use these tools to create your own Java projects. You will, of course, also learn the Java language, which C++ programmers will find familiar.

For more information on topics touched upon in this chapter, please refer to the following:

- Chapter 14, "Portfolio Manager and Project Manager," shows you how to set up your own projects and portfolios.
- Chapter 15, "Source Editor," describes how to use Java workshop's editor.
- Chapter 16, "Build Manager and Source Browser," gives you the inside scoop on these two important tools.
- Chapter 17, "Debugger," describes how to use Java Workshop's debugger to locate and correct runtime errors.
- Chapter 18, "Visual Java," describes how to design applets with Java workshop's powerful program generator.

PART II

The Java Language

CHAPTER 3

Keywords, Data Types, and Operators

Like any other computer language, Java uses keywords and operators to define the language. You use these language elements to create expressions and statements that the Java interpreter can understand. If you've worked with C or C++, Java is familiar territory. But even if you've had no experience with C or C++, you'll discover that Java is built upon the principles that are used to design just about every high-level computer language. In this chapter, you get an introduction to Java and how you use it to write the statements that comprise a Java program. ■

About Java's keywords.

Every computer language has a set of keywords that defines the language. Java's keywords are especially familiar to C and C++ programmers.

How to create identifiers in Java.

You can name your variables, constants, and functions just about anything. However, there are a few rules you must follow.

How to use Java's data types.

Java can handle data in many forms, including integer, floating point, character, and Boolean. Learning how to handle these data types is integral to forming Java expressions.

How Java defines variable scope.

Where a variable can be used in a program depends on where it's declared. Variable scope determines variable visibility in different parts of your program.

How to use Java's operators.

Like all computer languages, Java defines a set of mathematical, comparison, and logical operators that you can use to build expressions. Before you can program in Java, you must know how to use these operators.

Keywords

Every computer language features a set of reserved keywords that have special meaning within that language. They are called reserved keywords because they cannot be used as variable names or for any other purpose than that for which they are intended. A modern, high-level language, Java has a rich set of keywords, many of which you'll recognize from other computer languages, particularly C or C++. These keywords follow.

abstract	else	int	short
boolean	extends	interface	static
break	final	long	sure
byte	finally	native	switch
case	float	new	synchronized
cast	for	null	this
catch	future	operator	throw
char	generic	outer	throws
class	goto	package	transient
const	if	private	try
continue	implements	protected	var
default	import	public	void
do	inner	rest	volatile
double	instanceof	return	while

NOTE Although the keywords listed above are reserved and cannot be used as identifiers in a program, not all of them are currently implemented in Java, but are reserved for use in future versions of the Java language. Examples of currently unused keywords are `const` and `goto`.

Throughout the remainder of this book, you get a chance to use most of the keywords defined in the Java programming language. For now, though, you examine how Java handles identifiers, including variable and constant names.

Identifiers

Every computer program contains *identifiers*, which are user-defined names for data items and code blocks. In Java, as with many computer languages, you use identifiers to define variables, functions, and symbolic constants. (As you'll learn in Chapter 5, "Object-Oriented Programming and Java," Java usually refers to variables as "data members" and to functions as "methods.") Although you can name these identifiers almost anything you like, there are rules you must follow. You can't, after all, just type a bunch of characters on your keyboard and expect Java to accept them. First, every Java identifier must begin with one of these characters:

A–Z

a–z

_

$

The preceding characters are any uppercase letter from A through Z, any lowercase letter from a through z, an underscore, and the dollar sign.

Following the first character, the rest of the identifier can use any of these characters:

A–Z

a–z

_

$

0–9

As you may have noticed, this second set of characters is similar to the first. In fact, the only difference is the addition of the digits from 0 through 9.

NOTE Java identifiers can also use Unicode characters above the hexadecimal value of 00C0. If you don't know about Unicode characters, don't panic; you won't be using them in this book. Briefly put, Unicode characters expand the symbols that can be used in a character set to include characters that are not part of the English language. ■

Using the rules given, the following are valid identifiers in a Java program:

```
number
number2
amount_of_sale
$amount
```

The following identifiers are not valid in a Java program:

```
1number
amount of sale
&amount
item#
```

Constants

Often programmers need to define values that remain unchanged throughout a program. An example might be the value of a mathematical symbol like pi. Other examples include values that might change in the future, but never change during a session with the program, such as the state sales-tax rate. By creating a *symbolic constant* to represent such values, the programmer can use the symbol throughout the program, rather than hard-coding such values.

Because the symbol is defined in only one place in the program, it's a simple matter to revise a program when necessary. When the state sales-tax rate changes, for example, the programmer need only give the symbolic constant representing the tax rate the new value; any program lines that reference the symbolic constant automatically use the new value after the program is recompiled. Another advantage of symbolic constants is that they make programs easier to understand by replacing meaningless numbers with English-like symbols.

To define a symbolic constant in Java, you use the `final` keyword. (You C and C++ programmers will be tempted to use the `const` keyword, but don't bother. The `const` keyword, for some strange reason, is not used in the current version of Java.) In the case of the sales-tax program, you could choose a word like `SALESTAX` to represent the current sales-tax percentage for your state. Then, at the beginning of your program, you set `SALESTAX` to be equal to the current state sales tax. In the Java language, such a line of program code might look like this:

```
final float SALESTAX = 0.06;
```

In the preceding line, the keyword `final` tells Java that this data object is going to be a constant. The `float` is the data type, which, in this case, is floating point. (You'll learn more about data types later in the next section.) The word `SALESTAX` is the symbolic constant. The equals sign tells Java that the word should be equal to the value on the right, which, in this case, is 0.06.

Data Types

In attempting to give you a quick introduction to constants and other kinds of identifiers, the preceding sections skipped over a very important attribute of all constants and variables: data type. Java has eight different data types, which are `byte`, `short`, `int`, `long`, `float`, `double`, `char`, and `boolean`. In this section, you learn what kinds of values these various data types represent.

Integer Values

The most common values used in computer programs are integers, which represent whole number values such as 12, 1988, and -34. Integer values can be both positive or negative, or even the value 0. The size of the value that's allowed depends on the integer data type you choose. Java features four integer data types, which are `byte`, `short`, `int`, and `long`. Although some computer languages allow both signed and unsigned integer values, all of Java's integers are signed, which means they can be positive or negative. (Unsigned values, which Java does not support, can hold only positive numbers.)

The first integer type, `byte`, takes up the least amount of space in a computer's memory. When you declare a constant or variable as byte, you are limited to values in the range -128 to 127. In Java, you declare a byte value like this:

```
byte identifier;
```

In the preceding line, *byte* is the data type for the value, and *identifier* is the variable's name. You can also simultaneously declare and assign a value to a variable like this:

```
byte count = 100;
```

After Java executes the preceding line, your program will have a variable named count that currently holds the value of 100. Of course, you can change the contents of count at any time in your program. It only starts off holding the value 100.

The next biggest type of Java integer is `short`. A variable declared as `short` can hold a value from -32,768 to 32,767. You declare a `short` value like this:

```
short identifier;
```

or

```
short identifier = value;
```

In the above line, `value` can be any value from -32,768 to 32,767, as described previously. In Java, `short` values are twice as big in memory—16 bits—as `byte` values.

Next in the integer data types is `int`, which can hold a value from -2,147,483,648 to 2,147,483,647. The `int` data type can hold such large numbers because it takes up 32 bits of computer memory. You declare `int` values like this:

```
int identifier;
```

or

```
int identifier = value;
```

The final integer data type in the Java language is `long`, which takes up a whopping 64 bits of computer memory and can hold truly immense numbers. Unless you're calculating the number of molecules in the universe, you don't even have to know how big a long number can be. I'd figure it out for you, but I've never seen a calculator that can handle numbers that big. You declare a `long` value like this:

```
long identifier;
```

or

```
long identifier = value;
```

Floating-Point Values

Whereas integer values can hold only whole numbers, the floating-point data types can hold values with both whole number and fractional parts. Examples of floating-point values include 32.9, 123.284, and -43.436. As you can see, just like integers, floating-point values can be either positive or negative.

Java includes two floating-point types, which are `float` and `double`. Each type allows greater precision in calculations. Floating-point numbers can become very complex when they're used in calculations, particularly in multiplication and division. For example, when you divide 3.9 by 2.7, you get 1.44444444. In actuality, though, the fractional portion of the number goes on forever. That is, if you were to continue the division calculation, you'd discover that you keep getting more and more fours in the fractional part of the answer. The answer to 3.9 divided by 2.7 is not really 1.44444444, but rather something more like 1.4444444444444444. But even that answer isn't completely accurate. A more accurate answer would be 1.4444444444444444444444444444444444. The more 4s you add to the answer the more accurate the answer becomes—yet, because the 4s extend on into infinity, you can never arrive at a completely accurate answer.

Dealing with floating-point values frequently means deciding how many decimal places in the answer is accurate enough. That's where the difference between the `float` and `double` data types shows up. In Java, a value declared as `float` can hold a number in the range from around -3.402823 × 1038 to around 3.402823 × 1038. These types of values are also known as ***single-precision floating-point numbers*** and take up 32 bits of memory. You declare a single-precision floating-point number like this:

```
float identifier;
```

or

```
float identifier = value;
```

In the second line, `value` must be a value in the range given in the previous paragraph, followed by an upper- or lowercase F. However, you can write floating-point numbers in a couple of ways, with regular digits and a decimal point or with scientific notation. This value is the type of floating-point number you're used to seeing:

356.552

Now, here's the same number written using Java's rules, in both the number's normal form and in the form of scientific notation:

356.552f

3.56552e2f

Both of the preceding values are equivalent, and you can use either form in a Java program. The `e2` in the second example is the equivalent of writing $\times 10^2$ and is a short form of scientific notation that's often used in programming languages.

NOTE If you're not familiar with scientific notation, the value 3.402823 × 1038 is equal to 3.402823 times a number that starts with a 1 and is followed by 38 zeroes. Computer languages shorten this scientific notation to 3.402823e38.

The second type of floating-point data, `double`, represents a double-precision value, which is a much more accurate representation of floating-point numbers because it allows for more decimal places. A `double` value can be in the range from -1.79769313486232 × 10308 to 1.79769313486232 × 10308 and is declared like this:

```
double identifier;
```

or

```
double identifier = value;
```

Floating-point values of the `double` type are written exactly as their float counterparts, except you use an upper- or lowercase D as the suffix, rather than an F. Here's a few examples:

3.14d

344.23456D

3.4423456e2d

When using floating-point numbers in your programs, use the smallest data type you can. Floating-point numbers are notorious for slowing computer programs to a crawl. Unless you're doing highly precise programming, such as 3-D modeling, the single-precision float data type should do just fine.

Character Values

Often in your programs, you'll need a way to represent character values rather than just numbers. A character is a symbol that's used in text. The most obvious examples of characters are the letters of the alphabet, in both upper- and lowercase varieties. There are, however, many other characters, which include not only things such as spaces, exclamation points, and commas, but also tabs, carriage returns, and line feeds. The symbols 0 through 9 are also characters when they're not being used in mathematical calculations.

In order to provide storage for character values, Java features the `char` data type, which is 16 bits. However, the size of the `char` data type has little to do with the values it can hold. Basically, you can think of a `char` as being able to hold a single character. (The 16-bit length accommodates Unicode characters, which you don't need to worry about in this book.) You declare a `char` value like this:

```
char identifier;
```

or

```
char identifier = value;
```


In the second example, you're not only declaring the variable as a `char`, but also setting its value. In this case, `value` is a single character enclosed in single quotes.

Some characters can't be written with only a single symbol. For example, the tab character is represented in Java as `\t`, which is a backslash followed by a lowercase t. There are several of these special characters, as shown in table 3.1:

Table 3.1 Special Character Literals

Character	Symbol
Backslash	\\
Backspace	\b
Carriage return	\r
Double quote	\"
Form feed	\f
Line feed	\n
Single quote	\'
Tab	\t

Although the special characters in table 3.1 are represented by two symbols, the first of which is always a backslash, you still use them as single characters.

For example, to define a `char` variable as a backspace character, you might write something like the following in your Java program:

```
char backspace = '\b';
```

When Java's compiler sees the backslash, it knows that it's about to encounter a special character of some type. The symbol following the backslash tells the compiler which special character to use. Because the backslash is used to signify a special character, when you want to specify the backslash character itself, you must use two backslashes, which keeps the compiler from getting confused. Other special characters that might confuse the compiler because they are used as part of the Java language are single and double quotes. When you want to use these characters in your program's data, you must also precede them with a backslash.

Boolean Values

Many times in a program, you need a way to determine whether or not a specific condition has been met. For example, you might need to know whether a part of your program executed properly. In such cases, you can use Boolean values, which are represented in Java by the `boolean` data type. Boolean values are unique in that they can be only one of two possible values: `true` or `false`. You declare a `boolean` value like this:

```
boolean identifier;
```

or

```
boolean identifier = value;
```

In the second example, `value` must be `true` or `false` (or an expression that evaluates to `true` or `false`). In an actual program, you might write something like this:

```
boolean file_okay = true;
```

Table 3.2 summarizes Java's various data types.

Table 3.2 Summary of Java's Data Types

Types	Range of Values
`byte`	-128 to 127
`short`	-32,768 to 32,767

Types	Range of Values
`int`	-2,147,483,648 to 2,147,483,647
`long`	Huge
`float`	-3.402823e38 to 3.402823e38
`double`	-1.79769313486232e308 to 1.79769313486232e308
`char`	Symbols used in text
`boolean`	`true` or `false`

Variable Scope

When you write your Java programs, you can't just declare your variables willy-nilly. You have to consider how and where you need to use the variables. This is because variables have an attribute known as *scope*, which determines where in your program variables can be accessed. In Java, a variable's scope is determined by the program block in which the variable first appears. The variable is "visible" to the program only from the beginning of its program block to the end of the program block. When a program's execution leaves a block, all the variables in the block disappear, a phenomenon called "going out of scope."

Generally, in Java, a program block is a section of program code that starts with an opening curly brace ({) and ends with a closing curly brace (}). (Sometimes, the beginning and ending of a block are not explicitly defined.) Specifically, program blocks include things like classes, functions, and loops. As with most programming languages, Java allows program blocks within other program blocks, called *nested blocks*. The ability to nest program blocks adds a wrinkle to the idea of variable scope. Because a variable remains in scope from the beginning of its block to the end of its block, such a variable is also in scope in any blocks that are nested in the variable's block.

You can use variable scope to simplify the access of variables in a program. For example, you usually want to declare variables that you need in many places so that they are in scope in the entire class. That way, you can access the variables without having to pass them as arguments to functions. On the other hand, there are a lot of variables that you use only inside one particular program block. You can keep your program uncluttered by being sure to declare these types of variables only in the blocks in which they're used.

Math Operators

It's a rare computer program that doesn't need to perform mathematical operations on data. Java features a complete set of operators you can use to specify the mathematical operations your program needs to perform. These operators use the standard order of operations (also called operator precedence) and determine the order in which mathematical computations are performed. If you've ever taken algebra, you know that, long ago, mathematicians devised a standard set of symbols for mathematical operations and defined the order in which they're performed. These mathematical rules are also observed in programming languages like Java. Table 3.3 lists Java's mathematical operators in order of precedence.

Table 3.3 Mathematical Operators in Order of Precedence

Operator	Description
-	Negation
++	Increment
--	Decrement
*	Multiplication
/	Division
%	Modulus
+	Addition
-	Subtraction
=	Assignment

Operator precedence comes into play when you use several different operators in the same calculation. For example, look at the following line of Java source code:

```
answer = 3 + 5 * 3;
```

Go ahead and do the calculation. What did you get for an answer? If you got 18, you already know how operator precedence works. If you're new to this sort of thing, you probably got 24 for an answer, which is incorrect. The reason 18 is the correct answer is because operator precedence dictates that the multiplication be performed before the addition. If you look at table 3.3, you can see that multiplication comes before addition.

Casting a Result to a Different Data Type

Java doesn't allow implicit data conversion. That is, if you try to assign the result of an expression to the wrong data type, Java generates a compiler error. However, you can explicitly perform such data conversions by casting one data type to another. C and C++ programmers should be familiar with casting, but if you're familiar with some other computer language, you might not have used casting before. When you *cast* a value, you're telling Java that it's okay to convert one type of value to another. You do this by placing the data type you want in front of the calculation, in parentheses. For example, look at this line of Java code:


```
difference = 100 - 15 - 3.5f;
```

Because the calculation on the right side of the equals sign results in a floating-point number, `difference` must be a floating-point variable. If `difference` is an integer, then the result of the calculation must also be an integer. In the previous case, you can satisfy Java's compiler by using a type cast, which looks like this:

```
difference = (int)(100 - 15 - 3.5f);
```

Now, when Java executes the above line, it first calculates the result of `100-15-3.5f`, which is 81.5. Then, it converts the result to an integer by dropping the decimal portion of the value. This gives a result of 81. Finally, Java assigns the value of 81 to `difference`, which is an integer variable. In short, when you use a type cast, you're telling the compiler, "Yes, I know what I'm doing. I want the result converted."

NOTE Sometimes the minus sign is used as a negation operator, rather than a subtraction operator. For example, if you want to write a negative number, like negative ten, use the negation operator like this: -10. This is a case where the same symbol is used to mean different things. Java can tell the difference between the negation and a subtraction operator by the context in which the operator is used.

Multiplication and Data Types

Try to determine the result of the following calculation:

```
byte product = (byte)(20 * 20);
```

If you said the answer is 400, you'd be both right and wrong. While it is true that 20 times 20 is 400, `product` is only a `byte` variable, which means it can only hold values from -128 to 127. Unfortunately, Java just goes ahead and stuffs the answer into product whether it fits or not. (The `byte` type-cast, in fact, converts the answer to a `byte` before it's stuffed into product, but that's a minor complication.) In the preceding case, you'd end up with an answer of -112.

Be especially careful when you're performing more than one multiplication in a calculation. In such cases, if you're using the smaller data types like `byte` or `short`, numbers can really get out of hand. Most Java programmers use the `int` data type for their integer variables, which ensures that their variables have plenty of room for large numbers.

When a mathematical calculation gives you an answer that seems way out of whack, check to make sure that you're using data types that are large enough to hold the values used in the calculation. This is especially true for the result of the calculation. Many hard-to-find program bugs result from using the wrong data types for large values.

Integer versus Floating-Point Division

Look at this calculation:

```
int result = 3 / 2;
```

When you divide 3 by 2, you may start out with integers, but you end up with 1.5 for an answer, and 1.5 is, of course, a floating-point number. But when Java performs the division shown above, it performs integer division. That is, it drops any decimal portion in the answer, leaving `result` equal to 1. There are times when this is the type of division you want to perform. But if you want the precise answer to 3 / 2, you're going to have to change something. Maybe changing `result` to a floating-point variable will make a difference:

```
float result = 3 / 2;
```

When Java performs this calculation, you still end up with 1 as the answer. Why? Because, as I mentioned before, Java performs integer division on integer values like 3 and 2. To solve the problem, you must also convert 3 and 2 to floating-point values, like this:

```
float result = 3f / 2f;
```

Now, you get the correct result of 1.5. Actually, only one of the numbers to the right of the equals sign needs to be floating-point in order to get a floating-point answer. This line works, too:

```
float result = 3f / 2;
```


The Modulo Operator

In the previous section, you learned that integer division gives you a result that's equal to the number of times one number fits into another, regardless of the remainder. For example, you now know that, in Java, the answer to "3 divided by 2" is 1, meaning that 2 fits into 3 only once. Integer division throws away the remainder, but what if it's the remainder you're looking for? Then, you can use the modulo operator (%) like this:

```
result = expr1 % expr2;
```

This line results in the remainder of `expr1` divided by `expr2`. For example, the calculation:

```
int result = 11 % 3;
```

makes `result` equal to 2, because 3 goes into 11 three times with a remainder of 2. You probably won't use the modulo operator much, but it can be handy for special types of calculations.

The Increment Operator

You C and C++ programmers are way ahead of the game here, because the increment (and decrement) operators are used extensively in C programs. However, if you come to this book from a language like BASIC or Pascal, you won't have used these handy operators. Many times in a program, you want to increase a value by a specific amount. For example, if you use the variable `count` to keep track of how many times a part of your program executed, you need to add 1 to `count` each time you reach that part of the program. Many programmers do this kind of incrementing like this:

```
count = count + 1;
```

Here, the computer takes the value stored in `count`, increases it by 1, and then assigns the new value to `count`. Using Java's increment operator (++), you can replace the previous line with this one:

```
++count;
```

Another way to write the preceding line is like this:

```
count++;
```

There is, however, a subtle difference in the way the increment operator works when it's placed before (pre-increment) or after (post-increment) the value it's incrementing. The difference crops up when you use the operator in expressions. For example, look at these lines of Java program code:

```
int num1 = 1;
int num2 = ++num1;
```

Here, Java first sets the variable `num1` to 1. In the second line, Java increments `num1` to 2 and then assigns 2 to `num2`.

Now, look at these lines:

```
int num1 = 1;
int num2 = num1++;
```

This time, `num2` ends up as 1. Why? In the second line, Java doesn't increment `num1` until after it assigns the current value of `num1` (which is 1) to `num2`. Watch out for this little detail when you get started writing your own applets.

What if you want to increment a value by more than 1? The old-fashioned way would be to use a line like this:

```
num = num + 5;
```

Java has a special shortcut operator that handles the above situation, too. You use the shortcut operator like this:

```
num += 5;
```

The above line just says, "Add 5 to num."

The Decrement Operator

In computer programs, you don't always count forward. Often, you need to count backward as well. That's why Java has the decrement operator (– –), which works just like the increment operator, except it subtracts 1 instead of adding it. You use the decrement operator like this:

```
--num;
```

The above example uses the pre-decrement version of the operator. If you want to decrement the value after it's been used in an expression, use the post-decrement version, like this:

```
num--;
```

The set of operators wouldn't be complete without a decrement operator that enables you to subtract any value from a variable. The following line

```
num - 5;
```

tells Java to decrement num by 5.

Expressions

Without a doubt, expressions are the main building blocks of a program. This is because there are so many different kinds of expressions that a majority of the source-code lines in a program end up being—you guessed it—expressions. There are expressions that result in numerical values. There are expressions that result in strings. There are simple expressions, complex expressions, and all manner of expressions in between.

To put it simply, an expression is a line of code that can be reduced to a value or that assigns a value. For example, you know that the addition operator adds one expression to another, like this:

```
sum = expr1 + expr2;
```

In the preceding line, `expr1` can be something as simple as the variable `x` or as complex as `(4 + 5) * 2 * 5 / 7 + x / y`. The same goes for `expr2`, of course. And, in fact, the first example containing `expr1` and `expr2` is an expression itself!

But no matter how complicated, all expressions can be classified into one of three main categories:

- Numerical expressions combine numbers, variables, or constants using mathematical operators. An example is `2 + 3 / x`.
- Assignment expressions assign a value to a variable. An example is `num = 3`.
- Logical expressions are unique in that they result in a value of `true` or `false`. An example is `x < 3` (which reads "x is less than 3").

If you remember your high school math at all, you know that expressions often contain other simpler expressions. This is true for a Java expression, too. For example, look at the following assignment expression:

```
num = (5 - x) * (2 + y);
```

This is an assignment expression because it assigns a value to the variable `num`. However, the stuff on either side of the equals sign contains these other expressions:

```
num
(5 - x) * (2 + y)
```

Both of the above lines are numerical expressions because they can be reduced to a numerical value (assuming that you know the values of `num`, `x`, and `y`.

But, wait a second—you're not done yet. You can still find more sub-expressions. Look at the multiplication operation. Can you see that it's multiplying two expressions together? Those two expressions look like this:

```
(5 - x)
(2 + y)
```

And the above simplified expressions contain yet more sub-expressions. Those expressions are:

```
5
x
2
y
```

Expressions are *recursive*, meaning that the definition of an expression keeps coming back on itself. An expression contains expressions that contain other expressions, which themselves contain other expressions. How deep you can dig depends on the complexity of the original expression. But, as you saw demonstrated, even the relatively simple expression `num = (5 - x) * (2 + y)` has four levels of depth.

Comparison Operators

Another type of operator you can use to build expressions is the comparison operator. Comparison operators are used to create logical expressions, which, if you recall, result in a value of `true` or `false`. Table 3.4 lists the comparison operators used in Java programming. C and C++ programmers will find these operators very familiar. Table 3.5 shows some comparison expressions and how they evaluate to `true` or `false`.

Table 3.4 Java's Comparison Operators

Operator	Description
==	Equal to
<	Less than
>	Greater than
<=	Less than or equal to
>=	Greater than or equal to
!=	Not equal to

Table 3.5 Examples of Comparison Expressions

Expression	Result
3 + 4 == 7	true
3 + 4 != 7	false
3 + 4 != 2 + 6	true
3 + 4 < 10	true
3 + 4 <= 10	true
3 + 4 == 4 + 4	false
3 + 4 > 10	false
3 + 4 >= 7	true
3 + 4 >= 8	false

Logical Operators

The comparison operators enable you to compare two expressions. But another type of operator—logical operators—supercharges comparison operators so that you can combine two or more comparison expressions into a more complex logical expression. Table 3.6 lists Java's logical operators and what they mean.

Table 3.6 Java's Logical Operators

Operator	Description
&&	AND
||	OR
^	Exclusive OR
!	NOT

The AND (`&&`) operator requires all expressions to be true for the entire expression to be true. For example, the expression

```
(3 + 2 == 5) && (6 + 2 == 8)
```

is true because the expressions on both sides of the `&&` are true. However, the expression

```
(4 + 3 == 9) && (3 + 3 == 6)
```

is false because the expression on the left of the `&&` is not true. Remember this when combining expressions with AND. If any expression is false, the entire expression is false.

The OR operator (`¦¦`) requires only one expression to be true for the entire expression to be true. For example, the expressions

```
(3 + 6 == 2) ¦¦ (4 + 4 == 8)
```

and

```
(4 + 1 == 5) ¦¦ (7 + 2 == 9)
```

are both true because at least one of the expressions being compared is true. Notice that in the second case both expressions being compared are true, which also makes an OR expression true.

The exclusive OR operator (^) is used to determine if one and only one of the expressions being compared is true. Unlike a regular OR, with an exclusive OR, if both expressions are true, the result is false (weird, huh?). For example, the expression

```
(5 + 7 == 12) ^ (4 + 3 == 8)
```

evaluates to `true`, whereas these expressions evaluate to `false`:

```
(5 + 7 == 12) ^ (4 + 3 == 7)
(5 + 7 == 10) ^ (4 + 3 == 6)
```

The NOT (`!`) operator switches the value of (or negates) a logical expression. For example, the expression

```
(4 + 3 == 5)
```

is false; however, the expression

```
!(4 + 3 == 5)
```

is true.

Like all operators, comparison and logical operators have an order of operations, or operator precedence. When you evaluate a complex expression, you must be sure to evaluate any sub-expressions in the correct order. As you learned in the previous example, however, you can use parentheses to group expressions so that they're easier to understand or to change the order of operations. Table 3.7 lists the comparison and logical operators in order of precedence.

Table 3.7 Comparison and Logical Operators' Order of Operations

<table>
<tr><td>!</td><td>NOT</td></tr>
<tr><td>< > <= >=</td><td>Relational</td></tr>
<tr><td>== !=</td><td>Equality</td></tr>
<tr><td>^</td><td>Exclusive OR</td></tr>
<tr><td>&&</td><td>Logical AND</td></tr>
<tr><td>||</td><td>Logical OR</td></tr>
</table>

Of course, you wouldn't write expressions such as

```
(4 + 5 == 9) && !(3 + 1 == 3)
```

in your programs. They would serve no purpose because you already know how the expressions evaluate. However, when you use variables, you have no way of knowing in advance how an expression may evaluate. For example, is the expression

```
(num < 9) && (num > 15)
```

true or false? You don't know without being told the value of the numerical variable `num`. By using logical operators, though, your program can do the evaluation, and, based on the result—`true` or `false`—take the appropriate action.

From Here...

All computers must manipulate data in order to produce output. Java, like all programming languages, features many data types that you can use for constants and variables in your programs. These data types enable you to store everything from simple integers like 23 and -10 to strings and complex floating-point numbers.

Java also features mathematical and logical operators for standard operations such as addition, subtraction, multiplication, division, and comparing expressions. When you use these operators, always remember operator precedence.

Please refer to the following chapters for information on related topics:

- Chapter 4, "Controlling Program Flow," describes how to use comparison and logical expressions to control what parts of your program get executed.
- Chapter 6, "Applets and Graphics," shows how to display data in your Java applet's display area.
- Chapter 7, "Java Controls," discusses Java's many control objects and how you can use them to transfer data to and from your applet's users.
- Chapter 13, "Writing Java Applications," describes how to create stand-alone applications (applications that aren't applets) with Java.

CHAPTER 4

Controlling Program Flow

If programs had to be written so that each statement executed sequentially from the beginning to the end of the program, the world would not only have much bigger programs, there'd also be a lot of programmers in therapy. The ability to control what program statements are executed, as well as when they are executed, is a basic element of programming in almost every computer language. Thankfully, Java is no different. You can easily control a program's flow of execution by using decision-making code comprised of `if` and `switch` statements, as well as incorporating `while`, `do-while`, and `for` loops into Java programs. ■

How to use Java's `if` statement.

The `if` statement is the simplest tool for program decision making. When combined with else clauses, the `if` statement becomes a powerful decision maker.

How to use Java's `switch` statement.

For some program decision making, a `switch` statement is more appropriate than an `if` statement, although both can be used to obtain identical results.

How to program `while` loops.

Using a `while loop`, a program can repeatedly execute a block of code until a specified condition becomes false.

How to program `do-while` loops.

The `do-while` loop is a complement to the `while` loop, because, although it works similarly, its condition is checked at the end of the loop, rather than at the beginning, which means the loops always execute at least once.

How to program `for` loops.

The `for` loop enables you to specify exactly how many times the body of the loop executes.

Program Flow and Branching

Program flow is the order in which a program executes its statements. Most program flow is sequential, meaning that the statements are executed one by one in the order in which they appear in the program. However, there are Java commands that make your program jump forward or backward and skip over program code not currently required. These commands are said to control the program flow.

When a program breaks the sequential flow and jumps to a new section of code, it is called *branching*. When this branching is based on a decision, the program is performing conditional branching. When no decision-making is involved and the program always branches when it encounters a branching instruction, the program is performing unconditional branching. Unconditional branching is rarely used in modern programs, so the following sections deal with conditional branching.

The *if* Statement

Most conditional branching in a Java program occurs when the program executes an `if` statement, which compares data and decides what to do next based on the result of the comparison. For example, you've probably seen programs that print menus on-screen. To select a menu item, you often type the item's selection number. When the program receives your input, it checks the number you entered and decides what to do. You might use an `if` statement to create such a program.

Simple *if* Statements

A simple `if` statement includes the keyword `if` followed by a logical expression, which, as you learned in the previous chapter, is an expression that evaluates to either `true` or `false`. These expressions are surrounded by parentheses. You follow the parentheses with the statement that you want executed if the logical expression is true. For example, look at this `if` statement:

```
if (choice == 5)
    g.drawString("You chose number 5.", 30, 30);
```

In this case, if the variable `choice` is equal to 5, Java executes the call to `drawString()`. Otherwise, Java just skips the call to `drawString()`.

The syntax of languages such as Java is tolerant of the styles of various programmers, enabling programmers to construct programs that are organized in a way that's best-suited to the programmer and the particular problem. For example, the Java language is not particular about how you specify the part of an `if` statement to be executed. The statement

```
if (choice == 1)
    num = 10;
```

could also be written like this:

```
if (choice == 1) num = 10;
```

In other words, although the parentheses are required around the logical expression, the code to be executed can be on the same line or the following line after the `if` statement.

In the case of an `if` statement that contains only one program line to be executed, you can choose to include or do away with the curly braces that usually mark a block of code. With this option in mind, you could rewrite the preceding `if` statement like listing 4.1.

Listing 4.1 The *If* Statement with Braces

```
if (choice == 1)
{
    num = 10;
}
```

Another way you'll often see braces used with a Java `if` statement is shown here:

```
if (choice == 1) {
    num = 10;
}
```

In this case, the opening brace is on the `if` statement's first line.

NOTE The `if` statement, no matter how complex it becomes, always evaluates to either `true` or `false`. If the statement evaluates to `true`, the second portion of the statement is executed. If the statement evaluates to `false`, the second portion of the statement is not executed.

Multiple-Line *if* Statements

Listing 4.1 demonstrated the simplest `if` statement. This simple statement often fits your program's decision-making needs just fine. Sometimes, however, you want to perform more than one command as part of an `if` statement. To perform more than one command, enclose the commands within curly braces. Listing 4.2 uses this technique.

Listing 4.2 Multiple-line *if* Statement

```
if (choice == 1)
{
    num = 1;
    num2 = 10;
}
```

The *else* Clause

The `else` keyword enables you to use a single `if` statement to choose between two outcomes. When the `if` statement evaluates to `true`, the second part of the statement is executed. When the `if` statement evaluates to `false`, the `else` portion is executed. (When the `if` statement evaluates to neither `true` nor `false`, it's time to get a new computer!) Listing 4.3 demonstrates how `else` works.

Listing 4.3 Using the *else* Clause

```
if (choice == 1)
{
    num = 1;
    num2 = 10;
}
else
{
    num = 2;
    num2 = 20;
}
```

In listing 4.3, if `choice` equals 1, Java sets `num` to 1 and `num2` to 10. If `choice` is any other value, Java executes the `else` portion, setting `num` to 2 and `num2` to 20. As you can see, the `else` clause provides a default outcome for an `if` statement. A default outcome doesn't help much, however, if an `if` statement has to deal with more than two possible outcomes. That's the job of the `else if` clause. Listing 4.4 shows how to use the `else if` clause.

Listing 4.4 Using the *else if* Clause

```
if (choice == 1)
    num = 1;
else if (choice == 2)
    num = 2;
else if (choice == 3)
    num = 3;
```

When Java executes the program code in listing 4.4, if `choice` is 1, Java looks at only the first `if` section and skips over both of the `else if` clauses. That is, Java sets `num` to 1 and then continues on its way to whatever part of the program follows the final `else if` clause. Note that if `choice` doesn't equal 1, 2, or 3, Java must evaluate all three clauses in the listing, but doesn't do anything with `num`.

The *switch* Statement

Another way you can add decision-making code to your programs is with the `switch` statement. The `switch` statement gets its name from the fact that it enables a computer program to switch between different outcomes based on a given value. A `switch` statement does much the same job as an `if` statement, but it is more appropriate for situations where you have many choices, rather than only a few, as well as when different sets of values require the same outcome. Look at the `if` statement in listing 4.5.

Listing 4.5 A Typical *if* Statement

```
if (x == 1)
    y = 1;
if (x == 2)
    y = 2;
if (x == 3)
    y = 3;
else
    y = 0;
```

You could easily rewrite the preceding `if` statement as a `switch` statement, as shown in listing 4.6.

Listing 4.6 Changing an *if* Statement to a *switch* Statement

```
switch(x)
{
    case 1:
        y = 1;
        break;
    case 2:
        y = 2;
        break;
    case 3:
        y = 3;
        break;
    default:
        y = 0;
}
```

The first line of a `switch` statement is the keyword `switch` followed by the variable whose value determines the outcome. This variable is called the control variable. Inside the main switch statement (which begins and ends with curly braces) are a number of `case` clauses, one for each possible value of the `switch` control variable (the `x`, in this case). In the above example, if `x` equals 1, Java jumps to the `case 1` and sets `y` equal to 1. Then, the `break` statement tells Java that it should skip over the rest of the `switch` statement.

If `x` is 2, the same sort of program flow occurs, except Java jumps to the `case 2`, sets `y` equal to 2, and then breaks out of the `switch`. If the `switch` control variable is not equal to any of the values specified by the various `case` clauses, Java jumps to the `default` clause. The `default` clause, however, is optional. You can leave it out if you want, in which case Java will do nothing if there's no matching case for the control variable.

One tricky thing about `switch` statements is the various ways that you can use the `break` statement to control program flow. Look at listing 4.7.

Listing 4.7 Using *break* To Control Program Flow

```
switch(x)
{
    case 1:
        y = 1;
    case 2:
        y = 2;
        break;
    case 3:
        y = 3;
        break;
    default:
        y = 0;
}
```

In this example, funny things happen, depending on whether the control variable `x` equals 1 or 2. In the former case, Java first jumps to `case 1` and sets `y` equal to 1. Then, because there is no `break` before the `case 2` clause, Java continues executing statements, dropping through the `case 2` and setting `y` equal to 2. Ouch! The moral of the story is—make sure you have `break` statements in the right places.

If the outcome of listing 4.7 was really what you wanted to happen, you'd probably rewrite the `switch` statement to look like listing 4.8.

Listing 4.8 Rewriting Listing 4.7

```
switch(x)
{
    case 1:
    case 2:
        y = 2;
        break;
    case 3:
        y = 3;
        break;
    default:
        y = 0;
}
```

Here, just as in listing 4.7, `y` ends up equal to 2 if `x` equals 1 or 2. You run into this type of `switch` statement a lot in Java programs. If you're a C or C++ programmer, you've already seen a lot of this sort of thing, so you should feel right at home.

The *while* Loop

A `while` loop continues running until its control expression becomes `false`. The control expression is a logical expression, much like the logical expressions you use with `if` statements. In other words, you can use any expression that evaluates to `true` or `false` as a control expression for a `while` loop. Here's an example of a simple `while` loop:

```
num = 1;
while (num < 10)
    ++num;
```

Here the loop's control variable `num` is first set to 1. Then, at the start of the `while` loop, the program compares the value in `num` with 10. If `num` is less than 10, the expression evaluates to `true`, and the program executes the body of the loop, which in this case is a single statement that increments `num`. The program then goes back and checks the value of `num` again. As long as `num` is less than 10, the loop continues. But once `num` equals 10, the control expression evaluates to `false` and the loop ends.

NOTE Notice how, in the previous example of a `while` loop, the program first sets the value of the control variable (`num`) to 1. Initializing your control variable before entering the `while` loop is extremely important. If you don't initialize the variable, you don't know what it might contain, and therefore the outcome of the loop is unpredictable. In the previous example, if `num` happened to be greater than 10, the loop wouldn't happen at all. Instead, the loop's control expression would immediately evaluate to `false`, and the program would branch to the statement after the curly braces.

Although the previous example has only a single program line in the body of the `while` loop, you can make a `while` loop do as much as you want. To add more program lines, you create a program block using braces. This program block tells Java where the body of the loop begins and ends. For example, suppose you want to create a loop that not only increments the loop control variable, but also displays a message each time through the loop. You might accomplish this task as shown in listing 4.9.

Listing 4.9 Using a *while* Loop

```
num = 0;
while (num < 10)
{
    ++num;
    String s = String.valueOf(num);
    g.drawString("num is now equal to:", 20, 40);
    g.drawString(s, 20, 55);
}
```

CAUTION

Always initialize (set the starting value of) any variable used in a `while` loop's control expression. Failure to do so may result in your program skipping over the loop entirely. (Initializing a variable means setting it to its starting value. If you need a variable to start at a specific value, you must initialize it yourself.) Also, be sure to increment or decrement the control variable, whichever is appropriate, in the body of a loop. Failure to do this could result in an infinite loop, which is when the loop conditional never yields a true result. Such a loop would execute endlessly.

The *do-while* Loop

Java also features `do-while` loops. A `do-while` loop is much like a `while` loop, except a `do-while` loop evaluates its control expression at the end of the loop rather than at the beginning. So the body of the loop—the statements between the beginning and end of the loop—is always executed at least once. In a `while` loop, the body of the loop may or may not ever get executed. Listing 4.10 shows how a `do-while` loop works.

Listing 4.10 Using a *do-while* Loop

```
num = 0;

do
    ++num;
while (num < 10);
```

The difference between a `do-while` loop and a `while` loop are readily apparent when you look at the listing. As you can see, the loop's conditional expression is at the end instead of the beginning. That is, in the example listing, `num` is always incremented at least once. After Java increments `num`, it gets to the `while` line and checks whether `num` is less than 10. If it is, program execution jumps back to the beginning of the loop, where `num` gets incremented again. Eventually, `num` becomes equal to 10; this causes the conditional expression to be false so that the loop ends.

Previously, you saw an example of a `while` loop whose body contained multiple statements. By using braces to mark off a program block, you can do the same thing with a `do-while` loop. Listing 4.11 shows how to create a multiple line `do-while` loop.

Listing 4.11 A Multiple-line *do-while* Loop

```
num = 0;

do
{
    ++num;
    String s = String.valueOf(num);
    g.drawString("num is now equal to:", 20, 40);
    g.drawString(s, 20, 55);
}
while (num < 10);
```

In listing 4.11, `num` gets set to zero right before the loop starts. Then, the word `do` marks the beginning of the loop, after which the program increments `num`, creates a string from the current value of `num`, and displays the value on the screen. At the end of the loop, the program checks the value of `num`. If `num` is less than 10, the loop repeats; otherwise, the loop ends.

The *for* Loop

Probably the most often-used loop in programming is the `for` loop, which instructs a program to perform a block of code a specified number of times. There are many applications for a `for` loop, including tasks such as reading through a list of data items or initializing an array. You could, for example, use a `for` loop to instruct your computer to print 10,000 address labels, by reading a new address from a file each time through the loop and sending that address to the printer. Because you don't currently have an address file, however, let's say you want to print a name on the screen ten times. Listing 4.12 shows one way to do this in a Java program.

Listing 4.12 Printing a Name Ten Times

```
g.drawString("Alfred Thompson", 50, 50);
g.drawString("Alfred Thompson", 50, 65);
g.drawString("Alfred Thompson", 50, 80);
g.drawString("Alfred Thompson", 50, 95);
g.drawString("Alfred Thompson", 50, 110);
g.drawString("Alfred Thompson", 50, 125);
g.drawString("Alfred Thompson", 50, 140);
g.drawString("Alfred Thompson", 50, 155);
g.drawString("Alfred Thompson", 50, 170);
g.drawString("Alfred Thompson", 50, 185);
```

Look at listing 4.12. See all those calls to `drawString()`? To produce programs that are tightly written, shorter, and faster, always try to replace repetitive program code with program loops. Listing 4.12 can be streamlined easily by using a `for` loop, as shown in listing 4.13. The output of the second version is identical to the first, but now the listing is shorter and contains no redundant code.

Listing 4.13 Using a *for* Loop To Print Ten Names

```
int row = 0;

for (int x=0; x<10; ++x)
    g.drawString("Al Thompson", 25, 50 + (x * 15));
```

Look at the program line beginning with the keyword `for`. The loop starts with this line. The word foretells Java that you're starting a `for` loop. There are actually three elements inside the parentheses. The first part, `x=1`, is called the initialization section. The second part, `x<10`, is called the condition; the last part, `++x`, is called the increment.

All three sections of the `for` loop, which are separated by semicolons, reference the loop-control variable `x`. The loop-control variable, which can have any integer-variable name, is where Java stores the current loop count. Notice that the loop-control variable must have been previously declared as an `int` (integer) variable. You can place this declaration as part of the initialization part of the command (although doing so will probably slow the loop down a little).

The initialization section of the `for` statement is used to initialize the loop-control variable that controls the action. The condition section represents a Boolean condition that should be equal to `true` for the loop to continue execution. Finally, the increment, which is the third part of the statement, is an expression describing how to increment the control variable. The statement after the `for` statement is executed each time the loop's conditional expression is found to be true.

The previous example of a `for` loop increments the loop counter by 1. But suppose you want a `for` loop that counts from 5 to 50 by fives? This could be useful if you need to use the loop counter to display a value that needs to be incremented by a different number. You can do this by changing the sections of the `for` loop, like this:

```
for (x=5; x<=50; x+=5)
```

This loop doesn't start counting at 1. Rather, the loop variable begins with a value of 5. Then, thanks to the `x+=5` statement, the loop variable is incremented by 5 each time through the loop. Therefore, `x` goes from 5 to 10, from 10 to 15, and so on up to 50, resulting in ten loops.

You can also use a `for` loop to count backwards, like this:

```
for (x=50; x>=5; x-=5)
```

Notice that in the initialization part of the `for` statement, the higher value is used. Notice also that the increment clause uses a decrement operator; this causes the loop count to be decremented (decreased) rather than incremented.

Using Variables in Loops

Just as you can substitute variables for most numerical values in a program, you can also substitute variables for the literals in loops. In fact, you'll probably use variables in your loop limits as often as you use literals, if not more. Here's an example of how to use variables to control your `for` loops:

```
for (x=start; x<=end; x+=inc)
```

In the above partial `for` loop, the loop control variable `x` starts off at the value of the variable `start`. Each time through the loop, Java increments `x` by the value stored in the variable `inc`. Finally, when `x` is greater than the value stored in `end`, the loop ends. As you can see, using variables with loops enables you to write loops that work differently based on the state of the program.

From Here...

Making decisions based on the state of data is an important part of a computer program. Java's `if` and `switch` statements enable you to program such decisions into your Java applets. In addition, by using loops, you can easily program your applets to perform repetitive operations. A `while` loop may or may not ever execute depending on how the conditional expressions work out. On the other hand, a `do-while` loop always executes at least once because its conditional is evaluated at the end of the loop rather than at the start. The `for` loop is a versatile programming construct that enables you to create loops that run from a given starting value to a given ending value. The loop's operation also depends on the value of the loop's increment value, which enables you to use the loop-control variable to count forward or backward by any given amount.

Please refer to the following chapters for related topics:

- Chapter 3, "Keywords, Data Types, and Operators," describes the basic elements of the Java language.
- Chapter 6, "Applets and Graphics," is where you start applying the concepts you've learned so far toward the building of applets.
- Chapter 7, "Java Controls," discusses Java's many control objects. Using controls you can obtain input from the user and make program decisions based on that data.
- Chapter 13, "Writing Java Applications," describes how to create stand-alone applications, which use the same language basics as applets, with Java.

CHAPTER 5

Object-Oriented Programming and Java

Why object-oriented programming was invented.

Although object-oriented programming is more complex than procedural programming, it solves many problems inherent in previous types of programming.

About encapsulation, inheritance, and polymorphism.

For all intents and purposes, once you understand the principles of encapsulation, inheritance, and polymorphism, you'll understand object-oriented programming.

How to create your own classes and subclasses.

Java programs are comprised of classes that you write. Knowing how to apply object-oriented programming techniques is critical in learning how to write your own classes.

How to use Java Workshop to create and run applets.

Although Java Workshop's tools can't be thoroughly covered in a single chapter, this chapter gives you a quick introduction to using those tools to create your own applets.

Programming languages, like their spoken-language kin, evolve over time. They are constantly refined and focused to meet the ever-changing needs of their users. Like other modern programming languages such as C++, Java is a mixture of all the techniques developed over the years. Therefore, we'll start exploring object-oriented programming (OOP) by briefly looking at the history of programming languages. Knowing where object-oriented ideas came from will help you to better understand why they are an important part of modern programming languages. Once you understand why OOP was developed, you'll learn exactly what makes a programming language object-oriented. ■

From Switches to Objects

Back in the dark ages of computing, technicians programmed computers by flipping banks of switches, with each switch representing a single bit of information. In those days, even the simple programs required agonizing patience and precision. As the need for more sophisticated programs grew, so did the need for better ways to write these programs. The need to make computer programming quicker and simpler spurred the invention of assembly language and, shortly thereafter, high-level languages such as FORTRAN.

High-level languages enable programmers to use English-like commands in their programs and to be less concerned with the details of programming a computer and more concerned with the tasks that need to be completed. For example, in assembly language—a low-level language—it might take several instructions to display a line of text on the screen. In a high-level language, there's usually a single command, such as PRINT, that accomplishes this task.

With the advent of high-level languages, programming became accessible to more people; writing program code was no longer exclusively the domain of specially trained scientists. As a result, computing was used in increasingly complex roles. It was soon clear, however, that a more efficient way of programming was needed, one that would eliminate the obscure and tangled code that the early languages produced.

Programmers needed a new way of using high-level languages, one that would enable them to partition their programs into logical sections that represent the general tasks to be completed. Thus, the structured-programming paradigm was born. Structured programming encourages a top-down approach to programming in which the programmer focuses on the general functions that a program must accomplish rather than the details of how those functions are implemented. When programmers think and program in top-down fashion, they can more easily handle large projects without producing tangled code.

For example, consider an everyday task such as cleaning a house. Write out the steps needed to complete this task as follows:

> Go to the living room.
>
> Dust the coffee table.

Dust the end tables.

Vacuum the rug.

Go to the kitchen.

Wash the dishes.

Wipe the counters.

Clean the stove.

Wipe off the refrigerator.

Sweep the floor.

Go to the bedroom.

Make the bed.

Dust the bureau.

Vacuum the rug.

The preceding list of steps is similar, in theory, to how you'd program a computer without using a top-down approach. Using the top-down programming approach, you'd revise the "program" as follows:

```
TOP LEVEL
Clean the living room.
Clean the kitchen.
Clean the bedroom.
SECOND LEVEL
Clean the living room.
START
   Go to the living room.
   Dust the coffee table.
   Dust the end tables.
   Vacuum the rug.
END
```

Clean the kitchen.
START
  Go to the kitchen.
  Wash the dishes.
  Wipe the counters.
  Clean the stove.
  Wipe off the refrigerator.
  Sweep the floor.
END

Clean the bedroom.
START
  Go to the bedroom.
  Make the bed.
  Dust the bureau.
  Vacuum the rug.
END

If you're only interested in seeing what the "program" does, you can glance at the top level and see that these are instructions for cleaning the living room, kitchen, and bedroom. If, however, you want to know exactly how to clean the living room, you can go down one level in the top-down structure and find the detailed instructions for cleaning the living room. While the top-down approach tends to make programs longer, it also adds clarity to the program because you can hide the details until you really need them.

Today, the need for efficient programming methods is more important than ever. The size of the average computer program has grown dramatically and now consists of hundreds of thousands of code lines. (It's rumored that Windows 95 comprises as much as fifteen million lines of code.) With these huge programs, reusability is critical. Again, a better way of programming is needed—and that better way is object-oriented programming.

An Obvious, Yet Brilliant, Solution for Modern Programming

The world consists of many objects, most of which manipulate other objects or data. For example, a car is an object that uses speed and direction to transport people to a different location. This car object encapsulates all the functions and data that it needs to get its job done. It has a switch to turn it on, a wheel to control its direction, and brakes to slow it down. These functions directly manipulate the car's data, including direction, position, and speed.

When you travel in a car, however, you don't have to know the details of how these operations work. To stop a car, for example, you simply step on the brake pedal. You don't have to know how the pedal stops the car. You simply know that it works.

All these functions and data work together to define the object called a car. Moreover, all these functions work very similarly from one car to the next. You're not likely to confuse a car with a dishwasher, tree, or playground. A car is a complete unit—an object with unique properties.

You also can think of a computer program as consisting of objects. Instead of thinking of a piece of code that, for example, draws a rectangle on-screen, another piece of code that fills the rectangle with text, and still another piece of code that enables you to move the rectangle around on the screen, you can think of a single object: a window. This window object contains all the code that it needs in order to operate. It also contains all the data that it needs, including its size, location, and contents. This is the philosophy behind OOP.

Object-Oriented Programming

Object-oriented programming enables you to think of program elements as objects. In the case of a window object, you don't need to know the details of how it works, nor do you need to know about the window's private data fields. You need to know only how to call the various functions (called methods in Java) that make the window operate. Consider the car object discussed in the previous section. To drive a car, you don't have to know the details of how a car works. You only need to know how to drive it. What's going on under the hood is none of your business.

(And, if you casually try to make it your business, plan to face an amused mechanic who will have to straighten out your mess!)

But OOP is a lot more than just a way to hide the details of a program. To learn about OOP, you need to understand three main concepts that are the backbone of OOP. These concepts, which are covered in the following sections, are: encapsulation, inheritance, and polymorphism.

Encapsulation

One major difference between conventional structured programming and object-oriented programming is a handy thing called *encapsulation*. Encapsulation enables you to hide both the data fields and the methods that act on that data inside the object. (In fact, data fields and methods are the two main elements of an object in the Java programming language.) After you do this, you can control access to the data, forcing programs to retrieve or modify data only through the object's interface. In strict object-oriented design, an object's data is always private to the object. Other parts of a program should never have direct access to that data.

How does this data-hiding differ from a structured-programming approach? After all, you can always hide data inside functions, just by making that data local to the function. A problem arises, however, when you want to make the data of one function available to other functions. The way to do this in a structured program is to make the data global to the program, which gives any function access to it. It seems that you could use another level of scope—one that would make your data global to the functions that need it—but still prevent other functions from gaining access. Encapsulation does just that. In an object, the encapsulated data members are global to the object's methods, yet they are local to the object. They are not global variables.

Classes as Data Types

An object is just an instance of a data type. For example, when you declare a variable of type `int`, you're creating an instance of the `int` data type. A class is like a data type in that it is the blueprint upon which an object is based. When you need a new object in a program, you create a class, which is a kind of template for the object. Then, in your program, you create an instance of the class. This instance is called an object.

Classes are really nothing more than user-defined data types. As with any data type, you can have as many instances of the class as you want. For example, you can have more than one window in a Windows application, each with its own contents.

Think again about the integer data type (`int`). It's absurd to think that a program can have only one integer. You can declare many integers, almost as many as you want. The same is true of classes. After you define a new class, you can create many instances of the class. Each instance (called an object) has full access to the class's methods and gets its own copy of the data members.

Inheritance

Inheritance enables you to create a class that is similar to a previously defined class, but which still has some of its own properties. Consider a car-simulation program. Suppose that you have a class for a regular car, but now you want to create a car that has a high-speed passing gear. In a traditional program, you might have to modify the existing code extensively and might introduce bugs into code that worked fine before your changes. To avoid these hassles, use the object-oriented approach: create a new class by inheritance. This new class inherits all the data and methods from the tested base class. (You can control the level of inheritance with the `public`, `private`, and `protected` keywords.) Now, you only need to worry about testing the new code you added to the derived class.

NOTE The designers of OOP languages didn't pick the word "inheritance" out of a hat. Think of how children inherit many of their characteristics from their parents. But the children also have characteristics that are uniquely their own. In object-oriented programming, you can think of a base class as a parent and a derived class as a child. ■

Polymorphism

The last major feature of object-oriented programming is *polymorphism*. You can use polymorphism to create new objects that perform the same functions as the base object, but which perform one or more of these functions in a different way. For example, you may have a shape object that draws a circle on the screen. Using polymorphism, you can create a shape object that draws a rectangle instead. You do this by creating a new version of the method that draws the shape on the screen. Both the old circle-drawing and the new rectangle-drawing method have the same name (such as `DrawShape()`) but accomplish the drawing in a different way.

Using Encapsulation, Inheritance, and Polymorphism

Although you won't actually start using Java classes until later in this book, this is a good time to look at OOP concepts in a general way. As an example, I'll extend the car analogy you read earlier this chapter.

In that section I described a car as an object having several characteristics (direction, position, and speed) and several means (steering wheel, gas pedal, and brakes) to act on those characteristics. In terms of constructing a class for a car object, you can think of direction, position, and speed as the class's data fields and the steering wheel, gas pedal, and brakes as representing the class's methods.

The first step in creating an object is to define its class. For now, you'll use pseudocode to create a `Car` class. The base `Car` class might look like listing 5.1:

Listing 5.1 The Pseudocode for a Base *Car* Class

```
class Car
{
    data direction;
    data position;
    data speed;

    method Steer();
    method PressGasPedal();
    method PressBrake();
}
```

In this base `Car` class, a car is defined by its `direction` (which way it's pointed), `position` (where it's located), and `speed`. These three data fields can be manipulated by the three methods `Steer()`, `PressGasPedal()`, and `PressBrake()`. The `Steer()` method changes the car's direction, whereas the `PressGasPedal()` and

`PressBrake()` change the car's speed. The car's position is affected by all three methods, as well as by the direction and speed settings.

The data fields and methods are all encapsulated inside the class. Moreover, the data fields are private to the class, meaning that they cannot be directly accessed from outside of the class. Only the class's three methods can access the data fields. In short, listing 5.1 not only shows what a class might look like, it also shows how encapsulation works.

Now, suppose you want to create a new car that has a special passing gear. To do this, you can use OOP inheritance to derive a new class from the base `Car` class. Listing 5.2 is the pseudocode for this new class:

Listing 5.2 Deriving a New Class Using Inheritance

```
Class PassingCar inherits from Car
{
    method Pass();
}
```

You may be surprised to see how small this new class is. It's small because it implicitly inherits all the data fields and methods from the base `Car` class. Not only does the `PassingCar` class have a method called `Pass()`, it also has the `direction`, `position`, and `speed` data fields, as well as the `Steer()`, `PressGasPedal()`, and `PressBrake()` methods. The `PassingCar` class can use all these data fields and methods exactly as if they were explicitly defined in listing 5.2. This is an example of inheritance.

The last OOP concept that you'll apply to the car classes is polymorphism. Suppose that you now decide that you want a new kind of car that has all the characteristics of a `PassingCar`, except that its passing gear is twice as fast as `PassingCar`'s. You can solve this problem as shown in listing 5.3:

Listing 5.3 Using Polymorphism To Create a Faster Car

```
class FastCar inherits from PassingCar
{
    method Pass();
}
```

The `FastCar` class looks exactly like the original `PassingCar` class. However, rather than just inheriting the `Pass()` method, it defines its own version. This new version makes the car move twice as fast as `PassingCar`'s `Pass()` method does (the code that actually implements each method is not shown). In this way, the `FastCar` class implements the same functionality as the `PassingCar()` class but it implements that functionality a little differently.

NOTE Because the `FastCar` class inherits from `PassingCar`, which itself inherits from `Car`, a `FastCar` also inherits all the data fields and methods of the `Car` class. There are ways that you can control how inheritance works (using the `public`, `protected`, and `private` keywords), which you'll learn about later in this book.

Classes and Objects

In the previous sections, you learned that a class is the template for an object and that a class is a way to encapsulate both data (called *fields* in Java) and the functions (called *methods*) that operate on that data. You also learned about inheritance, which enables a class (called the *subclass*) to inherit the capabilities of a base class (called a *superclass* in Java). Finally, you discovered that polymorphism enables you to create methods that can be implemented differently in derived classes. In this section, you'll apply what you know about object-oriented programming toward creating Java classes.

Defining a Simple Class

As defined earlier, a class is sort of a template for an object. In this way, a class is equivalent to a data type such as `int`. The main difference is that Java already knows what an integer is. However, when you create a class, you must tell Java about the class's characteristics. You define a class by using the `class` keyword along with the class name, like this:

```
class MyClass
{
}
```

Believe it or not, the preceding lines are a complete Java class. If you save the lines in a file called `MyClass.java`, you could even compile the class into a .class file, although the file won't actually do anything if you try to run it. As you can see, the class definition begins with the keyword `class` followed by the name of the class. The body of the class is marked off by curly braces just like any other program block. In this case, the class's body is empty.

Because its body is empty, this example class doesn't do anything. You can, however, compile the class and even create an object from it. To create an object from a class, type the class's name followed by the name of the object. For example, the line below creates an object from the `MyClass` class:

```
MyClass myObject = new MyClass();
```

Declaring Fields for a Class

The `MyClass` example class doesn't do much yet. In order to be useful it needs both data fields and methods. You declare fields for your class in much the same way you declare any variable in a program: by typing the data type of the field followed by the name of the field, like this:

```
int myField;
```

The above line declares a data field of type integer. However, looking at the above line doesn't tell you much about how data fields are used with classes. To clear up this mystery, you can plug the above line into the `MyClass` class definition, as shown in listing 5.4.

Listing 5.4 Adding a Data Field to a Class

```
class MyClass
{
    int myField;
}
```

Now you can see that `myField` is a data field of the `MyClass` class. Moreover, this data field is, by default, accessible only by methods in the same package. (For now, you can think of a package as a file.) You can change the rules of this access by using the `public`, `protected`, and `private` keywords. A public data field can be accessed by any part of a program, inside or outside of the class in which it's defined. A protected data field can only be accessed from within the class or from within a derived class (a subclass). A private data field cannot even be accessed by a derived class.

Defining a Constructor

You have now added a data field to `MyClass`. However, the class has no methods and so can do nothing with its data field. The next step in defining the class, then, is to create methods. One special type of method, called a *constructor*, enables an object to initialize itself when it's created. A constructor is a public method (a method that can be accessed anywhere in a program) with the same name as the class. Listing 5.5 shows the `MyClass` class with its constructor in place.

Listing 5.5 Adding a Constructor to a Class

```
class MyClass
{
    int myField;

    public MyClass(int value)
    {
        myField = value;
    }
}
```

As you can see, the class's constructor starts with the `public` keyword. This is important because you want to be able to create an object from the class anywhere in your program, and when you create an object, you're actually calling its constructor. After the `public` keyword comes the name of the constructor followed by the constructor's arguments in parentheses. When you create an object of the class, you must also provide the required arguments.

For example, if you want to create an object from `MyClass`, you must supply an integer value that the class uses to initialize the `myField` data field. This integer is the `MyClass` constructor's single argument. You'd create an object of the class like this:

```
MyClass myObject = new MyClass(1);
```

This line not only creates an object of the `MyClass` class, but also initializes the `myField` data field to 1. The first word in the line tells Java that `myObject` is going to be an object of the `MyClass` class. The next word is the object's name. After the equals sign (an assignment operator, in this case) comes the keyword `new` and the call to the class's constructor.

Defining Methods

Other methods (functions that are part of a class) that you add to a class are just like the functions you've written in other programs you may have worked on. You just need to be sure to provide the proper type of access to your methods. That is, methods that must be callable from outside the class should be defined as public, methods that must be callable only from the class and its derived classes should be defined as protected, and methods that must be callable only from within the class should be declared as private.

Suppose `myField` is defined as private, but you want to be able to set the value of `myField` from outside of the `MyClass` class. Because that data field is defined as private, meaning it can be accessed only from within the same class, you cannot access it directly by name. To solve this problem, you can create a public method that can set the value for you. You might also want to create a method that returns the value of the field as well, as shown in listing 5.6:

Listing 5.6 Adding a Method to the Class

```
class MyClass
{
    private int myField;

    public MyClass(int value)
    {
        myField = value;
    }

    public void SetField(int value)
    {
        myField = value;
    }

    public int GetField()
    {
        return myField;
    }
}
```


NOTE According to the rules of strict object-oriented design, all class data fields should be declared as private. Some programmers would go so far as to say that you should not even provide access to data fields through public methods. However, you'll see these rules broken a lot, even by programmers in big companies like Microsoft, Borland, and Sun. As you become more familiar with object-oriented programming, you'll better understand why the rules were made and when it's appropriate to break them.

Using Classes in Applets

Now comes the moment you've been waiting for. You're about to create your first Java applet with Java Workshop, which will help you understand how classes work. Use the following steps.

1. Create a folder called Classes on the root directory of your C: drive. The Classes folder is where you'll store the Java programs you create in this book.
2. Create an Applet1 folder inside your Classes folder. The Applet1 folder is where you'll store the files for the applet you're creating in these steps.
3. Start Java Workshop. You'll see the window shown in figure 5.1.

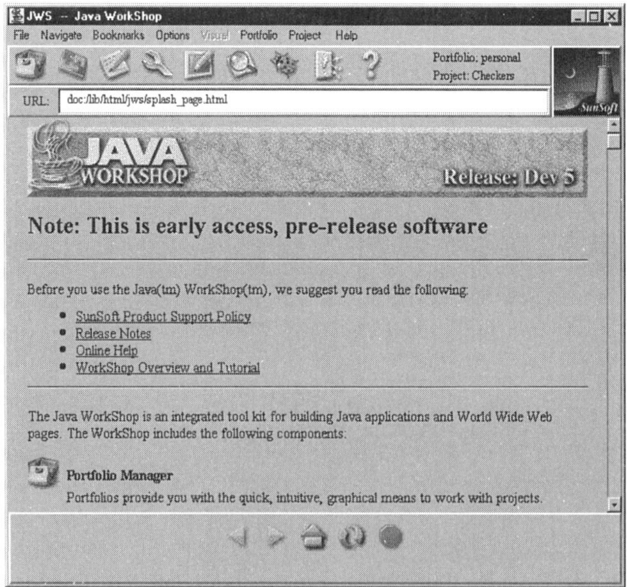

FIG. 5.1
This is Java Workshop when you first run it.

4. Using Java Workshop's text editor, type listing 5.6 and save it to your Classes\Applet1 folder under the name MyClass.java.
5. Type listing 5.7 and save it as Applet1.java in your Classes\Applet1 folder.

Listing 5.7 An Applet That Uses the *MyClass* Class

```
import java.awt.*;
import java.applet.*;
import MyClass;

public class Applet1 extends Applet
{
    MyClass myObject;
    TextField textField1;

    public void init()
    {
        myObject = new MyClass(1);
        textField1 = new TextField(20);
        add(textField1);
        textField1.setText("1");
    }

    public void paint(Graphics g)
    {
        String s = textField1.getText();
        int value = Integer.parseInt(s);
        myObject.SetField(value);
        value = myObject.GetField();
        s = String.valueOf(value);
        g.drawString("The data field of the object", 80, 80);
        g.drawString("is now set to this value:", 90, 95);
        g.drawString(s, 140, 125);
    }

    public boolean action(Event event, Object arg)
    {
        repaint();
        return true;
    }
}
```

6. Select Portfolio, Create from Java Workshop's menu bar. The Create Portfolio dialog box appears.
7. Type **c:\Classes\Using Java Workshop.psf** into the Portfolio text box, as shown in figure 5.2. Then, click the Create button to create the new portfolio.

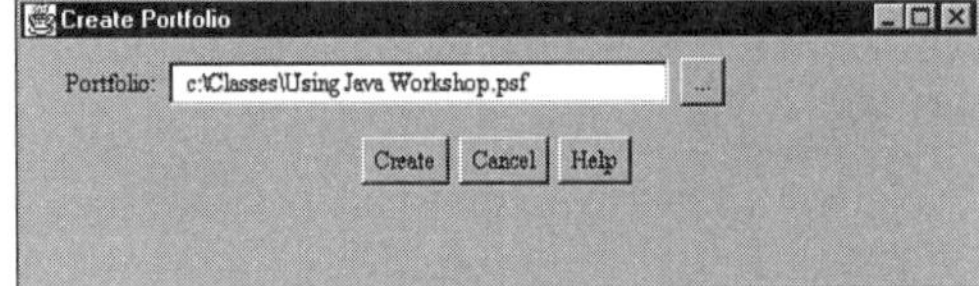

FIG. 5.2
You use the Create Portfolio dialog box to start a new portfolio.

You use portfolios to organize the source-code files that make up your various Java projects. You'll use the Using Java Workshop portfolio to organize all the programs you'll create in this book.

8. Select Project, Create, Applet from Java Workshop's menu bar. The property sheet for applet projects appears.
9. Type **Applet1** into the Name text box. Type **c:\Classes\Applet1** into the Source Directory text box, select the Yes option button for Existing Sources, and click the Add All in Directory button. Finally, type **Applet1.class** into the Main Class File text box (see fig. 5.3) and click the Apply button. Java Workshop starts the new Applet1 project.

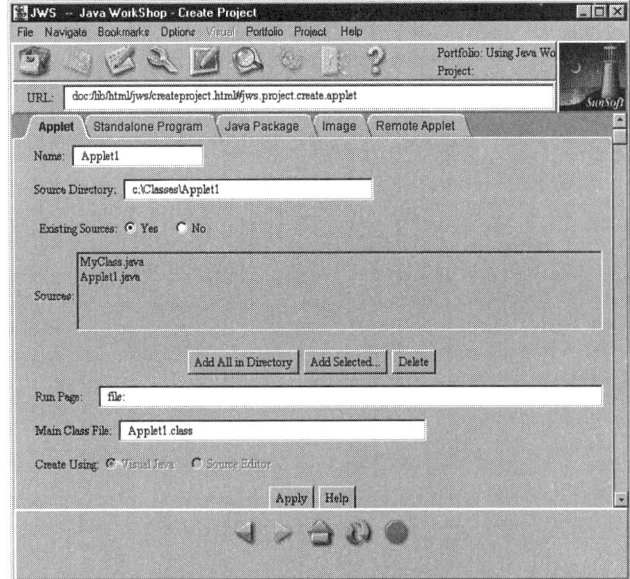

FIG. 5.3
You use this property sheet to create new projects.

Projects organize the source-code files for each individual program in a portfolio. You can think of a portfolio as a folder that contains all your Java projects, whereas the projects are similar to subfolders in the portfolio folder.

10. Click the Build Manager button (the one that looks like a wrench) in Java Workshop's main toolbar. Build Manager appears.
11. Click Build Manager's Build button (the first button on Build Manager's toolbar). Build Manager runs the Java compiler, javac, to compile your new applet (see fig. 5.4).

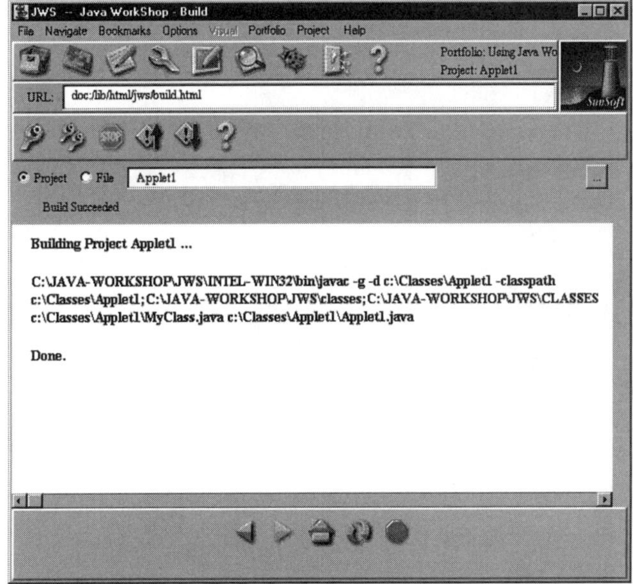

FIG. 5.4
Build Manager runs Java's compiler to compile your applet.

12. Click the Project Tester button (the one that looks like a light switch) on Java Workshop's toolbar to test your new applet. You'll see the window shown in figure 5.5.

The applet's display area shows the current setting of `MyClass`'s data field, `myField`. You can change this setting by typing a new value into the text box and pressing Enter.

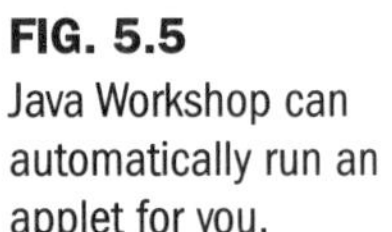

FIG. 5.5
Java Workshop can automatically run an applet for you.

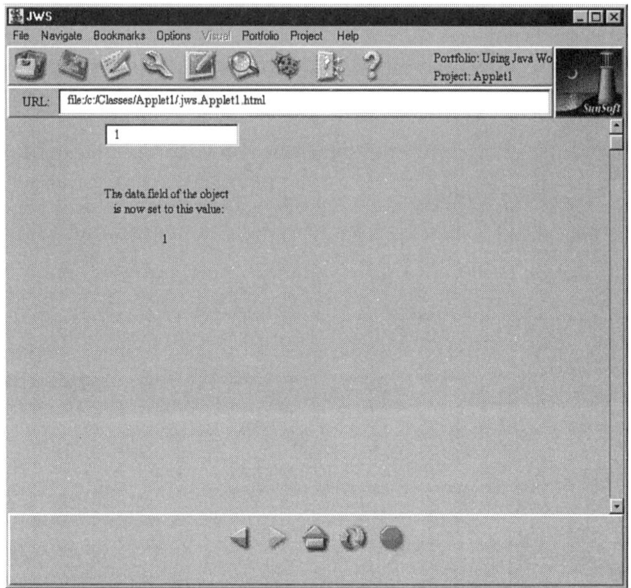

Understanding the Applet1 Applet

By now, you should have a good idea of how classes work, at least generally. (Don't worry about all the mysterious looking stuff in Applet1. You'll learn what it all means soon enough.) Still, you'll now examine parts of Applet1's source code. First, near the top of the source code is this line:

```
import MyClass;
```

Because the `MyClass` class is located in a different file than `Applet1`, you need to tell Java where to find it. The above line tells Java that it can find everything it needs to know about `MyClass` in the MyClass.class file, which you created when you compiled MyClass.java.

The next line of interest is this one, which is located at the top of Applet1's definition:

```
MyClass myObject;
```

This line tells Java that you'll be creating an object of the `MyClass` class and that the object will be called `myObject`.

At this point, you don't have the object created yet. You have to create the object, which Applet1 does in its `init()` method, using the `new` operator, like this:

```
myObject = new MyClass(1);
```

After this line executes, Java has created the object, which means you can now call the object's public methods to manipulate the object as is appropriate. Objects of the `MyClass` class have only two public methods (not counting the constructor). Applet1 calls these methods in its `paint()` method, like this:

```
myObject.SetField(value);
value = myObject.GetField();
```

In the first line, Applet1 calls the object's `SetField()` method, whose single argument is the value to which to set the `myField` data field. Due to its private access, this is the only way to set the value of `myField` outside of the class. If you tried to access `myField` with the line

```
myObject.myField = value;
```

you wouldn't even be able to compile the file. The compiler will generate an error telling you that you cannot access myField (see fig. 5.6).

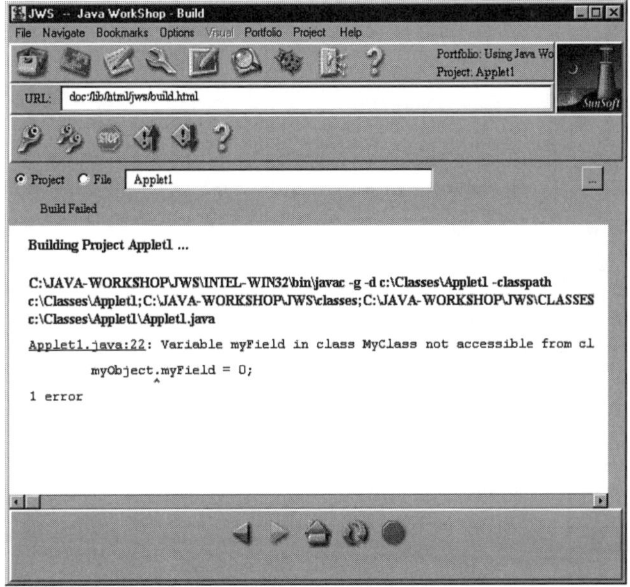

FIG. 5.6
The compiler complains when you ignore rules of access.

Using Inheritance

You may not know it, but you used inheritance when you created your first applet in the previous section. Specifically, you derived your applet class (`Applet1`) from Java's `Applet` superclass. By using inheritance in this way, you can take an existing class and create a new similar class that does things a little differently. The new class will have all the characteristics of its superclass, plus any new characteristics that you choose to add.

Creating a Subclass

You derive a new class from a Java superclass by using the `extends` keyword. This is an apt name for the keyword because by deriving a new class you usually extend the abilities of the original class. For example, when you create a new applet, you start the applet's class with a line that looks something like this:

```
public class MyApplet extends Applet
```

First, Java insists that all applet classes be declared as `public`. Next, you see the `class` keyword followed by the name of the class. Finally, comes the `extends` keyword followed by the name of the superclass. In English, the above line means that the public class `MyApplet` is derived from (is a subclass of) the existing `Applet` class.

As you've probably already figured out, `Applet` is a class that the Java makers created for you. This class contains all the basic functionality you need to create an applet. You need only extend (there's that word again) the specifics of the class in order to create your own applet class. Again, you did that with Applet1.

Adding Fields and Methods to the Subclass

One thing you can do when you create a subclass is to add your own data fields and methods. For example, when you derive your own applet class from Java's `Applet` class, although your class inherits tons of data fields and methods from the superclass, you'll undoubtedly need fields and methods not supplied in the superclass. Maybe your new applet is designed to play Tic-Tac-Toe. (Hmmmm. Where have I seen that before?) Obviously, when the fine programmers at Sun created the

Applet class, they didn't think to add the methods needed to play Tic-Tac-Toe. You'll have to add those methods yourself.

Take the MyClass class that you created earlier in this chapter (shown in listing 5.6). Suppose you want to create a new class that has a new data field called myNewField as well as a constructor and methods for setting and retrieving the value of this new data field. You might come up with something like listing 5.8.

Listing 5.8 Creating a Subclass

```
import MyClass;

class MySubClass extends MyClass
{
    private int myNewField;

    public MySubClass(int value)
    {
        super(value);
        myNewField = value;
    }

    public void SetNewField(int value)
    {
        myNewField = value;
    }

    public int GetNewField()
    {
        return myNewField;
    }
}
```


The file containing the MySubClass class first imports the MyClass file because Java will need the information contained in that file. In the constructor, the class first calls

```
super(value);
```

which ensures that the superclass (MyClass) is properly initialized by calling its constructor. The keyword super refers to the class's superclass. After calling the superclass's constructor, the MySubClass constructor initializes the new data field, myNewField. The new class also supplies new methods for setting and getting the value of myNewField. In short, MySubClass now has two data fields—myField, which it inherited from `MyClass`, and the new `myNewField`—and four methods—`SetField()` and `GetField()`, which it inherited from `MyClass`, and the new `SetNewField()` and `GetNewField()` methods.

Using the Subclass in a Program

Now that you have the `MySubClass` subclass, it might be nice to see how it works in a real programming situation. Applet2, which is shown in listing 5.9, does the honors of putting `MySubClass` to work. In most places, compared to Applet1, the applet merely replaces occurrences of `MyClass` with `MySubClass`. The `paint()` method (you'll learn more about `paint()` in Chapter 6, "Applets and Graphics") has to work a bit harder, though, calling all four of `MySubClass`'s methods to prove they work. To get Applet2 going, follow these steps:

1. Create an Applet2 folder inside your Classes folder. The Applet2 folder is where you'll store the files for the applet you're creating in these steps.
2. If necessary, start Java Workshop.
3. Using Java Workshop's text editor, type listing 5.8 and save it to your Classes\Applet2 folder under the name MySubClass.java.
4. Type listing 5.9 and save it as Applet2.java in your Classes\Applet2 folder.

Listing 5.9 Using a Subclass in a Program

```
import java.awt.*;
import java.applet.*;
import MySubClass;

public class Applet2 extends Applet
{
    MySubClass mySubObject;
    TextField textField1;
    TextField textField2;

    public void init()
    {
        mySubObject = new MySubClass(1);
        textField1 = new TextField(20);
        add(textField1);
        textField1.setText("1");
        textField2 = new TextField(20);
        add(textField2);
        textField2.setText("2");
    }
```

```
    public void paint(Graphics g)
    {
        String s = textField1.getText();
        int value = Integer.parseInt(s);
        mySubObject.SetField(value);
        value = mySubObject.GetField();
        s = String.valueOf(value);
        g.drawString("The myField data field", 80, 80);
        g.drawString("is now set to this value:", 90, 95);
        g.drawString(s, 140, 125);

        s = textField2.getText();
        value = Integer.parseInt(s);
        mySubObject.SetNewField(value);
        value = mySubObject.GetNewField();
        s = String.valueOf(value);
        g.drawString("The myNewField data field", 80, 155);
        g.drawString("is now set to this value:", 90, 170);
        g.drawString(s, 140, 200);
    }

    public boolean action(Event event, Object arg)
    {
        repaint();
        return true;
    }
}
```


5. Copy the MyClass.java file from the Classes\Applet1 folder to the Classes\Applet2 folder.
6. Select Portfolio, Choose, Using Java Workshop from Java Workshop's menu bar. Java workshop opens the Using Java Workshop portfolio.
7. Select Project, Create, Applet from Java Workshop's menu bar. The property sheet for applet projects appears.
8. Type **Applet2** into the Name text box. Type **c:\Classes\Applet2** into the Source Directory text box, select the Yes option button for Existing Sources, and click the Add All in Directory button. Finally, type **Applet2.class** into the Main Class File text box (refer to fig. 5.3) and click the Apply button. Java Workshop starts the new Applet2 project.
9. Click the Build Manager button in Java Workshop's main toolbar. The Build Manager appears.
10. Click Build Manager's Build button. Build Manager runs the Java compiler, javac, to compile your new applet.

11. Click the Project Tester button on Java Workshop's toolbar to test your new applet. You'll see the window shown in figure 5.7.

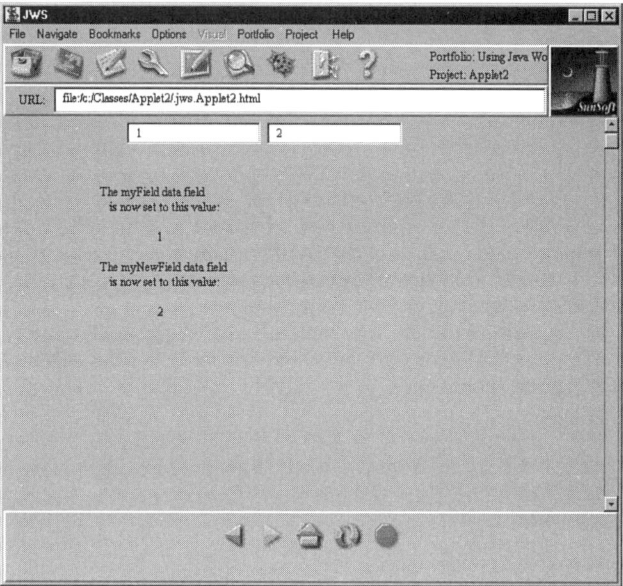

FIG. 5.7
Applet2 has two data fields you can set.

When you run Applet2 under Java Workshop, you see the window shown in figure 5.7. Use the first text box to enter values for the original `myField` data field. Use the second text box to enter values for `myNewField`. Whenever you press Enter, the applet reads the values from the boxes and calls `MySubClass`'s methods to set the new values and to retrieve the set values from the object.

Overriding Methods of the Superclass

When you override a method, you are creating a new version of a method that's part of the superclass. For example, in the applets you've created in this chapter, you've overridden methods like `init()`, `paint()`, and `action()`. All of these methods are defined in some general way in the `Applet` superclass. When you derive a new class from `Applet`, you can override these methods to perform the tasks you want them to perform, rather than the general tasks assigned to them by the `Applet` class. If you remember, overriding methods is taking advantage of what is known as polymorphism.

NOTE In general object-oriented programming discussions, the term "derive" means exactly the same thing as "subclass" (when the latter is used as a verb). Ditto for the terms "base class" and "superclass," which are the same thing. In other words, when you derive a new class from a base class, you are subclassing a new class from a superclass. ■

For example, when Java starts up an applet, it calls the applet's `init()` method. Here's how the `Applet` class defines `init()`:

```
public void init()
{
}
```

No, your eyes aren't fooling you. In the `Applet` class, the `init()` method does nothing at all. It's only there so you can override it in your own class. Here's how it all works: When you derive your applet class from `Applet`, your applet class inherits all of `Applet`'s data fields and methods. If you don't override a method, Java calls the original version as necessary. In other words, if you don't override `init()` in your applet class, when Java starts your applet, it calls the `Applet` class's version of `init()`, which does nothing. However, if you override `init()` in your class, Java is smart enough to call the new version rather than the original do-nothing version.

The *this* Keyword

There may be times when you need to explicitly refer to an object from within the object's methods. For example, you might need to pass a reference to the object as an argument in a method call. When you need to refer to the object explicitly, use the `this` keyword. In many cases, the `this` keyword is implicit in the method call or variable reference. For example, inside an object that has the data field `dataField`, the line

```
dataField = 1;
```

is the same as

```
this.dataField = 1;
```

In the first case, the `this` keyword is implicit, whereas in the second case, you've included it explicitly. If you needed to pass a reference to the object as an argument, you might write something like this:

```
SomeMethod(this);
```

Of course, the `SomeMethod()` method would have been written to accept an object of `this`'s type as its single argument.

From Here...

Java is an object-oriented language, meaning it not only enables you to organize your program code into logical units called objects, it also enables you to take advantage of encapsulation, inheritance, and polymorphism. Learning OOP, however, can be a little tricky. If you're a novice programmer, this chapter has probably left you confused. If so, read on to learn more about the Java language. Once you start writing Java programs, much of what you read here will make more sense. After finishing the book, you might want to reread this chapter to reinforce any concepts that may be unclear.

Classes are the single biggest hurdle to jump when making the transition from normal procedural programming to object-oriented programming (OOP). Just think of classes as a way to provide another level of abstraction to your programs. In your non-OOP programs, you had program elements—called programs, files, and procedures—listed in the order of their level of abstraction. Now, you can add classes to the end of the list, right between files and procedures.

Please refer to the following chapters for related topics:

- Chapter 3, "Keywords, Data Types, and Operators," describes the basic elements of the Java language.
- Chapter 6, "Applets and Graphics," is where you start learning what makes an applet tick.
- Chapter 13, "Writing Java Applications," describes how to create stand-alone applications, which use the same language basics as applets, with Java.
- Chapter 14, "Portfolio Manager and Project Manager," describes in detail how to use Java's portfolio and project managers.
- Chapter 15, "Source Editor," provides detailed instructions for Java Workshop's text editor.
- Chapter 16, "Build Manager and Source Browser," fully documents Java Workshop's Build Manager, to which you were introduced in this chapter.

PART III

Writing Java Applets

CHAPTER 6

Applets and Graphics

In the previous chapter, you got a chance to create and run your first applet. Although you learned a lot about Java's classes, most of the code in the applets you created in that chapter probably looked pretty strange. If so, you'll be happy to know that, starting in this chapter, you'll fill in those blanks, learning how applets do what they do. Specifically, it's now time to learn not only applet basics, but also how to draw graphics and text in an applet's display. ■

How to write a simple applet.

Although applets are much like other programs you may have written in other languages, there are a few rules of which you must be aware.

About an applet's life stages.

Every Java applet goes through stages as it loads, runs, and exits. Knowing about these stages enables you to control how your applet performs start-up and ending tasks.

How to draw graphics in an applet's display area.

Java features a special graphics class that enables you to do everything from drawing a simple line to displaying text in a variety of fonts.

How to draw complex shapes like polygons and ovals.

Some graphical shapes are easier to draw than others, but this chapter gets you started by describing how the graphics methods work.

How to properly display text in an applet.

How you display text in an applet depends on the size of the font. Java enables you to obtain information about the current font so that you can space text exactly as needed in your applet.

The Simplest Java Applet

The Java programming language and libraries enable you to create applets that are as simple or as complex as you like. In fact, you can write the simplest Java applet in only a few lines of code, as shown in listing 6.1.

Listing 6.1 The Simplest Java Applet

```
import java.applet.*;

public class MyApplet extends Applet
{
}
```

The first line of listing 6.1 tells the Java compiler that this applet uses some or all of the classes defined in the applet package (the asterisk acts as a wildcard, just as in DOS file names). All of the basic capabilities of an applet are provided for in these classes, which is why you can create a usable applet with so few lines of code.

The second line of code declares a new class called `MyApplet`. This new class is declared as public so that the class can be accessed when the applet is run in a Web browser, in Java Workshop, or in the Appletviewer application. If you fail to declare the applet class as public, the code compiles fine, but the applet refuses to run. In other words, all applet classes must be public.

As you can see, you take advantage of Object-Oriented Programming (OOP) inheritance to declare your applet class by subclassing Java's `Applet` class. This inheritance works as it did when you created your own classes in Chapter 5, "Object-Oriented Programming and Java." The only difference is that `Applet` is a class that's included with the Java Developer's Kit (JDK), rather than a class you created yourself.

You can actually compile and run the applet shown in listing 6.1. Just follow the procedures you learned in Chapter 5, which are summarized below:

1. Create a new folder for the project inside your Classes folder. In this case, call the new folder MyApplet.
2. Type the listing and save it in the new project's folder. In this case, you should name the source-code file MyApplet.java.

3. Create a new project for the program. In this case, name the project MyApplet.
4. Use Build Manager to compile the program.
5. Use Project Tester to run the program.

After you compile listing 6.1, the MyApplet.class file, which is the byte-code file that can be executed by the Java system, appears in your Classes\MyApplet folder. When you run the program with Project Tester, Java Workshop automatically creates an HTML document that Workshop uses to load and run the new applet. In the case of the MyApplet project, the HTML document file is called .jws.MyApplet.html. You can use this HTML document as the basis for the final HTML document when you run the applet inside a Web browser such as Netscape Navigator 2.0.

An Applet's Life Cycle

Every Java applet you create inherits a set of default behaviors from the `Applet` class. In most cases, these default behaviors do nothing, unless you override some of `Applet`'s methods in order to extend the applet's basic functionality. Although a simple applet, like MyApplet in listing 6.1, doesn't seem to do much, a lot is going on in the background. Some of this activity is important to your understanding of applets, and some of it can stay out of sight and out of mind. Part of what goes on in a simple applet is the execution of the applet's life cycle. In this section, you see how to take advantage of each of these stages in your applets.

The Five Life-Cycle Stages

There are five parts to an applet's life cycle, each of which has a matching method that you can override to gain access to that cycle of the applet's life. The five stages of an applet's life cycle are shown in the following list:

- *Initialization stage.* This is the part of an applet's life cycle in which the applet object is created and loaded. At this point, it's appropriate to create objects needed by the applet, as well as initialize values that must be valid when the applet runs. The initialization stage occurs only once in the applet's life cycle. You can tap into the initialization stage by overriding the `Applet` class's `init()` method.

- *Start stage.* This stage occurs when the system starts running the applet. The start stage can occur right after the initialization stage or when an applet is restarted. This usually happens when the user switches back to the applet's page after viewing a different page in his or her Web browser. Unlike the initialization stage, the start stage can occur several times over the life of the applet. To provide your own start code, override the `Applet` class's `start()` method.
- *Paint stage.* The paint stage occurs whenever the applet's display must be drawn on the screen. This happens right after the applet's start stage, as well as whenever the applet's display must be restored or changed. This can happen when the applet is exposed from underneath another window or when the program changes the applet's display in some way and explicitly repaints the applet. Probably, every applet you write will have a `paint()` method, which is the method you override to provide your applet with its display.
- *Stop stage.* As you may have guessed, the stop stage is the counterpart to the start stage. Java executes this stage of the applet's life cycle when the applet is no longer visible on the screen, like when the user switches to a different Web page. The default behavior for this cycle is to keep the applet running in the background. If you want to handle the stop cycle differently, you should override the `Applet` class's `stop()` method.
- *Destroy stage.* This is the counterpart to the initialization stage and occurs when the system is about to remove the applet from memory. Like the initialization cycle, the destroy cycle occurs only once. If your applet has resources that need to be cleaned up before the applet exits, this is the place to do it. You tap into this cycle by overriding the `Applet` class's `destroy()` method.

NOTE To be entirely accurate, the paint stage isn't considered an actual part of the applet life cycle, but since an applet without a display is useless, I thought I'd include the paint cycle. The truth is, the `paint()` method isn't even defined in the `Applet` class. Rather, `Applet` inherits `paint()` from the `Component` class, a superclass in `Applet`'s long chain of inheritance, which goes from `Applet` to `Panel` to `Container` and finally to `Component`.

Overriding the Life-Cycle Methods

This talk about life cycles and overriding methods may have left you a little confused as to how all this actually applies to the applets you want to create. In the previous chapter, you managed to create applets without dealing with most of this stuff because the `Applet` class, from which you derived your own applet classes, handles the life-cycle methods in the default manner proscribed by the Java system. If you look at listing 6.2, you'll see a small applet that overrides default settings and can be used to provide custom behaviors for all the applet's life-cycle stages.

Listing 6.2 Overriding the Applet Life-cycle Methods

```
import java.applet.*;
import java.awt.*;

public class MyApplet2 extends Applet
{
    public void init()
    {
        // Place initialization cycle code here.
    }

    public void start()
    {
        // Place start cycle code here.
    }

    public void paint(Graphics g)
    {
        // Place paint cycle code here.
    }

    public void stop()
    {
        // Place stop cycle code here.
    }

    public void destroy()
    {
        // Place destroy cycle code here.
    }
}
```

Notice that in order to override the `paint()` method, you must import the `java.awt.*` libraries, which contain information about the `Graphics` class. The `Graphics` class enables you to display information and graphics in an applet's display area (or *canvas*, as the display area is sometimes called).

When you look for the previous methods in Java's source code, you discover that the default implementations of `init()`, `start()`, `paint()`, `stop()`, and `destroy()` all do nothing at all. If you want your applet to do something in response to these cycles, you have to provide the code yourself by overriding the appropriate method. You learn how to do that in the following sections.

Drawing Graphics

Almost all applets must create some sort of display, whether that display is as simple as a line of text or as sophisticated as an animation sequence. Because Windows is a graphical system, everything you see on the screen during a Windows session is displayed graphically. This is true even of text. Because of its graphical nature, a system like Java's must include the capability to handle device-independent graphics. In the following sections, you see not only how you can display various graphical shapes, but also how to query the system about the characteristics of the display.

The Applet's Canvas

Every applet has an area of the screen, called the canvas, in which it creates its display. The size of an applet's canvas depends on the size of the applet, which is in turn controlled by the parameters included in an HTML document's `<applet>` tag. Generally, the larger the applet appears in the HTML document, the larger the applet's visible canvas. Anything that you try to draw outside of the visible canvas doesn't appear on the screen.

You draw graphical images on the canvas by using coordinates that identify pixel locations. Chances are good that you've had some sort of computer-graphics experience before Java, so you know that the coordinates that define pixel locations on a computer screen are organized in various ways. Windows, for example, supports a number of different *mapping modes* that determine how coordinates are calculated in a window.

Thankfully, Java does away with the complications of displaying graphics in a window by adopting a single coordinate system. This coordinate system has its origin (point 0,0) in the upper-left corner, with the X axis increasing to the right, and the Y axis increasing downward, as shown in figure 6.1.

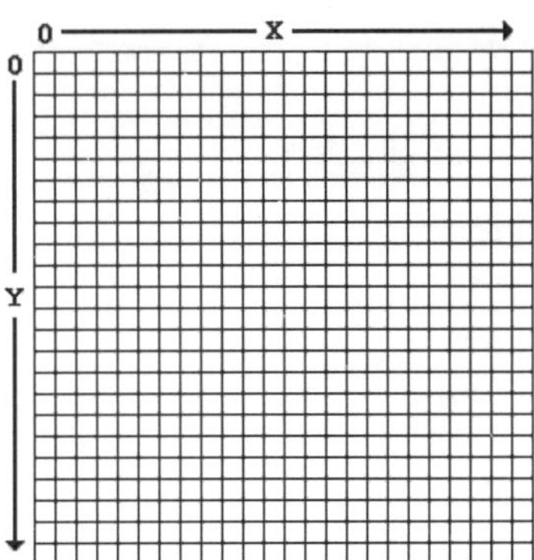

FIG. 6.1 An applet's canvas uses the typical computer-display coordinate system.

Using the Coordinate System

When you want to draw something on an applet's canvas, you use the coordinate system shown in figure 6.1. This coordinate system situates the system's origin in the applet's upper-left corner, just as it's shown in figure 6.1. For example, figure 6.2 shows an applet displaying a single line in its canvas. This line was drawn starting at coordinates 5,10, as shown in figure 6.3.

FIG. 6.2 This applet displays a single line.

Drawing Shapes

Java's `Graphics` class includes methods for drawing many different types of shapes, everything from straight lines to polygons. As you may have noticed in previous applets, a reference to a `Graphics` object is passed to the `paint()` method as its single argument. Because the `Graphics` class is part of the `awt` package, you have to include one of the following lines at the top of your applet's code to use the class:

```
import java.awt.Graphics
import java.awt.*
```

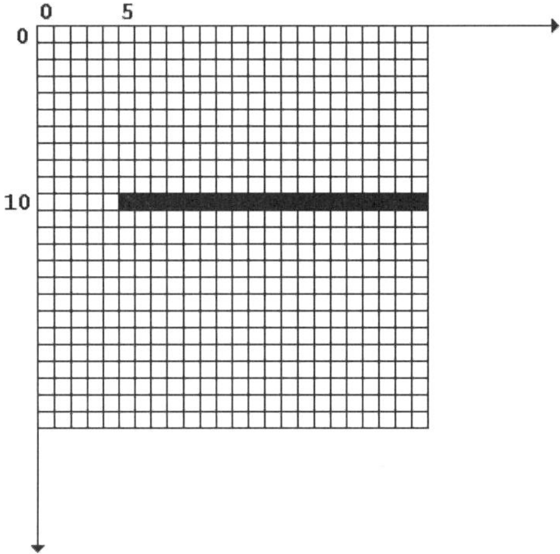

FIG. 6.3 The line in figure 6.2 is drawn at the coordinates 5,10.

The first line imports only the `Graphics` class, whereas the second line imports all the classes included in the `awt` package. Table 6.1 lists the most commonly used drawing methods in the `Graphics` class.

Table 6.1 Drawing Methods of the *Graphics* Class

Methods	Description
clearRect()	Erases a rectangular area of the canvas.
copyArea()	Copies a rectangular area of the canvas to another area.
drawArc()	Draws a hollow arc.
drawLine()	Draws a straight line.
drawOval()	Draws a hollow oval.
drawPolygon()	Draws a hollow polygon.
drawRect()	Draws a hollow rectangle.
drawRoundRect()	Draws a hollow rectangle with rounded corners.

Methods	Description
drawString()	Displays a text string.
fillArc()	Draws a filled arc.
fillOval()	Draws a filled oval.
fillPolygon()	Draws a filled polygon.
fillRect()	Draws a filled rectangle.
fillRoundRect()	Draws a filled rectangle with rounded corners.
getColor()	Retrieves the current drawing color.
getFont()	Retrieves the currently used font.
getFontMetrics()	Retrieves information about the current font.
setColor()	Sets the drawing color.
setFont()	Sets the font.

To draw a shape in an applet's display area, you only need to call the appropriate method and supply the arguments required by the method. These arguments are based on the coordinates at which you want to draw the shape. For example, the following code draws a straight line from coordinate 5,10 to 20,30:

```
g.drawLine(5, 10, 20, 30);
```

The `g` in the preceding code line is the `Graphics` object passed to the `paint()` method. As you can see, the `drawLine()` method takes four arguments, which are X,Y coordinate pairs that specify the starting and ending points of the line.

There may be times when you need to retrieve information about the system's currently set graphical attributes. Java's Graphics class supplies methods, like `getColor()`, `getFont()`, and `getFontMetrics()` to enable you to obtain this information.

Drawing a Rectangle

Most of the shape-drawing methods are as easy to use as the `drawLine()` method is. Suppose that you want to write an applet that draws a filled rounded rectangle inside a hollow rectangle. You'd then add calls to the `Graphics` class's fillRoundRect() and drawRect() to the applet's paint() method. Listing 6.3 is just such an applet. Figure 6.4 shows the applet running under Java Workshop.

Listing 6.3 Drawing Rectangles

```
import java.awt.*;
import java.applet.*;

public class RectApplet extends Applet
{
    public void paint(Graphics g)
    {
        g.drawRect(35, 15, 125, 200);
        g.fillRoundRect(50, 30, 95, 170, 15, 15);
    }
}
```

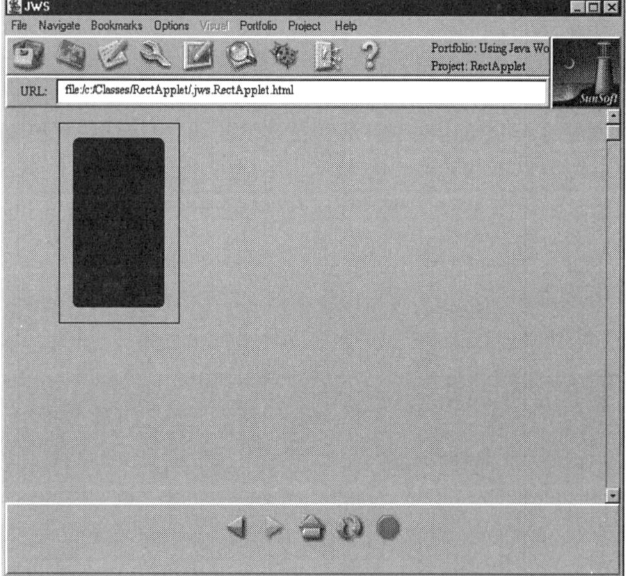

FIG. 6.4 This is RectApplet running under Java Workshop.

In RectApplet's paint() method, you can see the method call that produces the graphical display. The first line creates the outside rectangle. That method call looks like this:

```
g.drawRect(35, 15, 125, 200);
```

The `drawRect()` method's four arguments are the X,Y coordinates of the rectangle's upper-left corner and the width and height of the rectangle. The rounded filled rectangle is almost as easy to draw.

```
g.fillRoundRect(50, 30, 95, 170, 15, 15);
```

The first four arguments of the `fillRoundRect()` method are the same as those for the `drawRect()` method. The fifth and sixth arguments are the size of the rectangle that represents the rounded corners. Think of this rectangle as being placed on each corner of the main rectangle and a curved line drawn between its corners, as shown in figure 6.5.

FIG. 6.5 The coordinates for the rounded corners are given as the width and height of the rectangle that encloses the rounded corner.

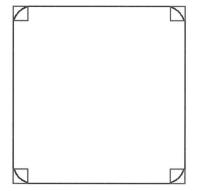

Shape-Drawing Applets

Some shapes you can draw with the `Graphics` class are more complex than others. For example, the `drawArc()` method requires six arguments in order to draw a simple curved line. Next you create a couple of new applets that enable you to experiment with the shape-drawing methods of the `Graphics` class to see how drawing other shapes works.

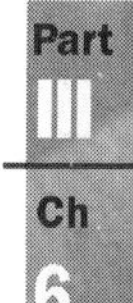

The ShapeApplet Applet

The first graphics applet you'll create is `ShapeApplet`, which enables you to switch from one shape to another in the applet's display. Listing 6.4 is ShapeApplet's source code. Figures 6.6 and 6.7 show what the applet looks like running under the Java Workshop.

Listing 6.4 An Applet That Draws Various Shapes

```
import java.awt.*;
import java.applet.*;

public class ShapeApplet extends Applet
{
    int shape;
    Button button;

    public void init()
    {
        shape = 0;
        button = new Button("Next Shape");
        add(button);
    }

    public void paint(Graphics g)
    {
        int x[] = {35, 150, 60, 140, 60, 150, 35};
        int y[] = {50, 80, 110, 140, 170, 200, 230};
        int numPts = 7;

        switch(shape)
        {
            case 0:
                g.drawLine(35, 50, 160, 230);
                break;
            case 1:
                g.drawRect(35, 50, 125, 180);
                break;
            case 2:
                g.drawRoundRect(35, 50, 125, 180, 15, 15);
                break;
            case 3:
                g.drawOval(35, 50, 125, 180);
                break;
            case 4:
                g.drawArc(35, 50, 125, 180, 90, 180);
                break;
            case 5:
                g.drawPolygon(x, y, numPts);
                break;
            case 6:
                g.fillPolygon(x, y, numPts);
                break;
        }
    }

    public boolean action(Event event, Object arg)
    {
        ++shape;
        if (shape == 7)
```

```
            shape = 0;
        repaint();
        return true;
    }
}
```

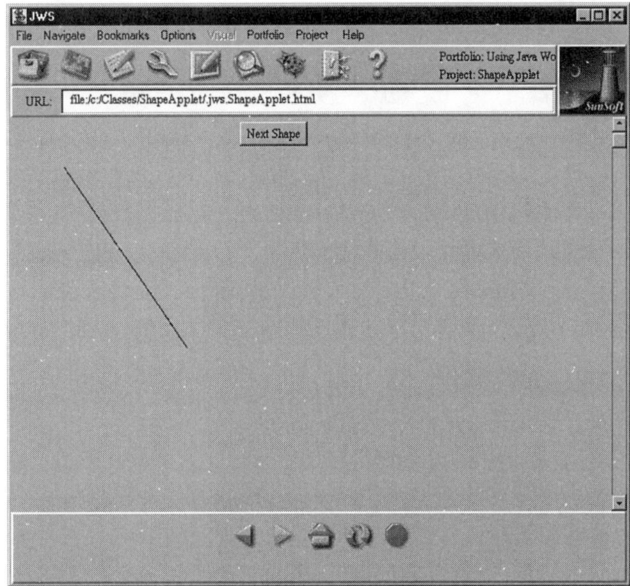

FIG. 6.6
This is what ShapeApplet looks like when it first runs.

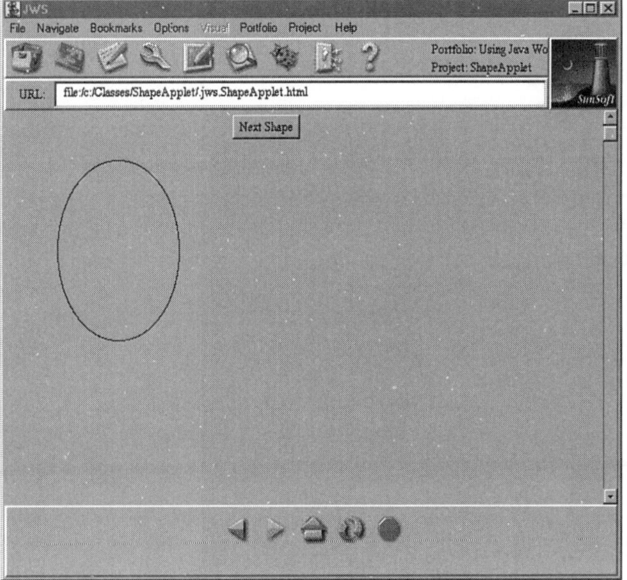

FIG. 6.7
This is ShapeApplet displaying an oval.

To run ShapeApplet, create a new project for the applet's source code, use Build Manager to build the applet's .class file, and use Project Tester to actually run the applet. When you run the applet under Java Workshop, you see the window shown in figure 6.6. To change the shape displayed in the applet's canvas, click the Next Shape button.

Understanding the ShapeApplet Applet

You don't need to concern yourself at this point with the button control that ShapeApplet uses to switch shapes, except to know that clicking the button causes Java to call the applet's `action()` method. Java calls `action()` whenever the user performs some action with controls in the applet. In this case, the action that `action()` responds to is the user's clicking the Next Shape button. In ShapeApplet, the `action()` method increments the shape counter, `shape`, and calls `repaint()`, which tells the applet to redraw itself. In the `paint()` method, the program uses the value of `shape` in a `switch` statement to determine which shape gets drawn.

The real meat of this program is the calls to the `Graphics` object's various shape-drawing methods. You already know about the first three: `drawLine()`, `drawRect()`, and `drawRoundRect()`. The call to `drawOval()`, however, is new and looks like this:

```
g.drawOval(35, 50, 125, 180);
```

As you can see, this method, which draws ovals and circles, takes four arguments. These arguments are the X,Y coordinates, width, and height of a rectangle that can enclose the oval. Figure 6.8 shows how the resultant oval relates to its enclosing rectangle.

FIG. 6.8
An oval's coordinates are actually the coordinates of an enclosing rectangle.

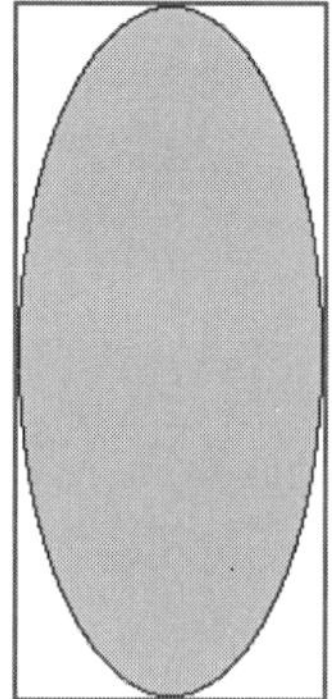

Next in `paint()` is the `drawArc()` method, which is the most complicated (at least, from an understanding point of view) of the shape-drawing methods. The call to `drawArc()` looks like this:

```
g.drawArc(35, 50, 125, 180, 90, 180);
```

The first four arguments are the same as the arguments for `drawOval()`: the X and Y coordinates, width, and height of the enclosing rectangle. The last two arguments are the angle at which to start drawing the arc and the number of degrees around the arc to draw.

To understand all this angle nonsense, take a look at figure 6.9, which shows how Java relates the arc's starting angle to the degrees of an oval. In the preceding example call to `drawArc()`, the fifth argument is 90, which means Java starts drawing the arc, within the arc's enclosing rectangle, at the 90-degree point. The sixth argument of 180 tells Java to draw around the arc 180 degrees (or halfway around the full 360 degrees). It doesn't mean that the ending point should be at the 180-degree point.

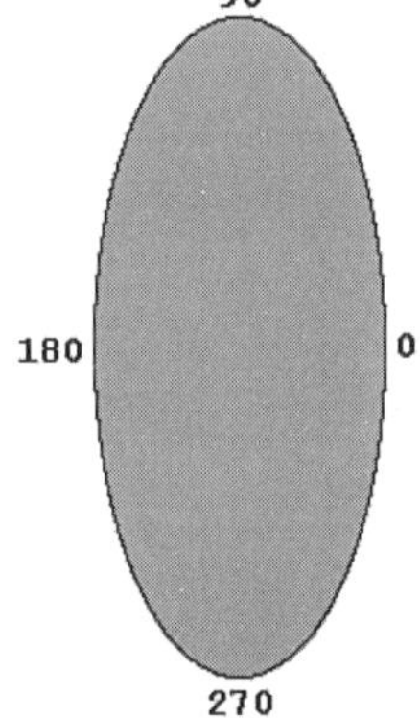

FIG. 6.9
The degrees of an oval start on the right side and travel counter-clockwise around the arc.

Drawing Arcs in an Applet

Because understanding the angles involved in drawing arcs can be a little confusing, now you'll create an applet called ArcApplet that enables you to enter different values for `drawArc()`'s fifth and sixth arguments and immediately see the results. Listing 6.5 is the source code for the applet.

Listing 6.5 An Arc-drawing Applet

```
import java.awt.*;
import java.applet.*;

public class ArcApplet extends Applet
{
    TextField textField1, textField2;

    public void init()
    {
        textField1 = new TextField(10);
        textField2 = new TextField(10);

        add(textField1);
        add(textField2);

        textField1.setText("0");
        textField2.setText("360");
    }

    public void paint(Graphics g)
    {
        String s = textField1.getText();
        int start = Integer.parseInt(s);

        s = textField2.getText();
        int sweep = Integer.parseInt(s);

        g.drawArc(35, 50, 125, 180, start, sweep);
    }

    public boolean action(Event event, Object arg)
    {
        repaint();
        return true;
    }
}
```

When you run ArcApplet using Java Workshop, you see the window shown in figure 6.10. Because the starting angle (in the first text box) is 0 and the drawing degrees (the second box) is 360, the arc is actually a full oval. By changing the values in the two boxes and pressing Enter, you can cause the applet to display different arcs. For example, figure 6.11 shows an arc that has a starting angle of 120 degrees and drawing degrees of 245.

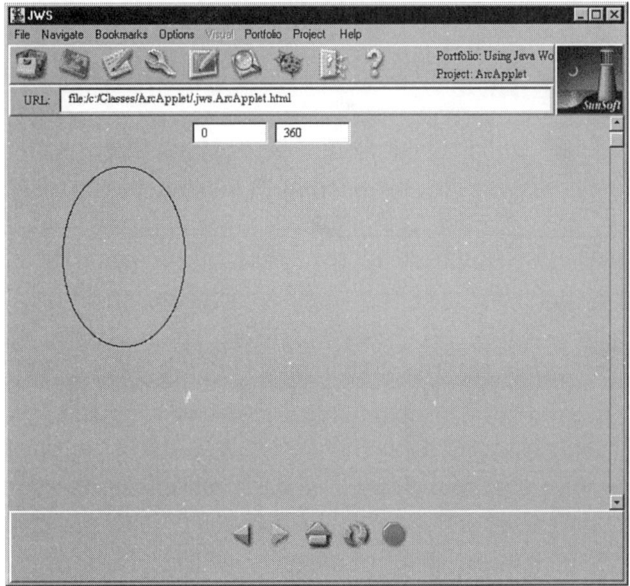

FIG. 6.10
This is ArcApplet at startup.

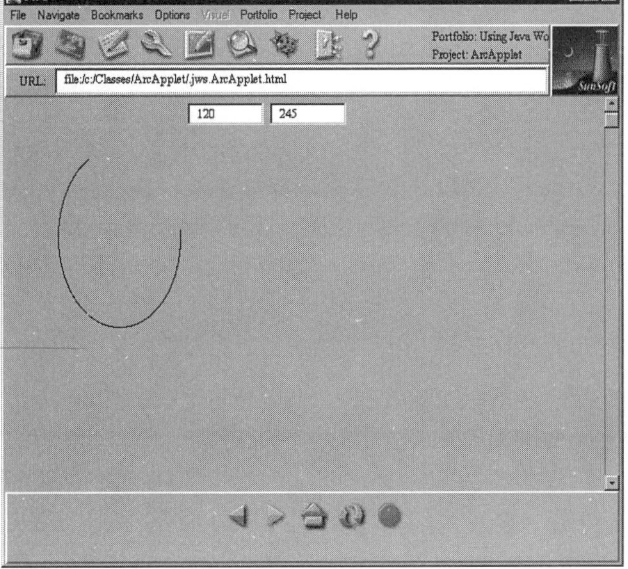

FIG. 6.11
You can use ArcApplet to experiment with different arc angle settings.

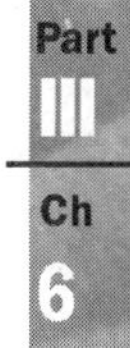

NOTE Most of the shape-drawing methods come in two versions, one that draws a hollow shape, and one that draws a filled shape. The method that draws the filled shape has the same name as the one that draws the hollow shape, except you change the word `draw` in the name to `fill`. For example, because `drawArc()` draws a hollow arc, the method `fillArc()` draws a filled arc.

Drawing Polygons

Polygons are simply many-sided shapes. For example, a triangle is a polygon (it is, in fact, the simplest polygon). Squares, rectangles, and hexagons are all polygons, as well. Because a polygon comprises many different lines, before you can draw a polygon in Java, you need to create arrays that contain the X,Y coordinates for each line in the polygon. In listing 6.4, ShapeApplet defines those arrays like this:

```
int x[] = {35, 150, 60, 140, 60, 150, 35};
int y[] = {50, 80, 110, 140, 170, 200, 230};
int numPts = 7;
```

The first array, called x[] in the preceding, is the X coordinates for each X,Y pair, and the second array, called y[], is the Y coordinates for each X,Y pair. When you look at the values defined in the arrays, you can see that the first line gets drawn from 35,50 to 150,80. Because all the lines in a polygon are connected, Java can continue drawing lines by using the previous ending point (in this case, 150,80) and the next coordinate pair, which is 60,110. Java continues to work through the arrays until it uses all the given coordinates. The actual method call that draws the polygon looks like this:

```
g.drawPolygon(x, y, numPts);
```

The `drawPolygon()` method's three arguments are the array holding the X coordinates, the array holding the Y coordinates, and the number of points defined in the arrays. You can use a literal value for the third argument, but it's often handy to define a variable as shown in the example (`numPts`). Then, if you change the arrays, you can change the variable at the same time and not have to worry about correcting any method calls that use the arrays along with point count.

Figure 6.12 shows the polygon drawn by the values given in the `x[]` and `y[]` arrays in the preceding. It looks more like a squiggly line than a polygon. That's because when you draw a hollow polygon, Java doesn't connect the starting and ending point. If you draw a filled polygon, though, you'll see that the connecting side is really there, as shown in figure 6.13.

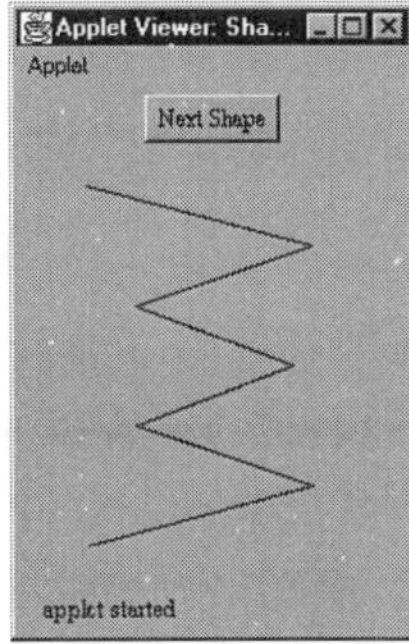

FIG. 6.12
A hollow polygon is always missing one side.

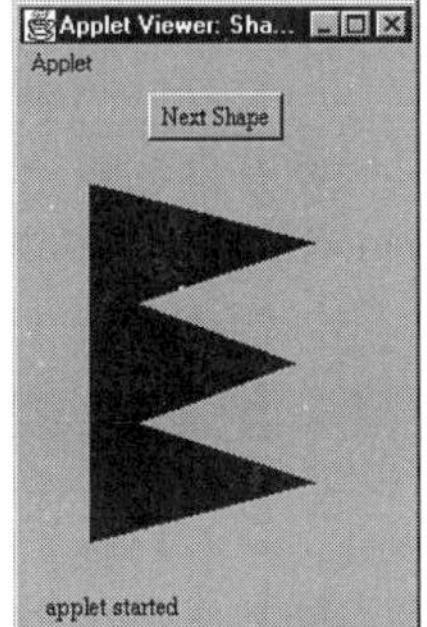

FIG. 6.13
A filled polygon actually looks like a polygon instead of a squiggly line.

NOTE If you need more control over your polygons, Java includes a `Polygon` class from which you can create polygon objects from the coordinate arrays. The `Polygon` class includes handy methods that enable you to add points to a polygon, determine whether a point is inside the polygon, and retrieve the polygon's bounding rectangle. You create a `Polygon` object with a line like `Polygon polygon = new Polygon(x, y, numPts)`. The arguments for the class's constructor are the same as those for the `drawPolygon()` method. The `Polygon` class's public methods are `addPoint(x, y)`, `getBoundingBox()` (which returns a `Rectangle` object), and `inside()` (which returns a `boolean` value).

Graphical Text

Now that you know how to draw all kinds of shapes in your applets, it's time to see how to use text and text fonts, as well. By combining graphical text with other drawing methods, you can create attractive applets for your Web pages. In the following sections, you learn how to display text, as well as how to create fonts and retrieve information about those fonts.

Displaying Text in an Applet

The easiest thing to display is a line of text. But since the text output is graphical, you need to use one of Java's graphical-text functions. The most commonly used is `drawString()`, which is part of the `Graphics` class contained in the `awt` package. You call `drawString()` like this:

```
g.drawString("Hello from Java!", 60, 75);
```

The arguments in the above call to `drawString()` tell Java to draw the text "Hello from Java!" at column 60 and row 75 of the display area. (The position is measured in pixels, not characters. A pixel is the smallest dot that can be displayed on the screen.) To display the text at a different location, just change the second and third arguments. Usually, you'll draw text in your applet's `paint()` method. As you know, Java calls `paint()` whenever the applet's display area needs to be redrawn. The `paint()` method always gets called when the applet first appears on the screen.

NOTE The Java compiler is case sensitive, meaning that it can differentiate between upper- and lower-case letters. For this reason, you have to be extra careful to type method names properly. For example, if you type `Paint()` instead of `paint()`, Java doesn't recognize the method and won't call it when the applet needs to be redrawn.

Getting Font Attributes

Every font that you can use with your Java applets is associated with a group of attributes that determines the size and appearance of the font. The most important of these attributes is the font's name, which determines the font's basic style. As shown in figure 6.14, there is a big difference between the Arial and Times Roman fonts as far as how they look. When you're setting up a font for use, the first thing that you concern yourself with is the name of the font.

You can easily get information about the currently active font. Start by calling the `Graphics` object's `getFont()` method, like this:

```
Font font = g.getFont();
```

The `getFont()` method returns a `Font` object for the current font. Once you have the `Font` object, you can use the `Font` class's various methods to obtain information about the font. Table 6.2 shows the most commonly used public methods of the `Font` class and what they do.

FIG. 6.14
The appearance of a font is determined by the font you choose.

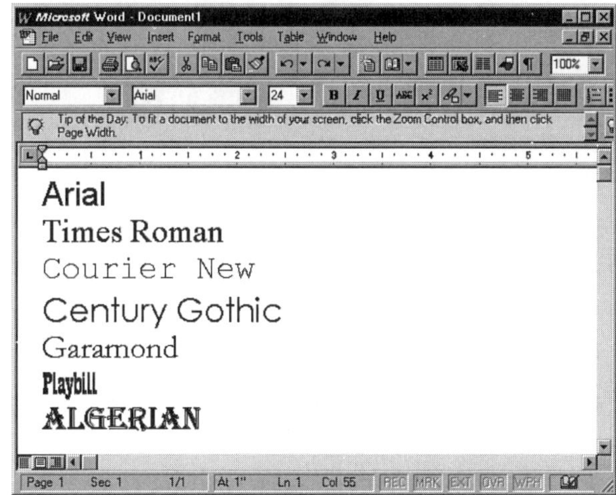

Table 6.2 The Font Class's Most Commonly Used Public Methods

Method	Description
getFamily()	Returns the family name of the font.
getName()	Returns the name of the font.
getSize()	Returns the size of the font.
getStyle()	Returns the style of the font, where 0 is plain, 1 is bold, 2 is italic, and 3 is bold italic.
isBold()	Returns a boolean value indicating whether or not the font is bold.
isItalic()	Returns a boolean value indicating whether or not the font is italic.
isPlain()	Returns a boolean value indicating whether or not the font is plain.
toString()	Returns a string of information about the font.

Displaying Font Attributes

As always, the best way to see how something works is to try it out yourself. With that end in mind, listing 6.6 is an applet that displays information about the currently active font using many of the methods described in table 6.2. Figure 6.15 shows the applet running under Java Workshop.

Listing 6.6 Getting Information about a Font

```
import java.awt.*;
import java.applet.*;

public class FontApplet extends Applet
{
    public void paint(Graphics g)
    {
        Font font = getFont();
        String name = font.getName();
        String family = font.getFamily();

        int n = font.getStyle();
        String style;
        if (n == 0)
            style = "Plain";
        else if (n == 1)
            style = "Bold";
        else if (n == 2)
            style = "Italic";
        else
            style = "Bold Italic";

        n = font.getSize();
        String size = String.valueOf(n);
        String info = font.toString();

        String s = "Name: " + name;
        g.drawString(s, 50, 50);
        s = "Family: " + family;
        g.drawString(s, 50, 65);
        s = "Style: " + style;
        g.drawString(s, 50, 80);
        s = "Size: " + size;
        g.drawString(s, 50, 95);
        g.drawString(info, 20, 125);
    }
}
```

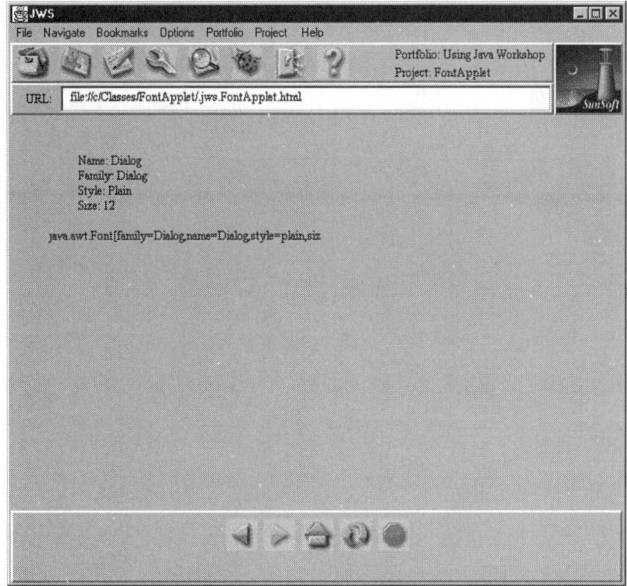

FIG. 6.15
This is FontApplet running under Java Workshop.

As you can see from listing 6.6, using the Font class's methods is fairly straightforward. Just call the method, which returns a value that describes some aspect of the font represented by the Font object.

Getting Font Metrics

In many cases, the information you can retrieve from a `Font` object is enough to keep you out of trouble. For example, you can properly space the lines of text by using the size returned by the `getSize()` method. Sometimes, though, you want to know more about the font you're using. For example, you might want to know the width of a particular character or even the width in pixels of an entire text string. In these cases, you need to work with text metrics.

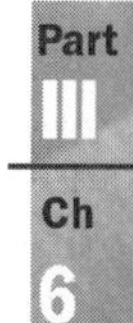

True to form, Java includes the `FontMetrics` class, which makes it easy to obtain information about fonts. You create a `FontMetrics` object like this:

```
FontMetrics fontMetrics = getFontMetrics(font);
```

You may recall that `getFontMetrics()`, which returns a reference to a `FontMetrics` object for the active font, is a method of the `Graphics` class. Its single argument is the `Font` object for which you want the font metrics.

Once you have the `FontMetrics` object, you can call its methods in order to obtain detailed information about the associated font. Table 6.3 lists the most commonly used methods.

Table 6.3 Commonly Used *FontMetrics* Methods

Method	Description
charWidth()	Returns the width of a character.
getAscent()	Returns the font's ascent.
getDescent()	Returns the font's descent.
getFont()	Returns the associated font object.
getHeight()	Returns the font's height.
getLeading()	Returns the font's leading (line spacing).
stringWidth()	Returns the width of a string.
toString()	Returns a string of information about the font.

NOTE If you haven't used fonts before, some of the terms, used in table 6.3 like, leading, ascent, and descent, may seem unfamiliar to you. Leading (pronounced "ledding") refers to the amount of white space between lines of text. Ascent is the height of a character, from the baseline to the top of the character. Descent is the size of the area that accommodates the descending portions of letters, such as the tail on a lowercase g. Height is the sum of ascent, descent, and leading. See figure 6.16 for examples of each.

FIG. 6.17 Ascent, descent, and leading determine the overall height of a font.

Displaying Font Metrics

Most of the methods listed in table 6.3 are self-explanatory. However, you probably want a chance to see them in action. Listing 6.7 is the source code for MetricsApplet. When you run the MetricsApplet applet, you see the window shown in figure 6.17. At the top of the window is a text box into which you can enter different strings of text. When you press Enter, the applet displays the length of the string in pixels. Immediately below the text box is information about the current font.

Listing 6.7 An Applet That Displays Text Metrics

```
import java.awt.*;
import java.applet.*;

public class MetricsApplet extends Applet
{
    TextField textField;

    public void init()
    {
        textField = new TextField(20);
        add(textField);
        textField.setText("Default string");
    }

    public void paint(Graphics g)
    {
        Font font = getFont();
        FontMetrics fontMetrics = g.getFontMetrics(font);
        int n = fontMetrics.getLeading();
        String leading = String.valueOf(n);
        n = fontMetrics.getAscent();
        String ascent = String.valueOf(n);
        n = fontMetrics.getDescent();
        String descent = String.valueOf(n);
        n = fontMetrics.getHeight();
        String height = String.valueOf(n);

        String s = textField.getText();
        n = fontMetrics.stringWidth(s);
        String width = String.valueOf(n);

        g.drawString("FONT INFO:", 55, 60);
        g.drawString("Leading: " + leading, 70, 80);
        g.drawString("Ascent: " + ascent, 70, 95);
        g.drawString("Descent: " + descent, 70, 110);
        g.drawString("Height: " + height, 70, 125);

        g.drawString("STRING INFO:", 55, 155);
        g.drawString("Width: " + width, 70, 175);
    }

    public boolean action(Event event, Object arg)
```

continues

Listing 6.7 Continued

```
{
        repaint();
        return true;
    }
}
```

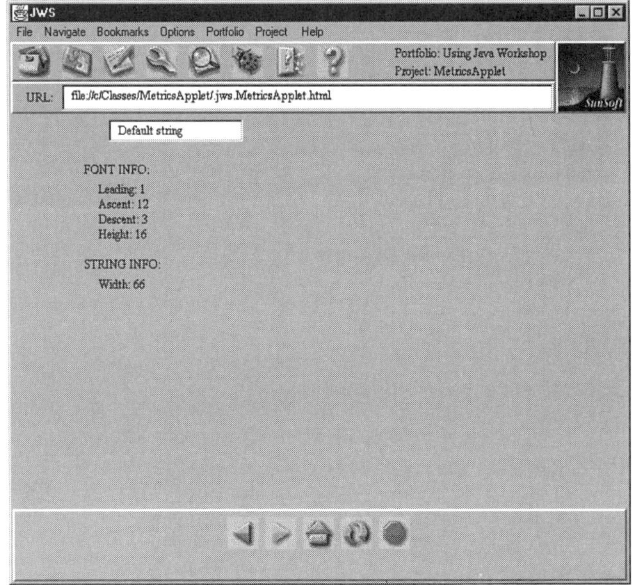

FIG. 6.17
This is MetricsApplet running under Java Workshop.

NOTE Because all of the applets you've written so far in this book haven't used text metrics when displaying text, you may wonder why you even need to bother with this stuff. Chances are that when you're running your applets under Windows 95 using the default font, everything will work fine. But remember that your applets may run on machines using other operating systems, and their default fonts may not be exactly the same size. Also, when you create your own fonts, you may not know the resultant font's size exactly. In order to position text accurately, you need to use font metrics.

Creating Fonts

You may think an applet that always uses the default font is boring to look at. In many cases, you'd be right. An easy way to spruce up an applet is to use different fonts. Luckily, Java enables you to create and set fonts for your applet. You do this by creating your own font object, like this:

```
Font font = new Font("TimesRoman", Font.PLAIN, 20);
```

The constructor for the `Font` class takes three arguments: the font name, style, and size. The style can be any combination of the font attributes that are defined in the `Font` class. Those attributes are `Font.PLAIN`, `Font.BOLD`, and `Font.ITALIC`.

Although you can create fonts with the plain, bold, or italic styles, at times, you may need to combine font styles. Suppose, for example, that you wanted to use both bold and italic styles. The line

```
Font font = new Font("Courier", Font.BOLD + Font.ITALIC, 18);
```

gives you an 18-point bold italic Courier font. (A point is a measurement of a font's height and is equal to 1/72 of an inch.)

Using the Font

After you've created the font, you have to tell Java to use the font. You do this by calling the Graphics class's `setFont()` method, like this:

```
g.setFont(font);
```

At this point, the next text you display in your applet uses the new font. However, when you request a certain type and size of font, you can't be sure of what you'll get. The system tries its best to match the requested font, but you still need to know at least the size of the font with which you ended up. You can get all the information you need by creating a `FontMetrics` object, like this:

```
FontMetrics fontMetrics = g.getFontMetrics(font);
```

To get the height of a line of text, call the `FontMetrics` object's `getHeight()` method, like this:

```
int height = fontMetrics.getHeight();
```

CAUTION

When creating a font, be aware that the user's system may not have a particular font loaded. In that case, Java chooses a default font as a replacement. This possible font substitution is a good reason to use methods like `getName()` in order to see whether you got the font you wanted. You especially need to know the size of the font, so you can be sure to position your text lines properly.

Displaying Different Sized Fonts

You wouldn't create a font unless you had some text to display. Before you can display your text, you need to know at least the height of the font. Failure to consider the font's height may give you text lines that overlap or that are spaced too far apart. You can use the height returned from the `FontMetrics` class's `getHeight()` method as a row increment value for each line of text you need to print. Listing 6.8, which is the source code for the FontApplet2 applet, shows how this is done. Figure 6.18 shows what the applet looks like.

Listing 6.8 Displaying Different Sized Fonts

```
import java.awt.*;
import java.applet.*;

public class FontApplet2 extends Applet
{
    TextField textField;

    public void init()
    {
        textField = new TextField(10);
        add(textField);
        textField.setText("32");
    }

    public void paint(Graphics g)
    {
        String s = textField.getText();
        int height = Integer.parseInt(s);

        Font font = new Font("TimesRoman", Font.PLAIN, height);
        g.setFont(font);
        FontMetrics fontMetrics = g.getFontMetrics(font);
        height = fontMetrics.getHeight();

        int row = 80;
        g.drawString("This is the first line.", 20, row);
        row += height;
        g.drawString("This is the second line.", 20, row);
        row += height;
        g.drawString("This is the third line.", 20, row);
        row += height;
        g.drawString("This is the fourth line.", 20, row);
    }

    public boolean action(Event event, Object arg)
```

```
        {
            repaint();
            return true;
        }
    }
```

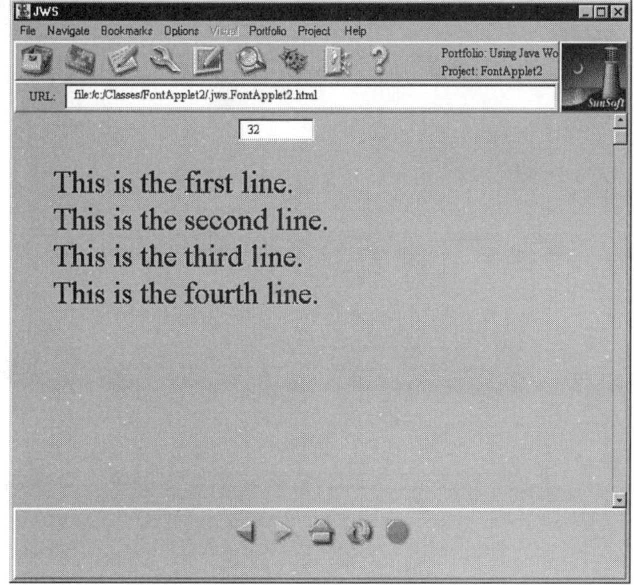

FIG. 6.18 This is FontApplet2 running under Java Workshop.

When you run FontApplet2, you see the window shown in figure 6.19. The size of the active font appears in the text box at the top of the applet, and a sample of the font appears below the text box. To change the size of the font, type a new value into the text box and press Enter. Figure 6.19, for example, shows the applet displaying 12-point font, whereas figure 6.20 is the applet displaying 120-point characters. As you can see, no matter what font size you choose, the lines are properly spaced (although large fonts overrun the boundaries of the applet's canvas).

The spacing of the lines is accomplished by first creating a variable to hold the vertical position for the next line of text:

```
int row = 80;
```

Here, the program not only declares the `row` variable, but also initializes it with the vertical position of the first row of text.

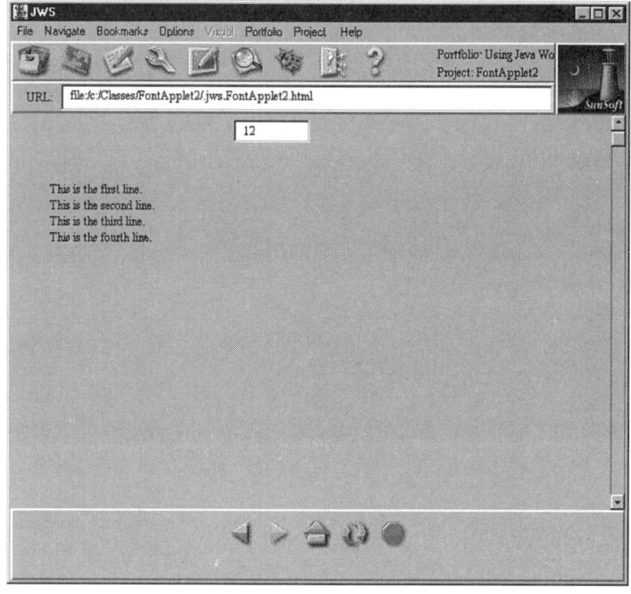

FIG. 6.19
FontApplet2 can display any size character you like. This is 12-point text.

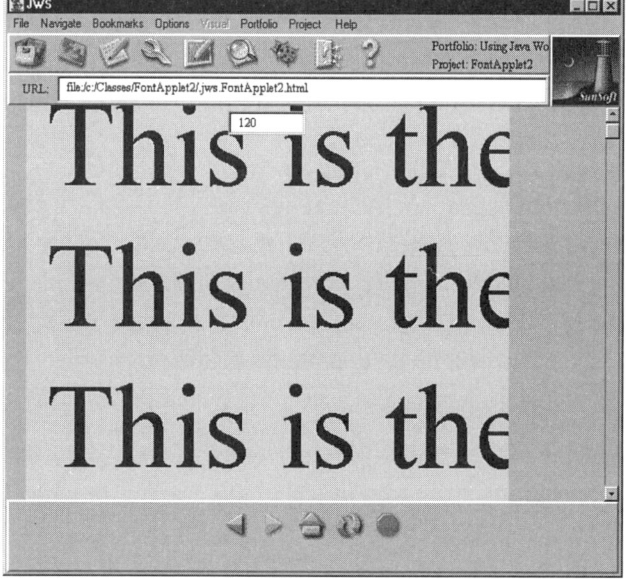

FIG. 6.20
This is FontApplet2 displaying 120-point text.

The applet then prints the first text line, using `row` for `drawString()`'s third argument:

```
g.drawString("This is the first line.", 20, row);
```

In preparation for printing the next line of text, the program adds the font's height to the `row` variable:

```
row += height;
```

Each line of text is printed, with row being incremented by the font's height in between, like this:

```
g.drawString("This is the second line.", 20, row);
row += height;
g.drawString("This is the third line.", 20, row);
```

From Here...

In this chapter, you got a quick look at the basic applet and the methods you can call on at various stages during the applet's life cycle. Java's `Graphics` class enables you to draw many types of shapes, including lines, rectangles, ovals, and arcs. You can use these shape-drawing methods to enhance the appearance of your applets.

In regular Windows programming, creating and using fonts is a meticulous and frustrating experience. Java, however, simplifies this task by offering the `Font` and `FontMetrics` classes. With just a few method calls, you can create the fonts you need for your applet.

- Chapter 5, "Object-Oriented Programming and Java," tells you more about classes and how they're used in Java.
- Chapter 7, "Java Controls," describes how to add graphical controls, such as buttons and scrolling lists, to your applet.
- Chapter 8, "Panels and the Layout Manager," shows how to organize the elements of your applet's display.
- Chapter 10, "Events and Configurable Applets," provides more information about how to handle events in your applets.
- Chapter 11, "Images, Sounds, and Communications," describes how to place graphical images (pictures) in your applet's display area.

CHAPTER 7

Java Controls

Many computer applications require that the user enter information that the program needs to perform its tasks. In a windowed, graphical environment, getting information from the user presents a challenge. This is because the currently executing application doesn't control the entire screen and so it can't just take control of the keyboard or other input device in order to obtain information from the user. That's why the developers of graphical user interfaces created the various controls—such as text boxes, buttons, and menus—that enable applications to interact with the user without bringing the rest of the system to a halt.

Because Java applets must run under many different windowed operating systems, the Java Developer's Kit provides classes for creating the basic controls needed by most graphical user interfaces. These controls include labels, text fields, buttons, radio buttons, check boxes, and choice menus. The following discussions show how to program these various controls. ■

How to use label, textfield, and text-area controls to display text.

Each of these text controls has its own set of advantages and disadvantages. When you learn to use them correctly, you can make your applets more attractive and easier to use.

About button and checkbox controls.

These two related controls enable you to easily accept commands and option selections from the user.

How to add choice menus and scrolling lists to an applet.

Java's choice menus and scrolling lists provide applet users with quick, easy, and accurate ways to make data selections in an applet.

About scrollbar controls.

Some Java controls have their own scrollbars, but you can create custom scrollbar controls for a variety of uses.

How to use canvases in an applet.

Java's canvases are nothing more than rectangular areas on which you can draw. Still, using canvases creatively helps your applets look their best.

Labels

Labels are the simplest of Java's controls, being little more than text strings you can place anywhere on your applet's display area. You create a label by calling the `Label` class's constructor, like this:

```
Label label = new Label(str, align);
```

The `Label` class's constructor takes two arguments, which are the text to display and an alignment value. The alignment value can be `Label.LEFT`, `Label.CENTER`, or `Label.RIGHT`. After creating the label, you add it to the applet by using the `add()` method, like this:

```
add(label);
```

Suppose that you want a centered label that displays the text `Java does labels!`. To do this, you use a line of Java code something like the following:

```
Label label = new Label("Java does labels!", Label.CENTER);
```

Of course, you can also store the text to display in a `String` object, like this:

```
String str = "Java does Labels!";
Label label = new Label(str, Label.CENTER);
```

One cool thing about labels is that they automatically retain their alignment when the size of an applet's display area changes. For example, figure 7.1 shows an applet displaying the centered label created in the previous example. In figure 7.2, the user has increased the size of the Appletviewer window. The label adjusts to the new space and automatically stays centered.

FIG. 7.1
Labels are great for creating text strings that align themselves automatically.

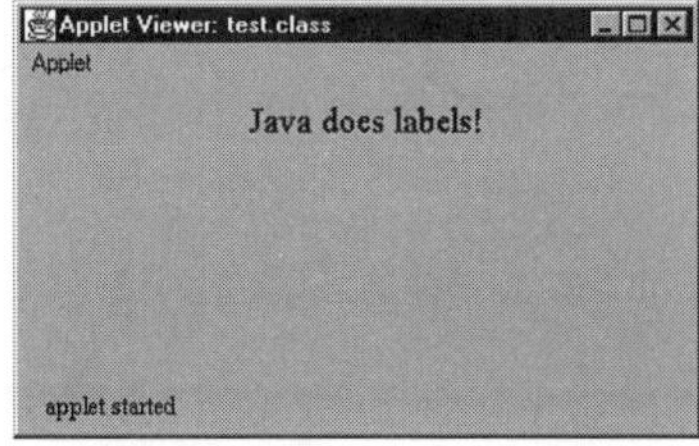

FIG. 7.2
Here, the label has repositioned itself so that, in spite of the enlarged window, the label stays centered.

After you create a `Label` object, you can use the class's methods to manipulate the label. Specifically, you can get or set the label's text and alignment, as shown by the methods listed in table 7.1.

Table 7.1 Methods of the *Label* Class

Method	Description
getAlignment()	Retrieves a label's alignment setting.
getText()	Retrieves a label's test string.
setAlignment()	Sets a label's alignment.
void setText()	Sets a label's text string.

The `getAlignment()` and `getText()` methods have no arguments. The argument for the `setAlignment()` is the alignment value (`Label.LEFT`, `Label.CENTER`, or `Label.RIGHT`), and the argument for `setText()` is the new text for the label.

NOTE A label's text is displayed using the currently set font. You can create labels that use different fonts by creating and setting the font before creating the label.

Buttons

In a previous applet, you used a button to enable the user to manipulate some feature of the applet. Buttons are a great way to trigger events in your applet because they're easy to create and manage, and most importantly, they're easy for the user to use. To create a button, you first call the `Button` class's constructor, like this:

```
Button button = new Button(str);
```

Here, `str` is the text string that you want to appear on the button.

Like other Java classes, `Button` features methods you can use to manipulate a button object. You use these methods to retrieve or set the button's text, like this:

```
String button.getLabel();
button.setLabel(str);
```

Adding buttons to your applets is easy. Just create the button, and then call the `add()` method to add the button to the applet. When the applet runs, the user is able to interact with the button, generating events that the applet can respond to as appropriate. For example, suppose that you want to add a button for setting a font. First, you create a button with an appropriate label, like this:

```
Button button = new Button("TimesRoman");
```

Then, you call the `add()` method to add the button object to the applet, as shown below:

```
add(button);
```

Now, when the applet appears in your Web page, the user can click the button to trigger an event that tells your applet which font to display.

Handling Multiple-Button Events

You respond to the button in the applet's `action()` method. When the user clicks the button, Java calls `action()`, and you do whatever you need to do in that method. However, what if you have more than one button? Then, you need some way to figure out which button was clicked so the applet can respond properly.

As it turns out, the `action()` method delivers two parameters to your program when it's called, as you can see by examining the function's signature:

```
public boolean action(Event evt, Object arg)
```

The first parameter, `evt`, is an `Event` object, and `arg`, the second parameter, is, in the case of a button, the button's label. (The value type of the second parameter changes depending on the interface object.) The `target` field of an `Event` object indicates the type of object that generated the event. To determine the object, you use the `instanceof` keyword, like this:

```
if (evt.target instanceof Button)
```

If this `if` statement is true, it was a button object that generated the event. To determine exactly which button caused the event, you examine the `arg` parameter, like this:

```
if (arg == str)
```

In this line, `str` is the button's label. If the comparison is true, you know exactly which button was clicked.

The ButtonApplet Applet

To get a better understanding of how button events work, take a look at the applet shown in listing 7.1. ButtonApplet displays three buttons in its display area. Whenever you click a button with a normal label, its label reverses itself, as shown in figure 7.3. When you click a button with an already reversed label, all the labels return to their normal state. Compile and run the applet by following the procedure summarized below:

1. Create a new folder for the project inside your Classes folder. In this case, call the new folder ButtonApplet.
2. Type the listing and save it in the new project's folder. In this case, you should name the source-code file ButtonApplet.java.
3. Create a new project for the program. In this case, name the project ButtonApplet.
4. Use Build Manager to compile the program.
5. Use Project Tester to run the program.

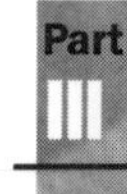

Listing 7.1 An Applet with Multiple Buttons

```
import java.awt.*;
import java.applet.*;

public class ButtonApplet extends Applet
{
```

continues

Listing 7.1 Continued

```
    Button button1;
    Button button2;
    Button button3;

    public void init()
    {
        button1 = new Button("Button1");
        button2 = new Button("Button2");
        button3 = new Button("Button3");

        add(button1);
        add(button2);
        add(button3);
    }

    public boolean action(Event evt, Object arg)
    {
        if (evt.target instanceof Button)
            HandleButtons(arg);
        return true;
    }

    protected void HandleButtons(Object label)
    {
        if (label == "Button1")
            button1.setLabel("1nottuB");
        else if (label == "Button2")
            button2.setLabel("2nottuB");
        else if (label == "Button3")
            button3.setLabel("3nottuB");
        else
        {
            button1.setLabel("Button1");
            button2.setLabel("Button2");
            button3.setLabel("Button3");
        }
    }
}
```

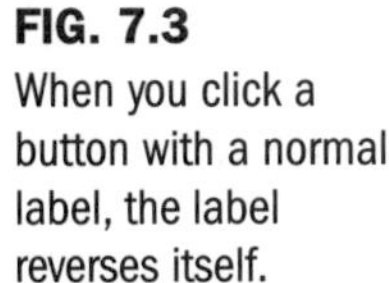

FIG. 7.3
When you click a button with a normal label, the label reverses itself.

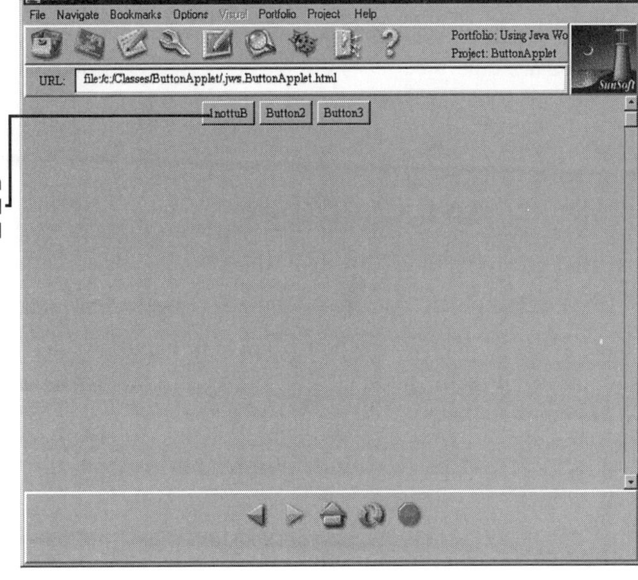

Checkboxes

Many applications (and applets) require that the user select from a list of options. Sometimes, the user can choose as many options as he or she likes (such as when combining various text attributes like bold and italic), and other times the user can select only one option in a list (such as when selecting a color). One way to provide these kinds of choices for your applet's users is to create and display checkbox controls.

To create a checkbox, you call the `Checkbox` class's constructor, like this:

```
Checkbox checkBox = new Checkbox(str, group, check);
```

Here, `str` is a text string for the checkbox's label, `group` is a reference to a `CheckboxGroup` object (used only for exclusive checkboxes), and a `boolean` value indicates whether the checkbox is selected (`true`) or not selected (`false`). After you create the checkbox, add it to the applet by calling the `add()` method, like this:

```
add(checkbox);
```

NOTE When the user can select many options from a list of checkboxes, the checkboxes are being used nonexclusively. When only one checkbox in a group can be selected at a time, the checkboxes are being used exclusively. Java's `Checkbox` class enables you to include both types of checkboxes in your applets.

Creating Nonexclusive Checkboxes

Suppose that you're writing an applet that requires the user to select from a list of books. Because you want the user to be able to select any, all, or none of the books, you must set up checkboxes in nonexclusive mode. First, you create the checkboxes, as shown in listing 7.2:

Listing 7.2 Creating Nonexclusive Checkboxes

```
checkbox1 =
    new Checkbox("The Adventures of Javaman", null, false);
checkbox2 =
    new Checkbox("Java by Example", null, false);
checkbox3 =
    new Checkbox("Java and the Single Guy", null, false);
```

As you know, the `Checkbox` constructor takes three arguments, which are the box's label, a reference to the checkbox's group (in this case, `null`, which means there is no group), and a `boolean` value, which indicates whether or not the box should be displayed as checked.

After creating the checkboxes, you add them to the applet as follows:

```
add(checkbox1);
add(checkbox2);
add(checkbox3);
```

Now, when you run your applet, the user sees a list of checkboxes, like those shown in figure 7.4. In the figure, none of the checkboxes has been selected. To select a checkbox, the user needs only to click the checkbox with the mouse. Because these are nonexclusive checkboxes, the user can select as many options as desired, as shown in figure 7.5.

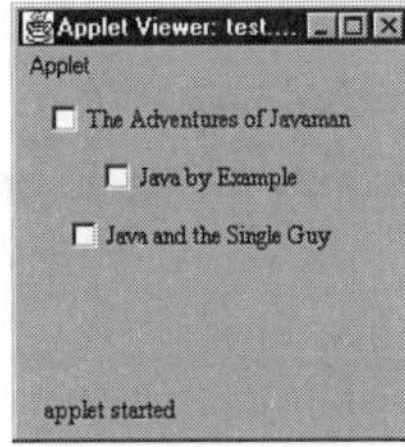

FIG. 7.4
Checkboxes enable the user to select from a list of options.

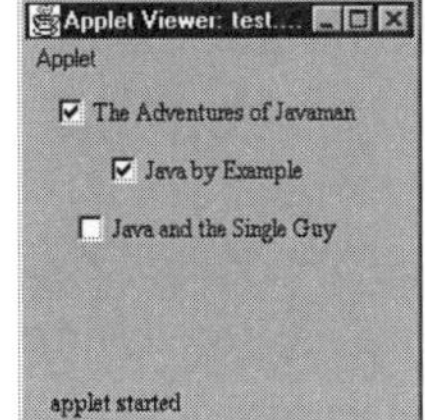

FIG. 7.5
Nonexclusive checkboxes enable the user to select as many options as desired.

Checkbox Groups

In order to create a list of exclusive checkboxes, you must first associate the checkboxes in the list with a `CheckboxGroup` object. The first step is to create the `CheckboxGroup`, like this:

```
CheckboxGroup group = new CheckboxGroup();
```

The `CheckboxGroup` constructor takes no arguments. After you create the `CheckboxGroup` object, you create the checkboxes themselves, giving a reference to the `CheckboxGroup` object as the constructor's second argument, as shown in listing 7.3.

Listing 7.3 Creating Exclusive Checkboxes

```
checkbox1 =
    new Checkbox("The Adventures of Javaman", group, true);
checkbox2 =
    new Checkbox("Java by Example", group, false);
checkbox3 =
    new Checkbox("Java and the Single Guy", group, false);
```

In listing 7.3, notice that the `CheckboxGroup` object, group, is given as the second argument of the `Checkbox` class's constructor for each of the checkboxes in the list. This tells Java to place the three checkboxes into the same group and to treat them as exclusive checkboxes, which means that only one can be selected at a time. Notice also, that the third argument for the first checkbox is `true`. This value tells Java that you want the first checkbox to be selected when Java displays the list.

As always, after creating the checkboxes, you must add them (as follows) to the applet, by calling the `add()` method for each checkbox in the group:

```
add(checkbox1);
add(checkbox2);
add(checkbox3);
```

Now, when the applet appears, the user sees a list something like that shown in figure 7.6. In the figure, the first option is selected. If the user decides to click a different option, the first option becomes unselected and the new one selected. Notice that exclusive checkboxes are round rather than square.

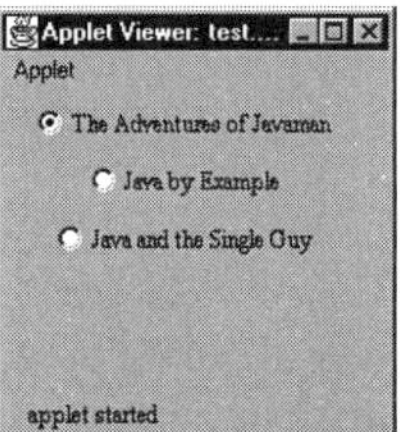

FIG. 7.6
Only one exclusive checkbox can be selected simultaneously.

Checkbox Methods

Just like other controls supported by Java, the `Checkbox` class features a number of methods that you can call in order to manipulate the control or obtain information about it. Table 7.2 lists the public methods for the `Checkbox` class.

Table 7.2 Methods of the *Checkbox* Class

Method	Description
getCheckboxGroup()	Returns the checkbox's group object.
getLabel()	Returns the checkbox's label.

Method	Description
getState()	Returns the checkbox's state.
setCheckboxGroup()	Sets the checkbox's group object.
setLabel()	Sets the checkbox's label.
setState()	Sets the checkbox's state.

The `get` methods, listed in table 7.2, require no arguments and return objects of the appropriate type. The `setCheckboxGroup()` method requires a reference to a `CheckboxGroup` object as its single argument, whereas `setLabel()` and `setState()` require a text string and a `boolean` value, respectively, as their single argument.

NOTE Checkboxes that are set to exclusive mode are also known as radio buttons because, like the station-selection buttons on a radio, only one can be selected at a time.

The CheckboxApplet Applet

Depending on what your applet needs to do, you can handle the checkboxes in a couple of ways. The easiest way to handle checkboxes is to use their methods to determine the information you need in an applet. Listing 7.4, for example, is an applet that tracks the state of a set of checkboxes; it displays their current states every time there are changes. Figure 7.7 shows the applet running under Java Workshop. To compile and run the applet, create a new folder for the project inside your Classes folder, create a new project for the program, type the listing and save it in the new project's folder, use Build Manager to compile the program, and, finally, use Project Tester to run the program.

Listing 7.4 Handling Checkboxes in an Applet

```
import java.awt.*;
import java.applet.*;

public class CheckboxApplet extends Applet
{
    Checkbox checkbox1;
    Checkbox checkbox2;
```

continues

Listing 7.4 Continued

```
Checkbox checkbox3;

    public void init()
    {
        checkbox1 = new Checkbox("Option 1", null, true);
        checkbox2 = new Checkbox("Option 2", null, false);
        checkbox3 = new Checkbox("Option 3", null, false);

        add(checkbox1);
        add(checkbox2);
        add(checkbox3);
    }

    public void paint(Graphics g)
    {
        Font font = g.getFont();
        FontMetrics fontMetrics = g.getFontMetrics(font);
        int height = fontMetrics.getHeight();

        boolean checked = checkbox1.getState();
        if (checked)
            g.drawString("Option1 selected", 20, 120);
        else
            g.drawString("Option1 not selected", 20, 120);

        checked = checkbox2.getState();
        if (checked)
            g.drawString("Option2 selected", 20, 120 + height);
        else
            g.drawString("Option2 not selected", 20, 120 + height);

        checked = checkbox3.getState();
        if (checked)
            g.drawString("Option3 selected", 20, 120 + 2 * height);
        else
            g.drawString("Option3 not selected", 20, 120 + 2 * height);
    }

    public boolean action(Event evt, Object arg)
    {
        repaint();
        return true;
    }
}
```

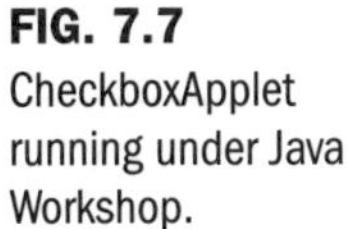

FIG. 7.7
CheckboxApplet running under Java Workshop.

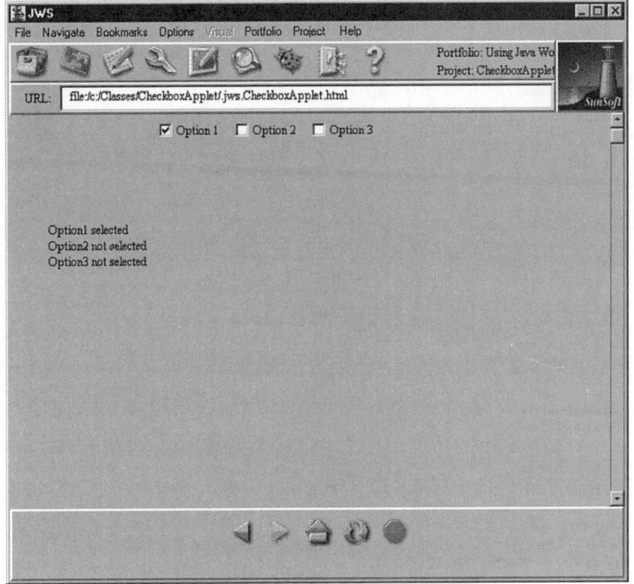

Responding to a Checkbox Event

Most of Java's user-interface controls generate events when they're clicked. The checkbox controls are no different. However, unlike button controls, which send both a reference to the control and the control's label as parameters to the `action()` method, checkboxes send only a reference to the control, with the second `action()` parameter always being the `boolean` value `true`. This anomaly makes it a little more difficult to handle checkbox controls when you need to respond directly to the event generated by the control.

To respond to a checkbox event, you must use the `Event` object's `target` field to call the checkbox's methods in order to determine which checkbox caused the event. If you don't remember, the `Event` object is passed as the `action()` method's first argument.

First, you obtain a reference to the checkbox, like this:

```
Checkbox checkbox = (Checkbox)evt.target;
```

Then, with a reference to the checkbox in hand, you can call whatever `Checkbox` class members you need in order to determine which checkbox caused the event and to deal with the event appropriately. Probably the best way to determine which checkbox you're dealing with is to get the object's label, like this:

```
String label = checkbox.getLabel();
```

You can then compare the returned string to the labels for each checkbox object.

The CheckboxApplet2 Applet

To demonstrate how to use the previously presented technique in an actual programming situation, you now examine CheckboxApplet2. The source code for the applet is shown in listing 7.5. Use the methods you've learned to compile and run the program under Java Workshop.

Listing 7.5 Responding to Checkbox Events

```
import java.awt.*;
import java.applet.*;

public class CheckboxApplet2 extends Applet
{
    Checkbox checkbox1;
    Checkbox checkbox2;
    Checkbox checkbox3;

    public void init()
    {
        checkbox1 = new Checkbox("Option 1", null, true);
        checkbox2 = new Checkbox("Option 2", null, false);
        checkbox3 = new Checkbox("Option 3", null, false);

        add(checkbox1);
        add(checkbox2);
        add(checkbox3);
    }

    public boolean action(Event evt, Object arg)
    {
        if (evt.target instanceof Checkbox)
            ChangeLabel(evt);
        repaint();

        return true;
    }

    protected void ChangeLabel(Event evt)
```

```
        {
            Checkbox checkbox = (Checkbox)evt.target;
            String label = checkbox.getLabel();

            if (label == "Option 1")
                checkbox.setLabel("Changed 1");
            else if (label == "Option 2")
                checkbox.setLabel("Changed 2");
            else if (label == "Option 3")
                checkbox.setLabel("Changed 3");
            else
            {
                checkbox1.setLabel("Option 1");
                checkbox2.setLabel("Option 2");
                checkbox3.setLabel("Option 3");
            }
        }
    }
```

When you run the CheckboxApplet2 applet, you see a display containing three checkboxes. You can click on any of the checkboxes as normal, and their check state changes accordingly. However, when you click on a checkbox, its label also changes, as shown in figure 7.8, proving that the applet is responding to the event generated by the checkbox. If you click on a checkbox that still has its original label, that label changes. If you click on a label that has already been changed, all the checkbox labels revert to their starting text.

FIG. 7.8
Clicking the checkboxes in this applet changes their labels.

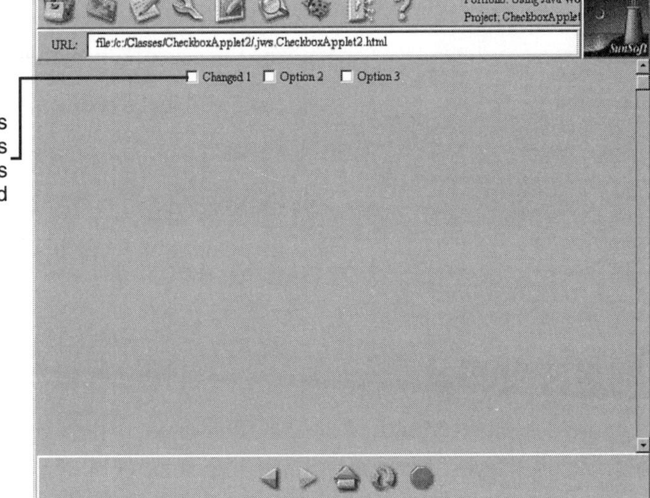

Textfields

A textfield object, which is an object of the `TextField` class, is much like a Windows edit control, providing a small box into which the user can type text. To create a textfield control, you call the `TextField` class's constructor, like this:

```
TextField textField = new TextField(str, size);
```

The constructor's two arguments are the default text, which should be displayed in the textfield control, and the size in characters of the control. After you create the control, add it to the applet by calling the `add()` method, like this:

```
add(textField);
```

TextField Methods

The `TextField` class features a number of public methods that you can use to manipulate textfield objects. By using these methods, you can set a textfield object's characteristics and obtain information about the object. Table 7.3 lists the most commonly used methods and their descriptions.

Table 7.3 Methods of the *TextField* Class

Method	Description
echoCharIsSet()	Returns `true` if the object's echo character is set. When set, echo characters appear in place of any character the user types.
getColumns()	Returns the size of the textfield object.
getEchoChar()	Returns the object's echo character, if set.
String getText()	Gets the text from the textfield object.
setEchoCharacter()	Sets the object's echo character.
setText()	Sets the text in the textfield object.

The EchoApplet Applet

Echo characters enable you to create textfield objects that display a special character when the user types. The most common use for echo characters is to set up text entry for things like passwords. For example, listing 7.6 is the source code for a short applet called EchoApplet that initializes a textfield object to use an asterisk as an echo character. When you run the applet and type something in the textfield control, you see the display in figure 7.9. You can change the echo character by clicking on the Change Echo button. Then, when you click on the textfield control to enter text, the text in the control changes to the new echo character, as shown in figure 7.10. The program switches between three different echo characters: an asterisk (*), a pound sign (#), and a dollar sign ($).

Listing 7.6 Using Echo Characters

```
import java.awt.*;
import java.applet.*;

public class EchoApplet extends Applet
{
    TextField textField;
    Button button;

    public void init()
    {
        textField = new TextField("", 25);
        button = new Button("Change Echo");

        textField.setEchoCharacter('*');

        add(textField);
        add(button);
    }

    public boolean action(Event evt, Object arg)
    {
        if (evt.target instanceof Button)
            ChangeEcho();

        return true;
    }

    protected void ChangeEcho()
    {
        char c = textField.getEchoChar();

        if (c == '*')
            textField.setEchoCharacter('#');
        else if (c == '#')
            textField.setEchoCharacter('$');
        else
            textField.setEchoCharacter('*');
    }
}
```

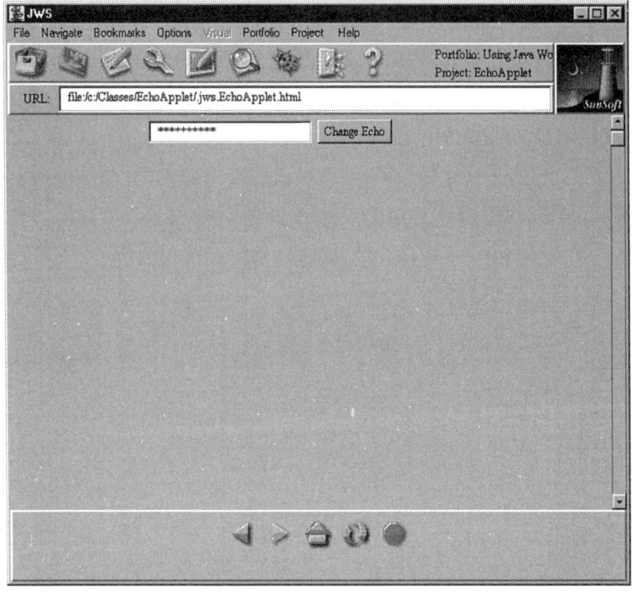

FIG. 7.9
When you start typing, you see asterisks instead of regular text characters.

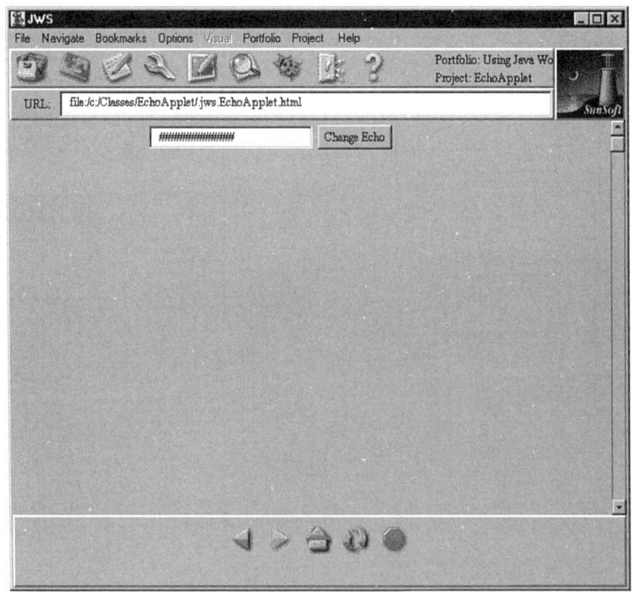

FIG. 7.10
When you click the Change Echo button, the applet switches to a different echo character.

NOTE A textfield control generates an event when the user presses Enter after typing in the control. You can capture this event in the applet's `action()` method.

Choice Menus

Choice menus are very similar to the drop-down lists. When the user selects the menu, a list of commands appears from which the user can choose. After the user makes a choice, the menu disappears. To create a choice menu, you must first create an instance of the `Choice` class, like this:

```
Choice menu = new Choice();
```

As you can see, the `Choice` class's constructor accepts no arguments.

After you have created the `Choice` object, you can add items to the menu by calling the object's `addItem()` method:

```
menu.addItem(str);
```

Here, `str` is the text that appears as the command in the menu. You can call `addItem()` as often as you need to build a complete menu. When you have the complete menu created, add it to the applet by calling the `add()` method.

As you can see, creating a menu is a fairly straightforward process. For example, to create a choice menu that enables the user to select between three font styles, you might use the code shown in listing 7.7.

Listing 7.7 Creating a Choice Menu

```
Choice menu = new Choice();
menu.addItem("Plain");
menu.addItem("Bold");
menu.addItem("Italic");
add(menu);
```

When the user runs the applet containing this menu, a menu like that shown in figure 7.11 appears. To display the menu, the user clicks on the arrow to the right of the text box displaying the current choice, and the menu appears, as shown in figure 7.12. To select a choice, the user merely clicks an entry in the menu.

FIG. 7.11 Java displays a choice menu as a text box with an arrow.

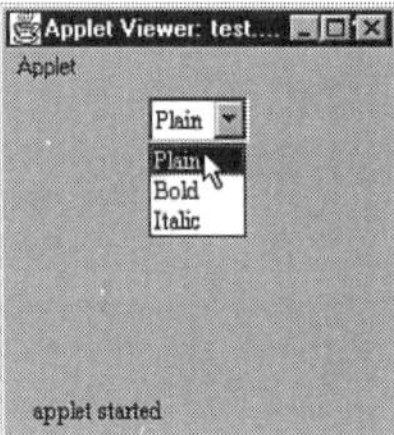

FIG. 7.12
Clicking the arrow displays the menu.

Choice Menu Methods

As you've no doubt guessed, the `Choice` class features a number of public methods that enable you to manipulate choice menus in various ways. Using these methods, you can do everything from determining the number of command entries in a menu to adding items to the menu. Table 7.4 lists the most commonly used methods and their descriptions.

Table 7.4 Methods of the *Choice* Class

Method	Description
countItems()	Returns the number of command items in the menu.
getItem()	Returns the command text for a given item.
addItem()	Adds an item to the menu.
getSelectedItem()	Returns a string representing the selected item.
getSelectedIndex()	Returns the index of the selected item.
select()	Selects the item with the given text string.

The ChoiceApplet Applet

A menu isn't much good unless you can determine which item the user selected so that the applet can carry out the user's command. As with most controls, when the user makes a selection from a choice menu, Java generates an event that you can capture in the `action()` method. In the case of a choice menu, `action()`'s first parameter is the menu instance, and the second parameter is the text of the selected menu item. By comparing the text to the items you added to the menu, you can determine which menu item the user chose.

The ChoiceApplet applet, whose source code is shown in listing 7.8, demonstrates creating and responding to choice menus in an applet. When you run the applet under Java Workshop, you see the window shown in figure 7.13. The text in the window is displayed using the currently selected color in the choice menu. To change the text color, just select a new menu item.

Listing 7.8 Using Choice Menus in an Applet

```
import java.awt.*;
import java.applet.*;

public class ChoiceApplet extends Applet
{
    Choice menu;
    Color color;

    public void init()
    {
        Choice menu = new Choice();

        menu.addItem("Black");
        menu.addItem("Red");
        menu.addItem("Green");
        menu.addItem("Blue");

        add(menu);

        color = Color.black;
    }

    public void paint(Graphics g)
    {
        Font font = new Font("TimesRoman", Font.BOLD, 24);
        int height = font.getSize();
        g.setFont(font);

        g.setColor(color);

        g.drawString("This text is drawn in", 32, 75);
        g.drawString("the color selected from", 32, 75+height);
        g.drawString("the above choice menu.", 32, 75+2*height);
    }

    public boolean action(Event evt, Object arg)
    {
        if (evt.target instanceof Choice)
            HandleMenu(arg);
```


continues

Listing 7.8 Continued

```
        return true;
    }

    protected void HandleMenu(Object item)
    {
        if (item == "Black")
            color = Color.black;
        else if (item == "Red")
            color = Color.red;
        else if (item == "Green")
            color = Color.green;
        else
            color = Color.blue;

        repaint();
    }
}
```

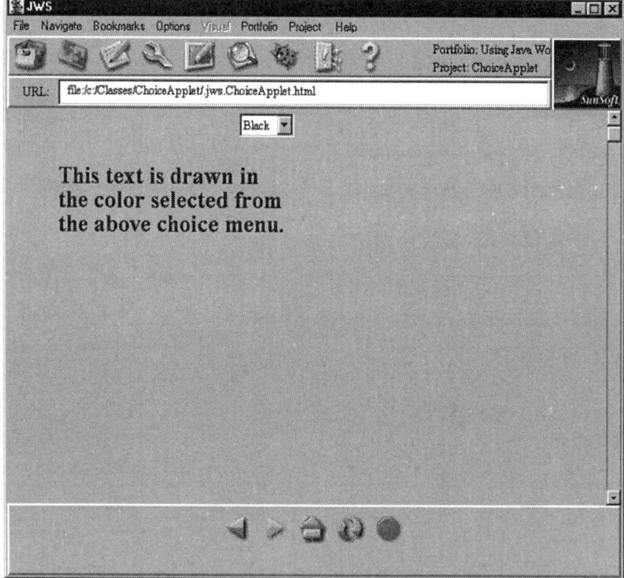

FIG. 7.13
ChoiceApplet displays text in the color selected from its choice menu.

Scrolling Lists

Whereas choice menus usually display a set of commands or options, scrolling lists are best used to display a list of items from which the user can choose. For example, you might use a scrolling list to enable the user to choose a state when filling out an address form. The scrolling list in this case would contain all 50 states. The user would only need to double-click on his or her state in order to complete that section of the form. Scrolling lists not only make it easy for users to enter information, but also ensure that the user makes a choice from a valid set of responses.

To create a scrolling list, you first call the `List` class's constructor, like this:

```
List list = new List(num, false);
```

The constructor's two arguments are the number of visible lines in the list and a `boolean` value indicating whether the list can support multiple selections. The list created in the preceding doesn't allow the user to select more than one item at a time.

When you have the list object created, you can add items to the list. You do this by calling the `List` object's `addItem()` method:

```
list.addItem(str);
```

Here, `str` is the text string for the item to add to the list.

NOTE You can add as many items as you like to a list. You are not limited to the number of items given as the `List` constructor's first argument. That value specifies only the size of the list box; that is, the value determines how many items are visible on the screen at one time.

Creating a Single-selection List

Suppose that you need to create a list that contains musical artists from which the user must select only one. First, you create the list object, next you add the names of the artists you want to include, finally, you add the list to the applet. Listing 7.9 shows the Java code that performs these tasks. Figure 7.14 shows the resultant list box in Appletviewer.

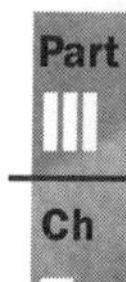

Listing 7.9 Creating a Single-selection List Box

```
List list = new List(10, false);
list.addItem("Pearl Jam");
list.addItem("Dream Theater");
list.addItem("Joe Satriani");
list.addItem("Oasis");
list.addItem("Alanis Morissette");
```

continues

Listing 7.9 Continued

```
list.addItem("Soul Asylum");
list.addItem("The Rembrandts");
list.addItem("Smashing Pumpkins");
list.addItem("Joan Osborne");
list.addItem("Bjork");
add(list);
```

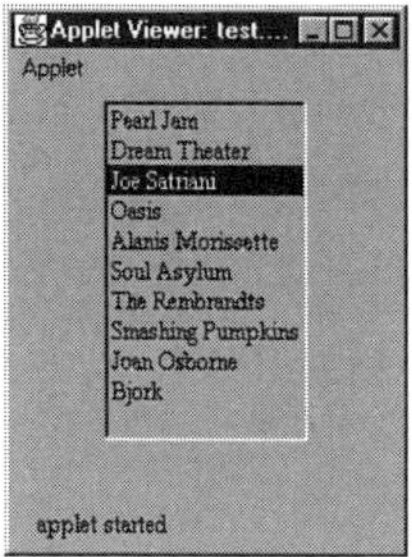

FIG. 7.14 In this list, only one item can be selected.

Because the `List` constructor's first argument is 10, and there are only 10 items in the list, all of the items are visible on the screen. Moreover, because the `List` constructor's second parameter is `false`, in the list created by listing 7.9, the user can select only a single artist at a time.

Creating a Multiple-selection List

When you display a list of musical artists such as that created by listing 7.9, you may want the user to select more than one. In this case, you can create a multiple-selection list, just by changing the `List` constructor's second argument to `true`, like this:

```
List list = new List(10, true);
```

As figure 7.15 shows, the new list enables the user to select as many artists as he or she likes.

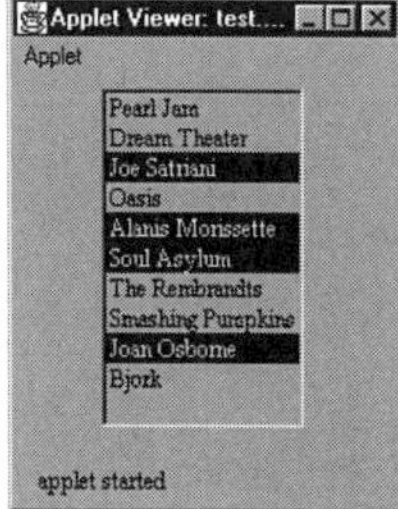

FIG. 7.15 Now the user can select more than one artist at a time.

Creating a Scrolling List

You may have noticed that in this section's title, the list controls are called "scrolling lists." So far, though, none of your lists have scrolled. In fact, they haven't even had scrollbars. Whenever the size of the list box (given as the constructor's first argument) is greater than or equal to the number of items in the list, the list doesn't need to scroll, so no scrollbar appears. However, as soon as the number of items exceeds the size of the list box, Java enables scrolling.

As an example, suppose that you were to change the first line of listing 7.9 to this:

```
List list = new List(5, false);
```

Now, you have a list that can display five items at a time. However, there are 10 items in your list, which means that, in order for the user to be able to see all the items, the list must scroll. Figure 7.16 shows the resultant scrolling list.

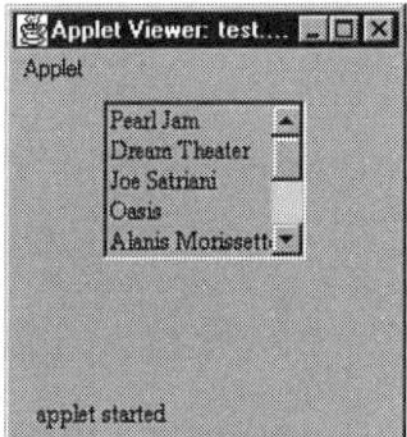

FIG. 7.16
The user must scroll this list to see all the items.

Methods of the *List* Class

Because there's so much you can do with a scrolling list control, the `List` class has a large set of public methods that you can call to manipulate a list. The most useful of these methods are listed in table 7.5. Although there are a lot of methods to learn in the table, the most important are `addItem()`, `getSelectedIndex()`, `getSelectedIndexes()`, `getSelectedItem()`, and `getSelectedItems()`. Using these five methods, you can create a basic scrolling list and enable the user to make selections from it. In the next section, in fact, you see how to determine which item the user selected.

Table 7.5 Most Useful Methods of the *List* Class

Method	Description
addItem()	Adds an item to the end of the list.
addItem()	Adds an item to a specific position in the list.
allowsMultipleSelections()	Returns a boolean value indicating whether or not the list supports multiple selections.
clear()	Clears all items from the list.
countItems()	Returns the number of items in the list.
delItem()	Deletes the item at the given position from the list.
delItems()	Deletes a group of items from the list.
deselect()	Deselects the item at the given index.
getItem()	Returns the item at the given index.
getRows()	Returns the size of the list box.
getSelectedIndex()	Gets the index of the selected item.
getSelectedIndexes()	Gets the indexes of a multiple selection.
getSelectedItem()	Returns the selected item in a list.
getSelectedItems()	Returns all the items in a multiple selection.
getVisibleIndex()	Returns the index of the last item that was made visible.
isSelected()	Returns a boolean value indicating whether the item at the given index is selected.
makeVisible()	Ensures that the item at the given index is visible.
replaceItem()	Replaces the item at the given index with a new item.
select()	Selects the item at the given index.
setMultipleSelections()	Toggles the multiple-selection mode.

The ListApplet Applet

By now, you've gotten used to working with the list of musical artists that I've used in the previous few examples. In this example, you put that list to the test by not only creating and displaying the list in an applet, but also by displaying the user's selection. Listing 7.10 is the source code for the ListApplet applet. Use Java Workshop to compile and run the applet.

Listing 7.10 An Applet with a Scrolling List

```
import java.awt.*;
import java.applet.*;

public class ListApplet extends Applet
{
    List list;

    public void init()
    {
        list = new List(5, false);

        list.addItem("Pearl Jam");
        list.addItem("Dream Theater");
        list.addItem("Joe Satriani");
        list.addItem("Oasis");
        list.addItem("Alanis Morissette");
        list.addItem("Soul Asylum");
        list.addItem("The Rembrandts");
        list.addItem("Smashing Pumpkins");
        list.addItem("Joan Osborne");
        list.addItem("Bjork");

        add(list);
        resize(300, 150);
    }

    public void paint(Graphics g)
    {
        g.drawString("CHOSEN ITEM:", 100, 110);
        String s = list.getSelectedItem();

        if (s == null)
            s = "None";

        g.drawString(s, 100, 130);
    }

    public boolean action(Event evt, Object arg)
    {
```

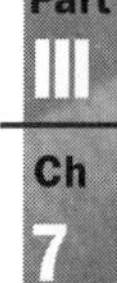

continues

Listing 7.10 Continued

```
            repaint();
            return true;
        }
    }
```

When you run ListApplet with Java Workshop, you see the list of music artists. When you double-click an item in the list, Java calls the applet's `action()` method, in which the applet calls the `repaint()` method. This forces Java to call the `paint()` method, where the applet retrieves the selected item and displays it (see fig. 7.17).

Notice the call to `resize()` in the `init()` method. The `resize()` method enables you to set the applet to any size you wish. This size overrides any size setting that's included in the HTML document that ran the applet.

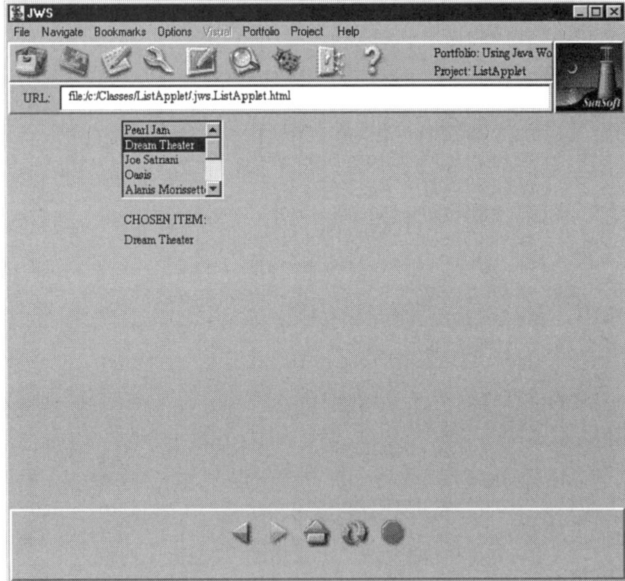

FIG. 7.17 The scrolling list in this applet enables you to choose a single musical artist.

The TextArea Control

Throughout this book, you've been using the textfield control to retrieve information from the user. In most cases, the textfield control works quite well, but it does have some limitations, the most serious being the fact that it can display only one line of text at a time. There may be situations where you'd like to display one or more paragraphs of text in your applet, in a control that enables the user to edit existing text, as well as enter his or her own text. This is where the text-area control is useful. The text-area control is a text box that acts like a simple word processor. When you display a text box, the user can type and edit multiple lines of text.

To create a text-area control, you call the `TextArea` class's constructor, like this:

```
TextArea textArea = new TextArea(str, rows, cols);
```

This constructor's three arguments are the string to display in the control, the number of rows in the control, and the number of columns. As with the other controls, after you create the `TextField` object, you add it to the applet by calling the `add()` method.

The TextAreaApplet Applet

As an example, suppose that you need to create a text-area control that starts off displaying eight lines of text. Listing 7.11 is an applet, called TextAreaApplet, which creates a text-area control that displays eight lines of text. Figure 7.18 shows what the applet looks like running under Java Workshop. When you run the applet, click on the text-area control's box, and try editing the text in the window. As you'll discover, not only can you edit the existing text, but you can also add new text.

Listing 7.11 The TextAreaApplet Applet

```
import java.awt.*;
import java.applet.*;

public class TextAreaApplet extends Applet
{
    TextArea textArea;

    public void init()
    {
        String s = "This is an example of a\n";
        s += "textarea control, which is not\n";
        s += "unlike a textfield control.\n";
        s += "The big difference is that a\n";
        s += "textarea control can hold many\n";
        s += "lines of text, whereas a\n";
        s += "textfield control deals with\n";
        s += "only one line of text at a time.\n";
```

continues

Listing 7.11 Continued

```
        textArea = new TextArea(s, 9, 30);
        add(textArea);

        resize(300, 180);
    }
}
```

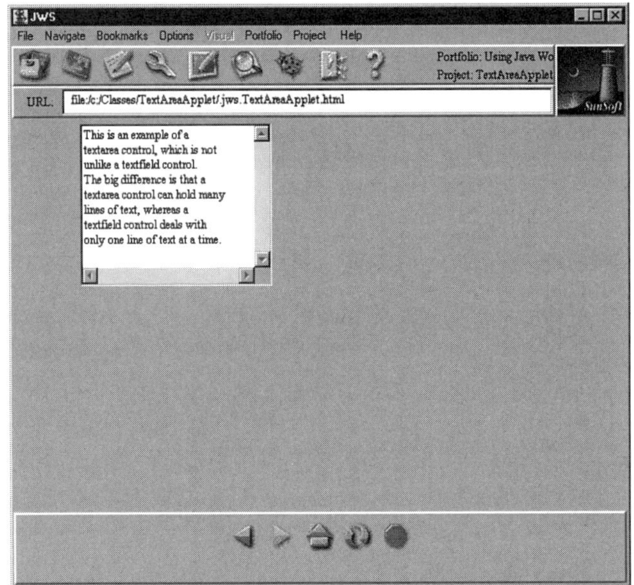

FIG. 7.18
The TextAreaApplet applet running under Java Workshop.

If you look at how the text-area control's display string is created in TextAreaApplet, you see that you can store multiple lines of text into a single `String` object. You do this by placing the newline character (`\n`) at the end of each line that you add to the string.

When you run TextAreaApplet, notice how all the text fits within the text box. Because the text is fully displayed, the control's scrollbars are inactive. However, if you were to edit the text and added more lines than the control can display, or made a line longer than the control can display, the control's scrollbars become active. Figure 7.19 shows TextAreaApplet after the user has added text that forces the scrollbars to become active. You can use the scrollbars to view the portions of the text that are offscreen.

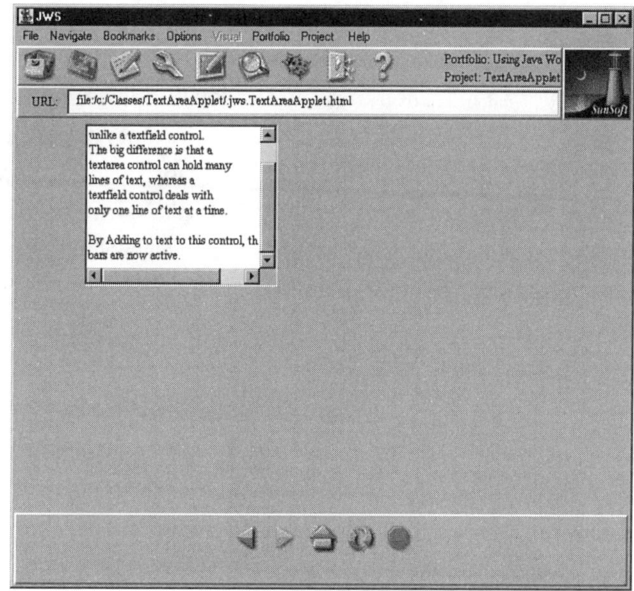

FIG. 7.19
When the text in the control cannot be fully displayed, a text-area control activates its scrollbars.

Methods of the *TextArea* Class

To enable you to manipulate the text easily, the `TextArea` class features a number of public methods. You can use these methods to modify the text in the control or to obtain information about the control. Table 7.6 shows the most useful methods and what they do.

Table 7.6 Useful Methods of the *TextArea* Class

Method	Description
appendText()	Appends text to the control.
getColumns()	Returns the number of columns in the control.
getRows()	Returns the number of rows in the control.
insertText()	Inserts text at the given position.
replaceText()	Replaces text specified by the starting and ending points.

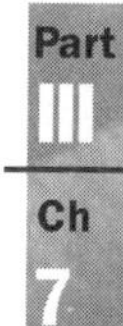

Scrollbars

Practically every application that runs under Windows supports scrollbars. In most cases, you use a scrollbar to move to different portions of a document. However, you can use these controls alternatively for selecting a value from a range. Although scrollbars are not as common in applets, Java does include a class for adding scrollbars to your programs. To create a scrollbar, you first call the `Scrollbar` class's constructor, like this:

```
Scrollbar scrollbar = new Scrollbar(orientation,
    start, page, min, max);
```

The constructor's five arguments are the scrollbar's orientation (can be `Scrollbar.HORIZONTAL` or `Scrollbar.VERTICAL`), the starting setting for the scrollbar, the scrollbar's page size (the amount the display scrolls when the user clicks above or below the scroll box), and the minimum and maximum values represented by the scrollbar.

After creating the scrollbar object, you add it to the applet by calling the `add()` method, like this:

```
add(scrollbar);
```

Suppose you need to create a scrollbar that enables the user to select a value from 1 to 100. You can create such a scrollbar like this:

```
Scrollbar scrollbar =
    new Scrollbar(Scrollbar.HORIZONTAL, 50, 0, 1, 100);
add(scrollbar);
```

The constructor's first argument tells Java that the scrollbar should be drawn horizontally on the display. The second argument tells Java that you want the scrollbar to start off set to the value of 50. The third argument is the page size, which represents the area in the slider covered by the scroll box. Finally, the fourth and fifth arguments give the scrollbar a minimum value of 1 and a maximum value of 100.

These settings enable the user to select a value from 1 to 100. So, why is the scrollbar's page size set to zero? Doing this forces the scroll box in the scrollbar to center on the selected value. It also enables the user to select the maximum value of 100. To understand why this is necessary, imagine that the scrollbar's scroll box represents the page of data that's currently displayed (such as in a word processor document). The scroll box then starts on the selected value and ends on the selected value plus the page size. Figure 7.20 illustrates this concept. The scrollbar in the figure was created like this:

```
Scrollbar scrollbar =
    new Scrollbar(Scrollbar.HORIZONTAL, 50, 10, 1, 100);
```

Because the scrollbar's starting value is 50, and the scrollbar's page size is 10, the scroll box covers the area of the slider from 50 to 60. If the user were to drag the scroll box to its maximum value, the scroll box would cover the area in the slider from 90 to 100, as shown in figure 7.21. In this case, the page size of 10 makes it impossible for the user to actually select the value of 100. This is because, if the user could select the value 100, the scroll box would have to cover the slider area from 100 to 110. But, the scrollbar's maximum value is 100.

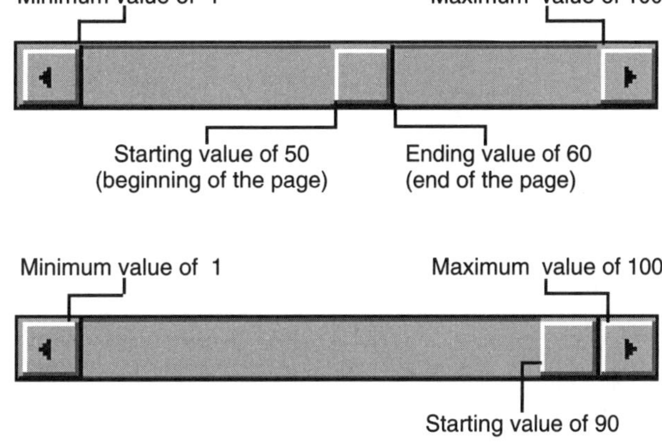

FIG. 7.20 The scroll box covers an area from the selected value to the selected value plus the page size.

FIG. 7.21 The maximum setting starts at 90 and goes to 90 plus the page size, which equals the maximum value of 100.

When using a scrollbar to select specific values rather than areas of a document, you can either set the page size to zero or set the maximum to the maximum you want plus the page size. Both of the scrollbars shown in listing 7.12 operate the same way.

Listing 7.12 Two Scrollbars That Work the Same

```
Scrollbar scrollbar =
    new Scrollbar(Scrollbar.HORIZONTAL, 50, 10, 1, 110);
Scrollbar scrollbar =
    new Scrollbar(Scrollbar.HORIZONTAL, 50, 0, 1, 100);
```

Figure 7.22 shows the scrollbar produced by either of the above examples. Notice that the scroll box is now centered on 50. When the scroll box is at its maximum position now, it indicates a value of 100.

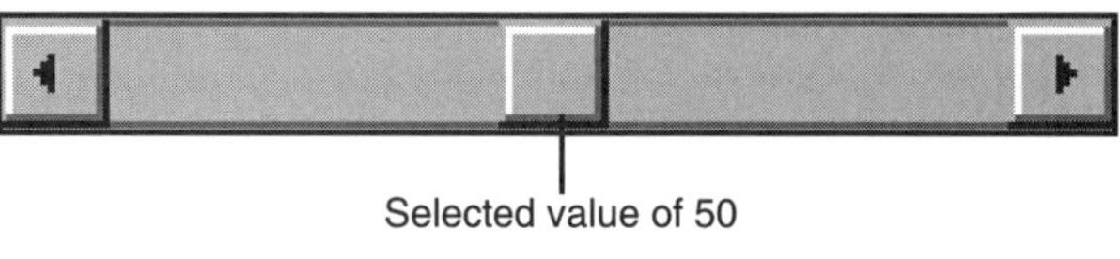

FIG. 7.22 This scrollbar enables the user to select any value within its minimum and maximum range.

Responding to a Scrollbar

Because of the many different types of events a scrollbar generates, you need to capture its events in the class's `handleEvent()` method, rather than in `action()`, as you did with other controls. Like `action()`, `handleEvent()` is a method that's defined in one of your applet's superclasses (in this case, `Component`). The `handleEvent()` method handles all the specific event messages that are generated by the typical windowing system. Table 7.7 lists some of the events to which the `handleEvent()` method can respond.

Table 7.7 Most Common Events That Can Be Handled by handleEvent()

Event	Description
ACTION_EVENT	An event that can be handled by `action()`.
GOT_FOCUS	The component received the focus.
KEY_PRESS	A key on the keyboard was pressed.
KEY_RELEASE	A key on the keyboard was released.
LIST_DESELECT	An item in a list was deselected.
LIST_SELECT	An item in a list was selected.
LOST_FOCUS	The component lost the focus.
MOUSE_DOWN	The user pressed a mouse button.
MOUSE_DRAG	The user dragged the mouse pointer.
MOUSE_ENTER	The mouse pointer entered an area.
MOUSE_EXIT	The mouse pointer left an area.
MOUSE_MOVE	The user moved the mouse.
MOUSE_UP	The user released a mouse button.

Event	Description
SCROLL_ABSOLUTE	The user moved a scrollbar's scroll box.
SCROLL_LINE_DOWN	The user clicked a scrollbar's down arrow.
SCROLL_LINE_UP	The user clicked a scrollbar's up arrow.
SCROLL_PAGE_DOWN	The user clicked in a scrollbar below the scroll box.
SCROLL_PAGE_UP	The user clicked in a scrollbar above the scroll box.
WINDOW_DEICONIFY	The window has been restored from an icon state.
WINDOW_DESTROY	The window has been destroyed.
WINDOW_EXPOSE	The window has been activated.
WINDOW_ICONIFY	The window has been reduced to an icon.
WINDOW_MOVED	The window has been moved.

As you can see from the list in table 7.7, there are five event messages associated with a scrollbar. These messages are `SCROLL_ABSOLUTE`, `SCROLL_LINE_DOWN`, `SCROLL_LINE_UP`, `SCROLL_PAGE_DOWN`, and `SCROLL_PAGE_UP`. You can respond to these event messages when you want to customize how the scrollbar functions. (You learn how to handle event messages in Chapter 10, "Events and Configurable Applets.") However, you don't need to get into such details when you just need to know where the user set the scrollbar. Instead, you can override `handleEvent()` and check for the scrollbar object in that method. If the user generates an event with the scrollbar, you can then call the scrollbar's methods to determine what change was made. Table 7.8 lists the most useful methods of the `Scrollbar` class:

Table 7.8 Most Useful Methods of the *Scrollbar* Class

Method	Description
getLineIncrement()	Returns the line increment.
getMaximum()	Returns the maximum value.
getMinimum()	Returns the minimum value.

continues

Table 7.8 Continued

Method	Description
getOrientation()	Returns the orientation.
getPageIncrement()	Returns the page increment.
getValue()	Returns the currently set value.
getVisible()	Returns the page size.
setLineIncrement()	Sets the line increment.
setPageIncrement()	Sets the page increment.
setValue()	Sets the selected value.
setValues()	Sets all the slider's values.

The ScrollbarApplet Applet

Now that you know how to use a scrollbar, you can put together an applet that demonstrates the concepts involved. Listing 7.13 is just such an applet. Called ScrollbarApplet, this applet enables you to manipulate a scrollbar with your mouse and see the results on the screen. Figure 7.23 shows the applet when it first starts up.

Listing 7.13 An Applet That Uses a Scrollbar

```
import java.awt.*;
import java.applet.*;

public class ScrollbarApplet extends Applet
{
    Scrollbar scrollbar;
    String s;

    public void init()
    {
        BorderLayout layout = new BorderLayout();
        setLayout(layout);

        scrollbar = new Scrollbar(Scrollbar.HORIZONTAL,
            50, 0, 1, 100);
        add("South", scrollbar);
```

```
            s = "50";
            Font font = new Font("TimesRoman", Font.BOLD, 72);
            setFont(font);
            resize(200, 200);
        }

        public void paint(Graphics g)
        {
            g.drawString(s, 60, 120);
        }

        public boolean handleEvent(Event evt)
        {
            if (evt.target instanceof Scrollbar)
            {
                scrollbar = (Scrollbar)evt.target;
                int value = scrollbar.getValue();
                s = String.valueOf(value);
                repaint();
                return true;
            }
            else
            {
                boolean result = super.handleEvent(evt);
                return result;
            }
        }
    }
```

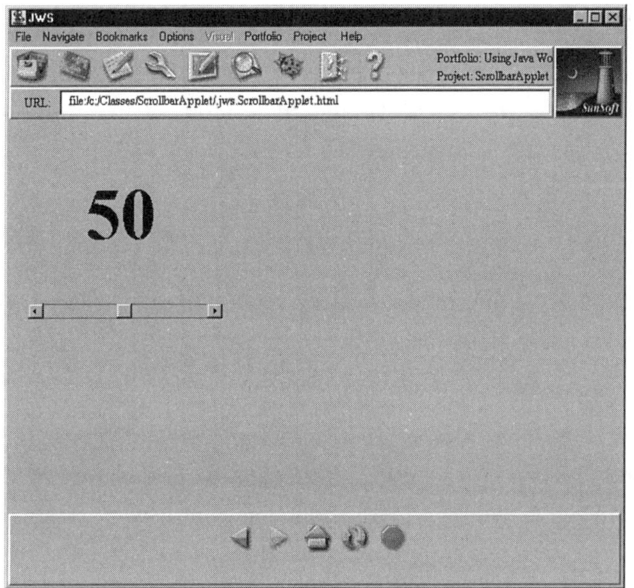

FIG. 7.23
This is ScrollbarApplet running under Java Workshop.

There are two things that you should be sure to notice in ScrollbarApplet. First, notice that the scrollbar isn't just added to the applet. It is, instead, added to the applet after the applet's layout manager has been set. This is because the size of the control bar is dependent upon the active layout manager and how the control is added to the manager. (For more information on layout managers, see Chapter 8, "Panels and the Layout Manager.") By creating a `BorderLayout` manager and adding the horizontal scrollbar to the "South" position, you get a scrollbar that stretches across the bottom of the applet. Failure to place the scrollbar properly in an appropriate layout manager results in a useless scrollbar like the one shown in figure 7.24, running in Appletviewer.

FIG. 7.24 The scrollbar in this applet was not placed properly in an appropriate layout manager.

Canvases

Canvases are nothing more than areas on which you can draw. You can combine canvases with other types of components, such as buttons, in order to build layouts that are attractive, as well as functional. The first step in creating a canvas is to call the `Canvas` class's constructor, like this:

```
Canvas canvas = new Canvas();
```

The `Canvas` constructor requires no arguments.

Once you have the canvas created, you add it to your layout just as you would any other component, by calling the `add()` method:

```
add(canvas);
```

To end this chapter, take a look at listing 7.14, which is an applet that creates a canvas class and uses the class to display a colored area on the screen. When you run the applet with Java Workshop, you see the window shown in figure 7.25. The applet displays two components: a button at the top of the applet, and a canvas below the button. When you click the button, the canvas changes color.

NOTE Often, you want to derive your own custom canvas class from Java's Canvas class. Then, you can more easily control what's drawn in the canvas, by overriding the canvas's `paint()` method. This is the approach that's used in the CanvasApplet applet.

Listing 7.14 An Applet That Displays a Custom Canvas

```
import java.awt.*;
import java.applet.*;

public class CanvasApplet extends Applet
{
    CustomCanvas canvas;

    public void init()
    {
        setLayout(new BorderLayout());

        Button button = new Button("Color");
        add("North", button);

        canvas = new CustomCanvas();
        add("South", canvas);

        resize(200, 250);
    }

    public boolean action(Event evt, Object arg)
    {
        if (arg == "Color")
            canvas.swapColor();

        return true;
    }
}

class CustomCanvas extends Canvas
{
    Color color;

    public CustomCanvas()
    {
        color = Color.black;
    }

    public void paint(Graphics g)
    {
        Rectangle r = bounds();
```

continues

Listing 7.14 Continued

```
        g.setColor(color);
        g.fillRect(0, 0, r.width, r.height);
        g.setColor(Color.white);
        g.drawString("CANVAS", 72, 90);
    }

    public void swapColor()
    {
        if (color == Color.black)
            color = Color.red;
        else if (color == Color.red)
            color = Color.green;
        else
            color = Color.black;

        repaint();
    }
}
```

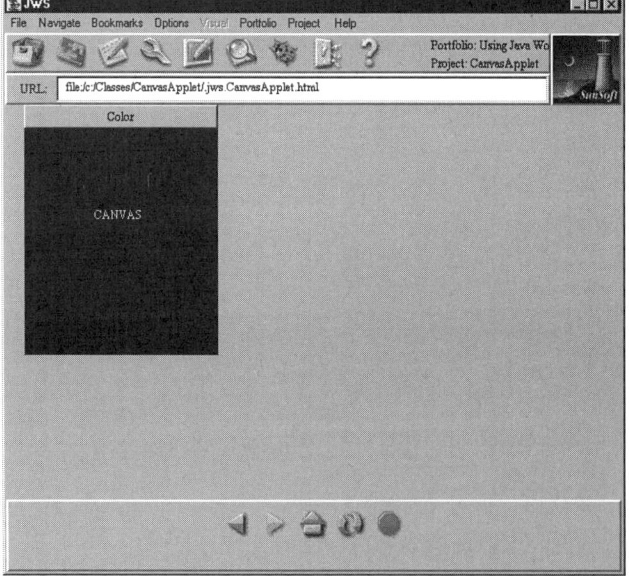

FIG. 7.25
This is CanvasApplet running in Java Workshop.

From Here...

Because a program running in a windowed environment cannot take exclusive control of a computer's resources, applets require special controls to send and retrieve information to and from the user. Such controls include labels, buttons, checkboxes, textfields, menus, scrolling lists, canvases, and scrollbars. Your applet can respond to most controls in its `action()` method.

Check out the following chapters for related information:

- Chapter 5, "Object-Oriented Programming and Java," tells you more about classes and how they're used in Java.
- Chapter 6, "Applets and Graphics," provides a primer on Java's `Graphics` class.
- Chapter 8, "Panels and the Layout Manager," shows how to organize the elements of your applet's display.
- Chapter 9, "Windows, Menu Bars, and Dialog Boxes," suggests alternative ways to retrieve commands and input from your applet's user.
- Chapter 10, "Events and Configurable Applets," provides more information on how to handle events in your applets.

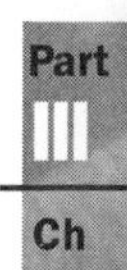

CHAPTER 8

Panels and the Layout Manager

Up until the previous chapter, when you've added controls to your applets, you've let Java place those controls wherever it felt like it. The only way you could control positioning was by changing the size of the applet. Obviously, if you're going to produce attractive applets that are organized logically, you need some way to tell Java exactly where you want things placed. Java's layout managers were created for exactly this purpose. Working in conjunction with layout managers are components called panels, which enable you to organize other applet components. ■

- **How to use panels to organize controls.**

  You can use objects of the Panel class to hold multiple controls, making those controls easier to organize as a group.

- **Java's five layout managers.**

  Java's layout managers enable you to create interesting displays by positioning elements in various ways.

- **How to create layouts that work similarly to Windows 95's tabbed dialog boxes (also called property sheets).**

  The CardLayout manager is the key to creating groups of controls that can change with a click of a button.

- **How to create displays with complex control layouts.**

  The GridBagLayout manager is the most complex and versatile of Java's layout managers.

Panels

A *panel* is a special type of container object that acts as a parent to other components that you want to organize in your applet. For example, you can add several panels to an applet, each with their own layout. By using panels in this way, you can create many different creative displays. Creating a panel is as easy as calling the `Panel` class's constructor, like this:

```
Panel panel = new Panel();
```

As you can see, the `Panel` class's constructor requires no arguments.

Once you create a panel, you add it to the applet in the normal way, by calling the `add()` method:

```
add(panel);
```

Using panels can be a little confusing at first, so an example is in order. Suppose you need to create an applet that displays four buttons, but you don't want Java to place the buttons one after the other in the display, which Java will do with its default layout. Instead, you want the buttons displayed in two rows of two. One way to accomplish this is to add two panels to the applet and then add two buttons to each panel. Although the size of the applet affects the positions of the panels, the buttons automatically go where the panels go, making positioning a little easier. Listing 8.1 shows how to use panels to hold button objects, whereas figure 8.1 shows what the applet's display looks like under Java Workshop.

Listing 8.1 An Applet That Uses Panels

```
import java.awt.*;
import java.applet.*;

public class PanelApplet extends Applet
{
    Panel panel1, panel2;
    Button button1, button2, button3, button4;

    public void init()
    {
        panel1 = new Panel();
        panel2 = new Panel();

        add(panel1);
        add(panel2);
```

```
        button1 = new Button("Button1");
        button2 = new Button("Button2");
        button3 = new Button("Button3");
        button4 = new Button("Button4");

        panel1.add(button1);
        panel1.add(button2);
        panel2.add(button3);
        panel2.add(button4);

        resize(200, 200);
    }
}
```

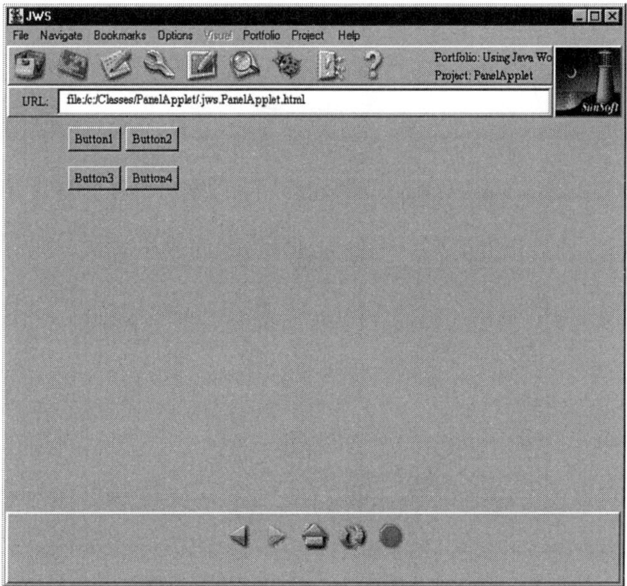

FIG. 8.1
Using panels, you can more easily organize components in an applet.

Notice how, when adding the panels to the applet, the program calls the `PanelApplet` class's `add()` method (which adds the panels to the applet's display). However, when adding the buttons, the program calls the panel objects' `add()` method (which adds the buttons to the panels). This is how you build a hierarchy of components into your applets. In this case, you have a stack three components high, with the applet's display on the bottom, the two panels on top of that, and the four buttons on top of the panels. As you create more sophisticated applets, this type of component stacking will be more common.

Panels are a kind of generic container for organizing components in an applet. As you'll discover in the next section, you can combine panels with layout managers to create truly complex displays.

Layout Managers

Layout Managers are special objects that determine how elements of your applet are organized in the applet's display. When you create an applet, Java automatically creates and assigns a default layout manager. In many of the applets you've created so far in this book, the default layout manager determined where your controls appeared. You can, however, create different types of layout managers to better control how your applets look. The layout managers you can use are:

- FlowLayout
- GridLayout
- BorderLayout
- CardLayout
- GridBagLayout

Each of these layout managers is represented by a class of the same name. To create a layout manager for your applet, you first create an instance of the appropriate layout class and then call the `setLayout()` method to tell Java which layout object you want to use. In the following sections, you get a chance to see the various layout managers in action.

The FlowLayout Manager

As mentioned in the previous section, when you create an applet, Java assigns a default layout manager to it. It just so happens that this default manager is an object of the `FlowLayout` class. The FlowLayout manager places controls, in the order in which they're added, one after the other in horizontal rows. When the layout manager reaches the right border of the applet, it begins placing controls on the next row. In its default state, the FlowLayout manager centers controls on each row. However, you can set the alignment when you create the layout manager for your applet, like this:

```
FlowLayout layout = new FlowLayout(align, hor, ver);
SetLayout(layout);
```

The `FlowLayout` constructor takes three arguments, which are the alignment (`FlowLayout.LEFT`, `FlowLayout.CENTER`, or `FlowLayout.RIGHT`), the horizontal spacing between components, and the vertical spacing.

Suppose that you want to arrange three buttons in an applet using a FlowLayout manager set to left alignment. Listing 8.2 shows how you'd create the manager and the buttons for the applet. Figure 8.2 shows the resultant control layout when an applet using the layout is run under Appletviewer. Figures 8.3 and 8.4 show the center and right alignments for the same controls.

Listing 8.2 Creating a FlowLayout Manager

```
FlowLayout layout =
    new FlowLayout(FlowLayout.LEFT, 10, 10);
setLayout(layout);
button1 = new Button("Button1");
button2 = new Button("Button2");
button3 = new Button("Button3");
add(button1);
add(button2);
add(button3);
```

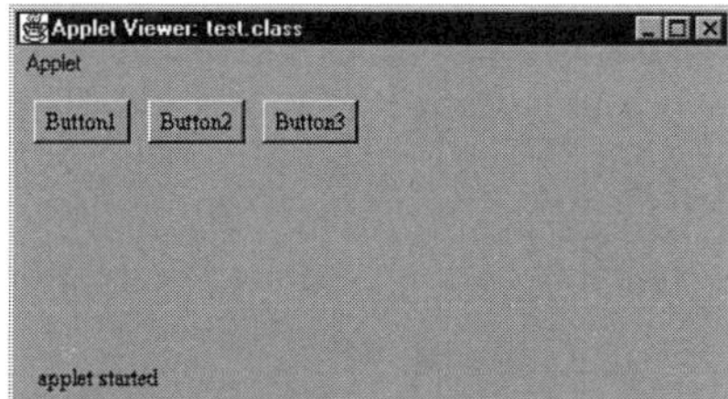

FIG. 8.2 These buttons are left-aligned by the FlowLayout manager.

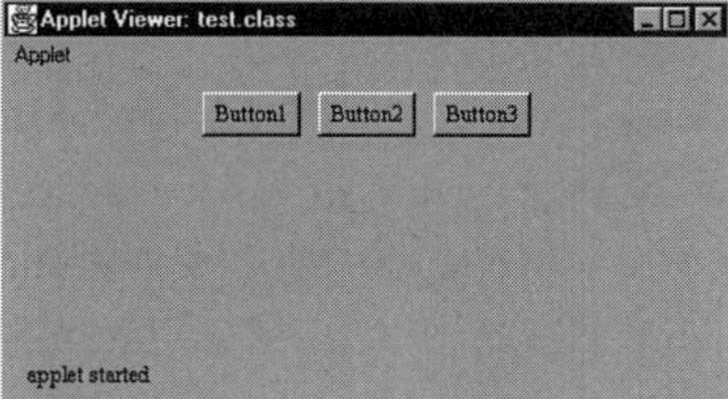

FIG. 8.3 These buttons are center-aligned by the FlowLayout manager.

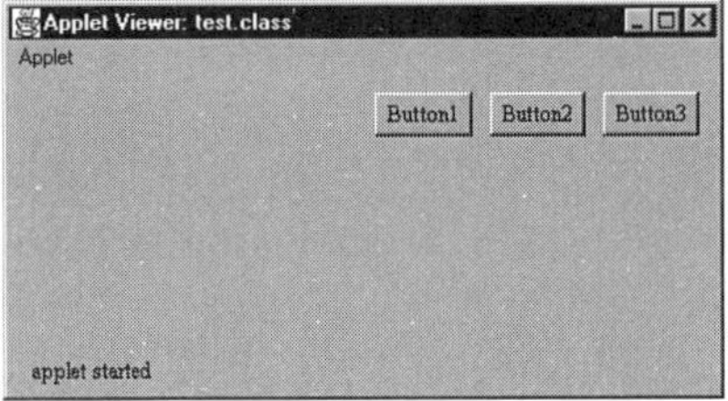

FIG. 8.4
These buttons are right-aligned by the FlowLayout manager.

NOTE The `FlowLayout()` constructor shown in this chapter takes four arguments. However, you can actually construct a FlowLayout object with no arguments, `FlowLayout()`, or with a single argument for the alignment, `FlowLayout (FlowLayout.LEFT)`. Many of Java's classes have multiple constructors.

The GridLayout Manager

Once you start creating more sophisticated applets, you'll quickly discover that the FlowLayout manager may not give you the control you need to create the kind of display you want for your applet. When you need more control over the placement of components, you can try the GridLayout manager.

Java's GridLayout manager organizes your applet's display into a rectangular grid, similar to the grid used in a spreadsheet. Java then places the components you create for the applet into each cell of the grid, working from left to right and top to bottom. You create a GridLayout manager like this:

```
GridLayout layout = new GridLayout(rows, cols, hor, ver);
SetLayout(layout);
```

The constructor's four arguments are the number of rows in the grid, the number of columns, and the horizontal and vertical space between the grid cells.

To test the GridLayout manager, suppose you want to place four buttons into a 2×2 grid, with no space between the buttons. Listing 8.3 shows how you'd create the manager and the buttons for the applet. Figure 8.5 shows the resultant control layout under Appletviewer. Figure 8.6 shows the same layout manager, except it's created with a horizontal and vertical spacing of 10. Figure 8.7 shows the layout with a single row of four cells.

Listing 8.3 Creating a GridLayout Manager

```
GridLayout layout =
    new GridLayout(2, 2, 0, 0);
setLayout(layout);
button1 = new Button("Button1");
button2 = new Button("Button2");
button3 = new Button("Button3");
button4 = new Button("Button4");
add(button1);
add(button2);
add(button3);
add(button4);
```

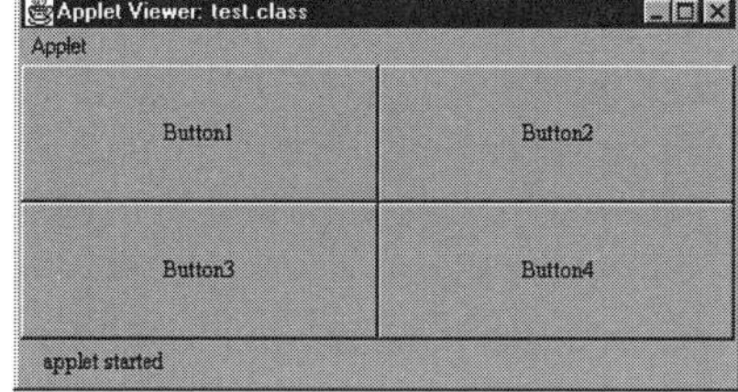

FIG. 8.5 This GridLayout manager is set to two rows and two columns.

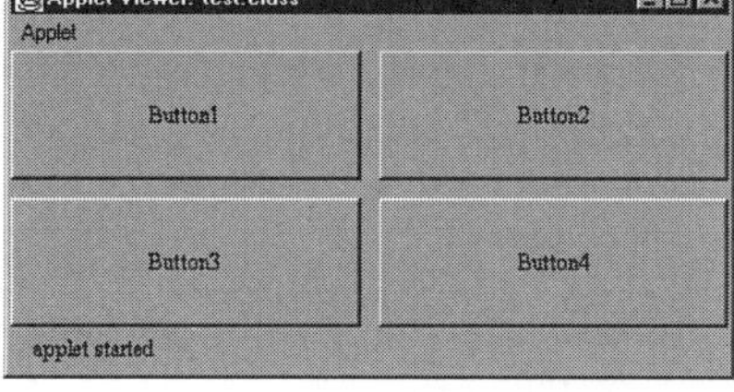

FIG. 8.6 This is the same GridLayout manager with horizontal and vertical spacing.

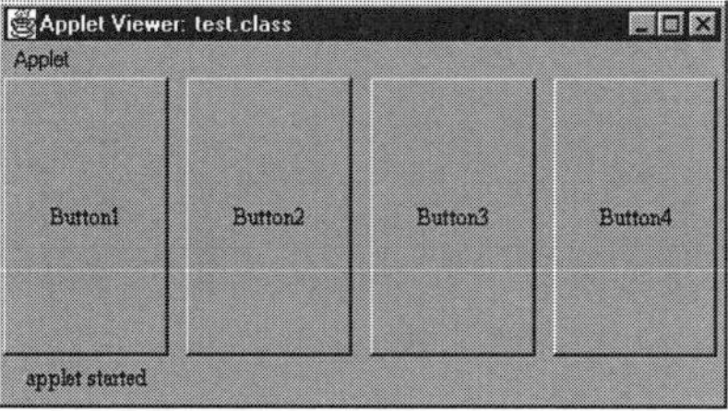

FIG. 8.7 This GridLayout manager has one row and four columns.

The BorderLayout Manager

You'll probably use the GridLayout manager most of the time, but there may be cases where you need to put together something a little more unusual. One layout you can try is provided by the BorderLayout manager, which enables you to position components using the directions `North`, `South`, `East`, `West`, and `Center`. You create a BorderLayout manager object like this:

```
BorderLayout layout = new BorderLayout(hor, ver);
setLayout(layout);
```

This constructor's two arguments are the horizontal and vertical spacing between the cells in the layout.

After you create the BorderLayout object, you must add the components using a different version of the `add()` method:

```
add(position, object);
```

Here, `position` is where to place the component and must be the string `North`, `South`, `East`, `West`, or `Center`. The second argument, `object`, is the component you want to add to the applet.

Suppose you have five buttons that you want to place in the five areas supported by a BorderLayout manager. First, you create and set the manager. Then, you create the five buttons and add them to the applet, using the special version of `add()` that includes the object's position as the first argument. Listing 8.4 shows how this is done. Figure 8.8 shows the resultant display. Figure 8.9 shows the same applet with the BorderLayout manager with horizontal and vertical spacing.

Listing 8.4 Creating a BorderLayout Manager

```
BorderLayout layout = new BorderLayout(0, 0);
setLayout(layout);
button1 = new Button("Button1");
button2 = new Button("Button2");
button3 = new Button("Button3");
button4 = new Button("Button4");
button5 = new Button("Button5");
add("North", button1);
add("South", button2);
add("East", button3);
add("West", button4);
add("Center", button5);
```

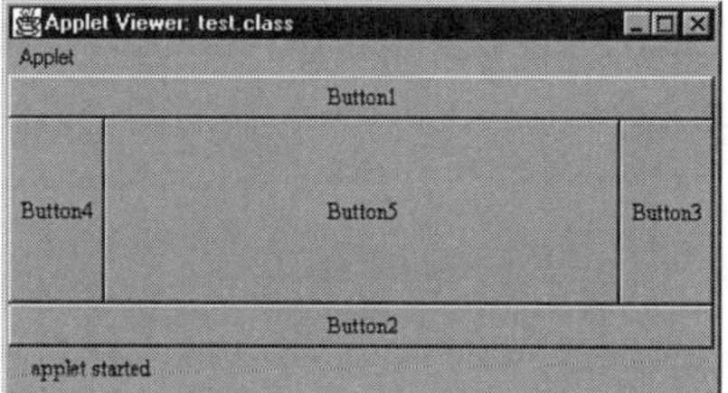

FIG. 8.8
This applet displays five buttons using a BorderLayout manager.

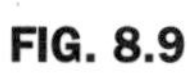

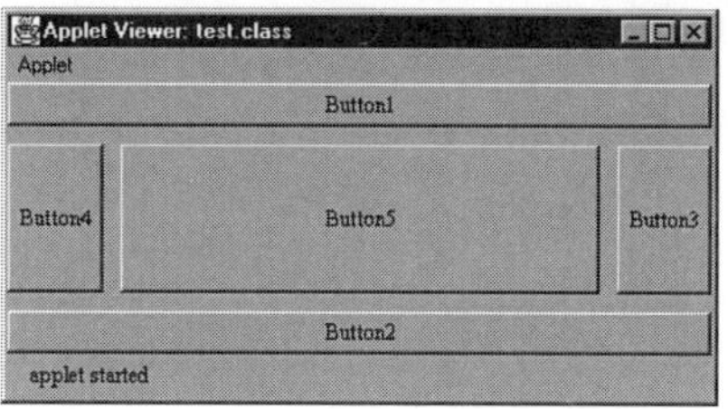

FIG. 8.9
This is the same applet with horizontal and vertical spacing.

The CardLayout Manager

One of the most complex layout managers is CardLayout. Using this manager, you can create a stack of layouts not unlike a stack of cards and then flip from one layout to another. This type of display organization is not unlike Windows 95's tabbed dialog boxes, usually called property sheets. To create a layout with the CardLayout manager, first create a parent panel to hold the "cards." Then, create the CardLayout object and set it as the panel's layout manager. Finally, add each "card" to the layout by creating the components and adding them to the panel.

To create a CardLayout manager, call its constructor and then add it to the applet, like this:

```
CardLayout cardLayout = new CardLayout(hor, ver);
panel.setLayout(cardLayout);
```

The constructor's two arguments are the horizontal and vertical spacing.

The CardLayout Manager Methods

Because the CardLayout manager enables you to switch between a stack of layouts, you need some way to tell the manager what to do. For this reason, the CardLayout manager has a number of public methods that you can call to specify which card is visible on the screen. Table 8.1 lists the most useful of these methods along with their descriptions.

Table 8.1 CardLayout Manager Methods

Method	Description
first()	Displays the first card.
last()	Displays the last card.
next()	Displays the next card.
previous()	Displays the previous card.
show()	Displays the specified card.

Creating a CardLayout Manager

Putting the CardLayout manager to work is a lot easier if you always keep in mind the hierarchy of components. At the bottom of the stack is the applet's display area. On top of this stack is the component (usually a panel) that will hold the "cards." On top of the parent component is the CardLayout manager, which you can think of as a deck of cards. The cards in this deck are the components that you add to the panel.

Listing 8.5 is an applet that demonstrates how all this works. The cards in this applet are the three buttons. When you run the applet, you see a single button in the display (see fig. 8.10). Click the button to switch to the next button in the stack. When you get to `button3` and click it, you end up back at `button1`. You can cycle through the buttons as often as you like.

Listing 8.5 An Applet That Uses a CardLayout Manager

```
import java.awt.*;
import java.applet.*;

public class CardApplet extends Applet
{
    CardLayout cardLayout;
    Panel panel;
    Button button1, button2, button3;
```

```
    public void init()
    {
        panel = new Panel();
        add(panel);

        cardLayout = new CardLayout(0, 0);
        panel.setLayout(cardLayout);

        button1 = new Button("Button1");
        button2 = new Button("Button2");
        button3 = new Button("Button3");

        panel.add("Button1", button1);
        panel.add("Button2", button2);
        panel.add("Button3", button3);
    }

    public boolean action(Event evt, Object arg)
    {
        cardLayout.next(panel);
        return true;
    }
}
```

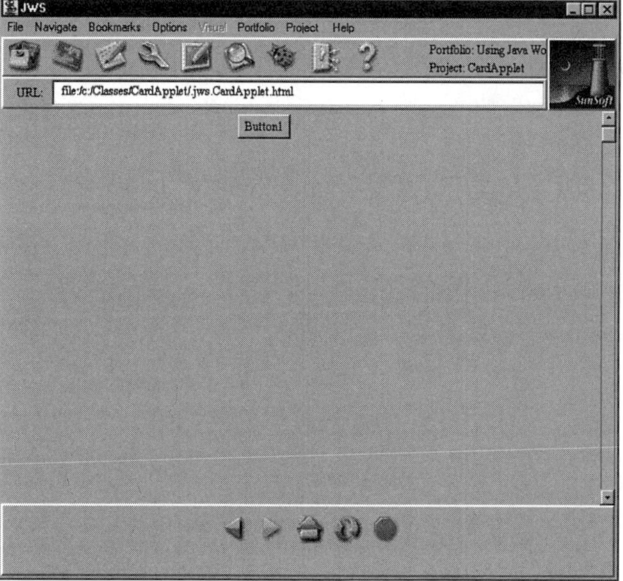

FIG. 8.10
Clicking the button switches the manager to the new card.

NOTE The stack of cards that are arranged by a CardLayout manager can be any type of component. For example, you can create several different panels, each with their own controls, and switch between the panels. This enables you to switch between whole sets of controls, just like Windows 95's property sheets.

The GridBagLayout Manager

The most complex of the layout managers is GridBagLayout, which pretty much lets you organize objects any way you like. However, the price for this power is meticulous planning and a lot of experimentation. At the time of this writing, the documentation for the GridBagLayout manager was sketchy and incomplete. I did the best I could to figure out exactly how this layout manager worked, but there's no question that to get the best out of GridBagLayout, you're going to have to spend some time experimenting with different layouts.

To create a layout using GridBagLayout, follow these steps:

1. Create a GridBagLayout object.
2. Set the layout manager.
3. Create a GridBagConstraints object.
4. Initialize and set the constraints for the object about to be added to the layout.
5. Add the object to the layout.
6. Repeat steps 4 and 5 for each object you're adding to the layout.

In the sections that follow, you'll learn how to perform each of the required steps to use a GridBagLayout manager.

Creating and Setting the GridBagLayout Manager

To create a GridBagLayout manager, call the class's constructor, like this:

```
GridBagLayout layout = new GridBagLayout();
```

The constructor requires no arguments. When you've created the `GridBagLayout` object, set the manager by calling `setLayout()`:

```
setLayout(layout);
```

This method's single argument is a reference to the layout object.

Creating and Setting a GridBagConstraints Object

Because the position of each component in a layout controlled by a `GridBagLayout` object is determined by the currently set `GridBagConstraints` object, you must create the `GridBagConstraints` object before you can start building your layout. To do this, call the class's constructor:

```
GridBagConstraints constraints = new GridBagConstraints();
```

Like the `GridBagLayout` class, the `GridBagConstraints` constructor requires no arguments. However, although the class's fields start off initialized to default values, you'll almost always change some of those values before adding components to the layout. You perform this task with a line like this:

```
constraints.fill = GridBagConstraints.BOTH;
```

This line sets the `GridBagConstraints` object's `fill` field to a constant defined in the class. Table 8.2 shows the fields of the `GridBagConstraints` class and what they mean.

Table 8.2 Fields of the GridBagConstraints Class

Field	Description
`anchor`	Where within a component's area the component should be placed. Predefined values are `GridBagConstraints.NORTH`, `GridBagConstraints.NORTHEAST`, `GridBagConstraints.EAST`, `GridBagConstraints.SOUTHEAST`, `GridBagConstraints.SOUTH`, `GridBagConstraints.SOUTHWEST`, `GridBagConstraints.WEST`, `GridBagConstraints.NORTHWEST`, and `GridBagConstraints.CENTER`.
`fill`	Determines how to size a component when the display area is larger than the component. Predefined values you can use are `GridBagConstraint.NONE`, `GridBagConstraint.HORIZONTAL`, `GridBagConstraint.VERTICAL`, and `GridBagConstraint.BOTH`.
`gridheight`	The number of cells in each column of a component's display area.
`gridwidth`	The number of cells in each row of a component's display area.
`gridx`	The X coordinate of the cell at the upper left of a component's display area.

continues

Table 8.2 Continued

Field	Description
`gridy`	The Y coordinate of the cell at the upper left of the component's display area.
`insets`	The minimum amount of space between a component and the edges of its display area.
`ipadx`	The amount of horizontal space around a component.
`ipady`	The amount of vertical space around a component.
`weightx`	Determines whether components stretch horizontally to fill the applet's display area.
`weighty`	Determines whether components stretch vertically to fill the applet's display area.

Once you have created and initialized the `GridBagConstraints` object, you must set the constraints by calling the layout object's `setConstraints()` method:

```
layout.setConstraints(component, constraints);
```

This method's two arguments are a reference to the component whose constraints you're setting and a reference to the constraints object. You need to call `setConstraints()` for each component you add to the layout. After setting the constraints for the component, you add the component to the layout in the normal way, by calling the `add()` method.

Using a GridBagLayout Manager in an Applet

As mentioned earlier, the only way to really understand how the GridBagLayout manager works is to experiment with it on your own. This book just doesn't have the room to cover every detail of using this complex manager. Still, I won't send you off without at least the basics. So, listing 8.6 is an applet, called GridBagApplet, that demonstrates how to create and use a GridBagLayout manager. Figure 8.11 shows what the applet looks like when it's run under Java Workshop.

Listing 8.6 A GridBagLayout Applet

```
import java.awt.*;
import java.applet.*;
public class GridBagApplet extends Applet
{
    public void init()
    {
        GridBagLayout layout = new GridBagLayout();
        setLayout(layout);

        GridBagConstraints constraints = new GridBagConstraints();

        Button button1 = new Button("Button1");
        Button button2 = new Button("Button2");
        Button button3 = new Button("Button3");
        Button button4 = new Button("Button4");
        Button button5 = new Button("Button5");
        Button button6 = new Button("Button6");
        Button button7 = new Button("Button7");
        Button button8 = new Button("Button8");
        Button button9 = new Button("Button9");

        constraints.fill = GridBagConstraints.BOTH;

        layout.setConstraints(button1, constraints);
        add(button1);

        constraints.gridwidth = GridBagConstraints.RELATIVE;
        layout.setConstraints(button2, constraints);
        add(button2);

        constraints.gridwidth = GridBagConstraints.REMAINDER;
        layout.setConstraints(button3, constraints);
        add(button3);

        constraints.gridwidth = GridBagConstraints.REMAINDER;
        layout.setConstraints(button4, constraints);
        add(button4);

        constraints.gridwidth = GridBagConstraints.RELATIVE;
        layout.setConstraints(button5, constraints);
        add(button5);

        constraints.gridwidth = GridBagConstraints.REMAINDER;
        layout.setConstraints(button6, constraints);
        add(button6);
```

continues

Listing 8.6 Continued

```
        constraints.gridwidth = 1;
        constraints.gridheight = 2;
        layout.setConstraints(button7, constraints);
        add(button7);

        constraints.gridwidth = GridBagConstraints.REMAINDER;
        constraints.gridheight = 1;
        layout.setConstraints(button8, constraints);
        add(button8);

        layout.setConstraints(button9, constraints);
        add(button9);

        resize(300, 200);
    }
}
```

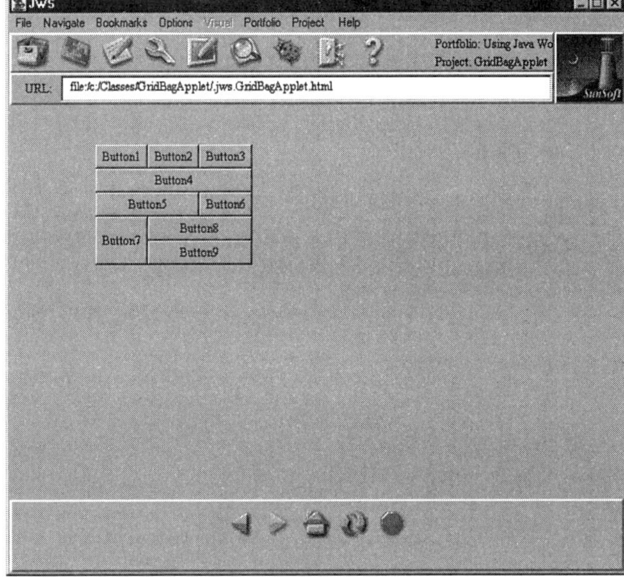

FIG. 8.11
The GridBagManager enables you to create unusual layouts.

Understanding the GridBagApplet Applet

Although GridBagApplet contains only the `init()` method, there's a lot going on in the program. In this section, you'll see, line by line, exactly how the applet works. The first two lines in the `init()` method look like this:

```
GridBagLayout layout = new GridBagLayout();
setLayout(layout);
```

This is where the applet creates its GridBagLayout object and sets it as the applet's layout. In the next line, the applet creates its GridBagConstraints object, like this:

```
GridBagConstraints constraints = new GridBagConstraints();
```

The applet will use this single `GridBagConstraints` object to set the constraints for each component added to the layout. Before components can be added, however, they must be created, which the applet does, as shown in listing 8.7.

Listing 8.7 Creating the Applet's Buttons

```
Button button1 = new Button("Button1");
Button button2 = new Button("Button2");
Button button3 = new Button("Button3");
Button button4 = new Button("Button4");
Button button5 = new Button("Button5");
Button button6 = new Button("Button6");
Button button7 = new Button("Button7");
Button button8 = new Button("Button8");
Button button9 = new Button("Button9");
```

After creating the buttons, the program can start adding them to the layout. But before the first button gets added, the constraints object must contain the appropriate values. In this case, only the `fill` field must be initialized since the first button component will use all the other default values:

```
constraints.fill = GridBagConstraints.BOTH;
```

Setting the `fill` field to `BOTH` ensures that the components (in this case, buttons) will expand both vertically and horizontally to completely fill their display areas. After initializing the constraints for the first button, the applet sets the constraints and adds the button:

```
layout.setConstraints(button1, constraints);
add(button1);
```

Now that you have the first button added, it's time to consider how the second button will fit in the layout. The value the applet initialized the `fill` field to will remain in effect for all buttons, so the applet doesn't need to change it again. However, the layout manager is going to want to know how `button2` should be placed. The following lines set the constraints and add the button:

```
constraints.gridwidth = GridBagConstraints.RELATIVE;
layout.setConstraints(button2, constraints);
add(button2);
```

By setting `gridwidth` to `GridBagConstraints.RELATIVE`, the applet tells the layout manager that this button is the next to the last component in this row, which will determine its width. The `button3` object is the last component for the first row, so it sets `gridwidth` to `GridBagConstraints.REMAINDER`:

```
constraints.gridwidth = GridBagConstraints.REMAINDER;
layout.setConstraints(button3, constraints);
add(button3);
```

The `REMAINDER` constant tells the layout manager that this control should fill the first row all the way to the end.

The `button4` component is the only object on its row, so it too uses a `gridwidth` of `REMAINDER`:

```
constraints.gridwidth = GridBagConstraints.REMAINDER;
layout.setConstraints(button4, constraints);
add(button4);
```

The first line above really isn't necessary since `gridwidth` was already set to `REMAINDER`. However, I like keeping this line because it tells me that I haven't forgotten something and that I do indeed want a width of `REMAINDER` for this button, too.

Because `button5` is both the first and next-to-last button in its row, it uses a width of `RELATIVE`:

```
constraints.gridwidth = GridBagConstraints.RELATIVE;
layout.setConstraints(button5, constraints);
add(button5);
```

Because there are only two buttons in this row, the `button6` component gets a width of `REMAINDER`:

```
constraints.gridwidth = GridBagConstraints.REMAINDER;
layout.setConstraints(button6, constraints);
add(butto\n6);
```

Now, things get a little tricky (like they weren't tricky enough, right?). If you look at figure 8.11, you'll see that `button7` is one cell wide but two cells high. `Button8` and `button9`, on the other hand, are two cells wide but only one cell high. Even though `button7` is technically the next-to-last button in its row, you don't want to give it the `RELATIVE` width because then Java will make the button twice as wide. So, the applet sets the width of `button7` to 1 and the height to 2, as shown in listing 8.8.

Listing 8.8 Setting *button7*'s Size

```
constraints.gridwidth = 1;
constraints.gridheight = 2;
layout.setConstraints(button7, constraints);
add(button7);
```

Because `button8` is the last button in its row, it gets the `REMAINDER` width. However, the button also must be set back to a normal one-cell height, as shown in listing 8.9.

Listing 8.9 Adding *button8*

```
constraints.gridwidth = GridBagConstraints.REMAINDER;
constraints.gridheight = 1;
layout.setConstraints(button8, constraints);
add(button8);
```

Finally, `button9` can use exactly the same restraints, which means simply setting the constraints and adding the button, like this:

```
layout.setConstraints(button9, constraints);
add(button9);
```

All the lines described in this section work together to create the applet's layout. Every layout will work differently, requiring that you carefully plan ahead how you want the applet's components laid out. There's almost an infinite number of ways to use the constraints along with the GridBagLayout manager.

You may wonder how changes to this example layout will affect the appearance of the applet. Suppose, for example, you left the `fill` field set to its default value of `GridBagConstraints.NONE`. You would then end up with a layout like that shown in figure 8.12. Figure 8.13 shows the applet (running under Appletviewer) with a `fill` setting of `GridBagConstraints.VERTICAL`.

Another change you might make is to set `weightx` and `weighty`, which tells Java how to use the extra space that usually surrounds the controls in the layout. For example, in GridBagApplet, if you set `weightx` to 1, you get a display like figure 8.14 because you've told Java that you want the layout to fill the entire horizontal space in the applet. Setting `weighty` stretches the layout in the vertical direction, as shown in figure 8.15, which has both `weightx` and `weighty` set.

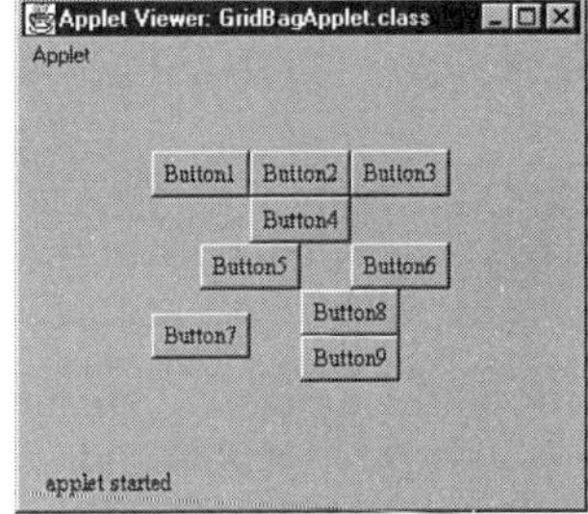

FIG. 8.12
The *fill* setting can make a huge difference in how a layout looks.

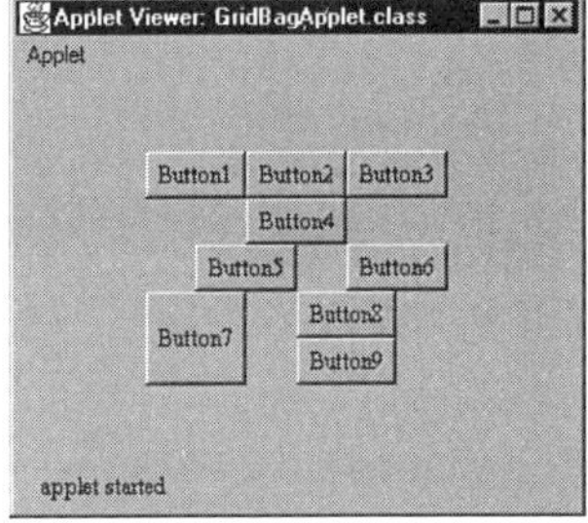

FIG. 8.13
The vertical *fill* stretches some controls vertically.

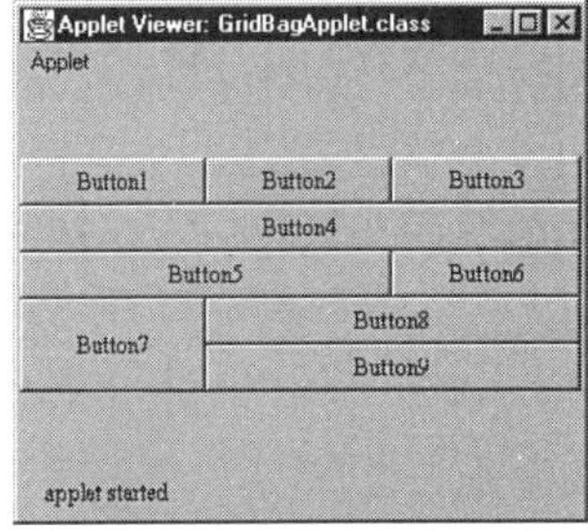

FIG. 8.14
Setting the *weightx* field stretches the layout horizontally.

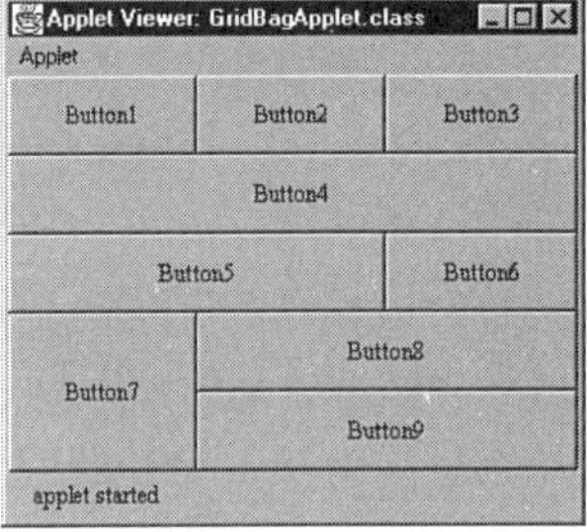

FIG. 8.15
Setting both *weightx* and *weighty* stretches the layout in both directions.

From Here...

Java gives you many options when it comes to creating a layout for the components that make up your applet. However, having so many possibilities at your fingertips can be daunting at first because there may be several ways to get the effect that you want. The more you learn to use Java's layout managers, the more easily you'll know which is the appropriate manager for a specific situation. Mastering the GridBagLayout manager especially requires time and patience.

For more information on related topics, please refer to the following chapters:

- Chapter 5, "Object-Oriented Programming and Java," tells you more about classes and how they're used in Java, as well as how to create, compile, and run applets using Java Workshop.
- Chapter 7, "Java Controls," shows how to create and program Java's many controls.
- Chapter 9, "Windows, Menu Bars, and Dialog Boxes," describes how to organize controls in special windows called dialog boxes.

CHAPTER 9

Windows, Menu Bars, and Dialog Boxes

How to create and display a window.

Applets can display additional windows. All you have to do is create and manage an object of Java's `Frame` class.

About adding components to a window.

Java's frame windows, just like an applet's display, can hold all kinds of controls.

How to create and manage menu bars.

Frame windows also can have menu bars that can contain menu items, checked menu items, and separator objects.

How to create and display dialog boxes.

Although they can only be used in conjunction with Java frame windows, you may find a use for dialog boxes, which enable you to prompt the user for information.

So far in this book, when you created and displayed an applet, you had a single window on the screen. This window was either Java Workshop, Appletviewer, or the browser you were using to display the applet. However, applets can create additional windows. Although you probably won't use this feature a lot, it's nice to know it's around in case you need it. Moreover, when you create a window in Java, you can add a full-featured menu bar that can contain commands, checked options, and separator objects. In this chapter, you learn to display windows and their menu bars as well as how to respond to menu commands. You even get a chance to create your own dialog boxes. ■

Displaying a Window

Java's libraries include a class called `Frame` that represents a frame window that you can create and display from within an application. To create a frame window, call the `Frame` class's constructor, like this:

```
Frame frame = new Frame("Frame Window");
```

This constructor's single argument is the window's title, which will appear in the window's title bar.

When you have the window created, you can display it by calling the window's `show()` method. To remove the window from the screen, call the `hide()` method. You can even size the window by calling `resize()` or position the window by calling `move()`.

Displaying a Window in an Applet

To demonstrate the basics of using the Frame class, listing 9.1 is the source code for an applet that can display a frame window. When you click the applet's button, the applet displays a frame window. When you click the button a second time, the applet removes the window from the screen. Figure 9.1 shows the applet and its frame window. Notice that when the button is clicked, the button's label switches between Show Window and Hide Window.

Listing 9.1 Displaying a Frame Window

```
import java.awt.*;
import java.applet.*;

public class FrameApplet extends Applet
{
    Frame frame;
    Button button;

    public void init()
    {
        frame = new Frame("Frame Window");
        button = new Button("Show Window");
        add(button);
    }

    public boolean action(Event evt, Object arg)
```

```
    {
            boolean visible = frame.isShowing();
            if (visible)
            {
                frame.hide();
                button.setLabel("Show Window");
            }
            else
            {
                frame.show();
                frame.resize(200, 100);
                button.setLabel("Hide Window");
            }

            return true;
        }
}
```


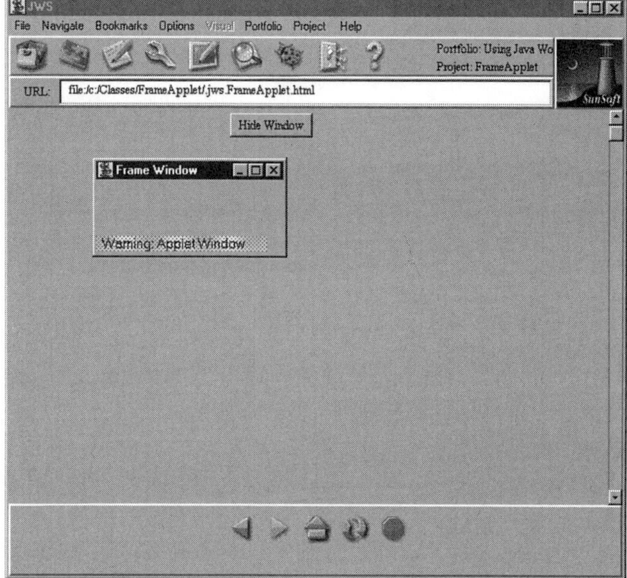

FIG. 9.1
Your Java applets can display additional windows.

Creating a Window Class

When you decide that your applet needs to display a frame window, you're usually better off creating a special class for the window. That way, you have complete control over how the window is constructed and displayed. To create a custom window class, simply derive your window class from Java's `Frame` class. Listing 9.2 is a rewritten version of FrameApplet, called FrameApplet2, that gives the frame window its own class. This new frame window also takes advantage of having its own class by overriding the `paint()` method to display text in the window. Figure 9.2 shows FrameApplet2 running under Java Workshop.

Listing 9.2 Creating a Frame-window Class

```
import java.awt.*;
import java.applet.*;

public class FrameApplet2 extends Applet
{
    CustomFrame frame;
    Button button;

    public void init()
    {
          frame = new CustomFrame("Custom Frame Window");
          button = new Button("Show Window");
          add(button);
    }

    public boolean action(Event evt, Object arg)
    {
        boolean visible = frame.isShowing();
        if (visible)
        {
            frame.hide();
            button.setLabel("Show Window");
        }
        else
        {
            frame.show();
            button.setLabel("Hide Window");
        }

        return true;
    }
}

class CustomFrame extends Frame
{
    CustomFrame(String title)
    {
        super(title);
    }

    public void paint(Graphics g)
    {
        resize(200, 100);
```

```
            g.drawString("This is a custom window.", 30, 30);
        }
    }
```

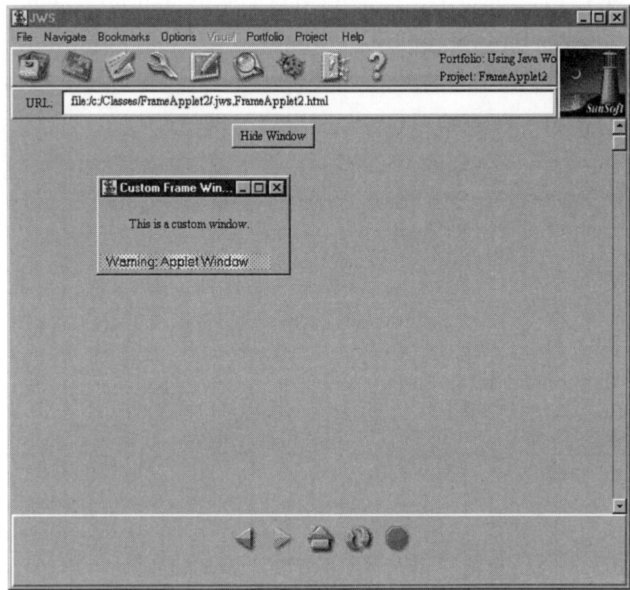

FIG. 9.2
This is FrameApplet2 running under Java Workshop.

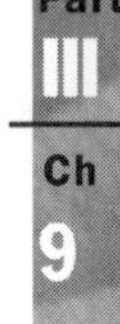

NOTE When you compile FrameApplet2, notice that, although both the FrameApplet2 and CustomFrame classes are defined in the same file, the Java compiler creates two class files called FrameApplet2.class and CustomFrame.class.

Adding Components to a Window

Frame windows are just like any other window you see when you create an applet. That is, you can add components organized into a variety of layouts and respond to the user's selections of these components. In fact, adding layouts and components to a frame window is not unlike doing the same thing with your applet's main window, which you did in the previous chapter. First you create and set the layout manager, and then you add the components as appropriate for the layout manager you've chosen.

Listing 9.3 is an applet called FrameApplet3 that not only creates a custom frame window, but also creates a simple layout for the window. This layout contains only a single button; however, you can create as sophisticated a layout as you like. Feel free to experiment further with this applet. Figure 9.3 shows FrameApplet3 running under Java Workshop, after the user has displayed the frame window. As you can see in the figure, the window has a single button labeled Close Window. When you click this button, the frame window's `action()` method responds by calling the `dispose()` method, which not only removes the window from the screen, but also destroys the window in memory.

Listing 9.3 Adding Components to a Window

```
import java.awt.*;
import java.applet.*;

public class FrameApplet3 extends Applet
{
    CustomFrame frame;
    Button button;

    public void init()
    {
          frame = new CustomFrame("Custom Frame Window");

          button = new Button("Show Window");
          add(button);
    }

    public boolean action(Event evt, Object arg)
    {
        boolean visible = frame.isShowing();
        if (visible)
        {
            frame.hide();
            button.setLabel("Show Window");
        }
        else
        {
            frame.show();
            button.setLabel("Hide Window");
        }

        return true;
    }
}

class CustomFrame extends Frame
{
    Button button;
```

```
        CustomFrame(String title)
        {
            super(title);

            FlowLayout layout = new FlowLayout();
            setLayout(layout);

            button = new Button("Close Window");
            add(button);
        }

        public void paint(Graphics g)
        {
            resize(200, 100);
            g.drawString("This is a custom window.", 30, 50);
        }

        public boolean action(Event evt, Object arg)
        {
            if (arg == "Close Window")
                dispose();

            return true;
        }
    }
```


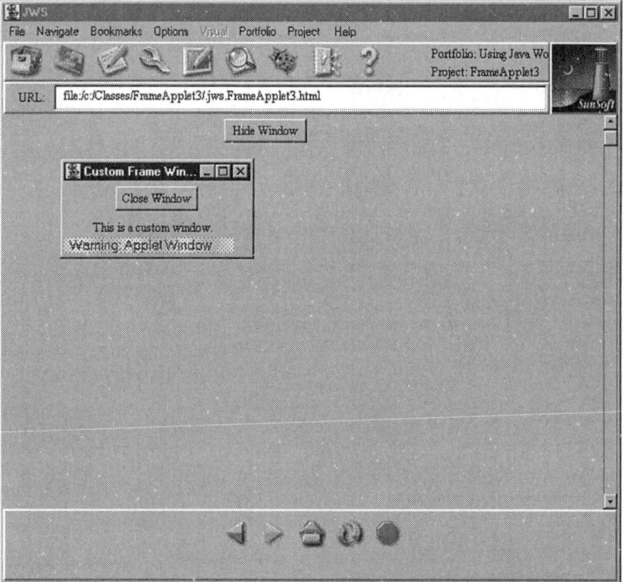

FIG. 9.3
This is FrameApplet3 running under Java Workshop.

Table 9.1 shows some useful methods you can use to manipulate a frame window. Some of these methods are defined in the `Frame` class, whereas others are inherited from the class's superclasses, such as `Window` and `Container`.

Table 9.1 Useful Frame-window Methods

Method	Description
add()	Adds components to the window.
dispose()	Deletes the window from memory.
getCursorType()	Returns the window's cursor type.
getIconImage()	Returns the window's icon object.
getLayout()	Returns the window's layout manager.
getMenuBar()	Returns the window's menu bar object.
getTitle()	Returns the window's title.
hide()	Removes the window from the screen.
isResizable()	Returns true if the window is resizable.
remove()	Removes components from the window.
removeAll()	Removes all components from the window.
setCursor()	Sets the window's cursor type.
setIconImage()	Sets the window's icon object.
setLayout()	Sets the window's layout manager.
setMenuBar()	Sets the window's menu bar.
setResizable()	Sets the window's resizable attribute.
setTitle()	Sets the window's title.
show()	Displays the window on the screen.

Using Menu Bars

Most Windows applications have menu bars, which enable the user to more easily locate and select the various commands and options supported by the program. The frame windows you create from within your applets also can have menu bars.

To create a menu bar in a window, follow these steps:

1. Create an object of the `MenuBar` class.
2. Call the window's `setMenuBar()` method to give the menu bar to the window.
3. Create objects of the `Menu` class for each menu you want in the menu bar.
4. Call the `MenuBar` object's `add()` method to add each menu object to the menu bar.
5. Create objects of the `MenuItem` or `CheckboxMenuItem` classes for each item you want to appear in the menus.
6. Call the menus' `add()` methods to add each item to its appropriate menu.

Each of these steps is covered in the sections that follow.

Creating and Setting a *MenuBar* Object

The first step in adding a menu bar to a frame window is to create the `MenuBar` object that'll hold all of the menus and commands. The menu bar in a window is the horizontal area near the top that contains the names of each of the menus in the menu bar. To create the `MenuBar` object, call the `MenuBar` class's constructor, like this:

```
MenuBar menuBar = new MenuBar();
```

As you can see, the `MenuBar()` constructor requires no arguments.

After you've created the `MenuBar` object, you have to tell Java to associate the menu bar with the frame window. You do this by calling the window's `setMenuBar()` method:

```
setMenuBar(menuBar);
```

At this point, you have an empty menu bar associated with the window. The next step is to add menus to the menu bar.

Adding Menus to a Menu Bar

After creating and setting the `MenuBar` object, you have the menu bar, but it contains no menus. To add these menus, first create objects of the `Menu` class for each menu you want in the menu bar, like this:

```
Menu fileMenu = new Menu("File");
Menu editMenu = new Menu("Edit");
Menu optionMenu = new Menu("Options");
```

The `Menu` class's constructor takes a single argument, which is the string that'll appear as the menu's name on the menu bar. The previous example lines create three menus for the menu bar.

After creating the `Menu` objects, you have to add them to the menu bar, which you do by calling the `MenuBar` object's `add()` method, like this:

```
menuBar.add(fileMenu);
menuBar.add(editMenu);
menuBar.add(optionMenu);
```

After Java executes the above three lines, you have a menu bar with three menus, as shown in figure 9.4. Note, however, that at this point the menus contain no commands. If you were to click on the menu names, no pop-up menus would appear.

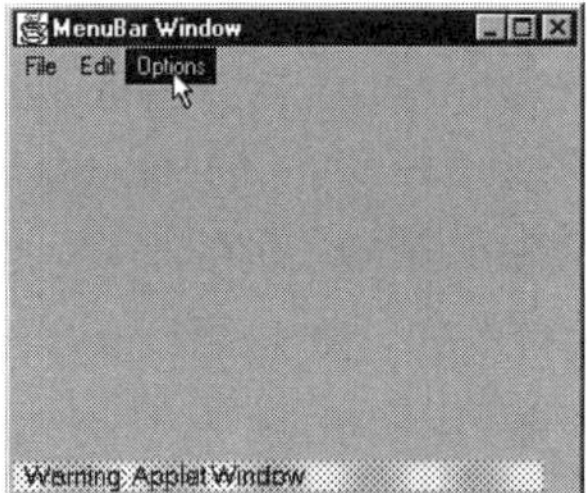

FIG. 9.4
This window's menu bar contains three empty menus.

Adding Menu Items to Menus

To add items to your menus, first create objects of the `MenuItem` or `CheckboxMenuItem` classes for each menu item you need. To add items to the Options menus you made previously, you might use Java code something like this:

```
MenuItem option1 = new MenuItem("Option 1");
MenuItem option2 = new MenuItem("Option 2");
MenuItem option3 = new MenuItem("Option 3");
```

The `MenuItem` constructor takes as its single argument the string that'll be displayed in the menu for this item.

After you create the menu items, you must call the appropriate `Menu` object's `add()` method. Those lines might look like this:

```
optionMenu.add(option1);
optionMenu.add(option2);
optionMenu.add(option3);
```

Now, when you display the frame window sporting the menu bar you've just created, you'll see that the Options menu contains a number of selections from which the user can choose (see fig. 9.5).

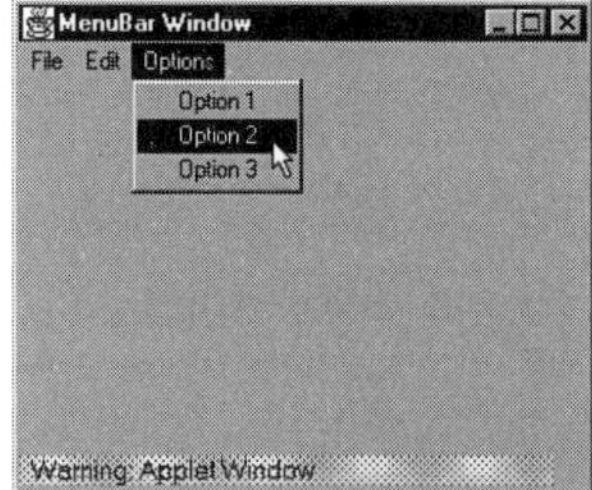

FIG. 9.5
Now the Options menu contains menu items.

Sometimes, you may have several groups of related commands that you'd like to place under a single menu. You can separate these command groups by using menu separators, which appear as horizontal lines in a pop-up menu. To create a menu separator, just create a regular `MenuItem` object with a string that contains a single hyphen (-).

Using a Menu Bar in a Frame Window

Now that you have this menu bar business mastered, it's time to put what you've learned to work. Listing 9.4 is an applet called MenuBarApplet. This applet displays a single button, which, when selected, displays a frame window with a menu bar. This menu bar contains a single menu with three items. The first two items are regular `MenuItem` objects. The third item is `CheckboxMenuItem`, which is a menu item that can display a check mark. Figure 9.6 shows MenuBarApplet with its frame window displayed and the Test menu visible. (Notice the menu separator above the checked item.)

Listing 9.4 An Applet That Uses a Menu Bar

```
import java.awt.*;
import java.applet.*;

public class MenuBarApplet extends Applet
{
    MenuBarFrame frame;
    Button button;

    public void init()
    {
          frame = new MenuBarFrame("MenuBar Window");

          button = new Button("Show Window");
          add(button);
    }

    public boolean action(Event evt, Object arg)
    {
        boolean visible = frame.isShowing();
        if (visible)
        {
            frame.hide();
            button.setLabel("Show Window");
        }
        else
        {
            frame.show();
            button.setLabel("Hide Window");
        }

        return true;
    }
}

class MenuBarFrame extends Frame
{
    MenuBar menuBar;
    String str;

    MenuBarFrame(String title)
    {
        super(title);
        menuBar = new MenuBar();
        setMenuBar(menuBar);
```

```
        Menu menu = new Menu("Test");
        menuBar.add(menu);

        MenuItem item = new MenuItem("Command 1");
        menu.add(item);
        item = new MenuItem("Command 2");
        menu.add(item);

        item = new MenuItem("-");
        menu.add(item);

        CheckboxMenuItem checkItem =
            new CheckboxMenuItem("Check");
        menu.add(checkItem);

        str = "";
        Font font = new Font("TimesRoman", Font.BOLD, 20);
        setFont(font);
    }

    public void paint(Graphics g)
    {
        resize(300, 250);
        g.drawString(str, 20, 100);
    }

    public boolean action(Event evt, Object arg)
    {
        if (evt.target instanceof MenuItem)
        {
            if (arg == "Command 1")
                str = "You selected Command 1";
            else if (arg == "Command 2")
                str = "You selected Command 2";
            else if (arg == "Check")
                str = "You selected the Check item";

            repaint();
            return true;
        }
        else
            return false;
    }
}
```

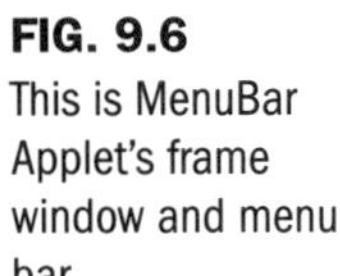

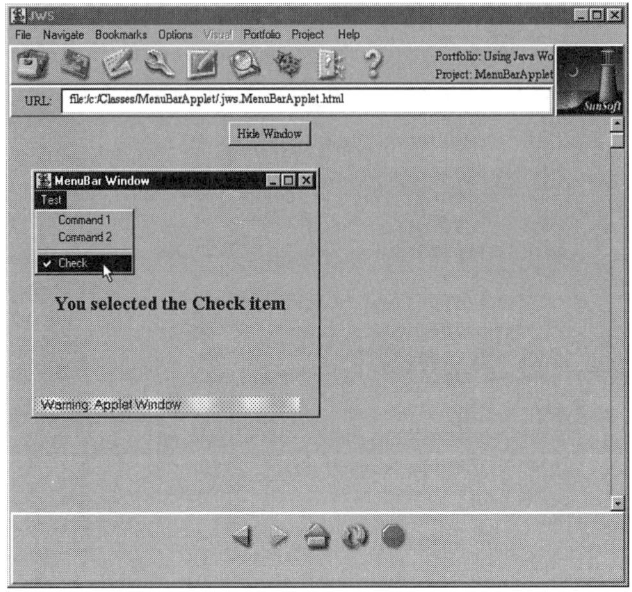

FIG. 9.6
This is MenuBar Applet's frame window and menu bar.

NOTE To determine the state (checked or unchecked) of a `CheckboxMenuItem` object, you can call its `getState()` method. This method returns `true` if the item is checked and `false` if the item is unchecked. In addition, you can set the item's state by calling its `setState()` method.

As you can see from MenuBarApplet's source code, you respond to menu-item selections in the same way you respond to other events in applets. This time, however, you have overridden two `action()` methods. The first, in the `MenuBarApplet` class, handles the applet's single button. The second overridden `action()` method, which is the one that handles the menu items, is in the `MenuBarFrame` class.

Using Dialog Boxes

In most cases, you'll add controls to your applet's display to present information to the user or to obtain information from the user. However, there may be times when you prefer to create a dialog box. For example, when the applet encounters some sort of error, a pop-up dialog box not only supplies the user with important information, but also immediately draws his attention to that information. Although Java supports dialog boxes, they, unfortunately, can only be associated with a frame window. This requirement limits their usefulness, but you still may want to use a dialog box at one time or another. To create, display, and handle a dialog box, perform the following steps:

1. Create the dialog box object.
2. Create and set a layout manager for the dialog box.
3. Create controls and add them to the dialog box.
4. Call the dialog's `show()` method to display the dialog box.
5. When the user clicks the OK or Cancel button, call the dialog's `hide()` method to remove the dialog box from the screen.
6. Extract and process the data—if any—entered into the dialog box's controls.

The following sections discuss these steps in greater detail.

Creating the Dialog Box

Java's dialog boxes are objects of the `Dialog` class. So, to create a dialog-box object, first call the `Dialog` class's constructor, like this:

```
Dialog dialog = new Dialog(frame, title, modal);
```

The constructor's three arguments are a reference to a frame window, the dialog box's title, and a `boolean` value indicating whether the dialog box is modal (`true`) or modeless (`false`). A modal dialog box, which is the most common of the two types, retains the focus until the user dismisses it. This forces the user to respond to the dialog box before continuing with the program. A modeless dialog box can lose the focus to another window, which means that the user can switch to another window even while the dialog box is still on the screen.

NOTE Although Java claims to support both modal and modeless dialog boxes, the constructor's argument doesn't seem to make any difference. In my experience, every Java dialog box is modeless. Maybe this inconsistency will be corrected by the time you read this book. ■

Creating the Dialog Box's Layout

Once you have the dialog box object created, you must give it a layout manager. If you fail to do this, any components you try to place in the dialog box will not appear. You perform this step exactly as you would for any other type of window or applet, by creating and setting the layout object:

```
FlowLayout layout = new FlowLayout();
dialog.setLayout(layout);
```

The next step is to create and add whatever controls you want to appear in the dialog box. You'll always have at least an OK button with which the user can dismiss the dialog box:

```
Button button = new Button("OK");
dialog.add(button);
```

Displaying the Dialog Box

Just like a frame window, a dialog box doesn't appear on the screen until you call its `show()` method like this:

```
dialog.show();
```

Once the dialog box is on the screen, the user can manipulate its controls in order to enter information into the dialog box's fields or to dismiss the dialog box from the screen.

Removing the Dialog Box

When the user clicks a dialog box's OK or Cancel buttons, that's your applet's signal to remove the dialog box from the screen, which you do by calling its `hide()` method:

```
dialog.hide();
```

The `hide()` method removes the dialog box from the screen, but the dialog box and its controls remain in memory so that you can access them in order to extract whatever information the user may have entered into the dialog box.

After you've removed the dialog box from the screen, you can use a control's methods to extract whatever information the user may have entered into the dialog's controls. For example, to get the entry from a text field control, you'd call the control's `getText()` method.

Methods of the *Dialog* Class

Like any class, `Dialog` provides a set of public methods that you can use to control the dialog box. `Dialog` also inherits many methods from its superclasses, `Window` and `Container`. Table 9.2 lists the most useful methods of the `Dialog` class, including those methods inherited from the `Window` and `Container` classes.

Table 9.2 Useful Methods of the *Dialog* Class (Including Inherited)

Method	Description
add()	Adds a component to the dialog box.
dispose()	Removes the dialog box from memory.
getLayout()	Returns the dialog's layout manager.
getTitle()	Returns the dialog box's title.
hide()	Removes the dialog box from the screen.
isModal()	Returns true if the dialog box is modal.
isResizable()	Returns true if the dialog box is resizable.
locate()	Returns the component at the given location.
remove()	Removes a component from the dialog box.
removeAll()	Removes all components.
setLayout()	Sets the dialog's layout manager.
setResizable()	Sets the resizable attribute.
setTitle()	Sets the dialog box's title.
show()	Displays the dialog box.

Creating a Dialog Box for Text Input

Your last task in this chapter is to put your newly acquired knowledge of dialog boxes to work. Listing 9.5 is an applet that enables you to display a frame window.

From the frame window's menu bar, you can select a command that displays a dialog box. This dialog box contains an OK button for dismissing the dialog box and a text field for entering information. When you dismiss the dialog box, the text you entered into the text field control appears in the frame window. Figure 9.7 shows the applet, the frame window, and the dialog box.

Listing 9.5 An Applet That Displays a Dialog Box

```
import java.awt.*;
import java.applet.*;

public class DialogApplet extends Applet
{
    DialogFrame frame;
    Button button;

    public void init()
    {
          frame = new DialogFrame("Dialog Window");

          button = new Button("Show Window");
          add(button);
    }

    public boolean action(Event evt, Object arg)
    {
        boolean visible = frame.isShowing();
        if (visible)
        {
            frame.hide();
            button.setLabel("Show Window");
        }
        else
        {
            frame.show();
            button.setLabel("Hide Window");
        }

        return true;
    }
}

class DialogFrame extends Frame
{
    MenuBar menuBar;
    Dialog dialog;
    TextField textField;
    String str;
```

```
DialogFrame(String title)
{
    super(title);

    menuBar = new MenuBar();
    setMenuBar(menuBar);
    Menu menu = new Menu("Test");
    menuBar.add(menu);
    MenuItem item = new MenuItem("Dialog box");
    menu.add(item);

    str = "";
}

public void paint(Graphics g)
{
    resize(300, 250);

    g.drawString("THE TEXT YOU ENTERED IS:", 70, 50);
    g.drawString(str, 70, 70);
}

public boolean action(Event evt, Object arg)
{
    if (evt.target instanceof MenuItem)
    {
        if (arg == "Dialog box")
            ShowDialogBox();
    }
    else if (evt.target instanceof Button)
    {
        if (arg == "OK")
        {
            dialog.hide();
            str = textField.getText();
            repaint();
        }
    }

    return true;
}

protected void ShowDialogBox()
{
    dialog = new Dialog(this, "Test Dialog", true);
    FlowLayout layout = new FlowLayout();
    dialog.setLayout(layout);

    textField = new TextField("", 20);
    Button button = new Button("OK");
```

continues

Listing 9.5 Continued

```
        dialog.add(button);
        dialog.add(textField);

        dialog.show();
        dialog.resize(200, 100);
    }
}
```

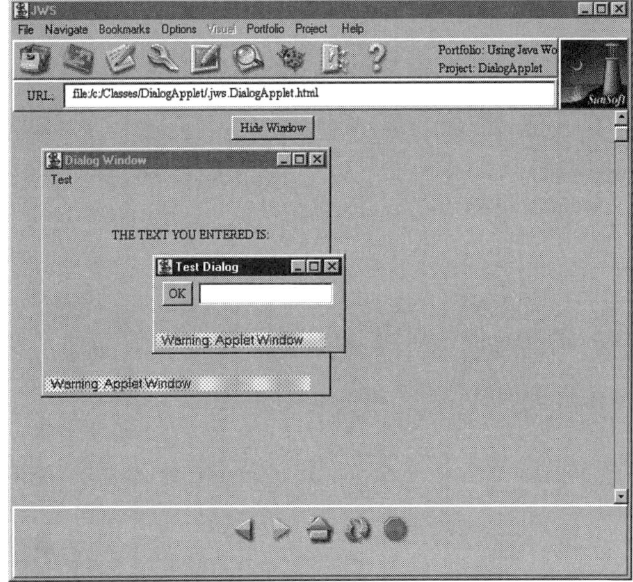

FIG. 9.7 This is DialogApplet running under Java Workshop.

NOTE In addition to normal dialog boxes, Java supports file dialog boxes for loading and saving files. The file dialog boxes are represented by the `FileDialog` class. However, because Java applets have extremely limited access to files, file dialog boxes are not covered here.

From Here...

Although it's an ability you may not frequently take advantage of, Java applets can display windows. The `Frame` class makes this possible, by providing the functionality for frame windows, which can be sized, moved, used to display components, and much more. A frame window can, in fact, even have a full-featured menu bar, just like the menu bars you see in many Windows applications. Creating a menu bar, however, requires knowing how to create and manipulate `MenuBar`, `Menu`, `MenuItem`, and `CheckboxMenuItem` objects.

You probably won't have much call for dialog boxes in your Java applets, but it's always good to know they're there when you need them. Using dialog boxes in conjunction with a frame window, you can inform the user of critical problems, as well as obtain information from the user without cluttering your main window with controls. Because dialog boxes are much like other display windows in Java, you can set up layout managers, add components, and control the dialog box using the many methods defined in the `Dialog` class or inherited from the class's superclasses.

Please refer to the following chapters for related information:

- Chapter 5, "Object-Oriented Programming and Java," tells you more about classes and how they're used in Java, as well as how to create, compile, and run applets using Java Workshop.
- Chapter 6, "Applets and Graphics," describes how to draw graphical shapes, which you can add to a frame window's display.
- Chapter 7, "Java Controls," shows how to create and program Java's many controls, which you can add to a frame window.
- Chapter 13, "Writing Java Applications," describes how to use Java to create stand-alone applications that have their own frame windows.

CHAPTER 10

Events and Configurable Applets

About Java's `Event` objects.

`Event` objects hold the information you need to respond to user interactions with your applet.

How to handle the mouse in an applet.

As one of the most common input devices in the world, the mouse is important to your applets, too. You need to know how to respond to mouse clicks and mouse movement.

How to respond to keyboard events.

Virtually all computers have keyboards, so odds are good that your applet's user will want to use his keyboard at one time or another. Luckily, capturing applet keyboard events is a snap.

How to create configurable applets.

To make your applets generally more useful, the applets must support parameters, which enable an HTML author to load and run applets using customized settings.

Up until now, your applets have responded to events generated by Java components like buttons, text fields, and list boxes. You've yet to examine how to respond to events generated by the most basic of a computer's controls, the mouse and the keyboard. Because virtually every computer has these important hardware controls, you can confidently take advantage of them in your applets to collect various types of input. In this chapter, you learn the secrets of mouse and keyboard handling in Java applets. You'll also discover how to enable other HTML authors to customize your applet to their own needs. This trick involves something called parameters. ■

The *Event* Object

In order to understand how to respond to various types of events, you need to know more about Java's `Event` class, an object of which is passed to any event-handling method. When you want to respond to a Java button control, for example, you override the `action()` method, whose first argument is an `Event` object. You then examine the target field of the `Event` object to determine whether it was the button control that generated the event. The `Event` class, however, defines many constants and data fields that provide information about the event represented by the object.

First, the `Event` class defines constants for all of the events to which an event-handling method can respond. In this chapter, you'll learn about some of these constants, which include `MOUSE_DOWN`, `MOUSE_UP`, and `KEY_PRESS`. The class also defines constants for special keys, such as `F1`, `PGUP`, `PGDN`, `HOME`, and so on. Finally, the `Event` class defines the data fields shown in table 10.1. How you use these data fields depends on the type of event represented by the `Event` object.

Table 10.1 Data Fields of the *Event* Class

Field	Description
Object arg	Event-specific information. With a button event, for example, this field is the button's label.
int clickCount	The click count for mouse events. A value of 1 means a single click and 2 means a double-click.
int id	The event's type, such as `MOUSE_DOWN`, `MOUSE_MOVE`, `KEY_PRESS`, and so on.
int key	The key for a key-related event. For a `KEY_PRESS` event, for example, this would be the key that was pressed.
int modifiers	The key modifiers, including the Shift and Control keys. The `Event` class defines constants such as `SHIFT_MASK` and `CTRL_MASK`.
Object target	The type of object—such as Button, TextField, and so on—that generated the event.
long when	The event's time stamp.
int x	The X coordinate associated with the event, usually used with mouse events to indicate the mouse's position at the time of the event.

Field	Description
int y	The Y coordinate associated with the event, usually used with mouse events to indicate the mouse's position at the time of the event.

The Mouse

Most people use their computer's mouse almost as much as its keyboard. I can vouch for this from first-hand experience, because my only bout with RSI (repetitive strain injury) came not from typing furiously all day, but from maneuvering my mouse to mark paragraphs, highlight words, click buttons, make list selections, bring up menus, and any number of other mousely tasks. The point is that the mouse is one of the most important input devices attached to your computer. To write complete applets, you're going to have to master responding to mouse events in your Java programs.

Luckily, responding to mouse input is a simple matter. Because responding to the events generated by the mouse are such an important and common task in modern programming, Java's classes already include special methods for responding to these events. Exactly what events are you expected to handle? A mouse generates six types of event messages that you can capture in your applets. These events are listed below, along with their descriptions and the method that handles them:

- `MOUSE_DOWN`. This event, which is handled by the `mouseDown()` method, is caused when the user presses the mouse button.
- `MOUSE_UP`. This event, which is handled by the `mouseUp()` method, is caused when the user releases the left mouse button.
- `MOUSE_MOVE`. This event, which is handled by the `mouseMove()` method, occurs when the user moves the mouse pointer on the screen.
- `MOUSE_DRAG`. This event, which is handled by the `mouseDrag()` method, is generated when the user moves the mouse pointer while holding down the left mouse button.
- `MOUSE_ENTER`. This event, which is handled by the `mouseEnter()` method, is sent when the mouse pointer enters the area owned by an applet or component.

- MOUSE_EXIT. This event, which is handled by the mouseExit() method, occurs when the mouse pointer leaves the area owned by an applet or a component.

In the sections that follow, you'll learn more about the most commonly used of these mouse events.

Handling Mouse Clicks

Without a doubt, the most commonly used mouse event in Java programs (and any other program written for a graphical user interface) is the MOUSE_DOWN event, which is generated whenever the user clicks within an applet. It's the MOUSE_DOWN event, for example, that lets Java know when an on-screen button component has been clicked. You don't have to worry about clicks on on-screen buttons (usually) because they're handled by Java. However, you can respond to MOUSE_DOWN events in your applets in order to accomplish other input tasks.

Java provides a couple of methods by which you can respond to mouse events. The easiest way to capture a MOUSE_DOWN event is to override the applet's mouseDown() method. Java automatically calls mouseDown() whenever the MOUSE_DOWN event is generated, which makes responding to this event easier than melting butter with a blowtorch. The mouseDown() method's signature looks like this:

```
public boolean mouseDown(Event evt, int x, int y)
```

The arguments passed to the function are an Event object and the X, Y coordinates of the mouse event. Although Java has already extracted the X, Y mouse coordinates for you, you can also get them from the Event object by examining the values stored in the x and y data fields, as described in table 10.1. (Because Java has already extracted the coordinates for you, though, it makes more sense to use the x and y parameters sent to the function.) What you do with these coordinates depends, of course, on your applet. In the next section, you'll see how to use the coordinates to display graphics on the screen.

NOTE Although most of Java's event-handling methods automatically receive as arguments the basic information you need about a specific event (such as the coordinates of a mouse click), you can extract whatever additional information you need from the Event object, which is always the first parameter in a message-handling method.

Using Mouse Clicks in an Applet

Listing 10.1 shows an example of using the `mouseDown()` method. The applet in listing 10.1 responds to mouse clicks by printing the word "Click!" wherever the user clicks in the applet. It does this by storing the coordinates of the mouse click in the applet's `coordX` and `coordY` data fields. The `paint()` method then uses these coordinates to display the word. Figure 10.1 shows MouseApplet running under Java Workshop.

Listing 10.1 Using Mouse Clicks in an Applet

```
import java.awt.*;
import java.applet.*;

public class MouseApplet extends Applet
{
    int coordX, coordY;

    public void init()
    {
        coordX = -1;
        coordY = -1;

        Font font =
            new Font("TimesRoman", Font.BOLD, 24);
        setFont(font);

        resize(400, 300);
    }

    public void paint(Graphics g)
    {
        if (coordX != -1)
            g.drawString("Click!", coordX, coordY);
    }

    public boolean mouseDown(Event evt, int x, int y)
    {
        coordX = x;
        coordY = y;
        repaint();
        return true;
    }
}
```

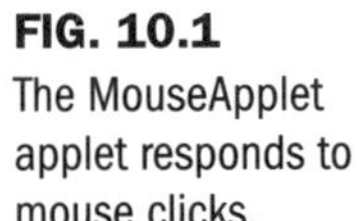

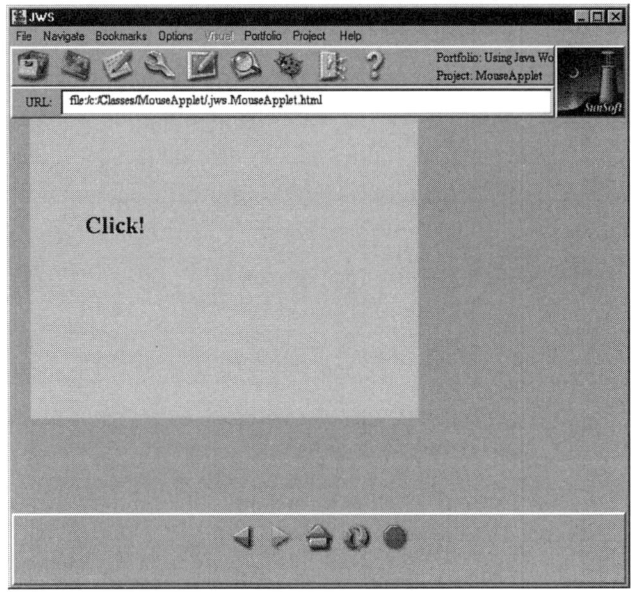

FIG. 10.1
The MouseApplet applet responds to mouse clicks.

NOTE When you run MouseApplet, you'll discover that the applet window gets erased each time the `paint()` method is called. That's why only one "Click!" ever appears in the window. ■

Handling Mouse Movement

Although mouse clicks are the most common type of mouse event to which your applet may want to respond, tracking the mouse pointer's movement can also be useful. Drawing programs, for example, enable you to draw shapes by tracking the movement of the mouse and displaying the results on the screen.

Unlike mouse clicks, though, which are rare and only occur when the user presses a mouse button, `MOUSE_MOVE` events come flooding into your applet by the hundreds as the user moves the mouse around the screen. Each one of these events can be handled in the `mouseMove()` method, whose signature looks like this:

```
public boolean mouseMove(Event evt, int x, int y)
```

Except for its name, the `mouseMove()` method looks exactly like the `mouseDown()` method, receiving as arguments an `Event` object and the X, Y coordinates at which the event occurred.

Responding to Mouse Movement in an Applet

Responding to mouse movement isn't something you have to do often in your applets. Still, it's a handy tool to have. You might, for example, need to track mouse movement when writing a game applet that uses the mouse as input. A more common use is in graphics programs that enable you to draw on the screen. Listing 10.2 is just such an applet.

When you run MouseApplet2 with Java Workshop, the applet's display area is blank. Click the mouse in the window to choose a starting point and then move the mouse around the window. Wherever the mouse pointer goes, it leaves a black line behind (see fig. 10.2). Although this is a very simple drawing program, it gives you some idea of how you might use a mouse to accomplish other similar tasks.

Listing 10.2 An Applet That Tracks Mouse Movement

```
import java.awt.*;
import java.applet.*;

public class MouseApplet2 extends Applet
{
    Point startPoint;
    Point points[];
    int numPoints;
    boolean drawing;

    public void init()
    {
        startPoint = new Point(0, 0);
        points = new Point[1000];
        numPoints = 0;
        drawing = false;
        resize(400, 300);
    }

    public void paint(Graphics g)
    {
        int oldX = startPoint.x;
        int oldY = startPoint.y;

        for (int x=0; x<numPoints; ++x)
        {
            g.drawLine(oldX, oldY, points[x].x, points[x].y);
            oldX = points[x].x;
            oldY = points[x].y;
        }
```

continues

Listing 10.2 Continued

```
    }

    public boolean mouseDown(Event evt, int x, int y)
    {
        drawing = true;
        startPoint.x = x;
        startPoint.y = y;
        return true;
    }

    public boolean mouseMove(Event evt, int x, int y)
    {
        if ((drawing) && (numPoints < 1000))
        {
            points[numPoints] = new Point(x, y);
            ++numPoints;
            repaint();
        }

        return true;
    }
}
```

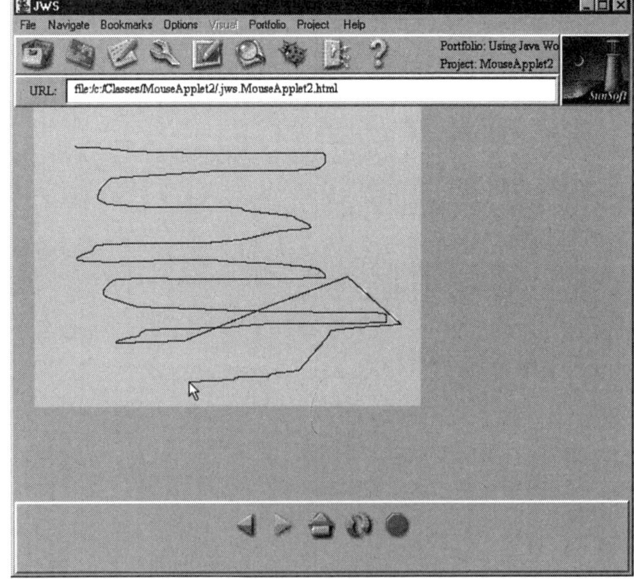

FIG. 10.2 This applet draws by tracking the movement of the mouse.

The Keyboard

The keyboard has been around even longer than the mouse; it has been the primary interface between humans and their computers for decades. Given the keyboard's importance, obviously, there may be times when you'll want to handle the keyboard events at a lower level than you can with something like a `TextField` control. Java responds to two basic key events, which are represented by the `KEY_PRESS` and `KEY_RELEASE` constants. As you'll soon see, Java defines methods that make it just as easy to respond to the keyboard as it is to respond to the mouse.

Responding to Key Presses

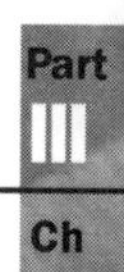

Whenever the user presses a key when an applet is active, Java sends the applet a `KEY_PRESS` event. In your applet, you can respond to this event by overriding the `keyDown()` method, whose signature looks like this:

```
public boolean keyDown(Event evt, int key)
```

As you can see, this method receives two arguments, which are an `Event` object and an integer representing the key that was pressed. This integer is actually the ASCII representation of the character represented by the key. To use this value in your programs, however, you must first cast it to a `char` value, like this:

```
char c = (char)key;
```

Predefined Key Constants

Some of the keys on your keyboard issue commands rather than generate characters. These keys include all the F keys, as well as keys like Shift, Ctrl, Page Up, Page Down, and so on. In order to make these types of keys easier to handle in your applets, Java's `Event` class defines a set of constants that represents these key's values. Table 10.2 lists these constants.

Table 10.2 Key Constants of the *Event* Class

Constant	Key
DOWN	The down arrow key.
END	The End key.
F1	The F1 key.
F2	The F2 key.
F3	The F3 key.
F4	The F4 key.
F5	The F5 key.
F6	The F6 key.
F7	The F7 key.
F8	The F8 key.
F9	The F9 key.
F10	The F10 key.
F11	The F11 key.
F12	The F12 key.
HOME	The Home key.
LEFT	The left arrow key.
PGDN	The Page Down key.
PGUP	The Page Up key.
RIGHT	The right arrow key.
UP	The up arrow key.

Key Modifiers

The `Event` class also defines a number of constants for modifier keys that the user might press along with the basic key. These constants include `ALT_MASK`, `SHIFT_MASK`, and `CTRL_MASK`, which represent the Alt, Shift, and Ctrl (or Control) keys on your keyboard. The `SHIFT_MASK` and `CTRL_MASK` constants are used in the `Event` class's methods `shiftDown()` and `controlDown()`, each of which returns a `boolean` value indicating whether the modifier key is pressed. (There currently is no `altDown()` method.) You can also examine the `Event` object's modifiers field to determine whether a particular modifier key was pressed. For example, if you want to check for the Alt key, you might use a line of Java code like this:

```
boolean altPressed = (evt.modifiers & Event.ALT_MASK) != 0;
```

By ANDing the mask with the value in the modifiers field, you end up with a non-zero value if the Alt key was pressed and a 0 if it wasn't. You convert this result to a boolean value by comparing the result with 0.

Using Key Presses in an Applet

Although capturing key presses is a fairly simple process, there's nothing like an example applet to put the theoretical stuff to the test. Listing 10.3 is an applet called KeyApplet that displays whatever key the user presses. Figure 10.3 shows the applet running under Java Workshop.

NOTE If you run KeyApplet under a browser like Netscape Navigator, click the applet with your mouse before you start typing. This ensures that the applet has the focus and will receive the key presses.

Listing 10.3 An Applet That Captures Key Presses

```
import java.awt.*;
import java.applet.*;

public class KeyApplet extends Applet
{
    int keyPressed;

    public void init()
    {
        keyPressed = -1;

        Font font =
            new Font("TimesRoman", Font.BOLD, 144);
        setFont(font);

        resize(200, 200);
    }
```

continues

Listing 10.3 Continued

```
    public void paint(Graphics g)
    {
        String str = "";

        if (keyPressed != -1)
        {
            str += (char)keyPressed;
            g.drawString(str, 40, 150);
        }
    }

    public boolean keyDown(Event evt, int key)
    {
        keyPressed = key;
        repaint();
        return true;
    }
}
```

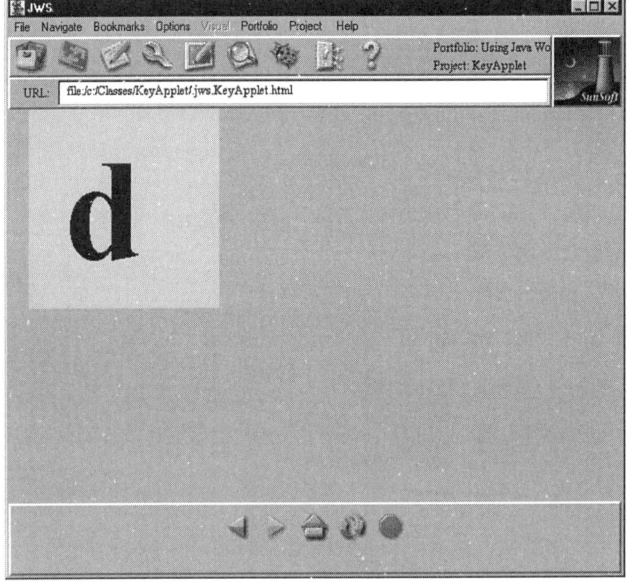

FIG. 10.3
This applet displays the last character typed.

Handling Events Directly

All of the events received by your applet are processed by the `handleEvent()` method, which the `Applet` class inherits from the `Component` class. When this method is not overridden in your applet, the default implementation is responsible for calling the many methods that respond to events. Listing 10.4 shows how the `handleEvent()` method is implemented in the `Component` class. By examining this listing, you can easily see why you only have to override methods like `mouseDown()` to respond to events. In the next section, you see how to customize `handleEvent()` in your own programs.

Listing 10.4 The Default Implementation of *handleEvent()*

```
public boolean handleEvent(Event evt) {
switch (evt.id) {
  case Event.MOUSE_ENTER:
    return mouseEnter(evt, evt.x, evt.y);

  case Event.MOUSE_EXIT:
    return mouseExit(evt, evt.x, evt.y);

  case Event.MOUSE_MOVE:
    return mouseMove(evt, evt.x, evt.y);

  case Event.MOUSE_DOWN:
    return mouseDown(evt, evt.x, evt.y);

  case Event.MOUSE_DRAG:
    return mouseDrag(evt, evt.x, evt.y);

  case Event.MOUSE_UP:
    return mouseUp(evt, evt.x, evt.y);

  case Event.KEY_PRESS:
  case Event.KEY_ACTION:
    return keyDown(evt, evt.key);

  case Event.KEY_RELEASE:
  case Event.KEY_ACTION_RELEASE:
    return keyUp(evt, evt.key);
```

continues

Listing 10.4 Continued

```
  case Event.ACTION_EVENT:
    return action(evt, evt.arg);
  case Event.GOT_FOCUS:
    return gotFocus(evt, evt.arg);
  case Event.LOST_FOCUS:
    return lostFocus(evt, evt.arg);
}
return false;
}
```

Although the default implementation of `handleEvent()` calls special methods that you can override in your applet for each event, you might want to group all of your event handling in one method to conserve on overhead, change the way an applet responds to a particular event, or even create your own events. To accomplish any of these tasks (or any others you might come up with), you can forget the individual event-handling methods and override `handleEvent()` instead.

In your version of `handleEvent()`, you must examine the `Event` object's `id` field in order to determine which event is being processed. You can just ignore events in which you're not interested. However, be sure to return `false` whenever you ignore a message, so that Java knows that it should pass the event up the object hierarchy. Listing 10.5 is a rewritten version of the MouseApplet2 applet, called MouseApplet3. This version overrides the `handleEvent()` method in order to respond to events.

Listing 10.5 Using the *handleEvent()* Method

```
import java.awt.*;
import java.applet.*;

public class MouseApplet3 extends Applet
{
    Point startPoint;
    Point points[];
    int numPoints;
    boolean drawing;

    public void init()
    {
        startPoint = new Point(0, 0);
        points = new Point[1000];
        numPoints = 0;
```

```
        drawing = false;
        resize(400, 300);
    }

    public void paint(Graphics g)
    {
        int oldX = startPoint.x;
        int oldY = startPoint.y;

        for (int x=0; x<numPoints; ++x)
        {
            g.drawLine(oldX, oldY, points[x].x, points[x].y);
            oldX = points[x].x;
            oldY = points[x].y;
        }
    }

    public boolean handleEvent(Event evt)
    {
        switch(evt.id)
        {
            case Event.MOUSE_DOWN:
                drawing = true;
                startPoint.x = evt.x;
                startPoint.y = evt.y;
                return true;
            case Event.MOUSE_MOVE:
                if ((drawing) && (numPoints < 1000))
                {
                    points[numPoints] = new Point(evt.x, evt.y);
                    ++numPoints;
                    repaint();
                }
                return true;
            default:
                return false;
        }
    }
}
```


Configurable Applets

All of the applets you've written so far have one thing in common. Outside of the starting size of the applet, none of your applets are configurable. That is, the user can't configure the applet to fit his needs. In many cases, it doesn't make sense to give the user configurable options. But, just as often, someone who wants to use your applet in his own home page will want to make minor changes without having to change and recompile the source code. In fact, the user probably won't even have access to the source code. In the following sections, you look at configurable applets, which enable the applet's user to modify how an applet looks and acts, all without having to change a line of Java code.

Types of Users

Before you read further, it might be a good idea to define exactly what a user is. When it comes to applets, you could say that there are two kinds of users. The first kind is a Net surfer who logs onto your home page and sees all the cool applets you've spent the last six months creating. Because this user is not installing your applets on his own Web pages—he's just a casual observer—he doesn't need access to the applet's parameters. In fact, if you want your Web pages to look right for different users, it just doesn't make sense to enable the surfer to configure an applet.

The other kind of user is the guy who found your applet on a server somewhere and wants to incorporate the applet into his own Web pages. Assuming that you've released your applet into the world for others to use, you want this type of user to find your applet to be as flexible as possible. However, you probably don't want to give this user your source code and expect him to make changes that require recompiling. After all, he could end up trashing the applet completely.

So, to make it easy for this user to modify the applet's appearance and functionality, you must build in support for parameters. To use these parameters, the user only needs to add a few lines to the HTML document that loads and runs the applet. For example, you may have written an applet that displays an awesome title on your home page. Now, you want to release the applet so that other netfolks can use it in their Web pages. However, these folks are going to want to display their own titles. So, you make the title string a parameter.

Parameters and Applets

When you want to use an applet that supports parameters, you must add the parameters and their values to the HTML document that loads and runs the applet.

You do this by using the <PARAM> tag, which has two parts. The NAME part of the tag specifies the parameter's name and the VALUE part specifies the parameter's value. For example, suppose you want to provide a title parameter for the title applet you read about in the previous section. The parameter tag might look like this:

```
<PARAM NAME=title VALUE="Big Al's Home Page">
```

Here, the name of the parameter is `title`. The applet will use this name to identify the parameter. The value of the `title` parameter in the above line is the text string `Big Al's Home Page`. The applet will retrieve this text string in order to display the title the user wants. A complete HTML document for the title applet might look something like listing 10.6.

Listing 10.6 Using a Parameter in an HTML Document

```
<title>Applet Test Page</title>
<h1>Applet Test Page</h1>
<applet
    code="TitleApplet.class"
    width=250
    height=150
    name="TitleApplet">
    <PARAM NAME=title VALUE="Big Al's Home Page">
</applet>
```

As you can see, the <PARAM> tag is enclosed between the `<applet>` and `</applet>` tags; the parameters are part of the applet's HTML code. Of course, since you've been using Java Workshop, you haven't had to write any HTML documents for your applets. You'll soon see how to specify parameters when using Java Workshop, but, for now, you might like to know how an applet retrieves parameters at run time. To retrieve a parameter, call the applet's `getParameter()` method, like this:

```
String param = getParameter(name);
```

The `getParameter()` method takes a single argument, which is a string containing the name of the parameter for which you want the value. The method always returns a string to your applet. This string is, of course, the part of the <PARAM> tag that follows the VALUE=.

Setting and Retrieving a Parameter's Value

Suppose that you've written an applet that displays a fancy greeting to the viewer. (How fancy the greeting is displayed depends upon the code you've written for the applet. Because how the applet actually displays this greeting is not important at this point, just pretend it does something really cool.) The parameter is defined in the HTML document like this:

```
<PARAM NAME=greeting VALUE="All Web Surfers Welcome!">
```

When the applet runs, it has to find out what greeting to display. So, in the applet's `init()` method is the following line:

```
String str = getParameter("greeting");
```

Now that the applet has the text stored in the `str` variable, it can manipulate and display it any way it needs to.

Using a Parameter in an Applet

Now that you know how to create HTML documents that set parameters, as well as how to obtain those parameters from within your applet, you'd probably like a real parameterized applet with which you can experiment. Listing 10.7 is an applet called ConfigApplet, which takes a single parameter. This parameter is the text string to display. To create this applet and its parameters, use the following steps.

1. In your Classes folder, create a folder called ConfigApplet. Type listing 10.7 and save it under the name ConfigApplet.java in the new ConfigApplet folder.

Listing 10.7 An Applet with a Single Parameter

```
import java.awt.*;
import java.applet.*;

public class ConfigApplet extends Applet
{
    String str;

    public void init()
    {
        str = getParameter("text");

        Font font = new Font("TimesRoman", Font.BOLD, 24);
        setFont(font);
```

```
    }

    public void paint(Graphics g)
    {
        g.drawString(str, 50, 50);
    }
}
```

2. Start Java Workshop and create a project for the ConfigApplet applet, using the settings shown in figure 10.4. (For more information on creating a project, refer back to Chapter 5, "Object-Oriented Programming and Java.")

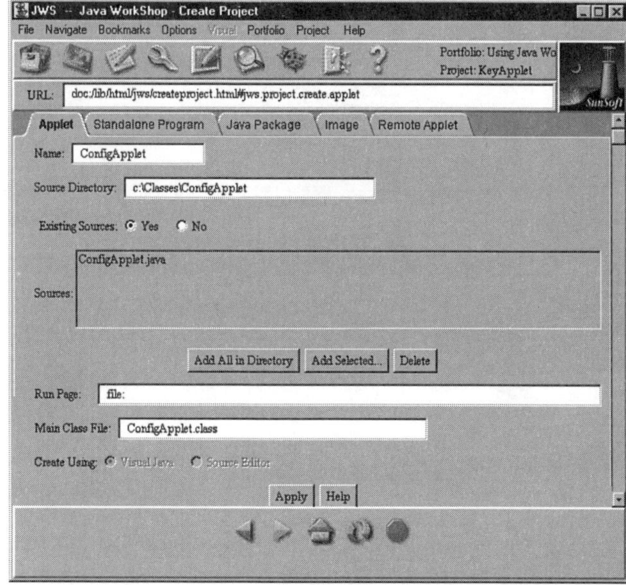

FIG. 10.4
These are the settings for ConfigApplet's project.

3. Choose ConfigApplet from Java's Project, Edit menu. The project's editable options appear in a tabbed dialog box.
4. Select the Run tab, and, in the parameter's area, enter **text** in the Name box and **Display Text** in the value box (see fig. 10.5).
5. Click the Add button to create the parameter. The parameter then appears in the Parameters box, as shown in figure 10.6.

   You've just created a parameter whose name is `text` and whose value is the string `Display Text`.

FIG. 10.5
You enter the parameter's name and value into the appropriate text boxes.

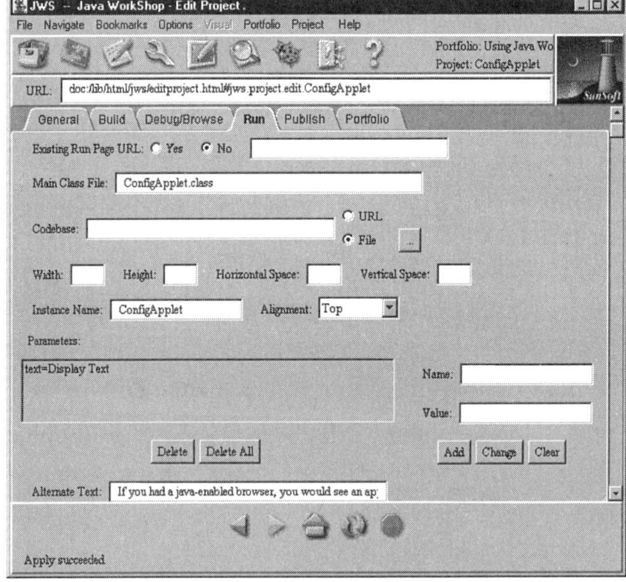

FIG. 10.6
When you click Add, Java Workshop adds the new entry to the applet's list of parameters.

6. Click the Apply button (you may have to use Java Workshop's scrollbar to reveal the button) to accept the changes to the applet (see fig. 10.7).

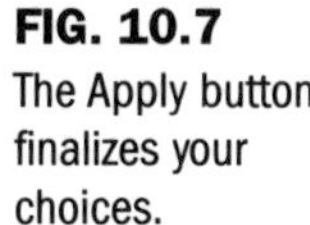

FIG. 10.7
The Apply button finalizes your choices.

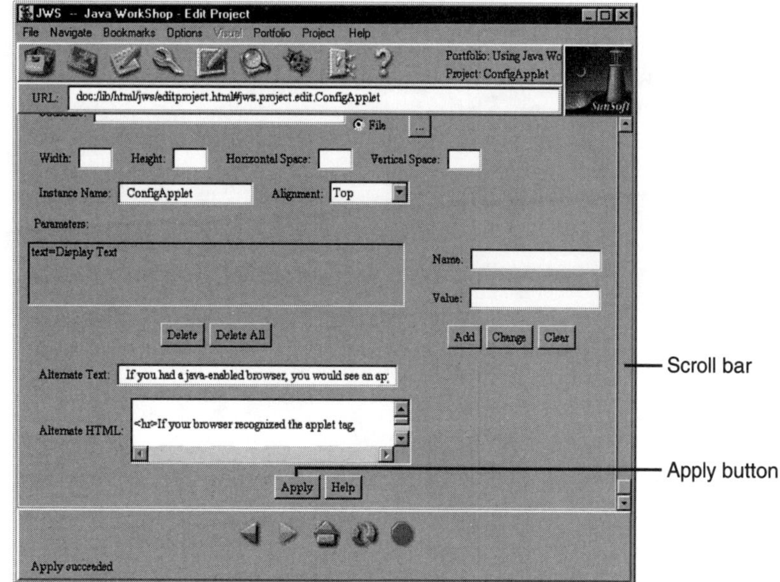

7. Use Build Manager and Project Tester to compile and run the applet.

When you run the applet under Java Workshop, you see the window shown in figure 10.8. As you can see, the string you defined for the `text` parameter appears in the window. This is because Java Workshop has added the `text` parameter to the project's HTML document, which is shown in listing 10.8. Try running the applet several times, each time changing the `text` parameter to a new text string. This will give you a good example of how parameters work from the HTML document writer's point of view. Changing the value of the parameter in the HTML document is all you need to do to display a different text string. You don't have to change the applet's source code at all.

NOTE When running ConfigApplet under Java Workshop, if you want to experiment with different values for the `text` parameter, you have to change the value using the Run page of the project's editable options. This is because Java Workshop creates a new HTML document each time you run the applet. If you want to edit the HTML file by hand, run the applet using Appletviewer or a Web Browser such as Netscape Navigator 2.0. ■

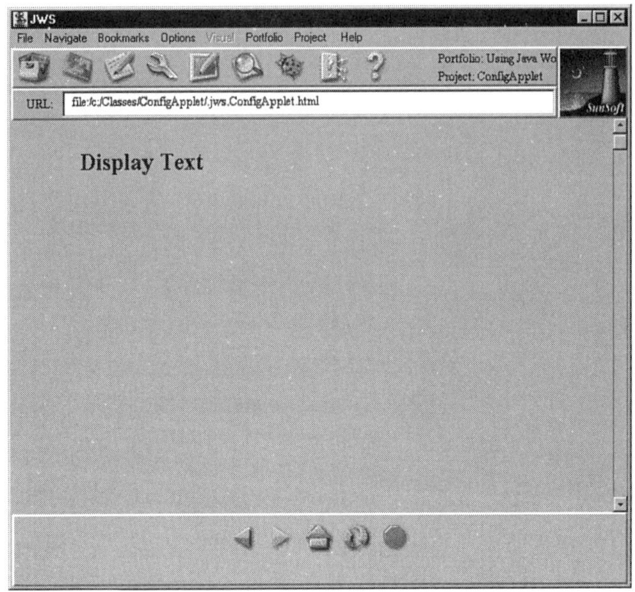

FIG. 10.8
The applet displays the string that you defined as the text parameter's value.

Listing 10 .8 The HTML Document Java Workshop Creates for ConfigApplet

```
<applet
   name="ConfigApplet"
   code="ConfigApplet.class"
   width="300"
   height="300"
   align="Top"
   alt="If you had a java-enabled browser, you would see an applet here."
>
<param name="text" value="Display Text">
   <hr>If your browser recognized the applet tag,
   you would see an applet here.<hr>
</applet>
```

Multiple Parameters

When you're writing an application that others may use in their Web pages, it's important that you make the applet as flexible as possible. One way to do this is to use parameters for any applet value that the user might like to customize. Adding multiple parameters is just a matter of adding additional <PARAM> tags to the HTML document and then retrieving the values of the parameters in the applet. In the next example, you take a look at ConfigApplet2, which gives the user much more control over how the applet displays the text string.

Suppose that you want to rewrite ConfigApplet so that the user can customize not just the text string the applet will display, but also the position of the text and the size of the font used to print the text. To do this, you need to create four parameters, one each for the text to display, the X position of the text, the Y position of the text, and the point size of the font. Listing 10.9 is the HTML document that Java Workshop creates to load and run the ConfigApplet2 applet, which is a new version of ConfigApplet. Notice that the HTML document now specifies four parameters for the applet. You can specify as many parameters as you need, in any order, for an applet. To get Java Workshop to create this HTML document, you must add the parameters shown in figure 10.9.

Listing 10.9 The HTML Document for ConfigApplet2

```
<applet
   name="ConfigApplet2"
   code="ConfigApplet2.class"
   width="300"
   height="300"
   align="Top"
   alt="If you had a java-enabled browser, you would see an applet here."
>
<param name="text" value="Display Text">
<param name="typesize" value="72">
<param name="xpos" value="20">
<param name="ypos" value="100">
   <hr>If your browser recognized the applet tag,
   you would see an applet here.<hr>
</applet>
```

The HTML document in listing 10.9 specifies that the applet is to display the text string `Display Text` in 72-point type and at position 20,100. The applet, of course, must call `getParameter()` to read these values into the applet. Moreover, the applet must call `getParameter()` once for each parameter. After retrieving the parameters, the applet must initialize itself such that it displays the text as requested. Listing 10.10 is the Java source code for ConfigApplet2, which accomplishes all these tasks. Figure 10.10 shows the applet running under Java Workshop, using the parameters given in the HTML document in listing 10.9.

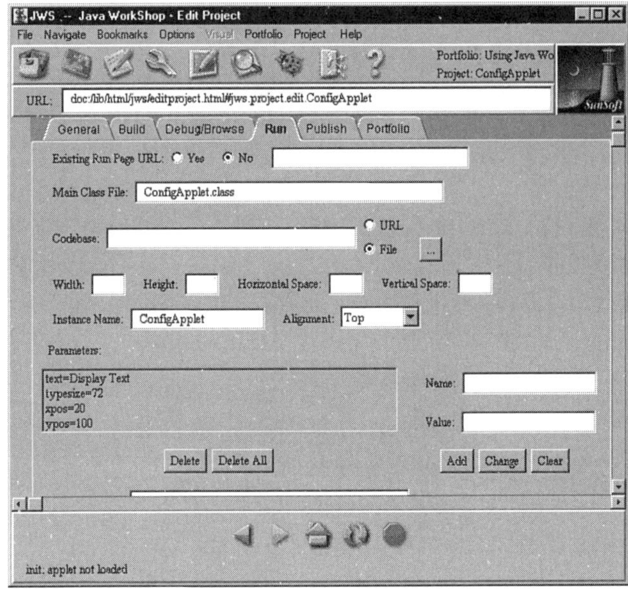

FIG. 10.9
You must specify four parameters for ConfigApplet2.

NOTE Because the `getParameter()` method always returns a string, you may have to convert some parameters before you can use them in your applet. For example, the ConfigApplet2 applet must convert its `typesize`, `xpos`, and `ypos` parameters from strings to integers.

Listing 10.10 The ConfigApplet2 Applet

```
import java.awt.*;
import java.applet.*;

public class ConfigApplet2 extends Applet
{
    String str;
    Point position;

    public void init()
    {
        String s;

        str = getParameter("text");

        s = getParameter("typesize");
        int typeSize = Integer.parseInt(s);
```

```
        s = getParameter("xpos");
        int xpos = Integer.parseInt(s);

        s = getParameter("ypos");
        int ypos = Integer.parseInt(s);

        position = new Point(xpos, ypos);

        Font font = new Font("TimesRoman", Font.BOLD, typeSize);
        setFont(font);
    }

    public void paint(Graphics g)
    {
        g.drawString(str, position.x, position.y);
    }
}
```


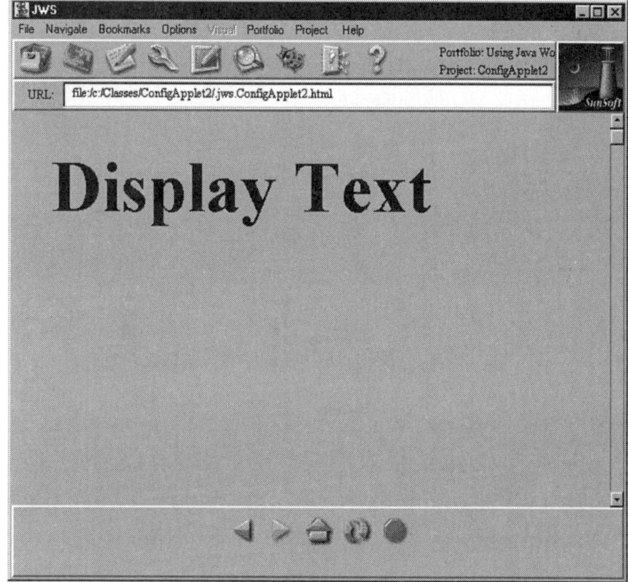

FIG. 10.10 This applet accepts four parameters that determine how the text is displayed.

Suppose you were to change the parameters in the HTML file to those shown in listing 10.11. You'd then completely change the way the text string is displayed in the applet, as shown in figure 10.11. As you can see, parameters can have a profound effect on the way an applet looks and acts.

Listing 10.11 New Parameters for ConfigApplet2

```
<PARAM NAME=text VALUE="New Text String">
<PARAM NAME=typesize VALUE=18>
<PARAM NAME=xpos VALUE=60>
<PARAM NAME=ypos VALUE=150>
```

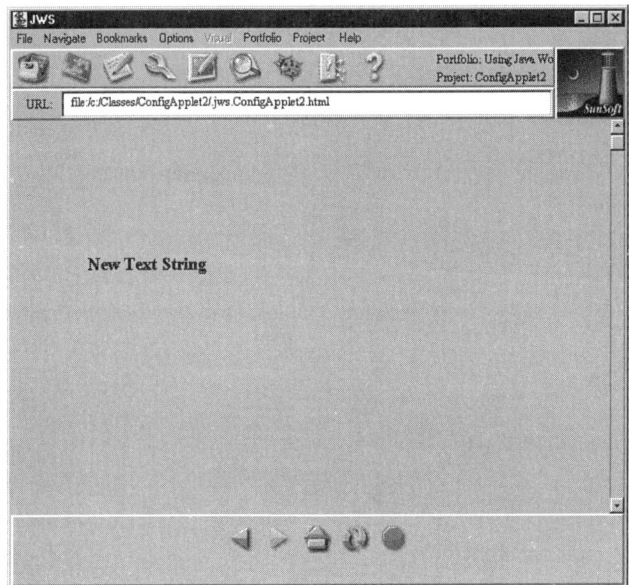

FIG. 10.11
Here's ConfigApplet2 running with different parameters.

Default Parameter Values

You might have noticed by now that there's a big problem with the ConfigApplet and ConfigApplet2 applets. Neither applet checks to ensure that the parameters it tries to retrieve exist. For example, what happens when the user who's writing the HTML document forgets to include the `text` parameter?

Relying on other people to provide your applet with the data it needs is a dangerous practice. Your applet should always check the validity of values returned from the `getParameter()` method. At the very least, you should be sure that the returned value is not null, which is the value `getParameter()` returns when a particular parameter doesn't exist (that is, the user forgot to define it in the HTML document or deliberately left it out, assuming that the applet will automatically use a default value for the missing one).

To ensure that your applet is in a runnable state after retrieving parameters, you must always check the parameter's values and supply default values for those parameters that are missing or invalid. For example, to make sure that your applet has a text string to display, you might use lines like this:

```
str = getParameter("text");
if (str == null)
    str = "Default Text";
```

NOTE If you decide to release your applets so other people can use them in their Web pages, be sure that you include a separate documentation file that describes the applet's parameters and shows how to use them.

You can now extend the ConfigApplet2 so that it provides default values for each parameter. When you've done this, the applet can run without generating errors no matter what parameters the user chooses to include or ignore. Listing 10.12 is the new version, called ConfigApplet3.

Notice that although the program now checks for missing parameters, it doesn't limit the values to any ranges or otherwise check their validity. Because the `text` parameter will always be a string, there's really nothing you need to check for (except null). However, you may want to limit the font size or make sure that the display location is inside the applet's window.

Listing 10.12 This Applet Provides Default Values for All Parameters

```
import java.awt.*;
import java.applet.*;

public class ConfigApplet3 extends Applet
{
    String str;
    Point position;

    public void init()
    {
        HandleTextParam();
        HandleTypeSizeParam();
        HandlePositionParam();
    }
```

continues

Listing 10.12 Continued

```
    public void paint(Graphics g)
    {
        g.drawString(str, position.x, position.y);
    }

    protected void HandleTextParam()
    {
        str = getParameter("text");
        if (str == null)
            str = "Default Text";
    }

    protected void HandleTypeSizeParam()
    {
        String s = getParameter("typesize");
        if (s == null)
            s = "24";
        int typeSize = Integer.parseInt(s);

        Font font = new Font("TimesRoman", Font.BOLD, typeSize);
        setFont(font);
    }

    protected void HandlePositionParam()
    {
        String s = getParameter("xpos");
        if (s == null)
            s = "20";
        int xpos = Integer.parseInt(s);

        s = getParameter("ypos");
        if (s == null)
            s = "50";
        int ypos = Integer.parseInt(s);

        position = new Point(xpos, ypos);
    }
}
```

From Here...

Because the keyboard and the mouse are two of the most important devices for accepting input from the user, it's important that you know how to handle these devices in your applets. Maybe most of your applets will work fine by leaving such details up to Java or maybe you'll want to have more control over the devices than the default behavior allows. You can capture most messages received by a Java applet by overloading the appropriate event handlers, such as `mouseDown()` and `keyDown()`. However, if you want to step back even further in your event-handling code, you can override the `handleEvent()` method, which receives all events sent to an applet.

By supporting parameters, your applets are more flexible, which makes it easier for other people to incorporate them into their Web-page designs. Even if you don't plan to release your applets, using parameters can make your applets more powerful and your own Web pages easier to fine tune. Using the <PARAM> tag is more sensible than having to reprogram and recompile an applet every time you want it to do something slightly different. Keep in mind, though, that all parameters must have default values built into the applet's source code. Otherwise, you could end up with an error-ridden applet, something that won't do much for your reputation as a Java guru.

For more information on related topics, please refer to the following chapters:

- Chapter 1, "Java Overview," explains how HTML documents load and run Java applets.
- Chapter 5, "Object-Oriented Programming and Java," provides step-by-step instructions for creating applet projects with Java Workshop.

CHAPTER 11

Images, Sounds, and Communications

If you've seen the applets that are floating around, you've undoubtedly noticed that many feature vivid graphics and even sound effects. When programming in a language such as C++, displaying graphics and playing sounds can be infamously difficult, thanks to the fact that these languages provide no direct support for handling these types of files. Even the Windows API, as immense as it is, provides little help when it comes to dealing with these graphical and aural chores. Java, on the other hand, was designed to make creating applets as easy as possible. For that reason, Java's classes handle almost all the difficulties associated with displaying images (commonly called bitmaps) and playing sounds. In the sections that follow, you'll use Java's power to add images and sounds to your applets. You'll also learn how to connect to Web sites from within an applet. ■

How to load and display images.

Applets can easily load and display GIF and JPEG types of images, thanks to Java's `Image` class.

How to add sound effects to an applet.

Java also features methods and classes for playing sound files from within an applet. By combining sounds and images, you can create attractive and useful applets.

How to gain greater control over sounds.

The easiest way to control a sound is simply to play it. However, Java's `AudioClip` class has extra abilities that give you added control over how your applet handles sound effects.

How to create `URL` objects.

Objects of Java's `URL` class enable you to reference Web locations from an applet.

How to connect to Web sites from an applet.

Once your applet has created an `URL` object, you can connect to the Internet and display the page referenced by the URL.

Image Types

In the world of computers, there are many types of images, each of which is associated with a specific file format. These image types are usually identified by their file extensions, which include PCX, BMP, GIF, JPEG (or JPG), TIFF (or TIF), TGA, and more. Each of these file types was created by third-party software companies to use with their products, but many became popular enough to grow into standards. The PCX graphics file type, for example, began as the format for PC Paintbrush files, whereas BMP files are usually associated with the Windows graphical interface.

If you were writing your Internet applications using a more conventional language like C++, you could choose to support whatever image type was most convenient for your use. This is because you'd have to write all the file-loading code from scratch, anyway. Java, on the other hand, comes complete with classes that are capable of loading image files for you. This convenience comes with a small price, however, since Java can load only GIF and JPEG image file formats. In this book, you'll use GIF files, which are more common, although JPEG files are rapidly gaining a reputation, especially for high-resolution, true-color images.

Loading and Displaying an Image

The first step in displaying an image in your applet is to load the image from disk. To do this, you must create an object of Java's `Image` class. This is easy to do; however, in order to do so, you need to create an `URL` object that holds the location of the graphics file. You could just type the image's URL directly into your Java source code. If you do this, however, you have to change and recompile the applet whenever you move the graphics file to a different directory on your disk. A better way to create the image's `URL` object is to call either the `getDocumentBase()` or `getCodeBase()` method. The former returns the URL of the directory from which the current HTML file was loaded, whereas the latter returns the URL of the directory from which the applet was run.

Using the *getDocumentBase()* Method

As mentioned previously, the `getDocumentBase()` method returns the URL of the directory from which the HTML document was loaded. If you're storing your images in the same directory (or a subdirectory of that directory) as your HTML files, you'd want to use this method to obtain an URL for an image.

Suppose you have your HTML documents in a directory called PUBLIC and the image you want, called IMAGE.GIF, is stored in a subdirectory of PUBLIC called IMAGES. A call to `getDocumentBase()` will get you the appropriate base URL. That call looks like this:

```
URL url = getDocumentBase();
```

As you'll soon see, once you have the URL, you can load the file by using the URL along with the relative location of the image, which in this case would be IMAGES/IMAGE.GIF. The full URL to the file would then be FILE:/C:/PUBLIC/IMAGES/IMAGE.GIF. If you decided to move your public files to a directory called MYHOMEPAGE, the call to `getDocumentBase()` will give you the URL for that new directory, without your having to change the applet's source code. This new URL, once you included the relative location of the image file, would be FILE:/C:/MYHOMEPAGE/IMAGES/IMAGE.GIF.

Using the *getCodeBase()* Method

The `getCodeBase()` method works similarly to `getDocumentBase()`, except that it returns the URL of the directory from which the applet was loaded. If you're storing your images in the same directory (or a subdirectory of that directory) as your .class files, you'd want to call `getCodeBase()` to obtain an URL for an image.

Suppose you have your .class files in a directory called CLASSES and the image you want (still called IMAGE.GIF) is stored in a subdirectory of CLASSES called IMAGES. A call to `getCodeBase()` will get you the base URL you need to load the image. That call looks like this:

```
URL url = getCodeBase();
```

Again, once you have the URL, you can load the file by using the URL along with the relative location of the image, which would still be IMAGES/IMAGE.GIF. The full URL to the file would then be FILE:/C:/CLASSES/IMAGES/IMAGE.GIF.

Loading an Image

Once you have the image's base URL, you're ready to load the image and create the `Image` object. You can complete both of these tasks at the same time by calling your applet's `getImage()` method, like this:

```
Image image = getImage(baseURL, relLocation);
```

The `getImage()` method's two arguments are the `URL` returned by your call to `getCodeBase()` or `getDocumentBase()` and the relative location of the image. For example, assuming that you've stored your .class files in the directory C:\CLASSES and your images in the directory C:\CLASSES\IMAGES, you'd have a code that looks something like this:

```
URL codeBase = getCodeBase();
Image myImage = getImage(codeBase, "images/myimage.gif");
```

After Java has executed the above lines, your image is loaded into the computer's memory and is ready to display.

Displaying an Image

Displaying the image is a simple matter of calling the Graphics object's `drawImage()` method, like this:

```
g.drawImage(myImage, x, y, width, height, this);
```

This method's arguments are the image object to display, the X and Y coordinates at which to display the image, the width and height of the image, and the applet's `this` reference.

When you want to display an image with its normal width and height, you can call a simpler version of the `drawImage()` method, which leaves out the width and height arguments, like this: `drawImage(image, x, y, this)`. This version of the method actually draws the image faster because it doesn't have to worry about reducing or expanding the image to the given width and height. It just blasts it onto the screen exactly as the image normally appears.

You may be wondering where you can get the width and height of the image. As it turns out (no doubt thanks to careful consideration by Java's programmers over hundreds of cups of coffee), the `Image` class has two methods, `getWidth()` and getHeight(), that return the width and height of the image. The complete code for displaying the image, then, might look like this:

```
int width = image.getWidth(this);
int height = image.getHeight(this);
g.drawImage(image, x, y, width, height, this);
```

As you can see, the getWidth() and getHeight() methods require a single argument, which is the applet's this reference.

You're now ready to write an applet that can display images. Listing 11.1 is the Java source code for an applet called ImageApplet that displays a small image using the techniques described previously in this chapter. When you run the applet with Java Workshop, you see the window shown in figure 11.1. Make sure the SNAKE.GIF image is in the same directory as the ImageApplet.class file, since that's where the program expects to find it.

Listing 11.1 An Applet That Displays an Image

```
import java.awt.*;
import java.applet.*;
import java.net.*;

public class ImageApplet extends Applet
{
    Image snake;

    public void init()
    {
        URL codeBase = getCodeBase();
        snake = getImage(codeBase, "snake.gif");
        resize(250, 250);
    }

    public void paint(Graphics g)
    {
        int width = snake.getWidth(this);
        int height = snake.getHeight(this);

        g.drawRect(52, 52, width+10, height+10);
        g.drawImage(snake, 57, 57, width, height, this);
    }
}
```

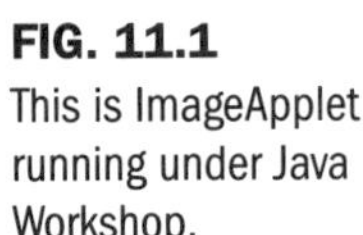

FIG. 11.1
This is ImageApplet running under Java Workshop.

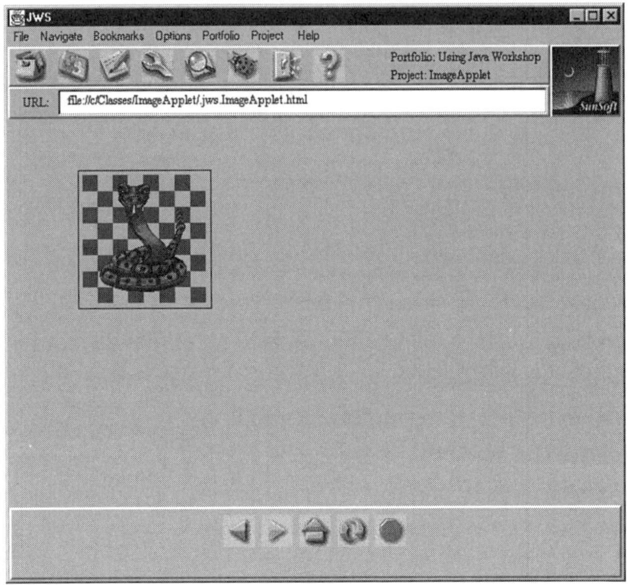

Notice how the applet imports the classes in the `net` package, which is where the `URL` class lives. If you fail to include this line at the top of the program, Java will be unable to find the `URL` class and the applet will not compile.

TIP By using different values for the `drawImage()` method's width and height arguments, you can display an image at any size you like. For example, to display an image at twice its normal size, just use 2*width and 2*height for the width and height arguments. To display the image at half its normal size, use width/2 and height/2. Figure 11.2 shows the snake image displayed at twice its normal size using Appletviewer. It doesn't even fit in the window!

FIG. 11.2
Here's the snake image at twice its size.

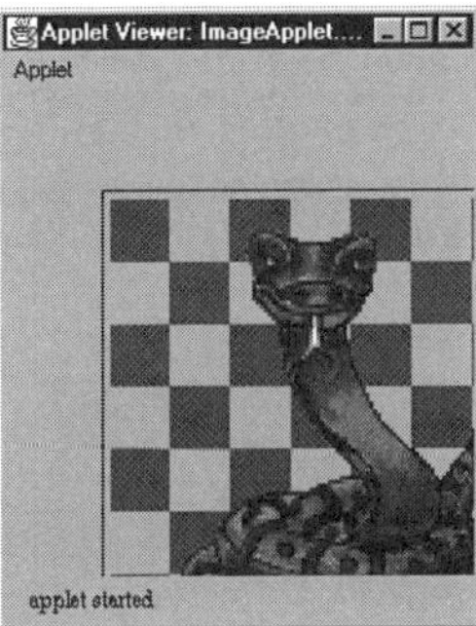

Playing a Sound

Just as there are many types of image files, so too are there many types of sound files. But, when it comes to applets, the only type of sound file you need to know about is the audio file, which has the file extension AU. This type of sound file, popularized on UNIX machines, is the only type of sound file that Java can currently load and play.

When you want to play a sound from beginning to end, you only have to call `getDocumentBase()` or `getCodeBase()` for the URL and then call `play()` to play the sound. A call to `play()` looks like this:

```
play(baseURL, relLocation);
```

The `play()` method's two arguments are the `URL` returned from a call to `getDocumentBase()` or `getCodeBase()` and the relative location of the sound file.

```
URL codeBase = getCodeBase();
play(codeBase, "audio/sound.au");
```


Playing a Sound in an Applet

Now you're ready to write an applet that plays a sound file. Listing 11.2 is the applet in question, called SoundApplet. When you run the applet with Java Workshop, you'll see the window shown in figure 11.3. Just click the button to hear the sound. Of course, you need to have a sound card properly installed on your system. You also must be sure that the SPACEMUSIC.AU (included with the Java Developer's Kit) sound file is in the same directory as the applet.

Listing 11.2 An Applet That Plays a Sound File

```
import java.awt.*;
import java.applet.*;
import java.net.*;

public class SoundApplet extends Applet
{
    Button button;

    public void init()
    {
```

continues

Listing 11.2 Continued

```
        BorderLayout layout = new BorderLayout();
        setLayout(layout);

        Font font = new Font("TimesRoman", Font.BOLD, 32);
        setFont(font);

        button = new Button("Play Sound");
        add("Center", button);

        resize(250, 250);
    }

    public boolean action(Event evt, Object arg)
    {
        if (evt.target instanceof Button)
        {
            URL codeBase = getCodeBase();
            play(codeBase, "spacemusic.au");
        }

        return true;
    }
}
```

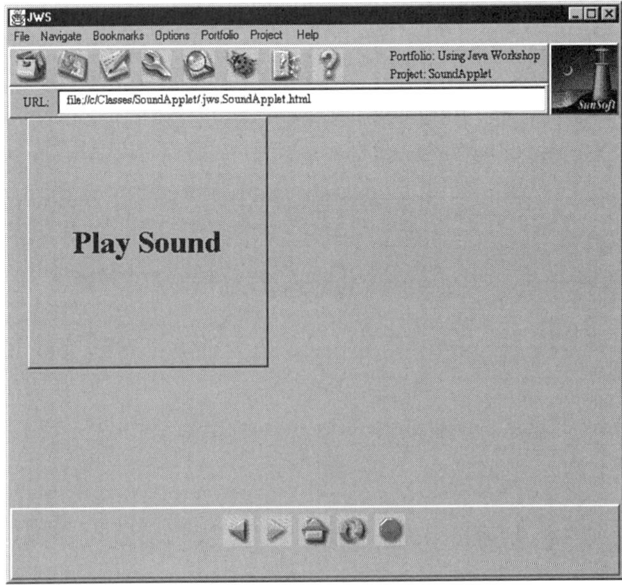

FIG. 11.3
Click the button to hear the applet's sound file.

Controlling Sounds

Although the applet's `play()` method is the easiest way to load and play sounds, it doesn't give you much control. You have only one option: play the sound from the beginning to the end. If you want a little more control over your sounds, you can create an `AudioClip` object and use the object's methods to control the sound. Unfortunately, even the `AudioClip` class doesn't give you much power, although you can play, stop, and loop the sound.

To create the AudioClip object, call the `getAudioClip()` method, like this:

```
AudioClip audioClip = getAudioClip(baseURL, relLocation);
```

This method's two arguments are the sound file's base URL and relative location.

Once you have the `AudioClip` object created and loaded, you can call its methods to control the sound. There are only three from which to choose: `play()`, `stop()`, and `loop()`. The `play()` method plays the sound once from the beginning to the end, `stop()` stops the sound whether or not it has finished playing, and `loop()` causes the sound to keep repeating until it's stopped.

Using an Audio Clip in an Applet

Although using audio clips is a little more complicated than simply loading and playing a sound using the applet's `play()` method, it's still a straightforward process. Listing 11.3 is an applet that creates an `AudioClip` object and enables the user to send commands to the object using the applet's command buttons. When you run the applet with Java Workshop, you see the window shown in figure 11.4. To play the sound once from the beginning to the end, click the Play button. To stop the sound at any time, click the Stop button. Finally, to play the sound over and over, click the Loop button.

Listing 11.3 An Applet That Creates and Displays an *AudioClip* object

```
import java.awt.*;
import java.applet.*;
import java.net.*;

public class SoundApplet2 extends Applet
```

continues

Listing 11.3 Continued

```
{
    AudioClip soundClip;

    public void init()
    {
        GridLayout layout = new GridLayout(1, 3, 10, 10);
        setLayout(layout);

        Font font = new Font("TimesRoman", Font.BOLD, 24);
        setFont(font);

        Button button = new Button("Play");
        add(button);
        button = new Button("Stop");
        add(button);
        button = new Button("Loop");
        add(button);

        URL codeBase = getCodeBase();
        soundClip = getAudioClip(codeBase, "spacemusic.au");

        resize(250, 250);
    }

    public boolean action(Event evt, Object arg)
    {
        if (arg == "Play")
            soundClip.play();
        else if (arg == "Stop")
            soundClip.stop();
        else if (arg == "Loop")
            soundClip.loop();

        return true;
    }
}
```

FIG. 11.4
This is Java Workshop running SoundApplet2.

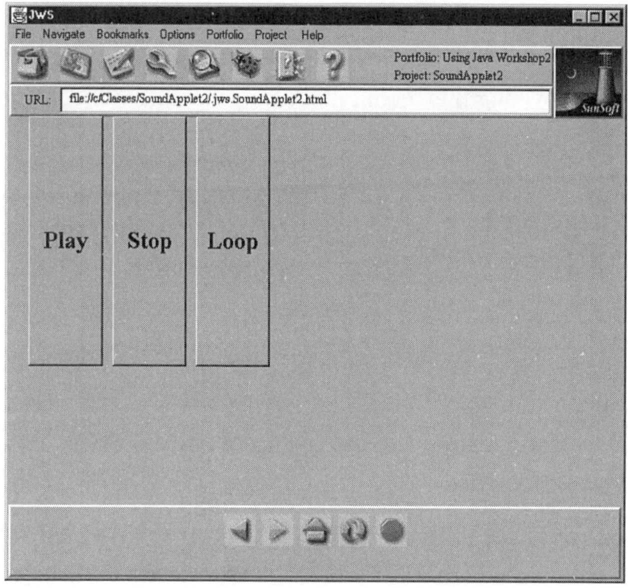

Communications

Not to state the obvious, but because applets are used on the Internet, they have the ability to perform a few types of telecommunications tasks. One of these tasks, connecting to other Web sites, is a snap to implement. Other tasks, such as accessing data in files, are difficult to implement because you constantly stumble over the security restrictions built into applets. Dealing with the intricacies of Internet security is beyond the scope of this book. If you're interested in this topic, you should pick up an advanced Java book. In the sections that follow, though, you'll get a chance to use Java to communicate over the Internet by connecting to URLs that the user supplies.

URL Objects

In the previous sections of this chapter, you got a quick introduction to `URL` objects when you obtained the location of graphics and sound files by calling the `getDocumentBase()` and `getCodeBase()` methods. You used the `URL` objects returned by these methods to display images and play sounds that were stored on your computer. In that case, the locations of the files were on your own system. What you didn't know then is that you can create an `URL` object directly by calling its constructor. Using this technique, you can create `URL` objects that represent other sites on the World Wide Web.

Although the `URL` class's constructor has several forms, the easiest to use requires a string argument holding the URL from which you want to create the object. Using this constructor, you create the `URL` object like this:

```
URL url = new URL(str);
```

This constructor's single argument is the complete URL of the location to which you want to connect. This URL string must be properly constructed or the URL constructor will throw an exception (generate an error). You'll soon learn what to do about such errors.

Suppose you want to create an URL object for the URL **http://www.sun.com**, which is where you can find lots of information about Java. You'd create the `URL` object like this:

```
URL url = new URL("http://www.sun.com");
```

If the `URL` construction goes okay, you can then use the `URL` object however you need to in your applet.

URL Exceptions

As mentioned previously, if the argument for the `URL` constructor is in error (meaning that it doesn't use valid URL syntax), the `URL` class throws an exception. Because the `URL` class is designed to throw an exception when necessary, Java gives you no choice except to handle that exception properly. This prevents the applet from accidentally attempting to use a defective `URL` object. You'll learn all the details about handling exceptions in Chapter 12, "Packages, Interfaces, Exceptions, and Threads." For now, though, you need to know how to handle the `URL` exception because your applets will not compile properly until you add the exception-handling code.

Basically, when you need to watch out for an exception, you enclose the code that may generate the error in a `try` program block. If the code in the block generates an exception, you handle that exception in a `catch` program block. (It's no coincidence that when code "throws" an exception, Java expects the program to "catch" that exception.) When you create an `URL` object from a string, you must watch out for the `MalformedURLException` exception, which is one of the many exceptions defined by Java. To do this, use the `try` and `catch` program blocks, as shown in listing 11.4.

Listing 11.4 Handing *URL* Exceptions

```
try
{
    URL url = new URL(str);
}
catch (MalformedURLException e)
{
    DisplayErrorMessage();
}
```


The Applet Context

Once you have the `URL` object created, you need a way to pass it on to the browser in which the applet is running. It is the browser, after all, that will make the Web connection for you. But, how do you refer to the browser from within your applet? You call the `getAppletContext()` method, which returns an `AppletContext` object. This `AppletContext` object represents the browser in which the applet is running. You call `getAppletContext()` like this:

```
AppletContext context = getAppletContext();
```

Once you have the context, you can link to the URL represented by the `URL` object you already created. You do this by calling the `AppletContext` object's `showDocument()` method, like this:

```
context.showDocument(url);
```

If all goes well, the above line will connect you to the requested URL.

Using an *AppletContext* to Link to an URL

Suppose that you want to enable the user to enter an URL string in your applet and then use `URL` and `AppletContext` objects to link to that URL. Listing 11.5 shows how you might accomplish this feat of Internet magic:

Listing 11.5 Linking to an URL

```
String str = GetURLStringFromUser();

try
{
    URL url = new URL(str);
    AppletContext context = getAppletContext();
    context.showDocument(url);
}
catch (MalformedURLException e)
{
    DisplayErrorMessage();
}
```

In listing 11.5, the program first calls a method that retrieves a text string from the user. This text string is the URL to which the user wants to connect. Then, the `try` program block starts. The first line inside the `try` block attempts to create an `URL` object from the string the user entered. Of course, because users often make mistakes when typing in long strings of characters, the string the user entered may not be a syntactically valid URL. In that case, program execution automatically jumps to the `catch` program block, where your applet displays an appropriate error message. If the `URL` object gets created okay, though, the program finishes the code in the `try` block, getting the `AppletContext` object and making the link to the URL. In this case, Java completely ignores the `catch` block.

Using an *AppletContext* in an Applet

Ready for a full-fledged example? Listing 11.6 is a complete applet that enables the user to link to an URL. Because this applet actually interacts with a browser and the Internet, you must have made your Internet connection before running the applet. Then, to run the applet, load its HTML document into a Java-compatible browser such as Netscape Navigator 2.0. When you do, you'll see a window similar to that shown in figure 11.5. In this figure, the user has already entered the URL he wishes to visit. In figure 11.6, the browser has made the requested connection. Figure 11.7 shows the browser when the user enters an invalid URL string.

Listing 11.6 An Applet That Connects to User-requested URLs

```
import java.awt.*;
import java.applet.*;
import java.net.*;

public class ConnectApplet extends Applet
{
    TextField textField;
    boolean badURL;

    public void init()
    {
        textField = new TextField("", 40);
        Button button = new Button("Connect");

        add(textField);
        add(button);

        badURL = false;
    }

    public void paint(Graphics g)
    {
        Font font = new Font("TimesRoman", Font.PLAIN, 24);
        g.setFont(font);

        int height = font.getSize();

        if (badURL)
            g.drawString("Bad URL!", 60, 130);
        else
        {
            g.drawString("Type the URL to which", 25, 130);
            g.drawString("you want to connect,",
                25, 130+height);
            g.drawString("and then click the Connect",
                25, 130+height*2);
            g.drawString("button.", 25, 130 + height*3);
        }
    }

    public boolean action(Event evt, Object arg)
    {
        String str = textField.getText();

        try
        {
```

continues

Listing 11.6 Continued

```
                URL url = new URL(str);
                AppletContext context = getAppletContext();
                context.showDocument(url);
            }
            catch (MalformedURLException e)
            {
                badURL = true;
                repaint();
            }

            return true;
        }
    }
```

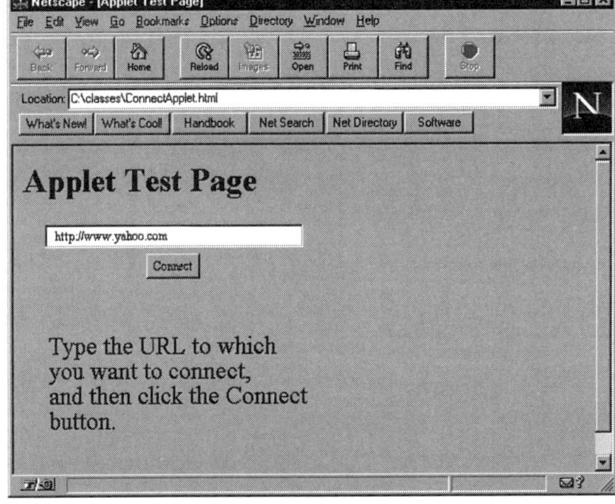

FIG. 11.5 Here, the user is ready to make a connection.

FIG. 11.6
If the URL is okay, the browser connects.

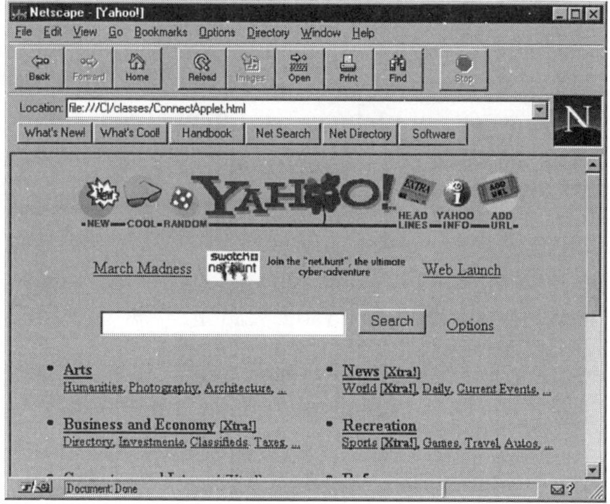

FIG. 11.7
If the URL is constructed improperly, the applet displays an error message.

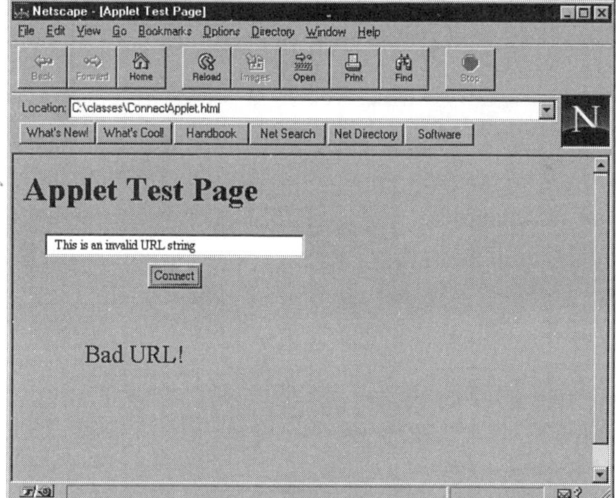

Creating a "Favorite URLs" Applet

Nothing, of course, says that the string from which you create an URL object must be typed in by the user at runtime. You can hard-code the URLs you want to use right in the applet's source code, which not only ensures that the URLs will always be correct (unless the associated server changes), but also makes it quick and easy to jump to whatever URL you want. Using this idea, you can put together an applet that gives you push-button control over your connections, selecting your URLs as easily as you'd select a radio station.

The ConnectApplet2 applet, shown in listing 11.7, is just such an applet. In its current version, it provides four buttons that give you instant connection to the Web sites represented by the buttons. Want to jump to Microsoft's Web page? Give the Microsoft button a click. Want to check out the latest news at Macmillan Computer Publishing? Click the Macmillan button. Of course, just as with the original ConnectApplet, you must have your Internet connection established before you run the applet. And, you must run the applet from a Java-compatible browser.

When you run the applet from Netscape Navigator 2.0, you see the window shown in figure 11.8. As you can see, the applet currently displays four buttons, one each for the Sun, Netscape, Microsoft, and Macmillan Web sites. Just click a button to jump to the associated site. (Figure 11.9 shows the browser after the user has clicked the Macmillan button.) When you're through with that site, use the browser's Back button to return to the ConnectApplet2 applet. Then, choose another site.

Sure, you can do the same sort of thing with an HTML document using Web links. But, let's face it, applets are a lot more fun.

Listing 11.7 A "Favorite URLs" Applet

```
import java.awt.*;
import java.applet.*;
import java.net.*;

public class ConnectApplet2 extends Applet
{
    boolean badURL;

    public void init()
    {
```

```
        GridLayout layout = new GridLayout(2, 2, 10, 10);
        setLayout(layout);

        Font font = new Font("TimesRoman", Font.PLAIN, 24);
        setFont(font);

        Button button = new Button("Sun");
        add(button);
        button = new Button("Netscape");
        add(button);
        button = new Button("Microsoft");
        add(button);
        button = new Button("Macmillan");
        add(button);

        badURL = false;
    }

    public void paint(Graphics g)
    {
        if (badURL)
            g.drawString("Bad URL!", 60, 130);
    }

    public boolean action(Event evt, Object arg)
    {
        String str;

        if (arg == "Sun")
            str = "http://www.sun.com";
        else if (arg == "Netscape")
            str = "http://www.netscape.com";
        else if (arg == "Microsoft")
            str = "http://www.microsoft.com";
        else
            str = "http://www.mcp.com";

        try
        {
            URL url = new URL(str);
            AppletContext context = getAppletContext();
            context.showDocument(url);
        }
        catch (MalformedURLException e)
        {
            badURL = true;
            repaint();
        }

        return true;
    }
}
```

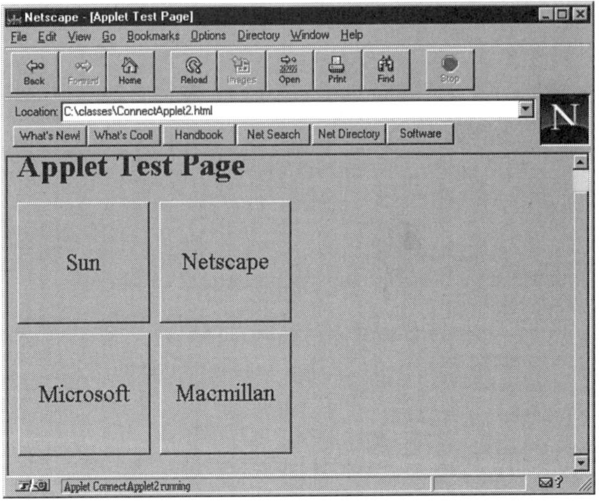

FIG. 11.8 ConnectApplet2 running under Netscape Navigator 2.0.

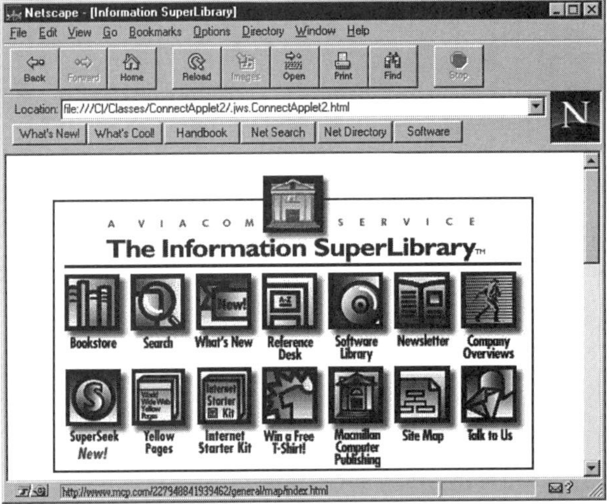

FIG. 11.9 This is ConnectApplet2 after the user has clicked the Macmillan button.

In listing 11.7, notice how, even though the URLs are hard-coded into the program, the `action()` method still surrounds the call to the `URL` constructor with the `try` and `catch` program blocks. This is because Java insists that the applet handles the exception if the `URL` class throws it. If you remove the exception handling, the applet won't compile. Anyway, having a little extra protection never hurts. Handling the exception is a good way to test whether your hard-coded URLs are valid. I've never known a programmer yet who didn't need to be protected from himself!

From Here...

Nothing spices up an applet more than vivid graphics and enjoyable sound effects. That's why Java's creators went to such lengths to ensure that you can easily add these important elements to your applets. Loading and displaying an image is as simple as obtaining the image's base URL, creating an `Image` object, and calling `drawImage()` to display the image on the screen. Sound effects are just as easy—if not easier—to handle. The simplest way is to call the applet's `play()` method, which will play the sound from the beginning to the end. However, if you want a little extra control over the sound, you can create an `AudioClip` object, whose methods enable you to play, stop, and loop the sound.

Although a running applet has to deal with many security considerations, it can usually connect to other Web sites. To do this, the applet creates an `URL` object representing the site to which the applet should connect. The applet then instructs the browser containing the applet to make the connection by calling the `AppletContext` object's `showDocument()` method. In spite of the telecommunications limitations inherent in applets, you can easily create Internet-aware applets.

For related information on the topics covered in this chapter, please refer to the following:

- Chapter 5, "Object-Oriented Programming and Java," tells you more about classes and how they're used in Java, as well as how to create, compile, and run applets using Java Workshop.
- Chapter 6, "Applets and Graphics," describes how to draw graphical shapes, which you can use along with images and sounds to create your applets' complete display.
- Chapter 7, "Java Controls," shows how to create and program Java's many controls, such as the buttons and text boxes you used in this chapter's applets.
- Chapter 8, "Panels and the Layout Manager," explains how to position applet display elements, which can be images or any other type of Java component.
- Chapter 13, "Writing Java Applications," describes how to use Java to create stand-alone applications in which you can also use images, sounds, or URLs.

CHAPTER 12

Packages, Interfaces, Exceptions, and Threads

How to organize your own classes into packages.

Java uses packages to create libraries of classes. You can do the same thing with the custom classes you write.

About using interfaces.

Java doesn't allow multiple inheritance. However, by using interfaces, you can attain much the same result you'd get by deriving a class from multiple base classes.

How to respond to exceptions.

Exceptions signal your applet that something went wrong. By handling exceptions, you can make your applets virtually bulletproof.

How to create and manage threads.

By using threads, your applet can handle more than one task concurrently.

About synchronizing threads.

When you start using threads, you'll quickly discover that some parts of your program should not be accessed by more than one thread at a time. Thread synchronization solves this problem.

As you write more and more Java source code, it's going to become difficult to find the snippets of code you need for your current project. You may, for example, have a number of classes that are related in some way, yet are scattered in separate files making it difficult to determine exactly what you have. One solution to this problem is *packages*, which enable you to organize your classes into logical groups.

You may also have a number of classes that contain capabilities that you'd like to use in a newly derived class. However, Java does not allow *multiple inheritance*, which is deriving a single class directly from two or more classes simultaneously. To get around this deliberate limitation,

Java uses something called *interfaces*, which enable the programmer to define capabilities for classes without implementing those capabilities until the classes that use the interface are defined.

When you write applets or applications using Java, sooner or later you're going to run into exceptions. An *exception* is a special type of error object that is created when something goes wrong in a program. After Java creates the exception object, it sends it to your program, which is an action called *throwing an exception*. It's up to your program to catch the exception. You do this by writing the exception-handling code.

Finally, when using Windows 95 (and other modern operating systems), you know that you can run several programs simultaneously. This ability is called *multitasking*. What you may not know is that many of today's operating systems also allow *threads*, which are separate processes that are kind of a step down from a complete application. A thread is a lot like a subprogram. An applet can create several threads—several different flows of execution—and run them concurrently. This is a lot like having multitasking inside multitasking. The user knows that he can run several applications at a time. The programmer knows that each application can run several threads at a time. ■

Packages

You may not realize it, but you've been using Java packages since the first applet you created. That's because all of Java's classes are organized into packages. You've been importing those packages into your source code with code similar to this:

```
import java.awt.*;
import java.applet.*;
```

If you examine either of these lines, you'll see that each starts with the word `java` followed by a package name and an asterisk, each element being separated by a dot. The use of the different names separated by the dots illustrates the hierarchy that Java's creators used when they created the Java packages. This hierarchy is used not only as a means of referring to class names in source code, but also as a way to organize the .class files that comprise a class library.

In the preceding two sample import lines, the asterisks mean that Java should import all of the classes of the awt and applet packages into the applet you're writing. If you want, you can streamline the import process by importing exactly the classes used in your source code. (When doing this, keep in mind that Java is case-sensitive.) You do this by replacing the asterisk with the name of the class you want to import. For example, to import only the `Button` class from the awt package, use this line:

```
import java.awt.Button;
```

However, because you frequently need to access more than a single class in a package, it's often more convenient to import all of the classes at once.

NOTE If you like, you can do without `import` statements. To do this, you need to use fully qualified package names when referring to a Java class. For example, to create a new button object, you could write `java.awt.Button button = new java.awt.Button(label)`. As you can see, however, such program lines become unwieldy, which is why Java supports the import statement. ■

Creating Your Own Packages

As you write your own classes, you're going to want to organize the related classes into packages just as Java does. You do this by organizing your classes into the appropriate folder hierarchy. For example, you may want to start with a folder called MyPackages in which you'll store the subdirectories and .class files that make up your class libraries. This folder should be in the folder in which your main source-code files are located. If you've been following the instructions given earlier in this book, you've been using a folder called Classes for this purpose.

To add a class to a package, put the following line at the top of the class's source code:

```
package PackageName;
```

Here, the keyword `package` tells Java that you want to add this class to a package. The name of this package will be `PackageName`. The `package` line must be the first line in the class's source code (except for blank lines or comments).

Suppose that you want to create a class called `DisplayClass` that returns a test string to be displayed in an applet. You want this class to be part of a package called `Display`. Listing 12.1 shows the source code for the `DisplayClass` class.

Listing 12.1 The *DisplayClass* Class

```
package MyPackages.Display;

public class DisplayClass
{
    public String GetDisplayText()
    {
        return "Display Text";
    }
}
```

NOTE When you examine listing 12.1, you may wonder how `DisplayClass` can reference Java's `String` class without including an `import` line at the top of the listing. The class gets away with this because Java automatically imports the `java.lang` package, where the `String` class is defined.

The first line of listing 12.1 determines not only the name of the package, but also the way it must be stored on your hard drive. That is, the DisplayClass.class file must end up in a folder called Display, which must be in a folder called MyPackages. To compile DisplayClass.java, follow these steps:

1. In your Classes folder, create a folder called Display. This is where you will store the source-code files and project file for the `Display` package.
2. Type in listing 12.1 and save it in the Display folder under the name DisplayClass.java.
3. Start Java Workshop and choose Project, Create, Java Package from the menu bar. The tabbed dialog box for packages appears in Java Workshop's display area.
4. Type **Display** in the Name text box. This is the new project's name.
5. Type **Display** in the Package Name text box. This is the new package's name.

6. Type **c:\Classes** in the Root Directory text box. This tells Java Workshop where to start the directory hierarchy for your package. In this case, after the package is created, you'll have the c:\Classes\MyPackages\Display folder hierarchy, which Java Workshop creates automatically based on the `package` line in your source code.
7. Type **c:\Classes\Display** in the Source Directory text box. This tells Java Workshop where the source code for the `Display` package is located, as well as where to store the project file Java Workshop will create.
8. Click the Yes button in the Existing Sources section. This tells Java Workshop that the source code has already been typed and placed in the Display folder.
9. Click the Add All in Directory button to add the source code to the project. Your DisplayClass.java file should appear in the Sources window, as shown in figure 12.1.
10. Click the Apply button to finalize the options you selected for the new package project.
11. Use Build Manager to compile the new package's source code (see fig. 12.2).

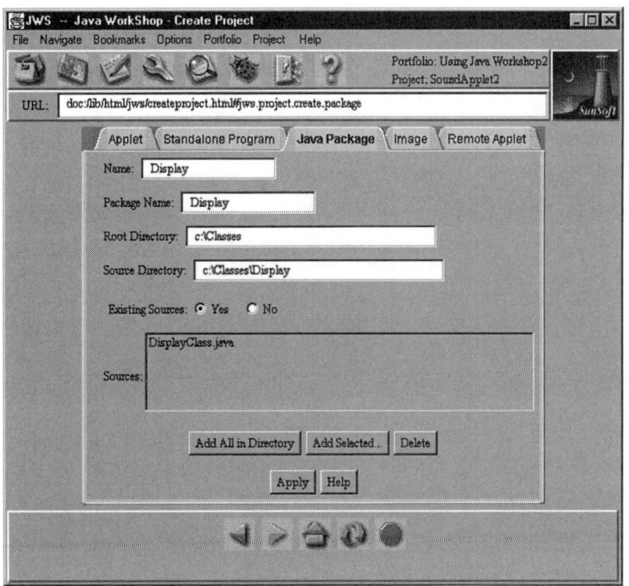

FIG. 12.1
The Sources pane shows the source-code files currently included in your project.

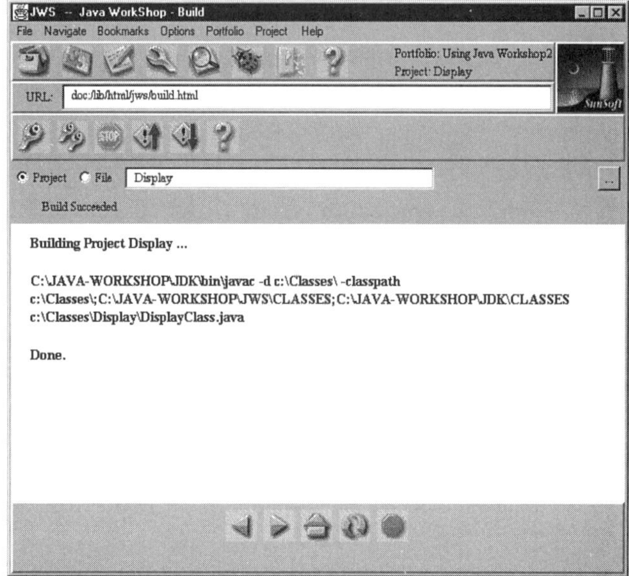

FIG. 12.2
Use Build Manager to compile the new package, just as with any other Java source code.

When you build the package, Java Workshop automatically creates the folders it needs for the package's folder hierarchy. That is, if you look in your Classes folder, you'll find the MyPackages\Display set of folders. Within c:\Classes\MyPackages\Display, you'll find the DisplayClass.class file, which is the compiled version of DisplayClass.java. Congratulations! You've just created your first package.

Using the New Package

Now that you've created a package, you'd probably like to use it in an applet. To do this, you must first import the class into the applet's source code file. You can then use the class exactly the same way you've been using Java's classes throughout this book. Listing 12.2 is an applet, called PackageApplet, that demonstrates how to use your new package.

Listing 12.2 An Applet That Uses the New Display Package

```
import java.awt.*;
import java.applet.*;
import MyPackages.Display.DisplayClass;
```

```
public class PackageApplet extends Applet
{
    String s;

    public void init()
    {
        Font font = new Font("TimesRoman", Font.PLAIN, 24);
        setFont(font);

        DisplayClass myClass = new DisplayClass();
        s = myClass.GetDisplayText();
    }

    public void paint(Graphics g)
    {
        g.drawString(s, 60, 80);
    }
}
```

Notice how the third line in listing 12.2 imports the `DisplayClass` class from the `Display` package. You also could have used the line import `MyPackages.Display.*`, as you did with the Java packages in the first two lines of the listing. Because there is currently only one class in the package, using the asterisk achieves exactly the same results as specifying the class's name in the import line. However, when you add other classes to the package, the asterisk will tell Java to include those classes, too.

To see how all this package stuff works with the PackageApplet applet, follow these steps:

1. Type in listing 12.2 and save it in your Classes folder (the same folder that contains your new MyPackages folder). If you prefer, you can copy the listings from this book's CD-ROM.
2. Create a new project for the applet, using the settings shown in figure 12.3.
3. Compile the applet using Build Manager.
4. Run the applet using Project Tester. You see the window shown in figure 12.4.

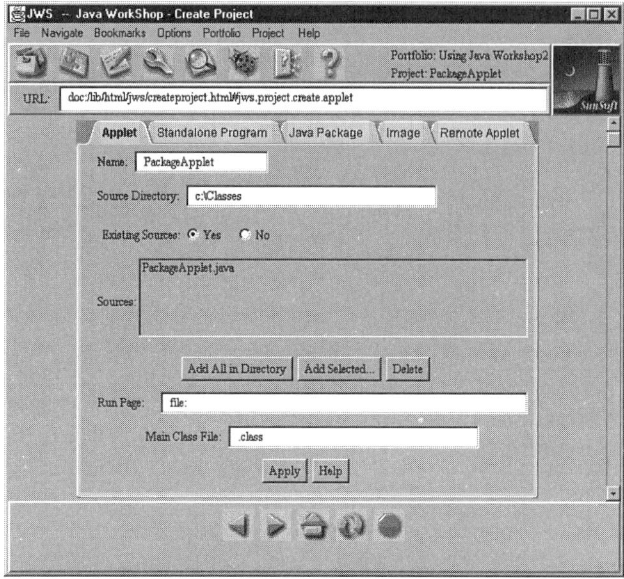

FIG. 12.3
The settings for the PackageApplet applet.

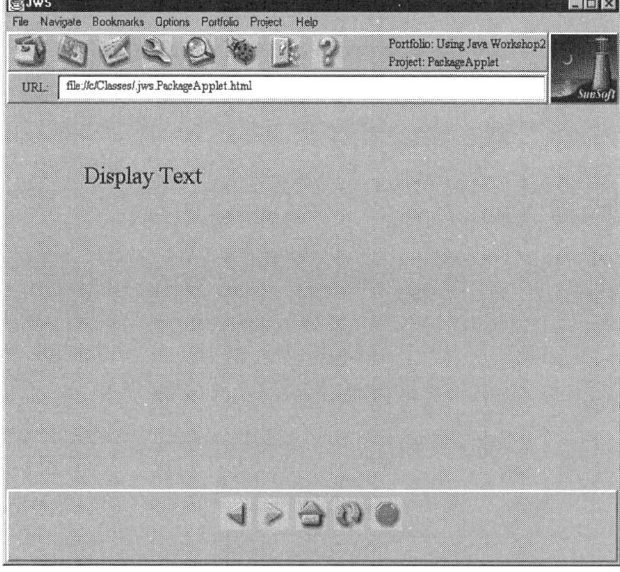

FIG. 12.4
This is PackageApplet running under Java Workshop.

When you run the PackageApplet applet, you see the window shown in figure 12.4. The text that's displayed in the applet is acquired by the call to the `DisplayClass` class's `GetDisplayText()` method. This class is part of your new `Display` class. When you run the applet, Java Workshop knows where to find the `Display` class because of the hierarchy of folders you created to mirror the `MyPackages.Display.DisplayClass` hierarchy. The folder hierarchy is, in fact, why you had to place the PackageApplet project in the Classes folder rather than a folder of its own (c:\Classes\PackageApplet) as you have with other projects so far in this book.

Extending the Package

Now that you have the package started, you can extend it simply by creating new classes that have the line package `MyPackages.Display` at the top of the source code. You store these source-code files in the Display folder. Thanks to the folder hierarchy you've developed, all of the .class files in the `Display` package will end up in the c:\Classes\MyPackages\Display folder. You can have one or a hundred. Follow these steps to add the `DisplayClass2` class to the `Display` package.

1. Type in listing 12.3 and save it in the `Display` folder, under the name DisplayClass2.java.
2. Start Java Workshop and choose Project, Edit, Display from the menu bar. The tabbed dialog box for editing the `Display` package appears in Java Workshop's display area.
3. Select the Build tab, and then click the Add All in Directory button to add the new `DisplayClass2` class to the Files In box (see fig. 12.5).
4. Click the Apply button to finalize your changes to the package. (You may have to scroll Java Workshop's window to see the Apply button.)
5. Use Build Manager to compile the new package's source code.

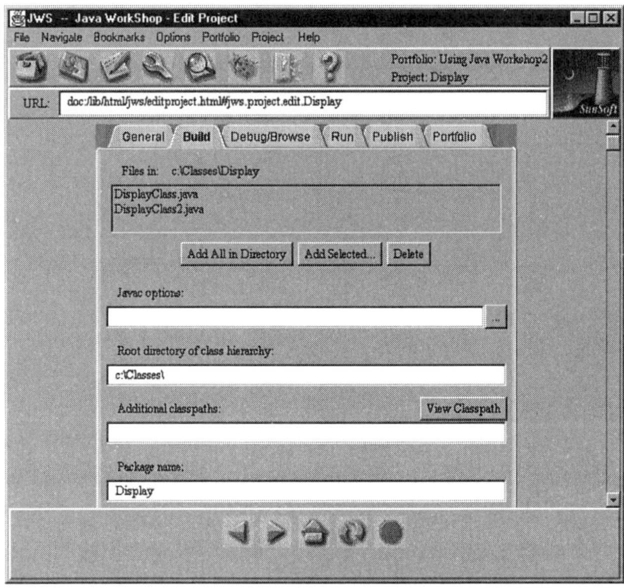

FIG. 12.5
The Build page of the tabbed dialog box enables you to add new classes to the package.

Listing 12.3 A Second Class for the *Display* Package

```
package MyPackages.Display;

public class DisplayClass2
{
    public String GetDisplayText()
    {
        return "More Display Text";
    }
}
```

When you're done with the previous steps, you'll have both the DisplayClass.class and DisplayClass2.class files in the c:\Classes\MyPackages\Display folder. To test the new class, you might use a program like the one shown in listing 12.4. Create PackageApplet2 similarly to how you created its predecessor, PackageApplet. When you run the applet under Java Workshop, you see the window shown in figure 12.6.

Listing 12.4 Using Both Classes in the *Display* Package

```
import java.awt.*;
import java.applet.*;
import MyPackages.Display.*;

public class PackageApplet2 extends Applet
{
    String s, s2;

    public void init()
    {
        Font font = new Font("TimesRoman", Font.PLAIN, 24);
        setFont(font);

        DisplayClass myClass = new DisplayClass();
        DisplayClass2 myClass2 = new DisplayClass2();
        s = myClass.GetDisplayText();
        s2 = myClass2.GetDisplayText();
    }

    public void paint(Graphics g)
    {
        g.drawString(s, 60, 80);
        g.drawString(s2, 60, 120);
    }
}
```


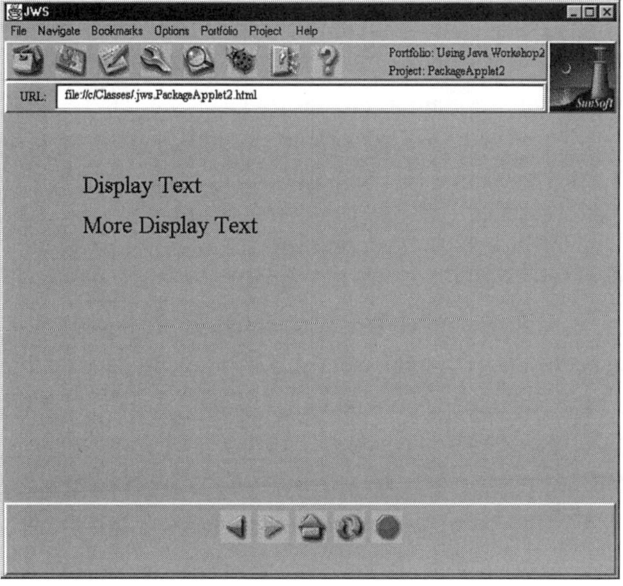

FIG. 12.6 This is PackageApplet2 running under Java Workshop.

Interfaces

Packages are fairly easy to understand, being little more than a way to organize related classes, whether supplied with Java or created by a programmer like yourself. Interfaces, on the other hand, are a concept that is a bit harder to grasp. To really understand Java's interfaces, you have to know about something called multiple inheritance, which is not allowed in Java, but which is often used in other object-oriented languages.

Multiple inheritance means creating a new class that inherits behavior directly from more than one superclass. To make this concept a little clearer, look at how you derive classes from superclasses in Java. For example, every applet you've created so far has been derived from Java's `Applet` class, like this:

```
public class AppletName extends Applet
```

The preceding line tells Java that you want to create a new class that inherits the data fields and methods of the `Applet` class. This is a sample of single inheritance. Now, suppose that you had a class of your own, called `MyClass`, that implemented some capabilities that you also want your new applet to inherit. In a language like C++, you simply add the class to a list of superclasses, like this:

```
public class AppletName extends Applet, MyClass
```

This would be an example of multiple inheritance if Java allowed such a thing. However, for many reasons, Java's designers decided that multiple inheritance was too cumbersome and unpredictable to be useful. They still liked the idea, though, of being able to declare a set of behaviors that can be inherited by one or more classes. So, they came up with interfaces.

The Basic Interface

An interface is very much like a class—with one important difference. None of the methods declared in an interface are implemented in the interface itself. Instead, these methods must be implemented in any class that uses the interface. In short, interfaces describe behaviors, but do not detail how those behaviors will be carried out.

Interfaces are so much like classes, in fact, that they are declared in almost exactly the same way. You just replace the `class` keyword with the `interface` keyword, like this:

```
interface MyInterface
{
}
```

The preceding example is a complete interface, meaning that it can be compiled, after which other Java programs can reference it. You compile an interface exactly the same way you compile a class. First, you save the interface's source code in a file with the .java extension. Then you use Java Workshop to compile the source code into byte-code form. Just like a normal class, the byte-code file will have the .class extension.

Missing from the preceding sample interface are the methods that describe the interface's behaviors. In the sections that follow, you'll learn how to add this important element to an interface.

Creating an Interface

Suppose that instead of creating a full-fledged class out of your `Display` package's `DisplayClass` class, you want to make it an interface. (Yes, just like classes, you can make interfaces part of a package.) Listing 12.5 shows how the source code would be modified.

Listing 12.5 Creating an Interface

```
package MyPackages.Display;

public interface DisplayInterface
{
    public String GetDisplayText();
}
```

The first line in listing 12.5 is exactly like the first line in listing 12.1, which shows the original class. The first line specifies that this interface is to be part of the `MyPackages.Display` package. The second line declares the interface. The only difference here is the use of the `interface` keyword in place of `class` and the new name, `DisplayInterface`.

Now, the real difference between a class and an interface becomes evident. Although listing 12.5 declares the `GetDisplayText()` method, it doesn't actually implement the method. That is, you can see from the interface that `GetDisplayText()` is supposed to return a `String` object, but there isn't a clue as to how that `String` object is created or what it contains. Those details are left up to any class that decides to implement the interface.

But before you worry about implementing the interface in a class, you have to compile the interface source code. To do that, follow these steps:

1. Type in listing 12.5 and save it in the `Display` folder under the name DisplayInterface.java.
2. Start Java Workshop and choose Project, Edit, Display from the menu bar. The tabbed dialog box for editing the `Display` package appears in Java Workshop's display area.
3. Select the Build tab, and then click the Add All in Directory button to add the new `DisplayInterface` interface to the Files In box (see fig. 12.7).
4. Click the Apply button to finalize your changes to the package. (You may have to scroll Java Workshop's window to see the Apply button.)
5. Use Build Manager to compile the new interface's source code. The `DisplayInterface` interface is now ready to use as part of the `Display` package.

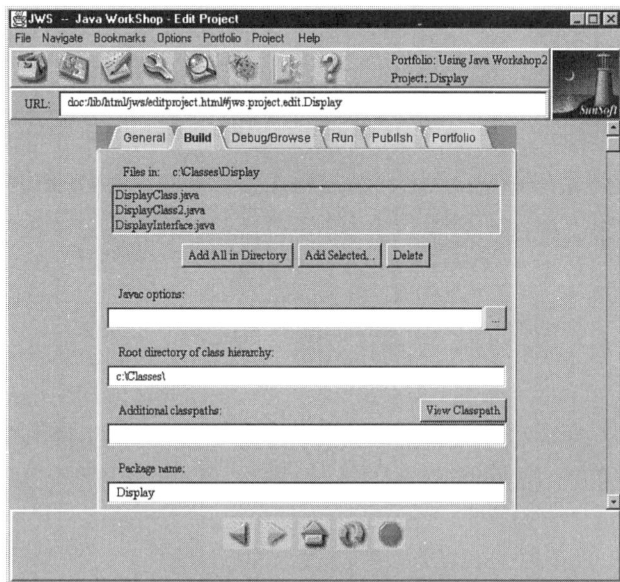

FIG. 12.7
You can add DisplayInterface from the Build page of the tabbed dialog box.

Implementing an Interface

Now that you have your new interface compiled, you can implement it in a class. This means not only telling Java that you'll be using the interface, but also implementing the interface within the new class. That is, every method that is listed in the interface's declaration must be defined in the class's source code. Listing 12.6 is a new applet, called InterfaceApplet, that shows how to implement the `DisplayInterface` interface. When you compile and run this applet (remember to store the project directly in the Classes folder so it has access to the MyPackages folder), you see exactly the same display as that produced by the original version, PackageApplet. Notice how the listing uses the `implements` keyword to tell Java that the applet will be implementing the `DisplayInterface` interface.

Listing 12.6 An Applet That Implements the *DisplayInterface* Interface

```
import java.awt.*;
import java.applet.*;
import MyPackages.Display.DisplayInterface;

public class InterfaceApplet extends Applet
    implements DisplayInterface
{
    String s;

    public void init()
    {
        Font font = new Font("TimesRoman", Font.PLAIN, 24);
        setFont(font);

        s = GetDisplayText();
    }

    public void paint(Graphics g)
    {
        g.drawString(s, 60, 80);
    }

    public String GetDisplayText()
    {
        return "Display Text";
    }
}
```

A class can implement as many interfaces as it needs to. To implement multiple interfaces, just list the interfaces after the `implements` keyword, separating each interface name from the others with a comma. Remember, however, that you must implement in your new class all the methods declared in all the interfaces you implement.

NOTE There's quite a lot to learn about interfaces. However, due to the skill level of this book and the fact that you probably won't have to worry about interfaces until you're an experienced Java programmer, only the basics have been presented here. Chances are good that you won't have to create interfaces at all. It's just good to know they're there in case you need them.

Exceptions

Chapter 11, "Images, Sounds, and Communications," gave you a quick look at exceptions and how they are handled in a program. Specifically, you had to be prepared to handle an exception when you created an `URL` object from a text string. This is because the text string may not use the proper syntax for an URL, making it impossible to create the `URL` object. In this case, the `URL` constructor throws an exception object called `MalformedURLException`. Listing 12.7 shows the code segment that handles this exception.

Listing 12.7 Handling an Exception

```
try
{
    URL url = new URL(str);
    AppletContext context = getAppletContext();
    context.showDocument(url);
}
catch (MalformedURLException e)
{
    badURL = true;
    repaint();
}
```

As you can see from the listing, you place the code that may cause the exception in a `try` program block, whereas the exception-handling code goes into a `catch` program block. In this case, the first line of the `try` block attempts to create an `URL` object from the string given in the variable `str`. If the string is not properly formatted for an URL, the `URL` constructor throws a `MalformedURLException`. When this happens, Java ignores the rest of the code in the `try` block and jumps to the `catch` block, where the program handles the exception. On the other hand, if the `URL` object gets created successfully, Java executes all the code in the `try` block and skips the `catch` block.

NOTE The `catch` program block does more than direct program execution. It actually catches the exception object thrown by Java. For example, in listing 12.7, you can see the exception object being caught inside the parentheses following the `catch` keyword. This is very similar to a parameter being received by a method. In this case, the type of the "parameter" is `MalformedURLException` and the name of the parameter is `e`. If you need to, you can access the exception object's methods through the `e` object.

Java defines many exception objects that may be thrown by the methods in Java's classes. How do you know which exceptions you have to handle? First, if you write an applet that calls a method that may throw an exception, Java insists that you handle the exception in one way or another. If you fail to do so, your applet will not compile. Instead, you'll receive an error message indicating where your program may generate the exception (see fig. 12.8).

Although Java Workshop's error messages are a clue that something is amiss, the clever programmer will look up a method in Java's documentation before using the method. Then, the programmer will know in advance whether that method requires exception-handling code. If you're interested in seeing the exceptions that are defined by a package, find the package's section in Java's online documentation where the classes and exceptions are listed (see fig. 12.9). (You can download Java's online documentation from the **http://java.sun.com** Web site. The Java Developer's Kit command on Java Workshop's Help menu connects you to the site if you're already online.)

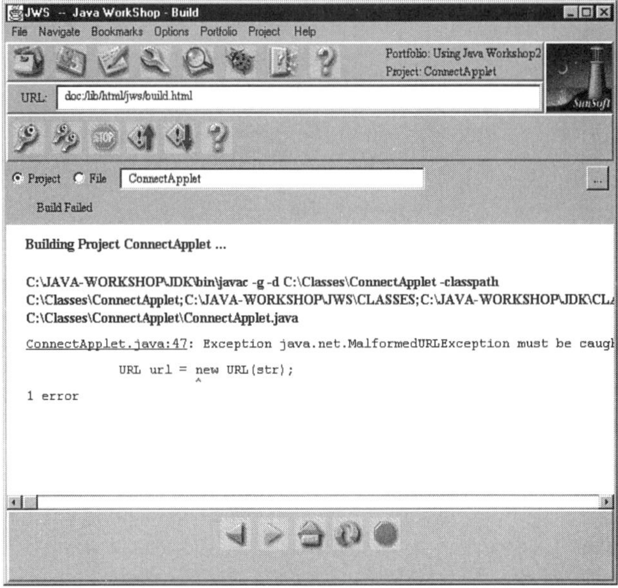

FIG. 12.8 Java Workshop gives you an error message if you fail to handle an exception in your applet.

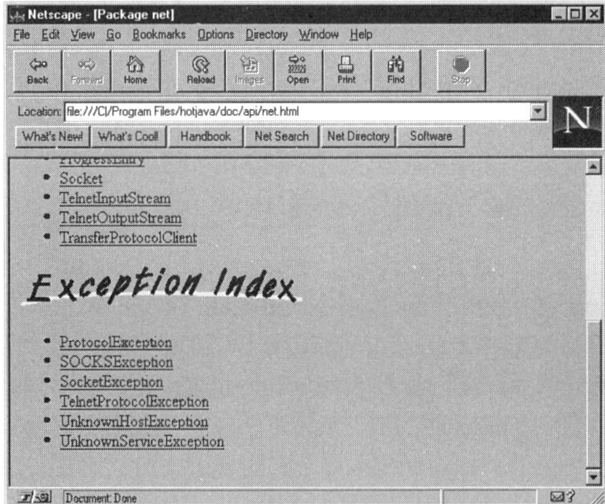

FIG. 12.9 Java's online documentation lists the exception objects that may be thrown by methods in a class.

The online documentation also lists all the methods that comprise a particular package. By looking up the method in the documentation (see fig. 12.10), you can see what types of arguments the method expects, the type of value the method returns, and whether the method may throw an exception. If the method shows that it can throw an exception, your code must handle the right type of exception or the program will not compile.

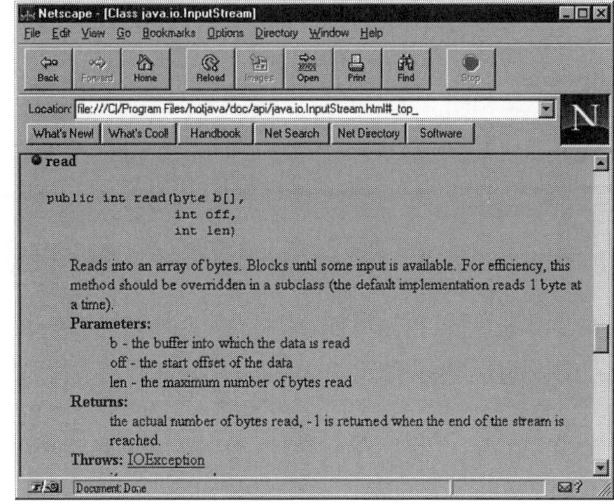

FIG. 12.10
The online documentation for a method shows the exception that the method may throw.

Throwing an Exception

One handy thing about exceptions is that you don't have to handle them in the same method in which the exception is generated. For example, in listing 12.8, the applet tries to create an `URL` object. If the `URL` creation fails, the `URL` constructor throws an exception that the `event()` method handles in its `catch` block. But what if, for some reason, you don't want to handle the exception in the same method in which you call the `URL` constructor? You can simply pass the buck, so to speak, by throwing the exception on up the method hierarchy. Listing 12.8 shows one way you might do this with the `MalformedURLException` exception.

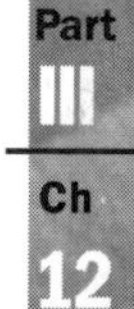

Listing 12.8 Throwing an Exception

```
public boolean action(Event evt, Object arg)
{
    try
        GetURL();
    catch (MalformedURLException e)
    {
        badURL = true;
        repaint();
    }

    return true;
}
```

continues

Listing 12.8 Continued

```
protected void GetURL() throws MalformedURLException
{
    String str = textField.getText();
    URL url = new URL(str);
    AppletContext context = getAppletContext();
    context.showDocument(url);
}
```

In this listing, the call to the `URL` class's constructor has been moved to a method called `GetURL()`. However, `GetURL()` does not directly handle the `MalformedURLException` exception. Instead, it passes the exception back to the `action()` method. Java knows that `GetURL()` wants to pass the exception because `GetURL()` adds the phrase `throws MalformedURLException` to its signature. Throwing the exception, however, doesn't relieve you from handling it eventually. Notice that in listing 12.8, the exception still gets handled in the `action()` method.

In short, you can handle an exception in two ways. The first way is to write `try` and `catch` program blocks exactly where you call the function that may generate the exception. The second way is to declare the method as throwing the exception, in which case you must write the `try` and `catch` program blocks in the method that calls the "throwing" method, as shown in listing 12.8.

Types of Exceptions

Java defines many different exception objects. Some of these you must always handle in your code if you call a function that may throw the exception. Others are generated by the system when something like memory allocation fails, an expression tries to divide by zero, a null value is used inappropriately, and so on. You can choose to watch for this second kind of exception or let Java deal with them.

You should always be on the lookout for places in your program where an exception could be generated. These places are usually associated with user input, which can be infamously unpredictable. However, programmers, too, have been known to make mistakes in their programs that lead to exception throwing. Some common exceptions you may want to watch out for at appropriate places in your applet are listed in table 12.1.

Table 12.1 Common Java Exceptions

Exception	Description
ArithmeticException	Caused by math errors such as division by zero.
ArrayIndexOutOfBoundsException	Caused by bad array indexes.
ArrayStoreException	Caused when a program tries to store the wrong type of data in an array.
FileNotFoundException	Caused by an attempt to access a non-existent file.
IOException	Caused by general I/O failures, such as inability to read from a file.
NullPointerException	Caused by referencing a null object.
NumberFormatException	Caused when a conversion between strings and numbers fails.
OutOfMemoryException	Caused when there's not enough memory to allocate a new object.
SecurityException	Caused when an applet tries to perform an action not allowed by the browser's security setting.
StackOverflowException	Caused when the system runs out of stack space.
StringIndexOutOfBoundsException	Caused when a program attempts to access a nonexistent character position in a string.

You can catch all types of exceptions by setting up your `catch` block for exceptions of type `Exception`, like this: `catch (Exception e)`. Call the exception's `getMessage()` method (inherited from the `Throwable` superclass) to get information about the specific exception that you've intercepted.

Determining the Exceptions to ExceptionsExceptionsHandle

Experienced programmers usually know when their code may generate an exception of some sort. However, when you first start writing applets with exception-handling code, you may not be sure what type of exceptions to watch out for. One way to discover this information is to see what exceptions get generated as you test your applet. Listing 12.9, for example, is an applet called ExceptionApplet that divides two integer numbers obtained from the user and displays the integer result (dropping any remainder). Because the applet must deal with user input, the probability of disaster is high. ExceptionApplet, however, contains no exception-handling code.

Listing 12.9 An Applet with No Exception Handling

```
import java.awt.*;
import java.applet.*;

public class ExceptionApplet extends Applet
{
    TextField textField1, textField2;
    String answerStr;

    public void init()
    {
        textField1 = new TextField(15);
        add(textField1);
        textField2 = new TextField(15);
        add(textField2);
        answerStr = "Undefined";
    }

    public void paint(Graphics g)
    {
        Font font = new Font("TimesRoman", Font.PLAIN, 24);
        g.setFont(font);
```

```
        g.drawString("The answer is:", 50, 100);
        g.drawString(answerStr, 70, 130);
    }

    public boolean action(Event evt, Object arg)
    {
        String str1 = textField1.getText();
        String str2 = textField2.getText();
        int int1 = Integer.parseInt(str1);
        int int2 = Integer.parseInt(str2);
        int answer = int1 / int2;
        answerStr = String.valueOf(answer);
        repaint();
        return true;
    }
}
```

You'll use this applet as the starting point for a more robust applet. Run the applet using Java Workshop. Then, enter a number into each of the two text boxes and press Enter. The program then divides the first number by the second number and displays the result (see fig. 12.11).

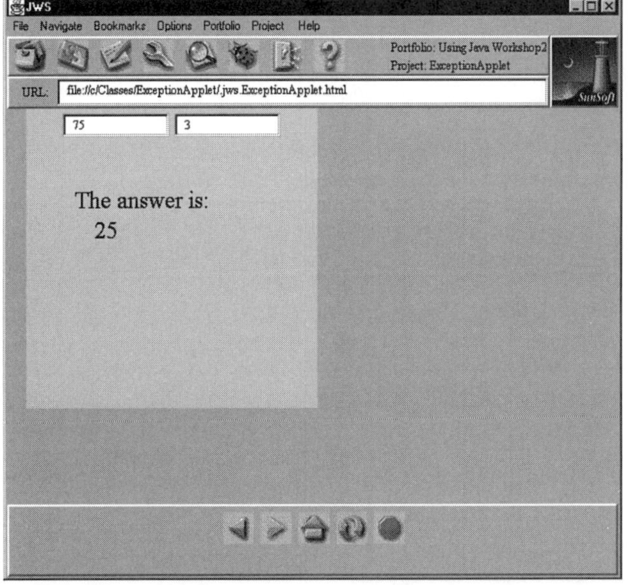

FIG. 12.11 ExceptionApplet divides the first number by the second.

As long as the user enters valid numbers into the text boxes, the program runs perfectly. What happens, though, if the user presses Enter when either or both of the text boxes are empty? Java immediately throws a `NumberFormatException` when the `action()` method attempts to convert the contents of the text boxes to integer values.

Catching a Runtime Exception

You now know that the user can cause a `NumberFormatException` if he or she leaves one or more text boxes blank or enters an invalid numerical value, like the string one. In order to ensure that your applet will not be caught by surprise, you now need to write the code that will handle this exception. Follow these steps to add this new code:

1. Load ExceptionApplet into Source Editor.
2. Replace the `action()` method with the new version shown in listing 12.10.

Listing 12.10 Handling the *NumberFormatException* Exception

```
public boolean action(Event evt, Object arg)
{
    String str1 = textField1.getText();
    String str2 = textField2.getText();

    try
    {
        int int1 = Integer.parseInt(str1);
        int int2 = Integer.parseInt(str2);
        int answer = int1 / int2;
        answerStr = String.valueOf(answer);
    }
    catch (NumberFormatException e)
    {
        answerStr = "Bad number!";
    }

    repaint();
    return true;
}
```

3. In the class declaration line, change the name of the class to `ExceptionApplet2`.
4. Save the new applet under the name ExceptionApplet2.java in a new folder called ExceptionApplet2 in your Classes directory.
5. Use Project Manager to create a new project for the applet.
6. Use Build Manager to compile the applet.
7. Use Project Tester to run the applet.

In listing 12.10, the `action()` method now uses `try` and `catch` program blocks to handle the `NumberFormatException` gracefully. Figure 12.12 shows what happens when the user leaves the text boxes blank. When the program gets to the first call to `String.valueOf()`, Java generates the `NumberFormatException` exception, which causes program execution to jump to the `catch` block. In the `catch` block, the program sets the display string to `Bad number!` The call to `repaint()` ensures that this message to the user gets displayed on the screen.

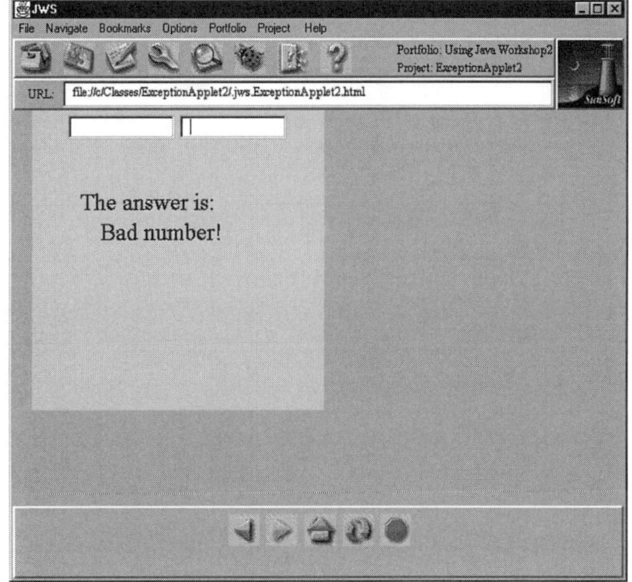

FIG. 12.12
ExceptionApplet2 handles the *NumberFormatException* gracefully.

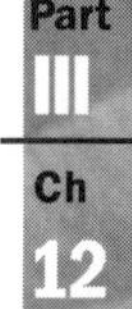

Handling Multiple Exceptions

So, here you are entering numbers into ExceptionApplet2's text boxes and getting the results. Without thinking, you enter a zero into the second box, Java tries to divide the first number by the zero, and *pow!* you have an `ArithmeticException` exception. What to do? You're already using your `catch` block to grab `NumberFormatException`; now, you have yet another exception to deal with.

The good news is that you're not limited to only a single `catch` block. You can, in fact, create `catch` blocks for any exceptions you think the program may generate. To see how this works with your new applet, follow these steps:

1. Load ExceptionApplet2 into Source Editor.
2. Replace the `action()` method with the new version shown in listing 12.11.

Listing 12.11 Handling Multiple Exceptions

```
public boolean action(Event evt, Object arg)
{
    String str1 = textField1.getText();
    String str2 = textField2.getText();

    try
    {
        int int1 = Integer.parseInt(str1);
        int int2 = Integer.parseInt(str2);
        int answer = int1 / int2;
        answerStr = String.valueOf(answer);
    }
    catch (NumberFormatException e)
    {
        answerStr = "Bad number!";
    }
    catch (ArithmeticException e)
    {
        answerStr = "Division by 0!";
    }

    repaint();
    return true;
}
```

3. In the class declaration line, change the name of the class to `ExceptionApplet3`.

4. Save the new applet under the name ExceptionApplet3.java in a new folder called ExceptionApplet3 in your Classes directory.
5. Use Project Manager to create a new project for the applet.
6. Use Build Manager to compile the applet.
7. Use Project Tester to run the applet.

If you examine listing 12.11, you'll see that the `action()` method now defines two `catch` program blocks, one each for the `NumberFormatException` and `ArithmeticException` exceptions. In this way, the program can watch for potential problems from within a single `try` block. Figure 12.13 shows what ExceptionApplet3 looks like when the user attempts a division by zero. If you discovered another exception that your program may cause, you can add yet another `catch` block.

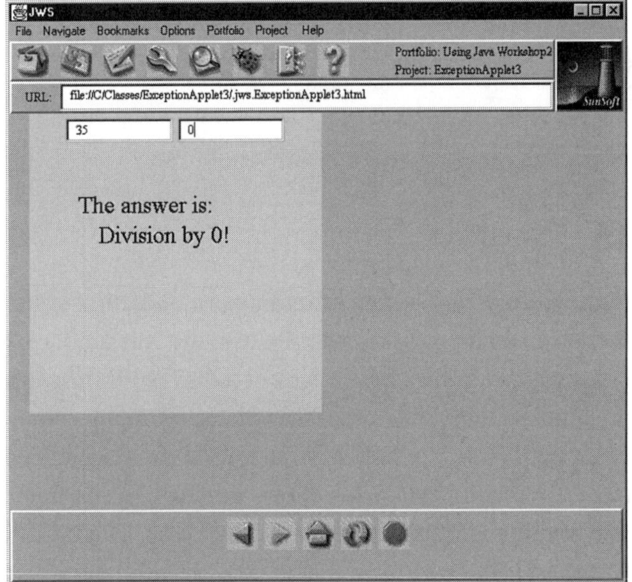

FIG. 12.13
ExceptionApplet3 catches division-by-zero exceptions.

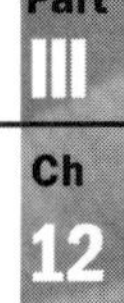

NOTE Although handling exceptions is a powerful tool for creating crash-proof programs, you should use them only in situations where you have little control over the cause of the exception, such as when dealing with user input. If your applet causes an exception because of a program bug, you should track down and fix the problem rather than try to catch the exception.

There may be times when you want to be sure that a specific block of code gets executed whether or not an exception is generated. You can do this by adding a `finally` program block after the last `catch`. The code in the `finally` block gets executed after the `try` block or `catch` block finishes executing. Listing 12.12 shows an example.

Listing 12.12 Using the *finally* Program Block

```
try
{
    // The code that may generate an exception goes here.
}
catch (Exception e)
{
    // The code that handles the exception goes here.
}
finally
{
    // The code here is executed after the try or
    // catch blocks finish executing.
}
```

Threads

When using Windows 95 (and other modern operating systems), you know that you can run several programs simultaneously. This ability is called multitasking. What you may not know is that many of today's operating systems also allow *threads*, which are separate processes that are kind of a step down from a complete application. A thread is a lot like a subprogram. An applet can create several threads—several different flows of execution—and run them concurrently. This is a lot like having multitasking inside multitasking. The user knows that he or she can run several applications at a time. The programmer knows that each application can run several threads at a time.

In Java, you can create threads in a couple of ways. The simplest way is to take an existing class and turn it into a thread. You do this by modifying the class so that it implements the `Runnable` interface, which declares the `run()` method required by all types of threads. (The `run()` method contains the code to be executed by a thread.) Previously, you learned how interfaces in Java enable you to add capabilities to classes simply by implementing the interface in that class. Now, you get a chance to put that idea to work.

The second way to create a thread is to write a completely separate class derived from Java's `Thread` class. Because the `Thread` class itself implements the `Runnable` interface, it already contains a `run()` method. However, `Thread`'s `run()` method doesn't do anything. You usually have to override the method in your own class in order to create the type of thread you want.

Converting a Class to a Thread

As mentioned in the preceding section, the first way to create a thread is to convert a class to a thread. To do this, you must perform several steps, as listed here:

1. Declare the class as implementing the `Runnable` interface.
2. Implement the `run()` method.
3. Declare a `Thread` object as a data field of the class.
4. Create the `Thread` object and call its `start()` method.
5. Call the thread's `stop()` method to destroy the thread.

The following sections look at each of these steps in detail.

Declaring the Class as Implementing the *Runnable* Interface

As you can see in step 1 in the preceding section, to create a thread from a regular class, the class must first be declared as implementing the `Runnable` interface. For example, if your class is declared as

```
public class MyApplet extends Applet
```

you must change that declaration to

```
public class MyApplet extends Applet
    implements Runnable
```

Implementing the *run()* Method

Now, because you've told Java you're about to implement an interface, you must implement every method in the interface. In the case of `Runnable`, that's easy because there's only one method, `run()`, the basic implementation of which looks like this:

```
public void run()
{
}
```

When you start your new thread, Java calls the thread's `run()` method, so it is in `run()` where all the action takes place. The preceding example of the `run()` method is the minimum you need to compile the new source code for the thread. However, in a real program, you'll add code to `run()` so that the thread does what you want it to do.

Declaring a *Thread* Object

The next step is to declare a `Thread` object as a data field of the class, like this:

```
Thread thread;
```

The `Thread` object will hold a reference to the thread with which the applet is associated. You will be able to access the thread's methods through this object.

Creating and Starting the Thread Object

Now it's time to write the code that creates the thread and gets it going. Assuming that your new threaded class is an applet, you'll often want to create and start the thread in the applet's `start()` method, as shown in listing 12.13.

Listing 12.13 Creating and Starting a *Thread* Object

```
public void start()
{
    thread = new Thread(this);
    thread.start();
}
```

NOTE In Chapter 6, "Applets and Graphics," you learned that `start()` is the method that represents the applet's second life-cycle stage. Java calls your applet's life-cycle methods in this order: `init()`, `start()`, `paint()`, `stop()`, and `destroy()`. Java calls the `start()` method whenever the applet needs to start running, usually when it's first loaded or when the user has switched back to the applet from another Web page. ■

Look at the call to the `Thread` constructor in listing 12.13. Notice that the constructor's single argument is the applet's `this` reference. This is how Java knows with which class to associate the thread. Right after the call to the constructor, the applet calls the `Thread` object's `start()` method, which starts the thread running. When the thread starts running, Java calls the thread's `run()` method, where the thread's work gets done.

Stopping the Thread

When the thread's `run()` method ends, so does the thread. However, because threads tend to run for quite a while, controlling things like animation in the applet, the user is likely to switch away from your applet before the thread stops. In this case, it's up to your applet to stop the thread. Because Java calls an applet's `stop()` method whenever the user switches away from the applet, the `stop()` method is a good place to stop the thread, as shown in listing 12.14.

Listing 12.14 Stopping a Thread

```
public void stop()
{
    thread.stop();
}
```

Using a Thread in an Applet

To understand about threads, you really have to use them. So in this section, you'll put together an applet that associates itself with a `Thread` object and runs the thread to control a very simple animated display. The animation in this case is simply a changing number that proves that the thread is running. Listing 12.15 is the applet in question, which is called ThreadApplet. Figure 12.14 shows the applet running under Java Workshop.

Listing 12.15 Using a Thread in an Applet

```
import java.awt.*;
import java.applet.*;

public class ThreadApplet extends Applet
  implements Runnable
{
    Thread thread;
    int count;
    String displayStr;
    Font font;

    public void start()
    {
        font = new Font("TimesRoman", Font.PLAIN, 72);
        setFont(font);

        count = 0;
        displayStr = "";

        thread = new Thread(this);
        thread.start();
    }

    public void stop()
    {
        thread.stop();
    }

    public void run()
    {
        while (count < 1000)
        {
            ++count;
            displayStr = String.valueOf(count);
            repaint();

            try
            {
         thread.sleep(100);
            }
            catch (InterruptedException e)
            {
            }
        }
    }

    public void paint(Graphics g)
    {
        g.drawString(displayStr, 50, 130);
    }
}
```

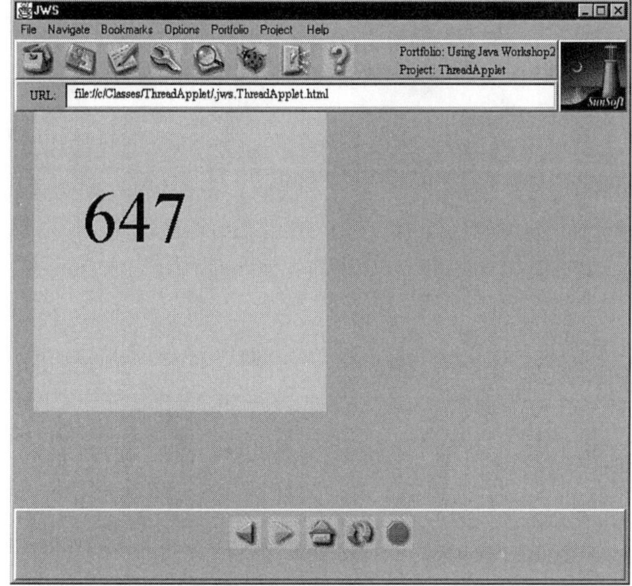

FIG. 12.14
ThreadApplet uses a thread to count to 1000.

There are a couple of interesting things in ThreadApplet of which you should be aware. First, notice that in `run()`, the thread loops 1000 times, after which the `while` loop ends. When the `while` loop ends, so does the `run()` method. This means that when you run ThreadApplet, if you let it count all the way to 1000, the thread ends on its own. However, what if you switch to a different Web page before ThreadApplet has counted all the way to 1000? Then, Java calls the applet's `stop()` method, which ends the thread by calling the thread's `stop()` method.

The next point of interest is what's going on inside `run()`. At the beginning of the loop, the program increments the counter, converts the counter's value to a string, and then repaints the applet so that the new count value appears in the window. That code should be as clear as glass to you by now. But what's all that code after the call to `repaint()`? That's where the thread not only times the animation, but also relinquishes the computer so that other threads get a chance to run. Simply, the call to the thread's `sleep()` method suspends the thread for the number of milliseconds given as its single argument. In this case, the sleep time is 100 milliseconds, or one tenth of a second. If you want the animation to run faster, change the 100 to a smaller value. To count slower, change the 100 to a larger value.

CAUTION

It's important that your threads don't dominate the computer's processor for longer than necessary. This is because other threads and processes are almost certainly in competition for the processor at the same time. If your thread will be running for a while, you should call the `sleep()` or `yield()` methods to give other processes a chance to run. This is more important on some systems than on others. Because you can't know for sure which system your applet will be running on, be a considerate thread programmer.

Notice that the call to `sleep()` is enclosed in a `try` block and followed by a `catch` block that's watching for `InterruptedException` exceptions. You have to catch this exception because the `sleep()` method throws it. If you fail to catch the exception, your program will not compile.

Deriving a Class from *Thread*

The second way to create a thread is to derive a new class from `Thread`. Then, in your applet's class, you create and start a thread object of your thread class. This leaves you with two processes going simultaneously, the applet and the thread object created in the class. By giving the thread class access to data and methods in the applet, the thread can easily communicate with the applet to perform whatever tasks it was written for.

Suppose that you want to write the same sort of applet as that shown in listing 12.15, but now you want a separate thread to control the counting process. Listing 12.16 shows how you might write the new class for the thread. (Don't try to compile this code yet. You'll use it in the next example in this chapter.)

Listing 12.16 A Class Derived from *Thread*

```
public class MyThread extends Thread
{
    ThreadApplet2 applet;
    int count;

    MyThread(ThreadApplet2 applet)
    {
        this.applet = applet;
    }

    public void run()
```

```
        {
            count = 0;
            while (count < 1000)
            {
                ++count;
                applet.displayStr = String.valueOf(count);
                applet.repaint();

                try
                {
                    sleep(100);
                }
                catch (InterruptedException e)
                {
                }
            }
        }
    }
```

The first thing to notice in this thread class is that its constructor takes as a single argument a reference to a `ThreadApplet2` object, which is the applet from which you'll be running this thread. The thread needs this reference so that it can communicate with the applet.

Next, look at `run()`. The thread still counts from zero to 1000, but now it accesses the applet object to create the display string and repaint the applet. In the original version of the program, the thread was directly associated with the class, rather than a completely separate process.

You'll now put that new thread class to work. To do this, you must have an applet that creates an object from the new thread class and calls that object's `start()` method to get the thread running. Listing 12.17 shows just such an applet, called ThreadApplet2. When you run the applet under Java Workshop, you'll see the same display that was created in the original version of the applet (ThreadApplet), but now the counting animation is being controlled by a separate thread class.

NOTE To compile listing 12.17, make sure you have both the MyThread.java and ThreadApplet2.java files in your Classes\ThreadApplet2 folder and that you've added both source-code files to the applet's project. Java Workshop will then compile both files when you compile the applet.

Listing 12.17 An Applet That Creates a Separate Thread

```
import java.awt.*;
import java.applet.*;
import MyThread;

public class ThreadApplet2 extends Applet
{
    MyThread thread;
    String displayStr;
    Font font;

    public void start()
    {
        font = new Font("TimesRoman", Font.PLAIN, 72);
        setFont(font);

        displayStr = "";

        thread = new MyThread(this);
        thread.start();
    }

    public void stop()
    {
        thread.stop();
    }

    public void paint(Graphics g)
    {
        g.drawString(displayStr, 50, 150);
    }
}
```

Synchronizing Multiple Threads

There may be times when you have several threads going, each competing for the same resources. This type of resource competition can be deadly for threads. For example, what if one thread tries to read from a string while another thread is still writing to that string? Depending on the situation, you'll get strange results. You can avoid these problems by telling Java where synchronization problems may occur so that Java can keep an eye out for unhealthy thread competition.

To put Java on guard, use the `synchronized` keyword when you define a method (or even a code block). When you mark a method as synchronized, Java creates a monitor object for the class. The first time a thread calls the synchronized method, Java gives the monitor object to that thread. As long as the thread holds the monitor object, no other thread can enter the synchronized section of code. You can think of the monitor object as a key. Unless a thread is holding the key, it can't unlock the door to the synchronized method.

Using synchronized methods makes sense only when more than one thread is vying for an applet's resources. For that reason, to demonstrate thread synchronization, you need to create two threads. Listing 12.18 is a thread class, called `MyThread2`, that can count either forward or backward, depending upon the values you give to the class's constructor. By creating two thread objects from this class, you can experiment with thread synchronization.

NOTE To compile listings 12.18 and 12.19, make sure you have both the MyThread2.java and ThreadApplet3.java files in your Classes\ThreadApplet3 folder and that you have added both source-code files to the project. Java will then compile both files when you compile the applet.

Listing 12.18 A Double-duty Thread

```
public class MyThread2 extends Thread
{
    ThreadApplet3 applet;
    boolean forward;
    int count;
    int increment;
    int end;
    int position;

    MyThread2(ThreadApplet3 applet, boolean forward)
    {
        this.applet = applet;
        this.forward = forward;
    }

    public void run()
    {
        InitCounter();
        DoCount();
    }

    protected void InitCounter()
    {
```

continues

Listing 12.18 Continued

```
        if (forward)
        {
            count = 0;
            increment = 1;
            end = 1000;
            position = 120;
        }
        else
        {
            count = 1000;
            increment = -1;
            end = 0;
            position = 180;
        }
    }

    protected void DoCount()
    {

        while (count != end)
        {
            count = count + increment;
            String str = String.valueOf(count);
            applet.SetDisplayStr(str, position);

            try
            {
                sleep(100);
            }
            catch (InterruptedException e)
            {
            }
        }
    }
}
```

When you construct a `MyThread2` thread object, you must pass two values as parameters: a reference to the applet and a `boolean` value indicating whether the thread should count forward or backward. The thread uses the `boolean` value in its `InitCounter()` method to set the values needed to accomplish the counting. These values are the starting count value (`count`), the counting increment (`increment`), the target count (`end`), and the position at which to display the count in the applet (`position`). Notice that the increment variable can be either 1 or –1. When the increment gets added to the count, a positive increment increases the count by one, whereas a negative increment decreases the count by one.

In its `run()` method, the thread calls the applet's `SetDisplayStr()` method, which, as you'll soon see, is the synchronized method. In other words, if the thread isn't holding the monitor object for `SetDisplayStr()`, it cannot enter the method. This prevents two running instances of the `MyThread2` thread from trying to change the display string at the same time.

Now it's time to look at the applet that's in charge of the threads. Listing 12.19 is the applet, which is called ThreadApplet3. This applet creates two objects of the `MyThread2` class: one that counts forward and one that counts backward. The applet's `SetDisplayStr()` method is where the synchronization comes into play because both threads will be trying to access this method.

When you run the applet, you'll see that when the first thread can display its count, the string will appear closer to the top of the display area. The second thread, however, displays its count below the first thread's. For this reason, when you get the applet going, you can sit back and watch the two threads battle over the `SetDisplayStr()` method.

Listing 12.19 An Applet That Uses Thread Synchronization

```
import java.awt.*;
import java.applet.*;
import MyThread2;

public class ThreadApplet3 extends Applet
{
    MyThread2 thread1;
    MyThread2 thread2;
    String displayStr;
    Font font;
    int position;

    public void init()
    {
        font = new Font("TimesRoman", Font.PLAIN, 72);
        setFont(font);

        displayStr = "";
        position = 120;

        thread1 = new MyThread2(this, true);
        thread2 = new MyThread2(this, false);
    }
```

continues

Listing 12.19 Continued

```
    public void start()
    {
       if (thread1.isAlive())
       thread1.resume();
       else
           thread1.start();

       if (thread2.isAlive())
           thread2.resume();
       else
           thread2.start();
    }

    public void stop()
    {
       thread1.suspend();
       thread2.suspend();
    }

    public void destroy()
    {
       thread1.stop();
       thread2.stop();
    }

    public void paint(Graphics g)
    {
       g.drawString(displayStr, 50, position);
    }

    synchronized public void SetDisplayStr(String str, int pos)
    {
       displayStr = str;
       position = pos;
       repaint();
    }
}
```

Understanding ThreadApplet3

The ThreadApplet3 applet is unique with regard to other applets in this book because it's the only applet that takes full advantage of the applet's life-cycle stages. In the `init()` method, the applet creates the two threads. The different `boolean` values given as the constructor's second argument cause the first thread to count forward and the second thread to count backward.

In the `start()` method, the applet calls each thread's `isAlive()` method (defined in Java's `Thread` class) to determine whether the thread has been started yet. The first time `start()` gets called, the threads have been created in `init()` but haven't been started. In this case, `isAlive()` returns `false`, and the applet calls each thread's `start()` method to get the threads rolling. If `start()` is not being called for the first time, it's because the user has switched back to the applet from another Web page. In this case, `isAlive()` returns `true`. The applet knows that it must call the threads' `resume()` method rather than `start()`.

In the `stop()` method, which gets called when the user switches to another Web page, rather than stopping the threads, the applet suspends them. The threads remain suspended until the applet calls their `resume()` methods, which, as you now know, happens in the `start()` method.

Finally, when Java calls the `destroy()` method, the applet is being stopped and removed from memory. The threads, too, should follow suit, so the applet calls each thread's `stop()` method.

CAUTION

When programming threads, you always have to watch out for a condition known as *deadlock*. Deadlock occurs when two or more threads are waiting to gain control of a resource, but for one reason or another, the threads rely on conditions that can't be met in order to get control of the resource. To understand this situation, imagine that you have a pencil in your hand and someone else has a pen. Now, assume that you can't release the pencil until you have the pen, and the other person can't release the pen until she has the pencil. Deadlock! A more computer-oriented example would be when one thread must access Method1 before it can release its hold on Method2, but the second thread must access Method2 before it can release its hold on Method1. Because these are mutually exclusive conditions, the threads are deadlocked and cannot run.

From Here...

Packages are a great way to create and organize class libraries. The more Java code you write, the more you'll appreciate the ability to create your own packages. Although you won't need to use interfaces for some time to come, interfaces are a unique element of the Java programming language. Although other object-oriented languages, such as C++, allow multiple inheritance, only Java supports the idea of interfaces, which can be powerful tools when they're needed.

One tool the programmer can use to create reliable programs is exceptions, which are objects created by Java when a program encounters a serious error. After Java creates an exception object, it throws the exception and expects some other part of the program to catch the exception.

Threads enable you to break an applet's tasks into separate flows of execution. These subprograms seem to run concurrently thanks to the task switching that occurs in multitasking systems. Remember that if there's a chance that two or more threads may compete for a resource, you need to protect that resource using thread synchronization.

Please refer to the following chapters for more information on the topics you just studied:

- Chapter 5, "Object-Oriented Programming and Java," tells you more about classes and how they're used in Java, as well as how to create, compile, and run applets using Java Workshop.
- Chapter 6, "Applets and Graphics," describes an applet's life cycle.
- Chapter 7, "Java Controls," shows how to create and program Java's many controls, such as the text boxes you used in this chapter's applets.
- Chapter 15, "Source Editor," describes how to use Java Workshop's built-in text editor.
- Chapter 17, "Debugger," shows how to find programming errors using Java Workshop's debugging tool.

CHAPTER 13

Writing Java Applications

The greater bulk of this book is dedicated to using Java Workshop to create applets for the Internet. However, Java is a full-fledged computer language that enables you to write complete, stand-alone applications. Although most Java Workshop users are interested in creating only applets (there are other, more powerful languages for creating applications), no introductory Java book would be complete without dabbling a little with Java applications. ■

How to write the simplest Java stand-alone application.

You'll be amazed at how small the source code for an application can be. It takes only a few lines of C-like code to create a runnable application.

About using Java Workshop to create and compile a stand-alone application.

You create and compile an application almost exactly as you've been creating your applets.

How to run a non-windowed Java application.

Java's interpreter makes it possible to run applications outside of Java Workshop. Windows 95's DOS window makes running Java DOS applications possible.

How to use arguments with your applications.

When running an application with Java's interpreter, the user can type a command-line from which the application can extract arguments. Using arguments in this way makes your applications more flexible.

About converting applets to applications.

There are only a few differences between applets and stand-alone applications. For that reason, you can easily convert any applet to a windowed application.

What Are Java Applications?

If you've run the HotJava browser, you've already had experience with Java applications. The HotJava browser was programmed entirely in Java, and it demonstrates how much you can do with Java, even when dealing with sophisticated telecommunications applications.

Much of what you've learned about applets can be applied toward writing applications. After all, the language doesn't change, just the way you use it does. Of course, conversely, some of what you learned about applets doesn't apply to the writing of applications. For example, because Java applications aren't run "on the Web," they don't have to deal with all the security issues that come up when running applets. A Java stand-alone application can access any files it needs to access, for example. (That's not to say that network security is never an issue with a stand-alone application, of course. HotJava is a stand-alone application, and it must deal heavily with security problems.)

If you've ever programmed in C or C++, you'll discover that writing applications in Java is similar. If you haven't programmed in those languages, rest assured that, by this point in the book, you already have 95 percent of the knowledge you need to write stand-alone Java applications.

The Simplest Java Application

You can create a runnable Java application in only a few lines of code. In fact, an application requires only one method called `main()`. C and C++ programmers will recognize `main()` as being the place where applications begin their execution. The same is true for Java applications. Listing 13.1 shows the simplest Java application.

Listing 13.1 The Simplest Java Application

```
class SimpleApp
{
    public static void main(String args[])
    {
        System.out.println("My first Java app!");
    }
}
```

If you look at the first line of listing 13.1, you'll see that even a Java stand-alone application starts off as a class. In this case, the class has no superclass—that is, the SimpleApp class is not derived from another class (although it could have been). The first line of the body of the class begins the `main()` method, which is where all Java applications begin execution. This method's single parameter is a String array containing the command line sent to the application when it was started.

Finally, the single line in `main()` prints a message on your computer's screen. Because this is not a Windows application, the class contains no `paint()` method. Instead, you display text by using the `println()` method of the System.out package.

To run the Java application, you must first compile it with Java Workshop and then run the byte-code file using Java's interpreter. You compile the program almost as you would an applet. The following example describes the entire process.

Building an Application

Building a Java application isn't any more difficult than building an applet, although the steps are slightly different. Use the following steps to compile and run the SimpleApp application.

1. Create a SimpleApp folder inside your Classes folder. The SimpleApp folder is where you'll store the files for the applet you're creating in these steps.
2. Using Java Workshop's text editor, type listing 13.1 and save it to your Classes\SimpleApp folder under the name SimpleApp.java.
3. Select Project, Create, Standalone Program from Java Workshop's menu bar. The tabbed dialog box for stand-alone application projects appears.
4. Type **SimpleApp** into the Name text box, type **c:\Classes\SimpleApp** into the Source Directory text box, select the Yes option button for Existing Sources, and click the Add All in Directory button. Finally, type **SimpleApp.class** into the Main Class File text box (see fig. 13.1) and click the Apply button. Java Workshop adds the project to the current portfolio.

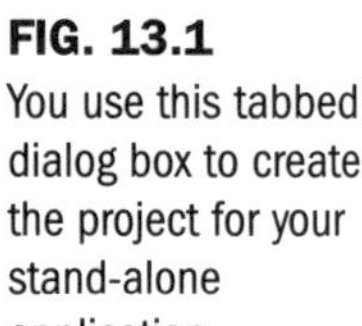

FIG. 13.1
You use this tabbed dialog box to create the project for your stand-alone application.

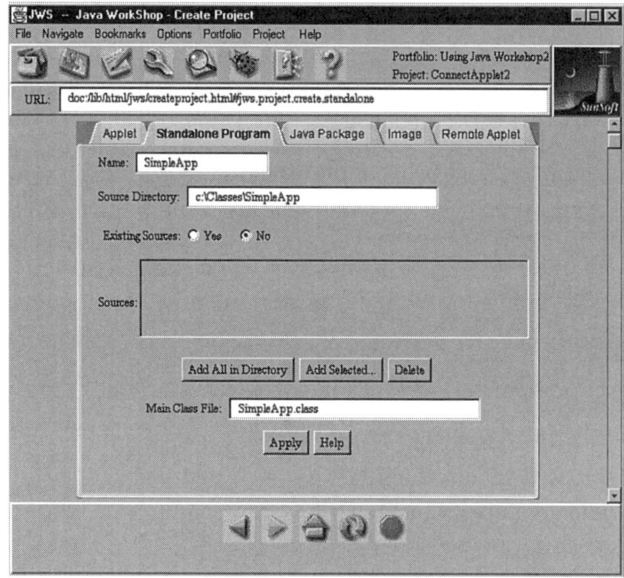

5. Click the Build Manager button (the one that looks like a wrench) in Java Workshop's main toolbar. The Build Manager appears.
6. Click Build Manager's Build button. Build Manager runs the Java compiler, javac, to compile your new application (see fig. 13.2).

FIG. 13.2
Build Manager runs Java's compiler to compile your stand-alone application.

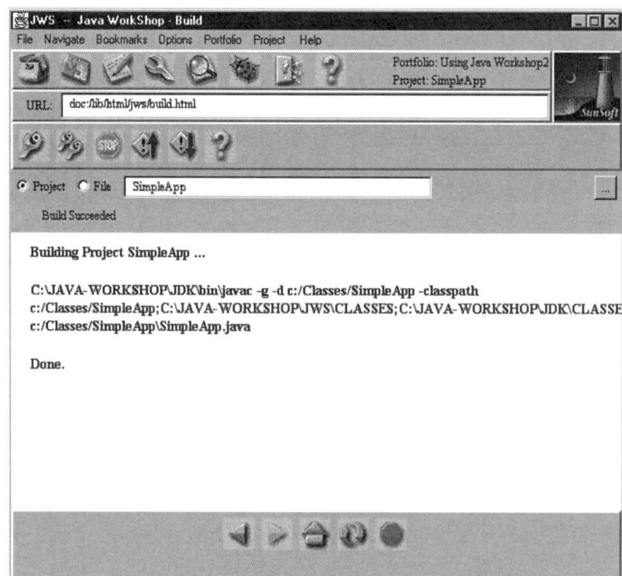

7. From Windows 95's Start, Programs menu, select the MS-DOS Prompt command. The MS-DOS window appears (see fig. 13.3), from which you can run DOS applications.

   This first simple applet does not run as a Windows application. Later in this chapter, you'll learn to write Windows applications with Java.

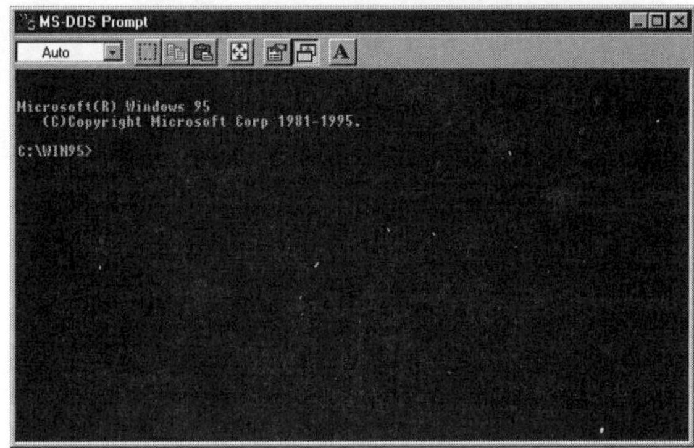

FIG. 13.3
You must run SimpleApp from the DOS window.

8. Type **path=c:\Java-WorkShop\Jws\intel-win32\bin** and press Enter.

   This adds the directory in which the Java tools are stored to your path so that the system can find the tools when you need them.

9. Type **set classpath=c:\classes\simpleapp;c:\java-workshop\jws\classes;c:\java-workshop\jdk\classes** and press Enter.

   This sets the CLASSPATH system variable, which tells Java where to find the .class files it needs to run the program.

10. Type **cd c:\Classes\SimpleApp** to switch to your Classes folder.

11. Type **java SimpleApp** to run the application. The message `My first Java app!` appears on the screen (see fig. 13.4).

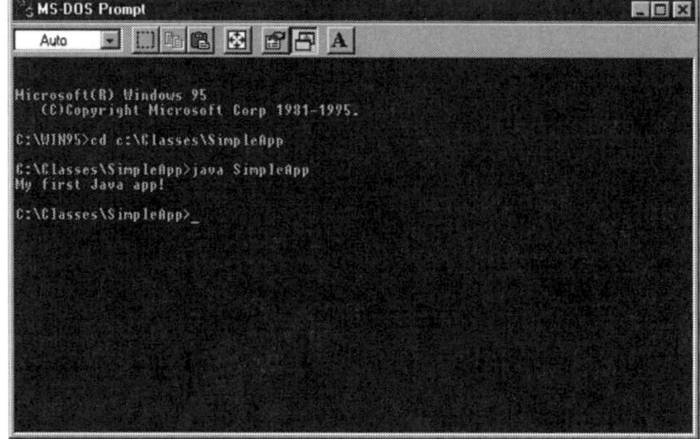

FIG. 13.4
The SimpleApp application prints a single line of text on the screen.

Getting an Application's Arguments

You probably know that when you start a program, you can sometimes append parameters to the command line to give the program information it needs to start. You can do the same thing with Java applications. For example, here's how you would start SimpleApp with two parameters:

```
java SimpleApp param1 param2
```

Of course, because SimpleApp ignores its parameters, the parameters in the command line don't mean anything. Suppose, however, you wanted to print a user-specified message a user-specified number of times. You might, then, write the Java application shown in listing 13.2. When you run this application (follow the steps you used to compile and run SimpleApp), add two parameters to the command line: the message to print (in quotes, if the message is more than one word) and the number of times to print the message. You'll get output like that shown in figure 13.5.

Listing 13.2 Using Command-line Arguments

```
class ArgApp
{
    String message;
    int count;

    void GetArgs(String args[])
    {
        String s = args[1];
        count = Integer.parseInt(s);
        message = args[0];
```

```
    }

    void PrintMessage()
    {
        for (int x=0; x<count; ++x)
            System.out.println(message);
    }

    public static void main(String args[])
    {
        ArgApp app = new ArgApp();
        app.GetArgs(args);
        app.PrintMessage();
    }
}
```

```
MS-DOS Prompt

Microsoft(R) Windows 95
   (C)Copyright Microsoft Corp 1981-1995.

C:\WIN95>cd c:\Classes\ArgApp

C:\Classes\ArgApp>java ArgApp "This is a test!" 10
This is a test!
This is a test!
This is a test!
This is a test!
This is a test!
This is a test!
This is a test!
This is a test!
This is a test!
This is a test!

C:\Classes\ArgApp>
```

FIG. 13.5
The ArgApp application prints a message the number of times given in the command-line arguments.

The ArgApp application not only shows you how to use command-line parameters, but also how to write a Java application that actually does something. The important thing to notice here is that you must first create an object of the ArgApp class before you can call its methods and access its data fields. This is because a class is just a template for an object; it doesn't actually become an object until you create an instance of the class with the new keyword.

One way to avoid having to create an object of the class is to declare all the class's data fields and methods as static. Such methods and data fields are accessible in memory, which is why the SimpleApp application in listing 13.1 runs. Its `main()` method is declared as static. Of course, it's a lot easier to just create an object of the class than it is to go through the source code and add static to everything.

Windowed Applications

You're probably thinking that it's a waste of time to write Java applications if you have to run them under the DOS or UNIX text-based operating system. All the action these days is in windowed applications. Yes, you can write windowed applications with Java, as the HotJava browser proves. But, if you've written conventional windowed applications, you're probably a little nervous about writing similar Java applications. After all, writing such applications with languages like C and C++ can be a nightmare.

The truth is, however, you already know almost everything you need to know to write your own stand-alone applications for GUI operating systems. You can take most any applet and convert it to a stand-alone application just by adding the `main()` method to the class. In `main()`, you have to perform some of the tasks that Java handles for you when running an applet. These tasks include creating, sizing, and displaying the application's window. The following example gives you the details.

Changing an Applet to an Application

As mentioned in the previous paragraph, you can convert almost any applet to an application simply by adding a `main()` method that performs a few housekeeping tasks. Listing 13.3 is an application that draws a face image in its own stand-alone frame window. This application began life as an applet. When you run the application, you see the window shown in figure 13.6.

Listing 13.3 Converting an Applet to an Application

```
import java.awt.*;
import java.applet.*;

public class FaceApp extends Applet
{
    public void init()
    {
        Button button = new Button("Close");
        add(button);
    }

    public void paint(Graphics g)
```

```
    {
        // Head.
        g.drawOval(40, 40, 120, 150);

        // Eyes.
        g.drawOval(57, 75, 30, 20);
        g.drawOval(110, 75, 30, 20);

        // Pupils.
        g.fillOval(68, 81, 10, 10);
        g.fillOval(121, 81, 10, 10);

        // Nose.
        g.drawOval(85, 100, 30, 30);

        // Mouth.
        g.fillArc(60, 130, 80, 40, 180, 180);

        // Ears.
        g.drawOval(25, 92, 15, 30);
        g.drawOval(160, 92, 15, 30);
    }

    public boolean action(Event evt, Object arg)
    {
        if (arg == "Close")
            System.exit(0);

        return true;
    }

    public static void main(String args[])
    {
        FaceApp app = new FaceApp();
        Frame frame = new Frame("Face Window");

        app.init();
        app.start();

        frame.add("Center", app);
        frame.resize(210, 300);
        frame.show();
    }
}
```

FIG. 13.6
The FaceApp application draws a face in a window.

Understanding the FaceApp Application

If you examine listing 13.3, you'll see that most of the FaceApp application is written exactly like any other applet you've written throughout this book. The big difference is the addition of the `main()` method, where this program's execution starts. Because you're no longer running the program as an applet, you have to perform some of the start-up tasks that Java automatically performs for applets. The first step is to create an object of the class and a frame window to hold the object, like this:

```
FaceApp app = new FaceApp();
Frame frame = new Frame("Face Window");
```

Next, you have to call the methods that get the object going. These methods are `init()` and `start()`, which are usually called by Java:

```
app.init();
app.start();
```

Note that, although the FaceApp class doesn't show a `start()` method, it does inherit it from the Applet class. It's true that even the inherited `start()` method doesn't do anything, but you might as well be consistent and call it anyway. That way, you won't forget that some applets do override the `start()` method, without which they won't run properly.

Now, you can add the FaceApp object to the frame window, like this:

```
frame.add("Center", app);
```

Finally, you must be sure to resize and show the window, like this:

```
frame.resize(210, 300);
frame.show();
```

If you fail to resize the application's window, all you'll see is the title bar, forcing the user to resize the window by hand. More importantly, if you fail to call `show()`, the application's window won't even appear on the screen. That's sure to leave your application's user feeling abused.

A Final Application Example

The previous stand-alone application (FaceApp) shows you how to convert an applet to an application. Unfortunately, you didn't end up with an application that interacts with the user. Moreover, in order to run the application, you relied on the fact that you already have Java Workshop installed on your system. When you give a Java stand-alone application to another user, you cannot be sure whether the user has installed Java Workshop. For that reason, you must include certain files with the application, as well as set certain system variables to enable the user to run your application.

Listing 13.4 is a stand-alone application that was created from Chapter 10's MouseApplet3 applet. To get this application up and running on your system, perform the steps that follow the listing below.

Listing 13.4 An Application That Accepts User Interaction

```
import java.awt.*;
import java.applet.*;

public class MouseApp extends Applet
{
    Point startPoint;
    Point points[];
    int numPoints;
    boolean drawing;

    public void init()
    {
        startPoint = new Point(0, 0);
        points = new Point[1000];
        numPoints = 0;
        drawing = false;
        resize(400, 300);
    }

    public void paint(Graphics g)
    {
```

continues

Listing 13.4 Continued

```
        int oldX = startPoint.x;
        int oldY = startPoint.y;

        for (int x=0; x<numPoints; ++x)
        {
            g.drawLine(oldX, oldY, points[x].x, points[x].y);
            oldX = points[x].x;
            oldY = points[x].y;
        }
    }

    public boolean handleEvent(Event evt)
    {
        switch(evt.id)
        {
            case Event.MOUSE_DOWN:
                drawing = true;
                startPoint.x = evt.x;
                startPoint.y = evt.y;
                return true;
            case Event.MOUSE_MOVE:
                if ((drawing) && (numPoints < 1000))
                {
                    points[numPoints] = new Point(evt.x, evt.y);
                    ++numPoints;
                    repaint();
                }
                return true;
            default:
                return false;
        }
    }

    public static void main(String args[])
    {
        MouseApp app = new MouseApp();
        Frame frame = new Frame("Mouse Window");

        app.init();
        app.start();

        frame.add("Center", app);
        frame.resize(210, 300);
        frame.show();
    }
}
```

1. Create a MouseApp folder inside your Classes folder. The MouseApp folder is where you'll store the files for the application you're creating in these steps.
2. Using Java Workshop's text editor, type listing 13.4 and save it to your Classes\MouseApp folder under the name MouseApp.java.
3. Select Project, Create, Standalone Program from Java Workshop's menu bar. The tabbed dialog box for stand-alone application projects appears.
4. Type **MouseApp** into the Name text box, type **c:\Classes\MouseApp** into the Source Directory text box, select the Yes option button for Existing Sources, and click the Add All in Directory button. Finally, type **MouseApp.class** into the Main Class File text box and click the Apply button. Java Workshop adds the project to the current portfolio.
5. Click the Build Manager button in Java Workshop's main toolbar. The Build Manager appears.
6. Click Build Manager's Build button. Build Manager runs the Java compiler, javac, to compile your new application.
7. Click the Project Tester button to run the application. Because MouseApp is a windowed program, you can run it from within Java Workshop.

When you run MouseApp from Java Workshop, you'll see the application's main window. Click somewhere in the window with your mouse, and then move the mouse around. A line follows the mouse pointer wherever it goes.

Because this application was created from an applet, there's one minor problem: The window will not close when you click the Close button. So, to end the application, press Ctrl+Alt+Delete on your keyboard. Then, select Mouse Window in the list of programs that appears, and click the End Task button.

When you compiled MouseApp, Java Workshop created a file called MouseApp.class, which is the byte-code file for the program. If you were to try to run this file by invoking the Java interpreter, you would get errors as the system tried to find the interpreter or tried to load Java classes. To run the application on a system that doesn't have Java Workshop installed, follow the procedures listed below:

1. Create a folder called MouseApp on the target system's hard drive, and copy the MouseApp.class file to this new folder. (You can also copy the MouseApp.java file if you want, but it's not necessary.)
2. From your system's Java-Workshop\Jdk\classes folder, copy the java and sun folders to the target system's new MouseApp folder.
3. From your system's Java-Workshop\Jws\intel-win32 folder, copy the bin folder to the target system's MouseApp folder.
4. From Windows 95's Start, Programs menu on the target system, select the MS-DOS Prompt command. The MS-DOS window appears from which you can run DOS applications.
5. Type **path=c:\MouseApp\bin** in order to tell the system where it can find Java's tools and DLLs.
6. Type **cd c:\MouseApp** to switch to the MouseApp folder.
7. Type **java Mouse App** to run the application.

CAUTION

At this time, there seems to be no definitive list of redistributable files for Java Workshop. For this reason, you must not assume that the above procedure for running a stand-alone application is the final procedure that will comply with Sun Microsystems' copyright of Java Workshop. Before redistributing any files that are included with Java Workshop, I strongly suggest that you contact Sun Microsystems for permission.

From Here...

Although Java is used almost exclusively for creating applets, it is possible to use Java to create stand-alone applications. These applications can be DOS-based (or UNIX, etc.) or be written for a windowed operating system such as Windows 95. The easiest way to create a windowed application is to write the program as if it were an applet and then add a `main()` method that creates the application object and the frame window that'll contain that object.

Please refer to the following chapters for more information on related topics:

- Chapter 5, "Object-Oriented Programming and Java," tells you more about classes and how they're used in Java, as well as how to create, compile, and run applets using Java Workshop.
- Chapter 6, "Applets and Graphics," describes how to use graphical methods such as those used to draw the face in FaceApp's window.
- Chapter 15, "Source Editor," describes how to use Java Workshop's built-in text editor.

PART IV

The Java Workshop Tools

CHAPTER 14

Portfolio Manager and Project Manager

- **How to create and delete portfolios.**

  Portfolios enable you to organize your projects into logical groups. Of course, you have to create a portfolio before you can use it. You might find it handy to be able to get rid of portfolios you no longer need.

- **How to select and import portfolios.**

  You can have as many different portfolios as you like, but you have to tell Java Workshop which portfolio you want to use. If you have to, you can even add existing portfolios to your portfolio list.

- **How to create and delete projects.**

  Projects enable you to organize the files that comprise an applet, stand-alone application, or other type of Java project. As with portfolios, you can both create and delete projects.

- **How to choose and import projects.**

  Before you start work, you select the project on which you want to work. You can also import existing projects from other portfolios and work on them.

Java Workshop has a few tricks up its sleeve when it comes to organizing your work. For example, when several programmers are working on different projects concurrently, each can use Portfolio Manager to maintain his own portfolio, ensuring that each programmer has access to only his own work. If you have many different types of applets and applications that you want to organize in some logical way, such as placing graphics-oriented programs and utilities in different groups, Java Workshop's Portfolio Manager enables you to handle these types of tasks, as well.

Moreover, each applet or application you create can be given its own project, which organizes all the source-code files needed by the program;

this enables you to set up different options for individual projects. Java Workshop's Project Manager gives you this organizational power over your various projects. ■

Using Portfolio Manager

As mentioned in the previous paragraph, Portfolio Manager enables you to organize projects into groups. These groups may represent different programmers' projects, or different types of programs that are related in some way. No matter how you decide to use Portfolio Manager, however, you can think of a portfolio as a virtual directory into which different projects can be stored. The difference is that, while a directory dictates a location on a disk, the projects in a portfolio can be located in many different places on a disk or even on the Web. You set the location for a project when you add it to the portfolio.

The first time you start up Java Workshop, there are already three portfolios created. These portfolios are named Personal, JDK, and AWT. The Personal portfolio contains two projects—Checkers and Blink—that Java Workshop refers to in its online tutorial. The JDK portfolio contains sample applets that you can access from Sun Microsystems Web site (see fig. 14.1). These applets are actually part of the Java Developer's Kit, from which the name JDK comes. The AWT portfolio contains several applets that test some of Java's graphical capabilities (see fig. 14.2). These applets, too, are located at Sun's Web site. If you want to run the applets in the JDK and AWT portfolios, you must have your Internet connection established first.

You can tell the type of projects included in a portfolio by the icon used to represent the project in Portfolio Manager's window. For example, an applet project's icon looks like a graphic on a page (representing the applet as part of an HTML document), whereas a package project's icon looks like a chest holding other projects.

FIG. 14.1
The JDK portfolio contains many sample applets.

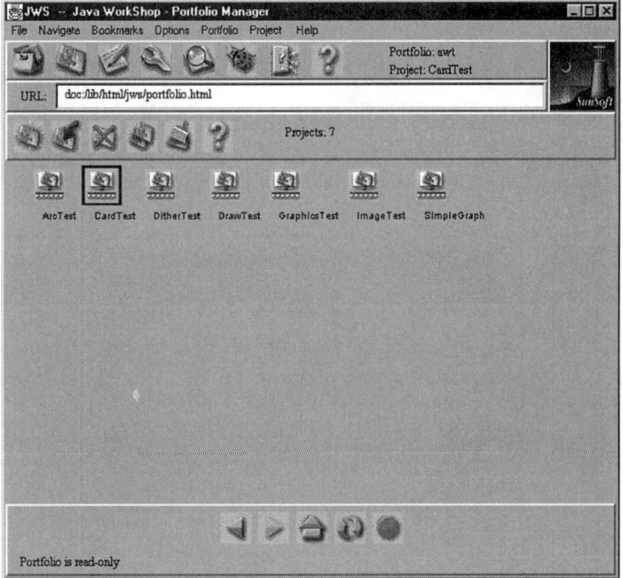

FIG. 14.2
The AWT portfolio contains graphical test applets.

Creating a New Portfolio

Of course, no one is forcing you to stick with the portfolios that come with Java Workshop. You can create your own custom portfolio. To do this, follow these steps.

1. Choose Portfolio, Create from Java Workshop's menu bar. The Create Portfolio dialog box appears (see fig. 14.3).

   This dialog box requests the name of the new portfolio file. As you can see in the dialog box's Portfolio text box, portfolio files end with the .psf file extension.

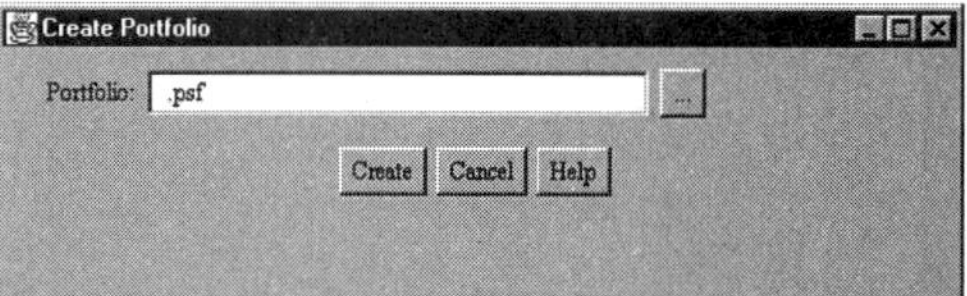

FIG. 14.3 The Create Portfolio dialog box requests the name of your new portfolio file.

2. Click the dialog box's browse button (the one marked with the ellipses). The Create Portfolio File dialog box appears.
3. Browse to the directory in which you want the portfolio file stored, type the name of the portfolio file in the dialog's File Name text box (see fig. 14.4), and then click the Open button. The Create Portfolio File dialog box closes, exposing the Create Portfolio dialog box again.

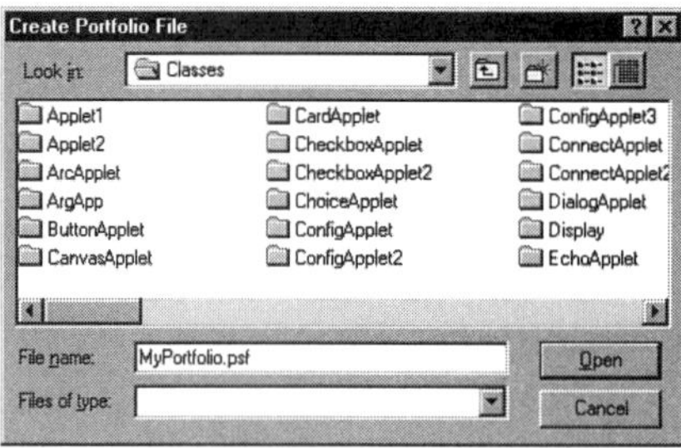

FIG. 14.4 You have to select the location in which Java Workshop should store your new portfolio file.

4. Click the Create button. Portfolio Manager creates the portfolio file and opens the new portfolio into Java Workshop (see fig. 14.5).

FIG. 14.5
When you create a new portfolio, Portfolio Manager automatically opens the portfolio so it's ready to go.

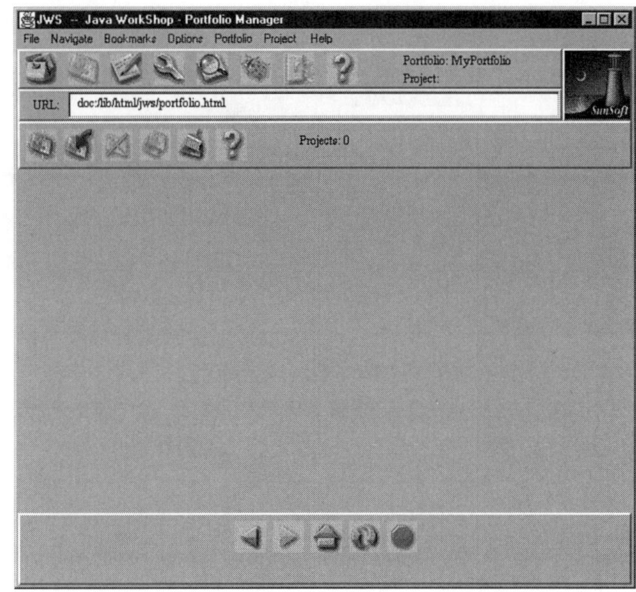

Once you've created your new portfolio, you'll want to add at least one project to it. See the section entitled "Creating a Project" for information on how to do this.

Choosing a Portfolio

As you now know, Java Workshop comes with three portfolios all ready to go. You'll also be adding your own to the collection. With all these different portfolios from which to choose, you need a way to tell Java Workshop which portfolio you want to access. You do this by selecting the portfolio from Java Workshop's menu bar. Select the Portfolio Choose menu item, and a submenu containing the various portfolios appears (see fig. 14.6). Select the portfolio you want, and Portfolio Manager opens the portfolio for you.

Removing a Portfolio

Once you get a lot of portfolios going, you'll need to do a little housekeeping now and then, to get rid of portfolios you're no longer using. You can accomplish this task quickly and easily; select the Portfolio Remove command from Java Workshop's menu bar. When you do, a submenu appears from which you can select the portfolio to remove (see fig. 14.7).

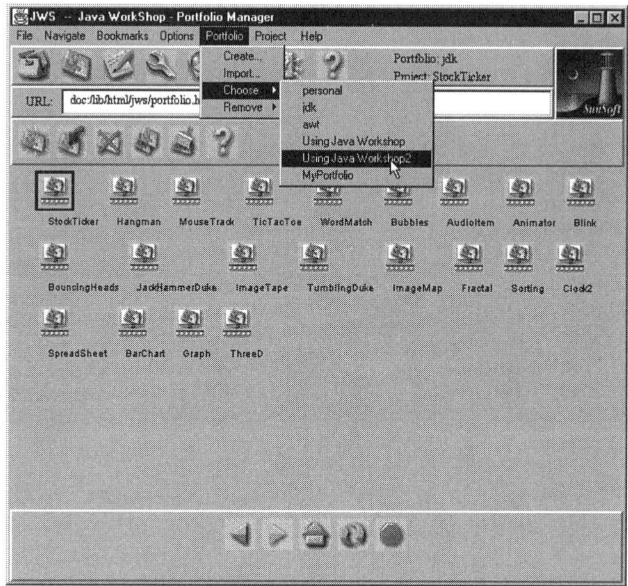

FIG. 14.6
You can choose a portfolio from Java Workshop's menu bar.

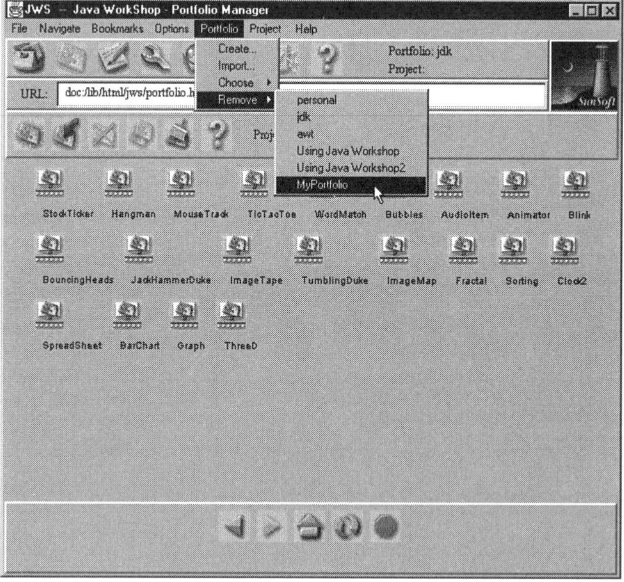

FIG. 14.7
Use the Portfolio Remove command to remove old portfolios from Java Workshop.

NOTE When you choose the Portfolio Remove command, Portfolio removes the portfolio only from the lists shown in the Portfolio Choose and Portfolio Remove submenus. No files—including the portfolio's .psf file—are removed from the disk. ■

Importing a Portfolio

Sometimes you may want to add an existing portfolio to the portfolios currently recognized by Java Workshop. Doing this enables you to select the portfolio from the menu bar, and add projects to the portfolio. To import an existing portfolio, choose the Portfolio, Import command. When you do, the Import Portfolio dialog box appears (see fig. 14.8). If the portfolio file's location is an URL, select the URL button; otherwise, leave the File Option button selected. In the case of a file, click the dialog box's Browse button to bring up the file browser. Use the file browser to locate and select the .psf file you want to import.

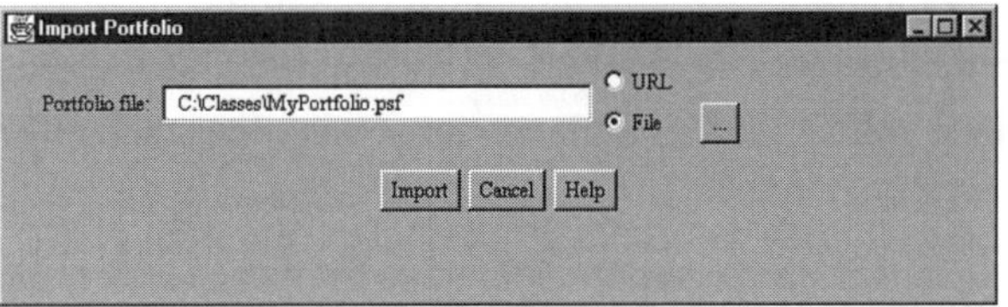

FIG. 14.8
You can import existing portfolio files into Java Workshop.

You can run a project from Portfolio Manager (assuming that the files have been fully compiled) by double-clicking the project in the Portfolio Manager window.

Using Project Manager

An empty portfolio is about as useful as a toothbrush without bristles. That is, your portfolios won't do you much good unless they contain projects on which you can work. And even if you're using a portfolio that already contains projects, you need a way to tell Java Workshop which project you want to open. Project Manager provides all the commands you need to control and edit your projects.

Creating a Project

If you're starting off with an empty portfolio, or if you want to add a new project to an existing portfolio, you must create a project. Portfolio Manager enables you to create five different kinds of projects, which are listed below:

- *Applets.* Applets are small programs that can be added to HTML documents. When the user opens the document, the applet is automatically loaded and run. Most of the programs you've created in this book have been applets.
- *Stand-alone programs.* Stand-alone programs are like any other application you might create with your favorite programming language. These programs cannot be part of an HTML document. Instead, you run a stand-alone program with the Java interpreter. Because the Java language is better suited for applets, Java stand-alone programs are not common.
- *Packages.* A package is a lot like a library in that a package enables you to organize different classes into related groups.
- *Images.* Images are graphical elements that can be added to HTML documents. Images can be aligned in various ways, and used as a target for mouse clicks. When used as a mouse target, images can act like buttons, triggering events.
- *Remote Applets.* A remote applet is simply an applet that's located on another computer. To access a remote applet, you need its URL.

To create a project, choose Project, Create from Java Workshop's menu bar. When you do, a submenu appears, listing the five types of projects you can create. Select the project type you want, and a tabbed dialog box appears. Each page of the tabbed dialog box accepts attributes for one of the five project types. Each project type requires that you enter different information. Figures 14.9 through 14.13 show the dialog boxes and the information you must enter into each.

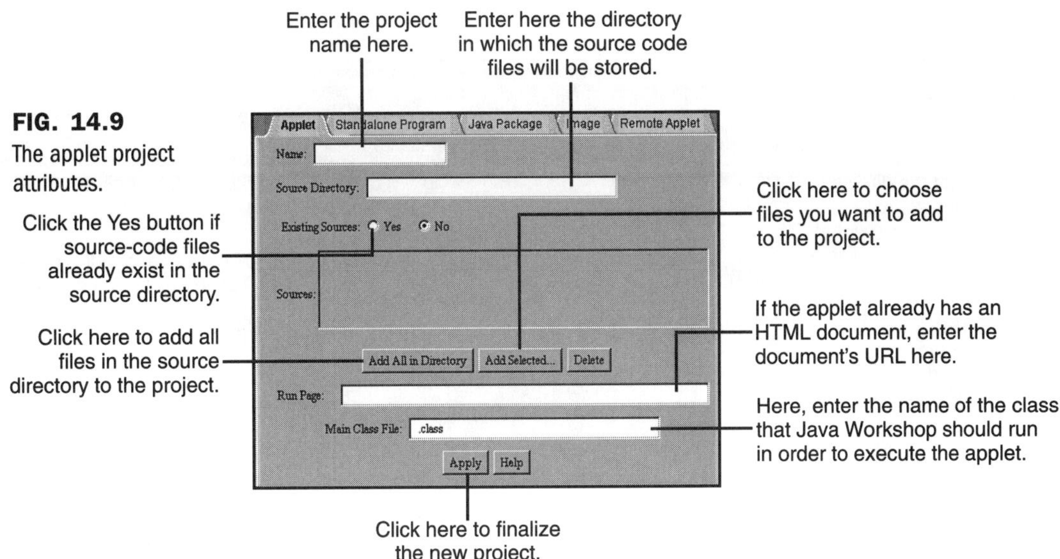

FIG. 14.9
The applet project attributes.

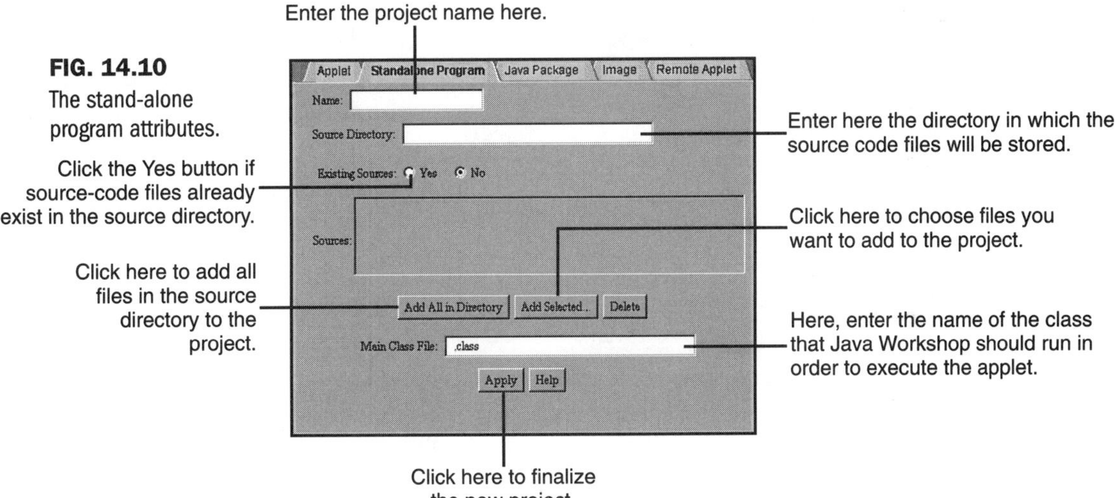

FIG. 14.10
The stand-alone program attributes.

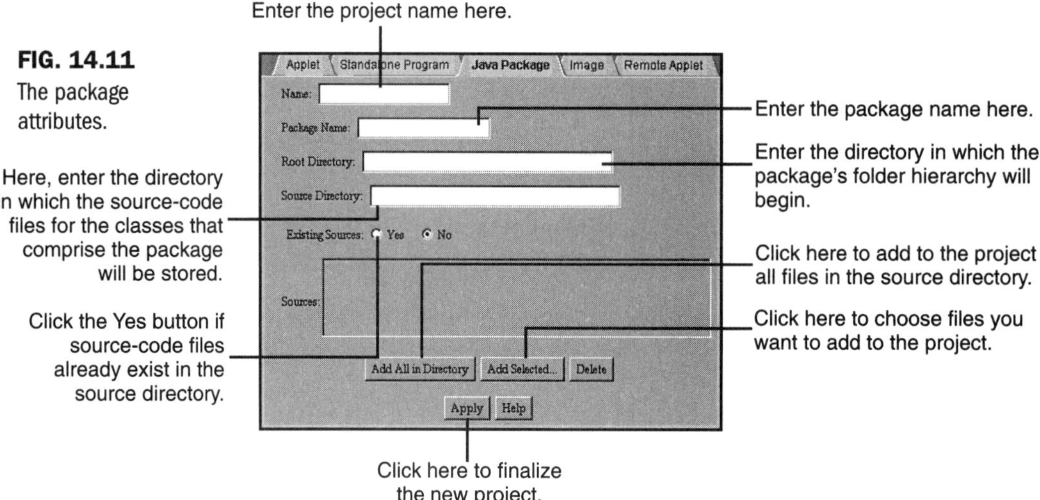
Enter the project name here.
Applet
Standalone Program
Java Package
Image
Remote Applet
Name:
Package Name:
Root Directory:
Source Directory:
Existing Sources: Yes No
Sources:
Add All in Directory
Add Selected...
Delete
Apply
Help
Enter the package name here.
Enter the directory in which the package's folder hierarchy will begin.
Here, enter the directory in which the source-code files for the classes that comprise the package will be stored.
Click here to add to the project all files in the source directory.
Click here to choose files you want to add to the project.
Click the Yes button if source-code files already exist in the source directory.
Click here to finalize the new project.

FIG. 14.11
The package attributes.

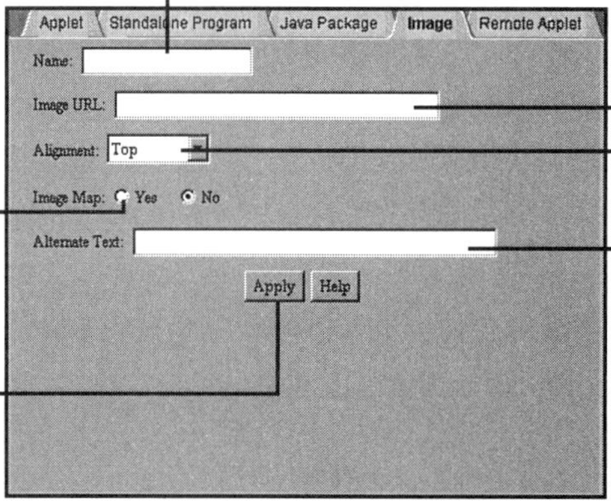

Enter the project name here.

Applet | Standalone Program | Java Package | Image | Remote Applet

Name:

Image URL:

Alignment: Top

Image Map: Yes No

Alternate Text:

Apply Help

Enter the image's URL here

Select the image's alignment here.

Select the Yes button if you'll be using the image as a mouse-click target.

Here, enter the text that should be displayed by browsers that can't display images.

Click here to finalize the new project.

FIG. 14.12
The image attributes.

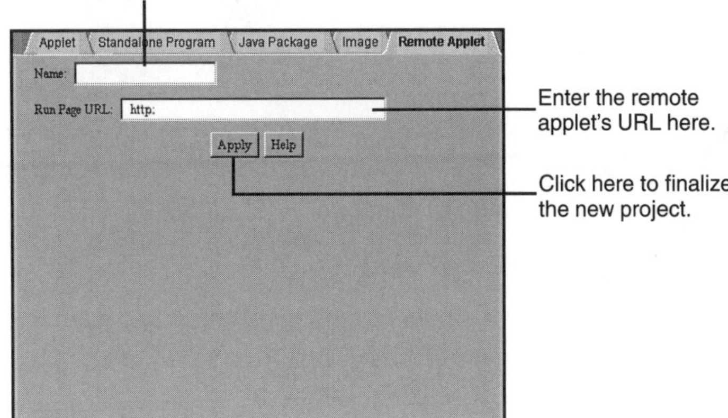

FIG. 14.13
The remote applet attributes.

Choosing a Project

Most portfolios contain many different projects. When you want to switch from one project to another, you can choose Project, Choose from Java Workshop's menu bar. When you do, you'll see a submenu listing the projects from which you can choose (see fig. 14.14). Just click on the project you want to make it active.

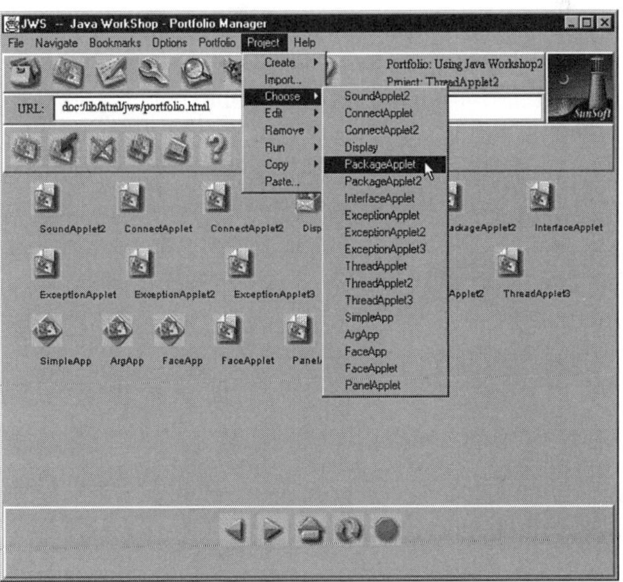

FIG. 14.14
Use the Project, Choose command to select a project.

Importing a Project

Often, you may want to add already existing projects to a portfolio. You can do this by using Project Manager's import function. There are two ways to import a project: copying or by reference. When you copy a project, you create a second project in a separate folder, whereas when you import a project by reference, you simply add the existing project as is to the portfolio. To import a project by reference, use the following steps:

1. Choose Project, Import from Java Workshop's menu bar. The Import Project dialog box appears (see fig. 14.15).

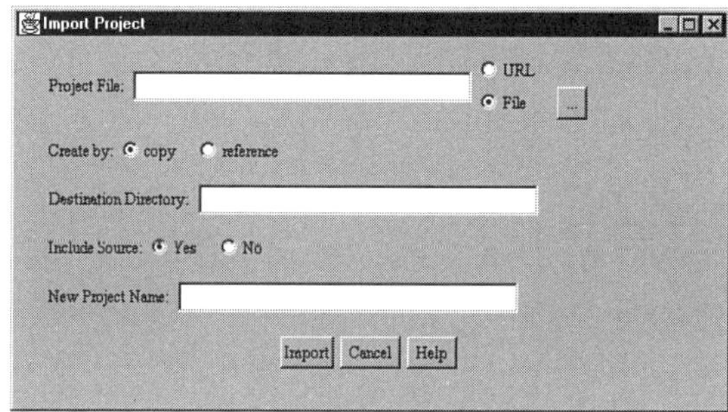

FIG. 14.15
The Import Project dialog box.

2. Use the browse feature (click the Browse button) to locate and select the project file for the project you want to import (see fig. 14.16).

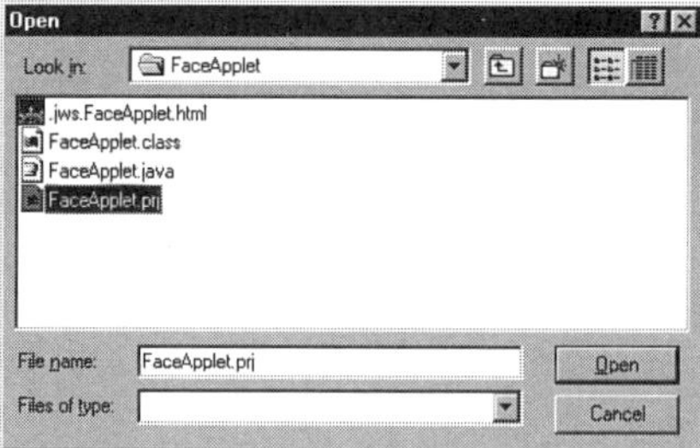

FIG. 14.16
Use the browser to find the project file you want to import.

3. Select the Reference button in the Import Project dialog box.
4. Click the Import button.

To import a project by copying, follow this set of steps:

1. Choose Project, Import from Java Workshop's menu bar. The Import Project dialog box appears.
2. Use the browse feature (click the Browse button) to locate and select the project file for the project you want to import.
3. Select the Copy button in the Import Project dialog box.
4. In the Destination Directory text box, enter the directory in which you want the new project's files stored.
5. If you want to copy the project's source-code files, select the Yes option button.
6. In the New Project Name text box, enter a name for the new project.
7. Click the Import button.

You can also use the Copy and Paste commands on the Project menu to import projects into a portfolio. Use Copy to duplicate the project you want to import. Then change to the portfolio into which you want to import the project and use Paste to perform the importing.

Editing a Project

After you've created a project, you're not stuck with the attributes you chose. You're also not stuck with the default attributes that Java Workshop supplies for the project. You can change many project attributes by choosing Project, Edit from Java Workshop's menu bar. When you do, you see the tabbed dialog box shown in figure 14.17. This dialog box has several pages that organize the many attributes for the project.

Some of the attributes in the tabbed dialog box are for advanced programmers only. Others provide a handy way for you to control your project. For example, in figure 14.17, you can see that you can change the type of project just by clicking an option button. On the Run page, you can specify the values Java Workshop uses when it creates your applet's HTML document (see fig. 14.18). You can specify the applet's width and height, alternative text, and even the parameters that should be passed to the applet when it runs.

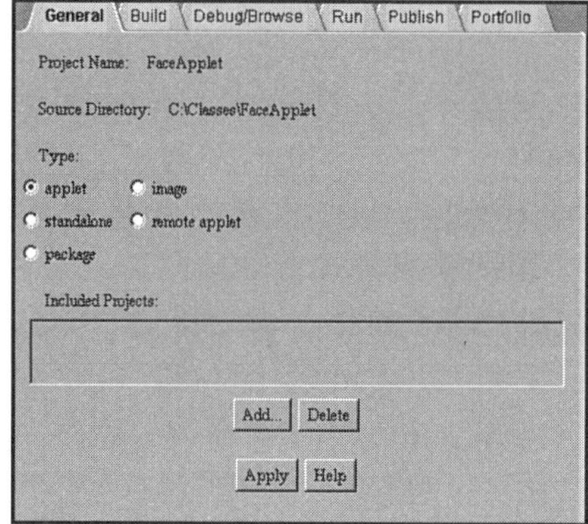

FIG. 14.17
You can change many of your project's attributes.

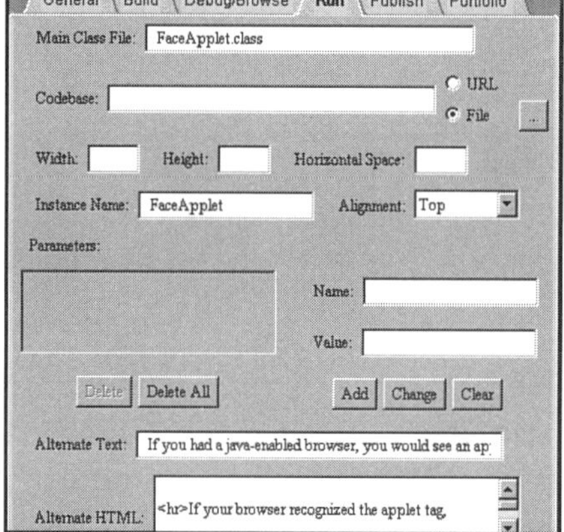

FIG. 14.18
Using the Run attributes, you can change how Java Workshop runs your applet.

Removing a Project

You know that you can add new projects to a portfolio, either by creating a new project or by importing an existing one. You may have guessed that you can also delete projects from a portfolio. To do this, choose Project, Remove from Java Workshop's menu bar. When you do, you'll see a submenu showing all the projects in the portfolio (see fig. 14.19). Simply select the project you want to remove. Project Manager removes the project from the portfolio but all the project's files remain on your hard drive.

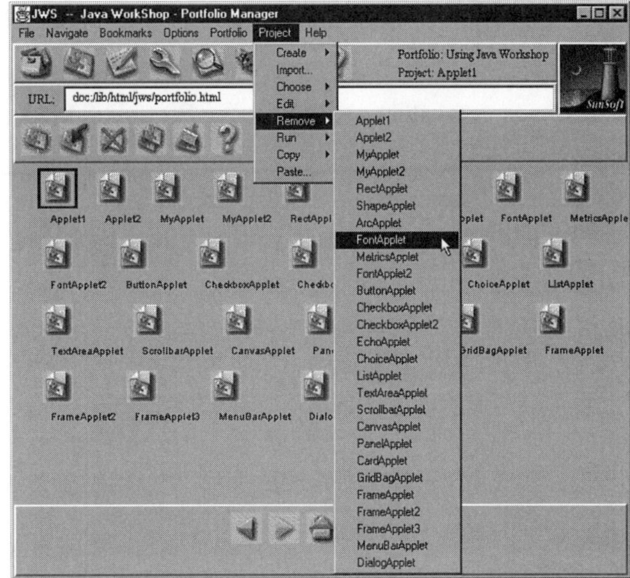

FIG. 14.19
Use the Project, Remove command to delete projects from a portfolio.

Running a Project

If you've already compiled the source code associated with a project, there are several ways you can run the program. One way is to select the project in the Portfolio Manager window and click the Project Tester button in Java Workshop's toolbar. Another way is to simply double-click the project's icon in the Portfolio Manager window. Finally, you can also run a project by choosing Project, Run from Java Workshop's menu bar.

From Here...

Using Portfolio Manager and Project Manager, you can keep your Java programs organized and set up exactly the way you want them. Such organization is especially important when you start to accumulate a lot of different projects or when you have several people working on different projects on the same system or network.

For more information on related topics, please refer to the following chapters:

- Chapter 5, "Object-Oriented Programming and Java," offers some hands-on experience in creating an applet using Portfolio Manager and Project Manager.
- Chapter 12, "Packages, Interfaces, Exceptions, and Threads," shows how to use Project Manager to create your own Java packages.
- Chapter 13, "Writing Java Applications," describes how to use Project Manager to create stand-alone programs.

CHAPTER 15

Source Editor

About running Source Editor.

There are two ways to get Source Editor up and running, depending on whether you're creating a new project or want to edit an existing source-code file.

How to open and save files.

Transferring files to and from disk is obviously an important part of using a text editor. Source Editor provides all the usual file commands.

About Source Editor's status bar.

The editor's status bar keeps you informed of your current file's status.

How to perform text-block operations.

Using text-block operations such as Cut-and-Paste and Search-and-Replace can save you a lot of development time.

How to control the text cursor.

Source Editor supports many of the cursor commands you've become accustomed to using with other text editors.

Virtually all computer programming requires that you write source code using some sort of text editor. Java is no exception. Although you can create Java source code with any text editor capable of saving ASCII (pure text) files, Java Workshop includes its own integrated editor called Source Editor. While Source Editor isn't as powerful as some editors with which you may be familiar, it's still an excellent workhorse for creating and editing Java source-code files. This chapter provides an introduction to using Source Editor. ■

Running Source Editor

Because Source Editor is an integrated tool of Java Workshop, you can run it simply by clicking its icon in Java Workshop's toolbar (see fig. 15.1). When you click the icon, Java Workshop runs Source Editor, loading the source-code file for the currently selected project (see fig. 15.2). Another way to run Source Editor is to create a new project, by choosing the Create, Using Source Editor option on the Applet page of the tabbed dialog box that appears when you start a new project. When you run Source Editor this way, Java Workshop automatically creates a source-code file for you. This source-code file represents a "do-nothing" applet—including overridden `init()`, `start()`, `stop()`, and `destroy()` methods—that you can modify as needed to create your specific applet.

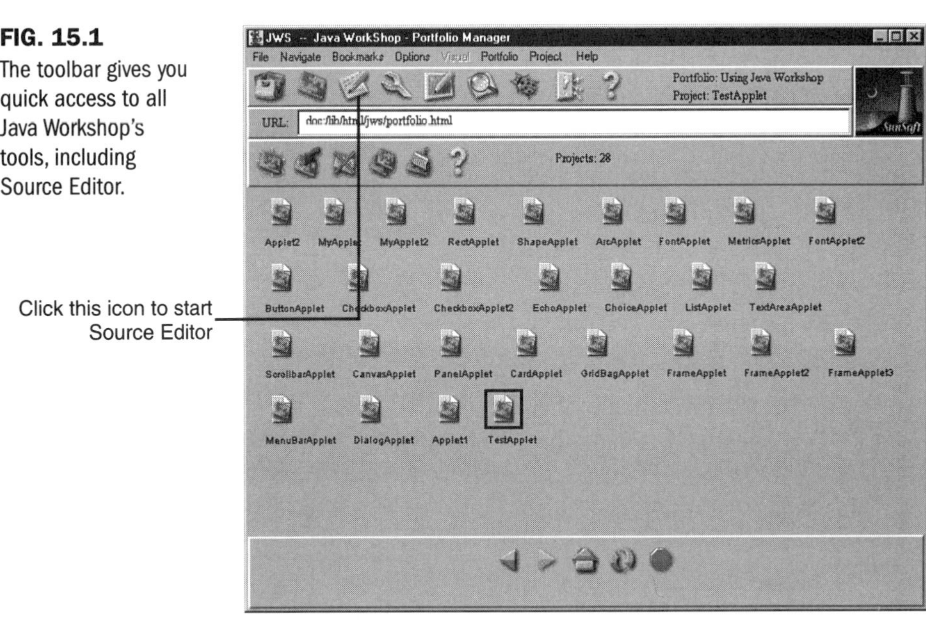

FIG. 15.1
The toolbar gives you quick access to all Java Workshop's tools, including Source Editor.

FIG. 15.2
Source Editor automatically loads the source code for the current project.

```
c:\Classes\Applet1\Applet1.java
File Edit View Version

import java.awt.*;
import java.applet.*;
import MyClass;

public class Applet1 extends Applet
{
    MyClass myObject;
    TextField textField1;

    public void init()
    {
        myObject = new MyClass(1);
        textField1 = new TextField(20);
        add(textField1);
        textField1.setText("1");
    }

    public void paint(Graphics g)
    {
        String s = textField1.getText();
        int value = Integer.parseInt(s);
        myObject.SetField(value);
        value = myObject.GetField();
        s = String.valueOf(value);
        g.drawString("The data field of the object", 80, 80);

Line: 1   Column: 1   Unchanged   Writable
```

The Status Bar

Source Editor's status bar contains helpful information about the currently loaded file (see fig. 15.3). This information includes the text cursor's current line and column position, an icon indicating the file's change status, the read/write access for the file, the file's version-control status, and editor reusability status. Table 15.1 lists the status bar's panels and meanings.

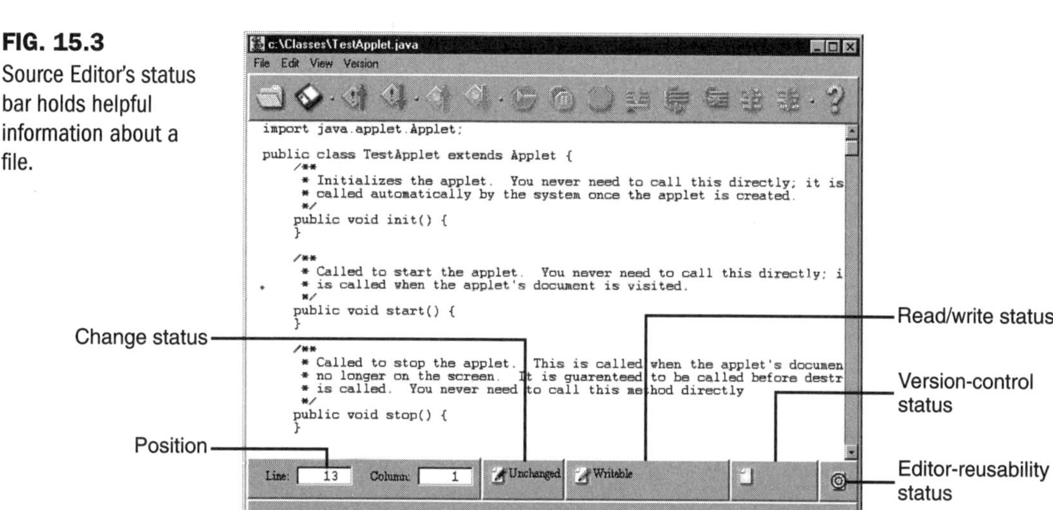

FIG. 15.3
Source Editor's status bar holds helpful information about a file.

Table 15.1 Source Editor's Status Bar

Panel	Description
Position	This is the line and column number at which the text cursor is currently positioned.
Change status	This panel will be marked as New, Changed, or Unchanged.
Read/write status	A writable file can be edited and saved. A read-only file can be edited, but must be saved under a new file name, preventing the original file from being modified.
Version-control status	When using a version-control system with the project, Checked In indicates that the file cannot be edited and Checked Out means that the file can be edited.
Editor-reusability status	A Target icon indicates that only a single copy of the editor will be shared between Java Workshop's various tools. A Multiple-page icon means that a new instance of the editor will be started each time a tool needs an editor.

File Handling

As with any text editor, you'll find Source Editor's file-handling commands in the application's File menu (see fig. 15.4). These commands enable you to create, open, save, and close files. You can also load and save files by clicking the Open and Save icons in Source Editor's toolbar. The remaining toolbar icons (except the Help icon) are used in conjunction with Java Workshop's debugger. For more information on the debugger, see Chapter 17, "Debugger." Table 15.2 lists the File menu's commands and their meanings.

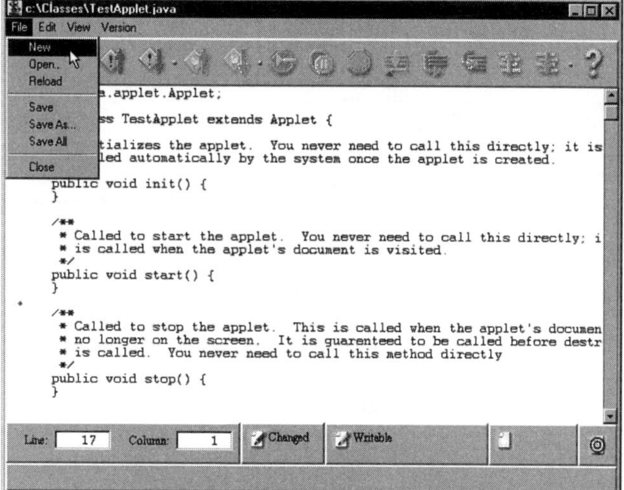

FIG. 15.4
The File menu holds Source Editor's file-handling commands.

Table 15.2 Commands on the File Menu

Command	Description
New	Creates a new, empty file.
Open	Opens an existing file.
Reload	Restores a file to its last-saved state, throwing away all editing done since the last save.
Save	Saves the current file.
Save As	Saves the current file under a new name.
Save All	Saves files in all active editors.
Close	Closes the file and the editor.

Editing Commands

Source Editor's Edit menu contains commands that make it easier to deal with blocks of text, and to find and replace occurrences of text in the file (see fig. 15.5). Table 15.3 lists the commands and their descriptions.

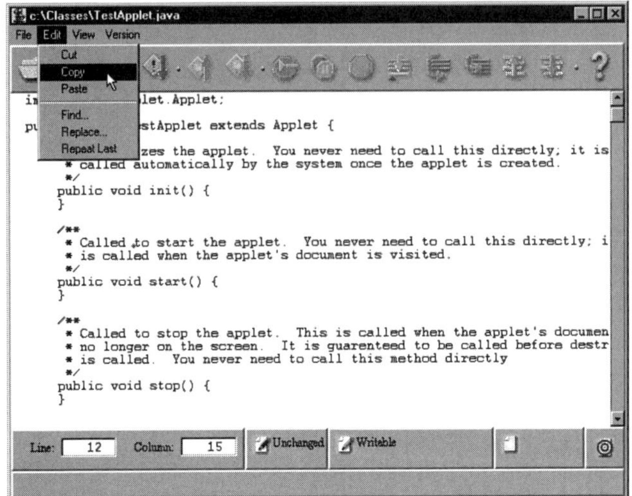

FIG. 15.5
Source Editor's Edit menu contains handy editing commands.

Table 15.3 Commands on the Edit Menu

Command	Description
Cut	Cuts the selected text to the clipboard.
Copy	Copies the selected text to the clipboard.
Paste	Pastes the clipboard's text at the cursor position.
Find	Finds a word or phrase in the text.
Replace	Replaces a word or phrase in the text.
Repeat Last	Repeats the last find or replace command.

In order to use commands that act on blocks of text, you must first define the text block with which you want to work. There are a couple of ways to define a text block, both result in the selected text appearing highlighted in the editor's window (see fig. 15.6). The first method to define a text block is to drag the mouse pointer over the text to be highlighted. When you release the mouse button, Source Editor highlights the selected text. You can also highlight text from the keyboard. To do this, use your keyboard's arrow keys to position the text cursor at the start of the block you want to select. Then, hold down the Shift key and position the text cursor (again using the arrow keys) at the end of the text block.

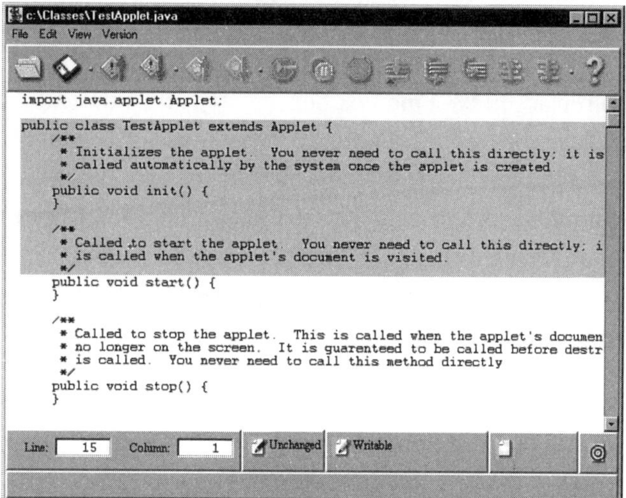

FIG. 15.6
A selected block of text appears highlighted in the editor window.

In addition to the common text-selection methods described in this section, there are a few other techniques you can try. For example, to highlight a single word, double-click it. Another way to select a text block is to click at the beginning of the block, then hold down the Shift key and click at the end of the block. Finally, you can select an entire line by triple-clicking it.

Search and Replace

As you learned in the previous section, the Edit menu contains commands you can use to find or replace text in a source-code file. To find a word or phrase, choose Edit, Find. When you do, you see the Find dialog box (see fig. 15.7). Type the word you want to find into the Find text box and click the OK button. Source Editor highlights the first occurrence of the word that it finds. To find the next occurrence, use the Edit menu's Repeat Last command.

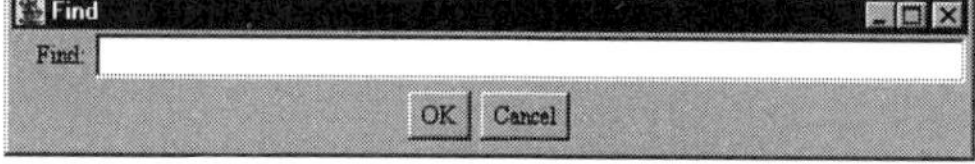

FIG. 15.7
You use the Find dialog box to locate a word or phrase in a source-code file.

To replace an occurrence of a word or phrase with new text, choose Edit, Replace. When you do, the Replace dialog box appears (see fig. 15.8). Type the text you want to replace in the Find text box, and type the new text in the Replace text box. Then, click the OK button. Source editor finds and highlights the first occurrence of the text to replace and displays the Ask dialog box (see fig. 15.9). Click the Replace button to replace only the selected occurrence. Click the Skip button to ignore the selected occurrence and move on to the next occurrence. Click the Replace All button to replace every occurrence of the text in the file with the replacement text. Finally, click the Cancel button to cancel the Replace command.

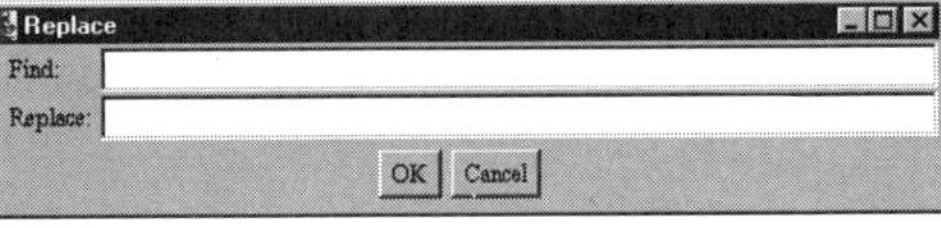

FIG. 15.8 The Replace dialog box enables you to replace one text string with another.

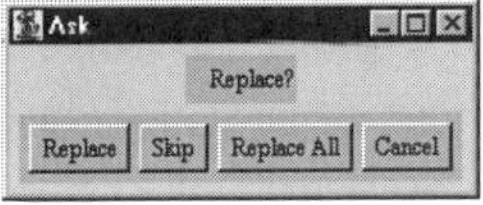

FIG. 15.9 The Ask dialog box offers several options for the Replace command.

Additional Menus

Source Editor's View and Version menus contain additional commands that you may or may not need to use. The View menu's New Window command is similar to the Open command, except it opens the selected file into a new instance of the editor. The View menu's Use For Tools Display command, on the other hand, sets the editor's reusability status. When Use For Tools Display Command is selected, the status bar's reusability panel displays a Target icon, indicating that all tools should use this editor instance. If Use For Tools Display is not selected, the status bar's reusability panel displays a Multi-page icon, indicating that all tools should open their own editor instance.

Finally, the Version menu is used only when you're running Java Workshop under a version-control system. It requires source-code files to be checked out before they can be edited, preventing two people from making changes to the same file concurrently. Because version-control systems are usually used only by programming teams, they are not covered in this book.

Controlling the Text Cursor

The text cursor indicates where any text you type appears in the file. For that reason, you obviously need a way to position the cursor where you need it. You can use your keyboard's four arrow keys to place the cursor anywhere in the text file. However, there are several special keys and key combinations that offer more flexibility. Those keys and their descriptions are listed in Table 15.4.

Table 15.4 Cursor Control Key

Key	Description
Ctrl+End	Places the cursor at the very end of the file.
Ctrl+Home	Places the cursor at the very start of the file.
Ctrl+PageDown	Places the cursor at bottom line of the current display.
Ctrl+PageUp	Places the cursor at top of the displayed page.
Ctrl+DownArrow	Scrolls the display down one line.
Ctrl+LeftArrow	Moves the cursor one word to the left.
Ctrl+RightArrow	Moves the cursor one word to the right.
Ctrl+UpArrow	Scrolls the display up one line.
End	Places the cursor at the end of the line.
Home	Places the cursor at the start of the line.
PageDown	Moves the cursor forward one page.
PageUp	Moves the cursor back one page.

From Here...

Source Editor provides you with a handy, built-in tool for developing source-code files under Java Workshop. You can also use Source Editor to write HTML documents or any other type of plain text file. When you learn about program debugging in Chapter 17, you'll discover that Source Editor also enables you to locate and correct errors quickly.

For more information on related topics, please consult the following chapters:

- Chapter 14, "Portfolio Manager and Project Manager," shows you how to create new projects.
- Chapter 16, "Build Manager and Source Browser," shows how to compile and browse the source-code files you create with Source Editor.
- Chapter 17, "Debugger," describes how the Source Editor fits into the program-debugging process.

CHAPTER 16

Build Manager and Source Browser

Two tools in the Java Workshop toolkit make it easier to compile and edit source-code files. First, Build Manager eliminates your need to run Java's compiler from a DOS command line. Moreover, in a multiple-file project, Build Manager keeps track of which files are current and which need to be recompiled. Build Manager even links to Source Editor, enabling you to quickly jump to places in your source code where corrections are needed. Source Browser, too, links to Source Editor, enabling you to not only see class hierarchies, but also to jump almost instantly to any method in your source code. ■

About compiling programs with Build Manager.

Build Manager takes all the sweat out of using Java's command-line compiler. You can compile a project with a single mouse click.

How to find syntax errors with Build Manager.

Because Build Manager communicates directly with Source Editor, you can quickly jump to error lines in your source-code files.

About Source Browser's class browsing.

Source Browser can display an inheritance hierarchy for your classes, as well as a list of the methods and variables included in a class.

How to find text strings with Source Browser.

You can locate specific text strings in your source-code files. Just tell Source Browser what to look for and watch it go.

Using Build Manager

After you've created a new project or edited an existing one, you need to compile the source code into a byte-code file that the Java interpreter can understand. If you use the JDK's command-line tools, you have to compile your source-code files by invoking the Java compiler (called javac). This is done by typing a command line at the DOS prompt. Since you're using Java Workshop, you can compile your applet using Build Manager and stay within the familiar Windows environment; you can also invoke the compiler with a single mouse click. In the following sections, you'll learn how to use Build Manager effectively with your projects.

Starting Build Manager

Assuming that you've already selected the project using Project Manager, compiling the project is just a matter of clicking the Build Manager button on Java Workshop's toolbar. (It's the button that looks like a wrench.) When you do, you see a window something like that shown in figure 16.1. In the figure, you can see that Build Manager has its own toolbar from which you select the commands you need to bring your project up-to-date.

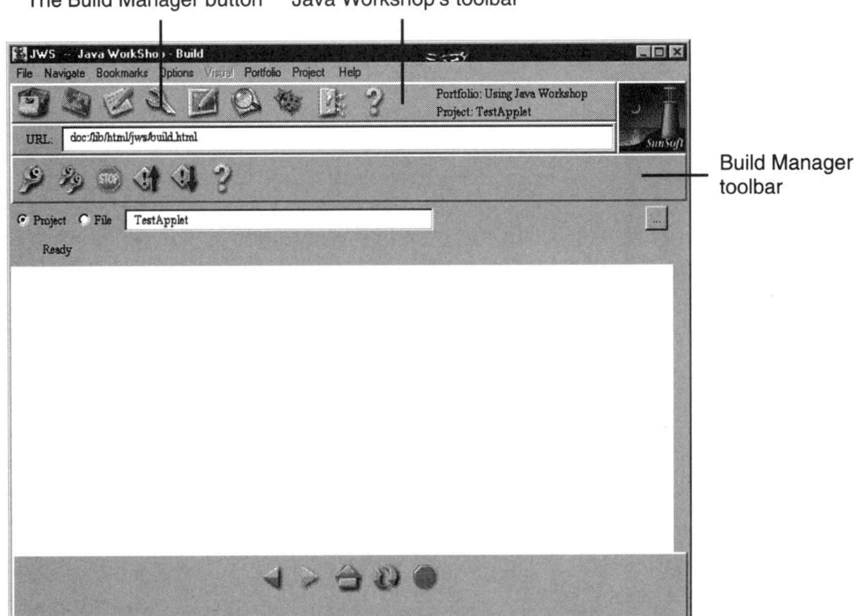

FIG. 16.1
Both Java Workshop and Build Manager sport their own toolbars.

Compiling a Project

Normally, to compile a project, you'd click the first button on Build Manager's toolbar (the one that looks like a single wrench and bolt). When you do, Build Manager invokes javac (the Java compiler) with the correct command line for your project. As the compiler works, status information appears in Build Manager's window (see fig. 16.2). If the project compiles successfully, Build Manager gives you the message `Done`. If you want to stop the build process any time while it's working, just click the stop-sign icon, which becomes enabled when Build Manager is working.

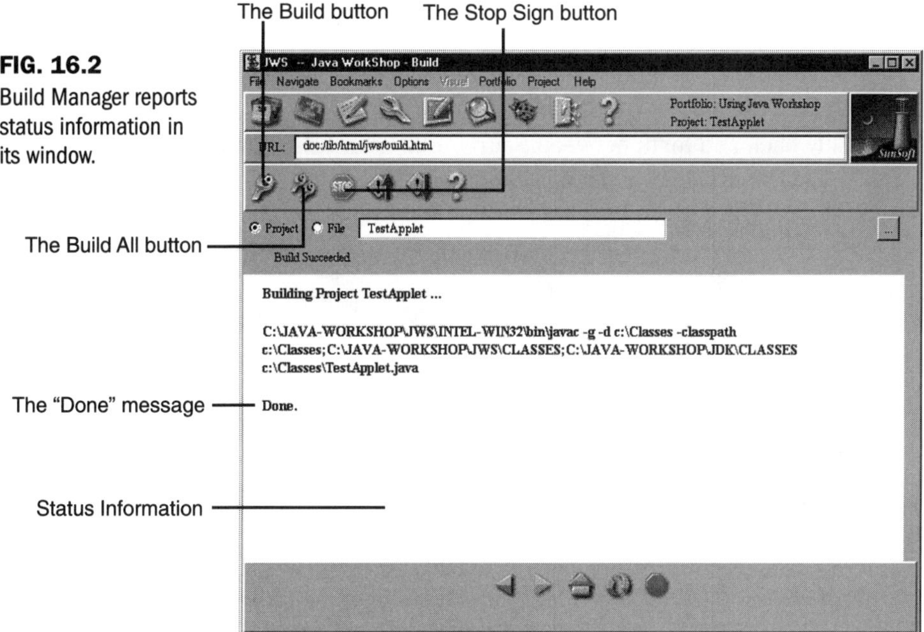

FIG. 16.2
Build Manager reports status information in its window.

If you're working on lengthy projects, you may have your source code in more than one file. For example, you might use three different custom classes in your applet, each of which is contained in its own source-code file. Because you may make changes in one file, but not in others, Build Manager keeps track of editing information and compiles only those files that have changed since the last compilation. This doesn't mean, however, that you can't compile the entire project any time you want. To override Build Manager's intelligent compilation, and compile every file in the project, click the second icon in Build Manager's toolbar (the one that looks like two wrenches and bolts). This tells Build Manager to compile every source-code file, even if a compiled file is already up-to-date.

Correcting Syntax Errors

Of course, more often than not, your source-code contains syntax errors that need to be corrected before Build Manager can successfully compile the project. When this happens, Build Manager lists the errors in its status display, as shown in figure 16.3. When there are errors listed in the build-status display, Build Manager enables the error-location buttons in Build Manager's toolbar (the buttons with arrows and exclamation points). By clicking one of these arrow buttons, you can call up Source Editor with the problem source-code line highlighted. Just correct the line, save the file, and recompile. Because Java Workshop enables you to jump so quickly back and forth between Source Editor and Build Manager, you can get even error-ridden source-code fixed and compiled quickly.

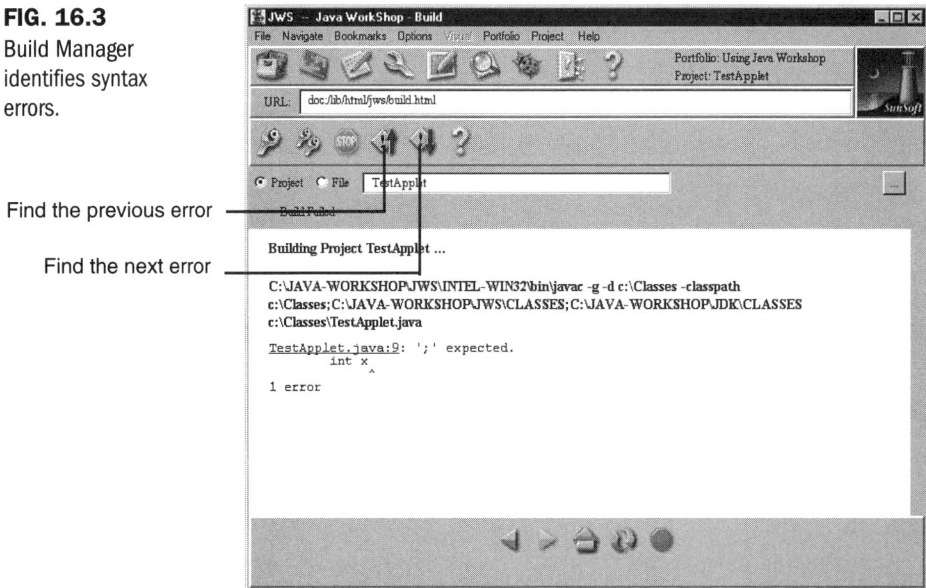

FIG. 16.3
Build Manager identifies syntax errors.

TIP You can also jump to an error in the source code by clicking on the file name in the error description that appears in Build Manager's window. Doing so loads Source Editor with the error line highlighted, the same as if you clicked one of the error buttons in the toolbar.

Selecting Projects or Files

When Java Workshop runs, there is always a current project selected. It is the currently selected project that Build Manager works on, not only compiling the files in the project, but also obtaining the compiler options from the project. As you know, you can select a project from Project Manager. However, you can also select a project by clicking the Ellipsis button to the right of the area below Build Manager's tool bar. If you click the Ellipsis button, Build Manager displays a window containing the projects in the currently selected portfolio (see fig. 16.4). To choose a project, click the project's name to highlight it and then click the OK button.

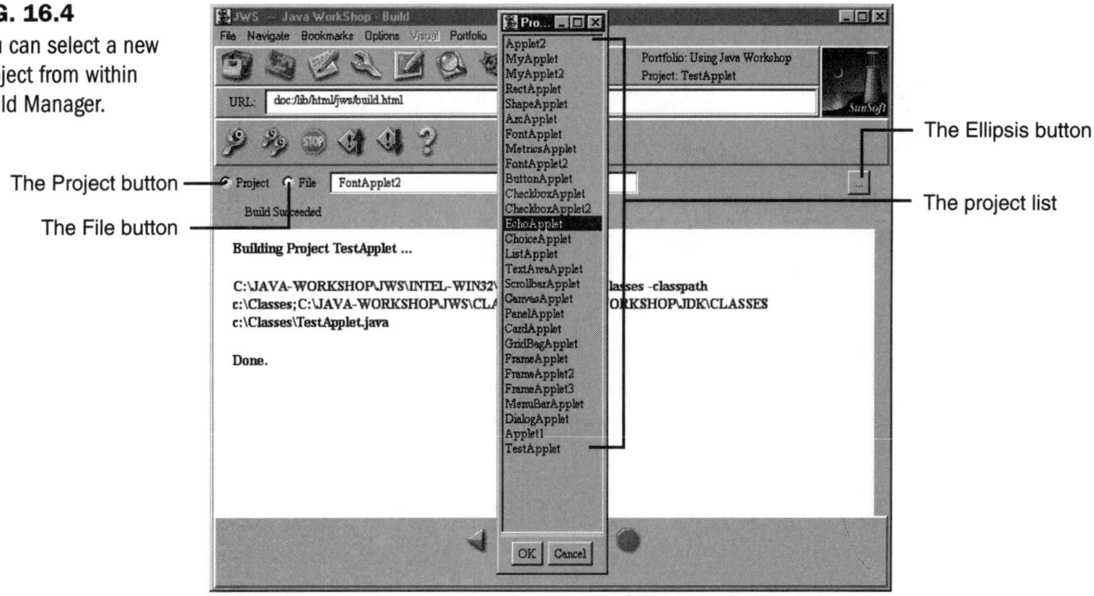

FIG. 16.4
You can select a new project from within Build Manager.

You can also select a single file for compilation by selecting the File Option button, clicking the Ellipsis button, and then choosing the file from the browser window that appears (see fig. 16.5). When you compile a single file, Build Manager uses the compiler options from the currently active project, even though the selected file may not be part of that project.

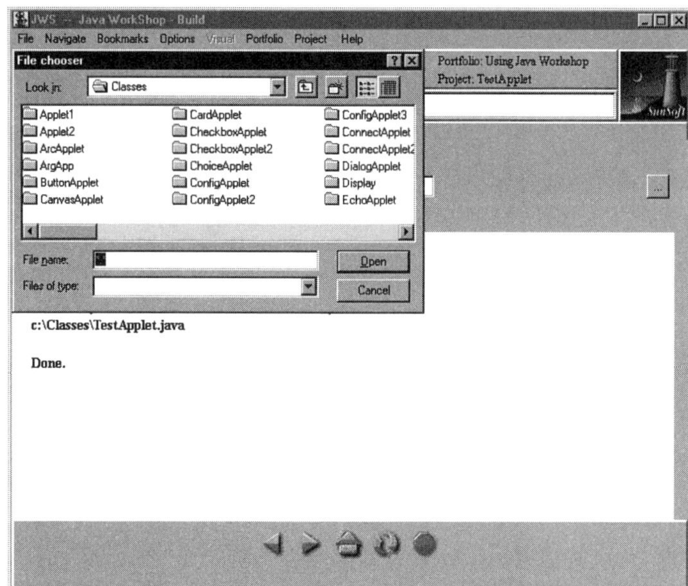

FIG. 16.5 You can compile single files, as well as whole projects, with Build Manager.

Using Source Browser

Source Browser is especially handy for applets that have a lot of source code. Using Source Browser, you can not only view the class hierarchy represented by a class in your program, but you can also use the list of methods and member variables to almost instantly jump to any method in a program. In the sections that follow, you'll learn how to use Source Browser to accomplish this task. You'll also learn how to use Source Browser to locate text strings in your source code.

Starting Source Browser

To start Source Browser, click its button (the one that looks like a magnifying glass) in Java Workshop's toolbar. When you do, Source Browser appears in Java

Workshop's main window (see fig. 16.6). As you can see from the figure, Source Browser displays two pages of options. The first page is for browsing classes and locating methods, and the second page is for finding text strings anywhere in your source-code files.

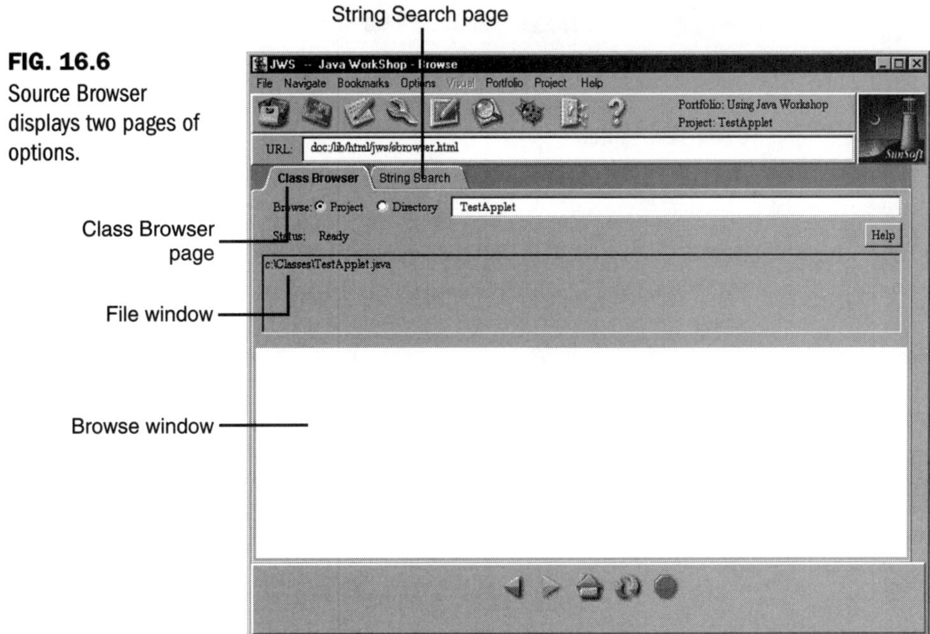

FIG. 16.6 Source Browser displays two pages of options.

Browsing a Project

When Source Browser starts, it's automatically set to browse the files in the currently active project. Because the Project Option button is selected, the file window shows all the files in the project. To browse the classes in a file, click the file's name in the file window. When you do, Source Browser constructs an inheritance tree, for the class in the file, and a list of methods and variables (see fig. 16.7).

If you use Java Workshop's scroll bars to scroll through the information in the browser window, you'll discover that Source Browser has also listed all the methods in your applet (see fig. 16.8). You can jump to any method in the source code just by clicking the method's name in the browser window. Source Editor then runs, loading the appropriate source-code file and jumping directly to the method on which you clicked.

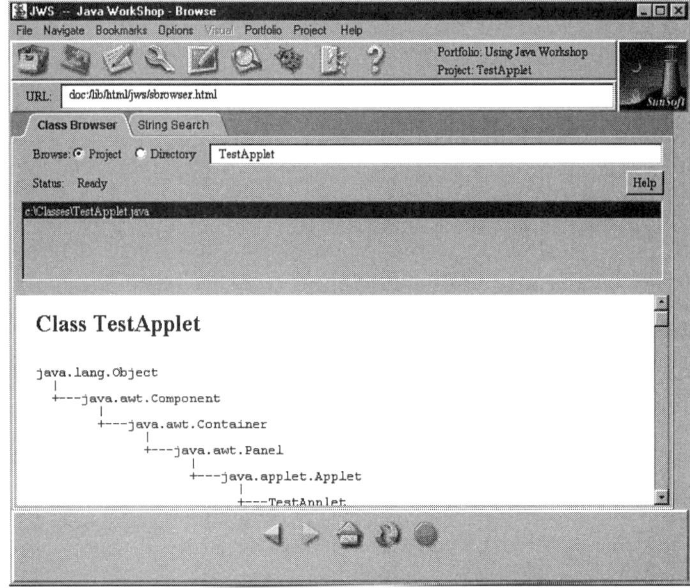

FIG. 16.7
Source Browser can display the inheritance tree for a class.

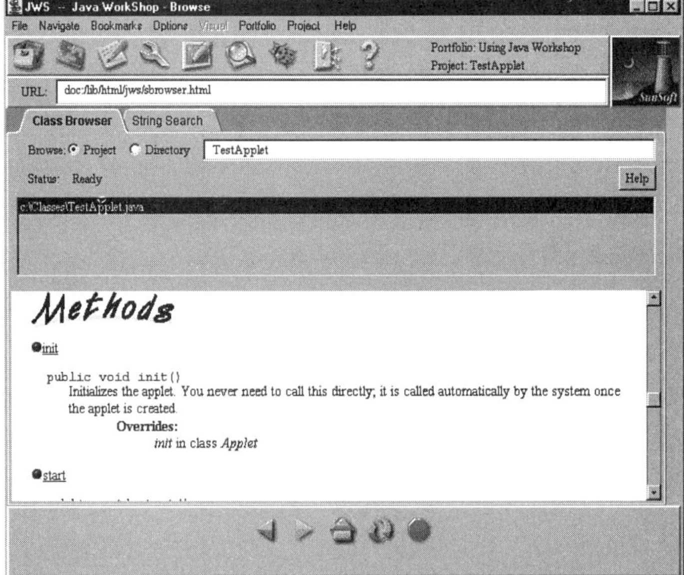

FIG. 16.8
Source Browser also lists the methods of the selected class.

Browsing Directories

Besides browsing classes associated with projects, you can browse the files located in a specific directory. To do this, select the Directory Option button, and then type the directory path and name into the text box to the right of the Directory button. When you do, the files in the directory appear in the file window; you can select them for browsing (see fig. 16.9).

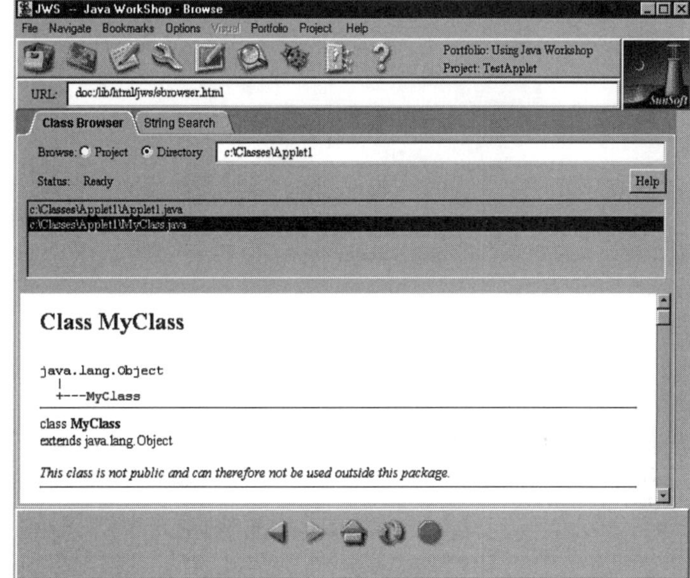

FIG. 16.9
You can also browse the files in a specific directory.

Searching for Strings

As mentioned previously, you can also use Source Browser to find occurrences of a given text string. The first step in this process is to select the String Search page of the Source Browser Display, which gives you the window shown in figure 16.10. As when class browsing, Source Browser starts a string search session; the Project button must be selected for the currently active project.

Type the text string for which to search into the String text box, select the Ignore Case button if you want to do a non-case-sensitive search. In most cases, you'll leave the default file types entered into the File Types text box as they appear. However, if you like, you can specify any file types you like. Just be sure to leave spaces between each file extension you list. To start the search, press Enter when the text cursor is in the String text box. Source Browser then scans the source-code files for occurrences of the target string and reports its findings in the display area (see fig. 16.11).

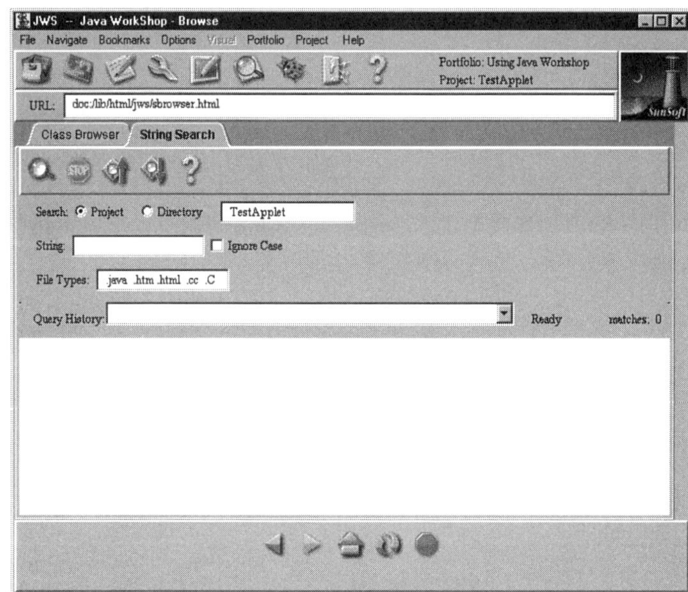

FIG. 16.10
Use the String Search page to find text strings in your files.

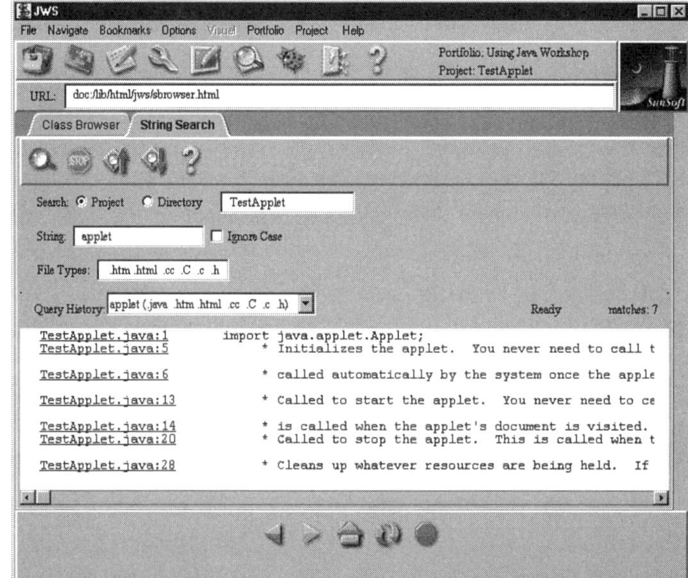

FIG. 16.11
Source Browser displays the matches it finds.

From Here...

Build Manager and Source Browser simplify the process of compiling your projects and correcting syntax errors in your source-code files. Because these two tools communicate directly with Source Editor, you can quickly locate errors, methods, and text strings anywhere in your files.

For more information on related topics, please refer to the following chapters:

- Chapter 2, "Introducing Java Workshop," provides an overview of the many tools included with Java Workshop.
- Chapter 14, "Portfolio Manager and Project Manager," shows you how to create new portfolios and projects.
- Chapter 15, "Source Editor," tells you how to use Java Workshop's editor to edit your source-code files.
- Chapter 17, "Debugger," describes how to use Java Workshop's debugger to locate and correct runtime errors.

CHAPTER 17

Debugger

How to run Java Workshop's Debugger tool.

Before you can start debugging your code, you have to get the debugger up on the screen.

How to debug with threads and stack frames.

Debugger can display all the threads in the currently running applet.

About Debugger's Expressions and Breakpoints pages.

Being able to check the value of variables is an essential part of the debugging process, as is being able to set or clear breakpoints in the code.

About Debugger's Exceptions, Classes, and Messages pages.

You can tell Debugger which exceptions to handle or ignore, get a listing of classes in the currently executing project, or view the messages that have been generated during the debugging session.

How to use Source Editor in a debugging session.

The editor can display your source code complete with highlighted breakpoints.

Debugging is an essential part of creating quality computer programs. Virtually no useful program is entirely bug-free, but it's the programmer's task to eliminate as many errors as possible before releasing his work into the world. These days, most programming suites include sophisticated debugging tools that enable the programmer to easily explore inside his application as it runs. Java Workshop, too, includes a debugging tool, aptly called Debugger, to assist you in creating robust applets and applications. ■

Starting Debugger

Getting Debugger up and running is as simple as clicking Debugger's button (the one that looks like a ladybug) in Java Workshop's toolbar. When you do, Java Workshop launches a debugging session for the currently active project. This process includes loading the project's source code into Source Editor and running a special debugging browser in which the applet you're debugging appears. Debugger then executes the applet and stops at the first line in the `init()` method. (For this reason, your applet must override `init()` in order for Debugger to automatically load and display the source code. If you don't override `init()` in your applet, Debugger doesn't automatically load the applet's source code.)

Debugger's Display Pages

When the debugging session has started, there are three windows on the screen. The first window is Java Workshop's main window, which now displays Debugger's six pages of debugging information and options. These six pages—labeled Threads/Stacks, Expressions, Breakpoints, Exceptions, Classes, and Messages—give you complete control over the debugging session. In the following sections, you see what each of these pages contains.

The Threads/Stacks Page

The Threads/Stacks page of the display shows the active threads for the applet (see fig. 17.1). The information displayed in the Threads/Stacks page is organized as a hierarchy, with the first level of the hierarchy being the active thread groups. In figure 17.1, you can see that the ShapeApplet applet is running with three active thread groups: system, main, and applet. The system thread group comprises system threads that you cannot manipulate, the main thread group holds the threads for the browser, and the applet thread group contains your applet's threads.

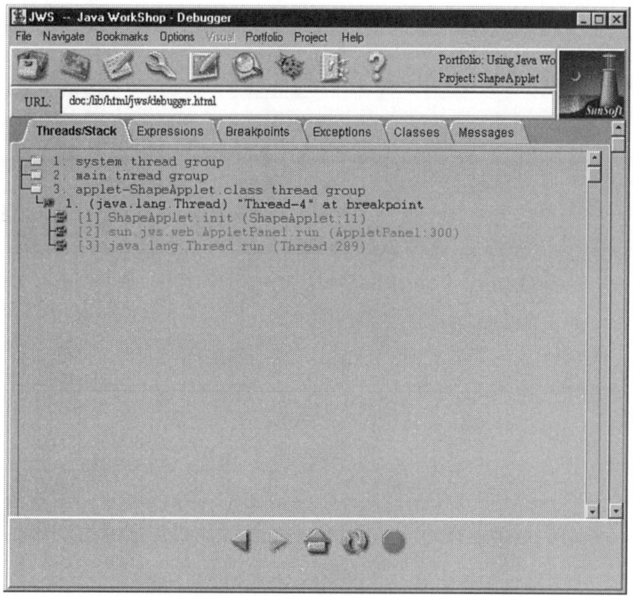

FIG. 17.1
This Debugger page displays thread and stack-frame information.

As you can see in figure 17.1, each thread group is represented by a folder icon. To view the threads within a group, click the group's icon. Figure 17.2, for example, shows the threads that comprise the main and applet thread groups. To the left of each thread is an icon that depicts the thread's current status. These icons, which you can find listed in Java Workshop's online documentation, indicate whether a thread is running, suspended, sleeping, stopped at a breakpoint, and so on.

To get to the third level of data, click the icon to the left of a thread. You then see the stack frames for the thread. (A stack frame represents a method call.) These stack frames are listed in the order in which they were called; the newest stack frame is at the top of the list. In figure 17.3, the user has opened thread 9's stack frame list. (The applet thread and its stack frames were initially displayed by Debugger at the start of the debugging session.)

If you click a stack frame's icon, you get to the final level of the thread-display hierarchy, which is a list of variables that are currently within the scope of the selected stack frame. Figure 17.4 shows the applet thread with its stack frame 2 opened to reveal the variable list.

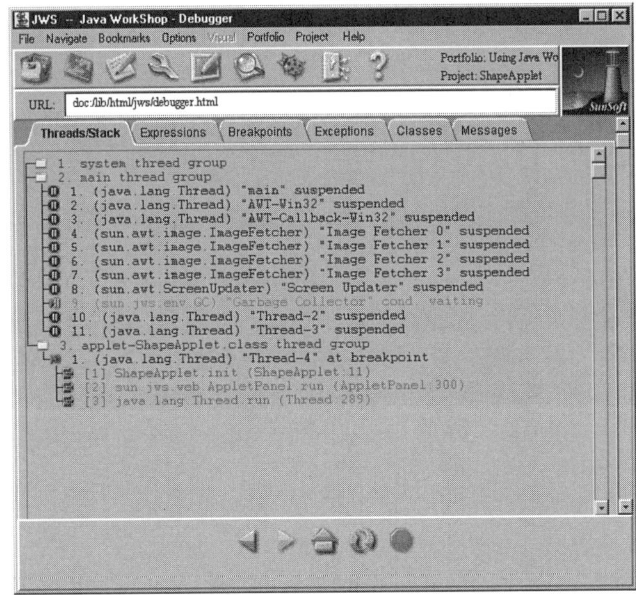

FIG. 17.2
Clicking a thread group's icon reveals the threads in the group.

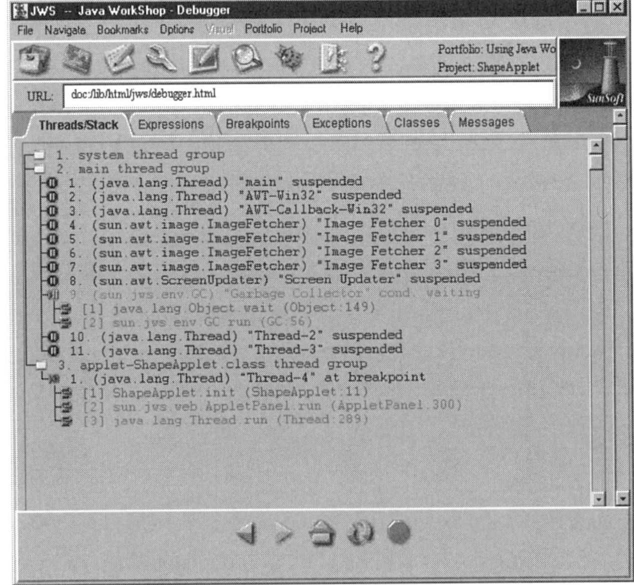

FIG. 17.3
The third level of information is a list of a thread's stack frames.

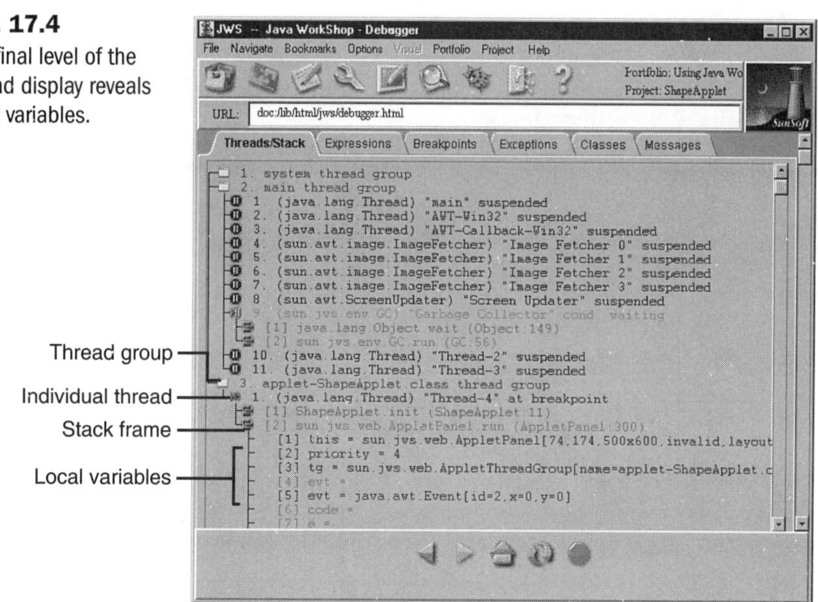

FIG. 17.4
The final level of the thread display reveals local variables.

If you scroll the Threads/Stacks page up as far as it goes, you discover a handy set of buttons that enables you to control any threads that you're allowed to manipulate (see fig. 17.5). Using these buttons you can suspend or resume threads, show the source code associated with a selected stack frame, and even step through a program.

The Expressions Page

Often, a hard-to-find bug in a program can be traced to variables being assigned the wrong values. By using Debugger's Expressions page, you can watch variables to see how their values are changing. Figure 17.6 shows the Expressions page set to watch a variable called `shape`. The variable's initial value is shown at the top of the list, with each successive evaluation being listed below the initial value.

It's up to you to tell Debugger which variables you want evaluated. You do this by entering the variable name into the first text box below the variable list and clicking the Evaluate button. If you don't see the text box on your screen, scroll Java Workshop's window upwards (see fig. 17.7).

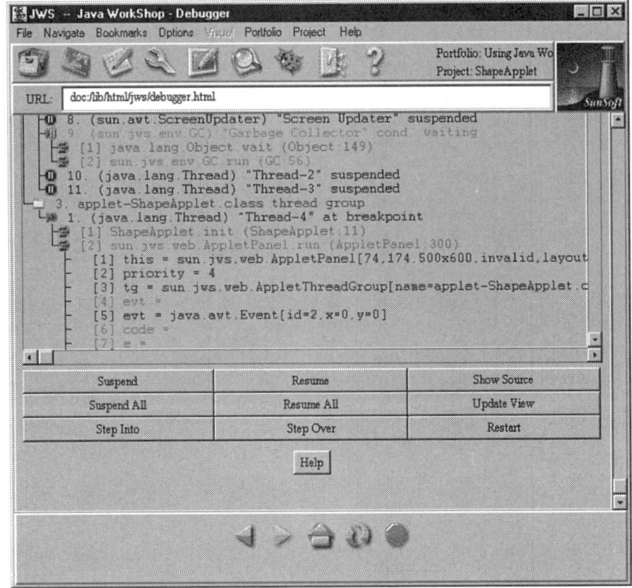

FIG. 17.5
You can use the Threads/Stacks page's buttons to control the displayed threads.

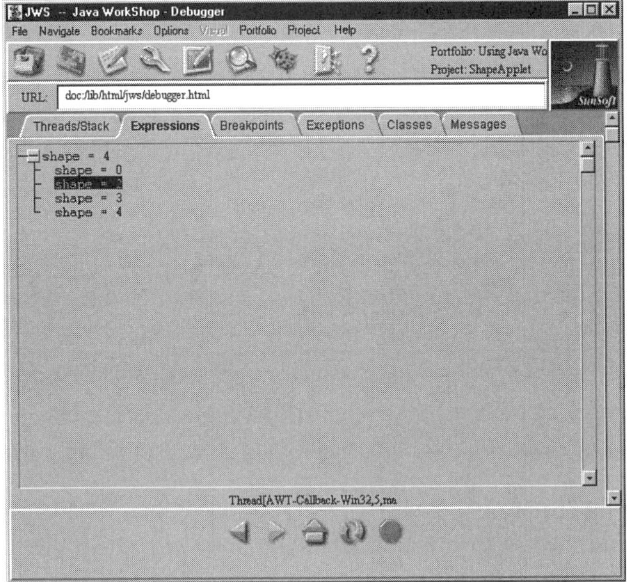

FIG. 17.6
The Expressions page lets you look at the values of variables.

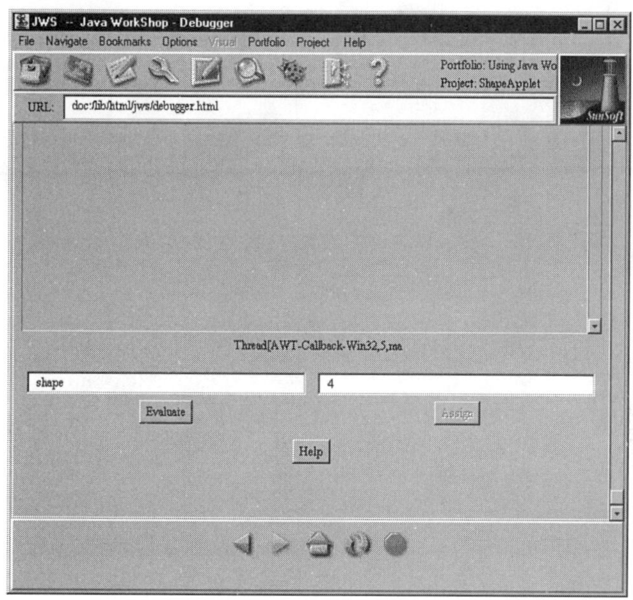

FIG. 17.7
Enter the name of the variable you want to evaluate into the first text box.

The Breakpoints Page

If you've done any program debugging, you already know that breakpoints are places in a program where you've instructed the debugger to halt execution and wait for another debugging command. In Java Workshop, you can view and manipulate the currently set breakpoints from Debugger's Breakpoint page (see fig. 17.8). In the top part of the page is a list of currently active breakpoints. Each entry in the list shows the class and the line number of the breakpoint.

Using the buttons and text boxes below the breakpoint list, you can set and clear breakpoints, as well as call up the source code for a selected breakpoint (see fig. 17.9). There are two ways you can set breakpoints. The first method requires that you enter the class name and the name of the method at which to halt execution into the text boxes in the Stop In Method panel. You can also select the exact line at which to halt execution, by entering the class name and line number in the text boxes in the Stop At Line panel.

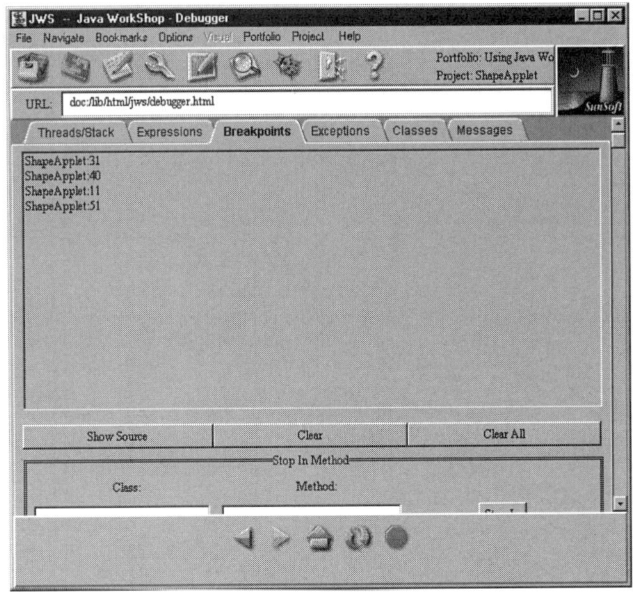

FIG. 17.8
The Breakpoints page lists the currently active breakpoints.

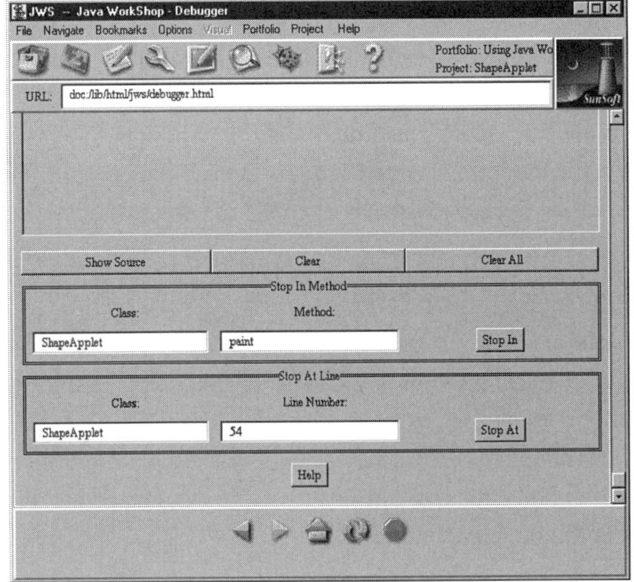

FIG. 17.9
You can use controls on the Breakpoints page to manipulate your breakpoints.

The Exceptions Page

In the Exceptions page, you can tell Debugger what to do about exceptions that are generated by your running project. Figure 17.10 shows the Exceptions page for the ShapeApplet applet. (In the figure, the page has been scrolled down in order to reveal the page's controls.) At the top of the page is the list of exceptions supported by Java. To the left of each entry in the list is the status for that exception. In the figure, you can see that all the exceptions are listed as "ignore," which means the Debugger will do nothing with the exceptions. If you want to catch an exception, first highlight the exception in the list by clicking it with your mouse, and then click the Catch button. Other buttons in the page enable you to ignore a single exception, ignore all exceptions, catch all exceptions, or view the associated source code.

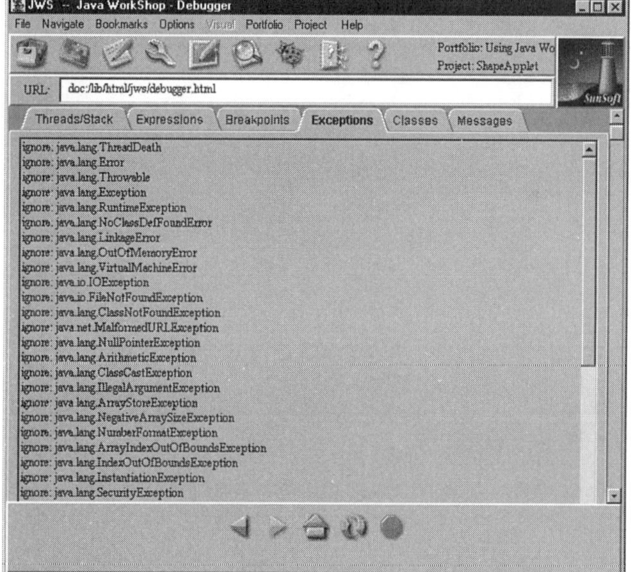

FIG. 17.10
Using this page, you can instruct the debugger to catch or ignore any of Java's exceptions.

The Classes Page

The Classes page is similar to the Threads/Stacks page, in that it lists its data in a hierarchy. But, rather than basing the hierarchy on threads and stack frames, the hierarchy is based on classes. The highest level of the hierarchy shows the classes in the project. By opening a class entry, you reveal the file and path name for the class's source code. If you open the file name entry, you see a list of the methods that comprise that class. In figure 17.11, ShapeApplet's ShapeApplet class is fully revealed, showing the class file and the methods in the class.

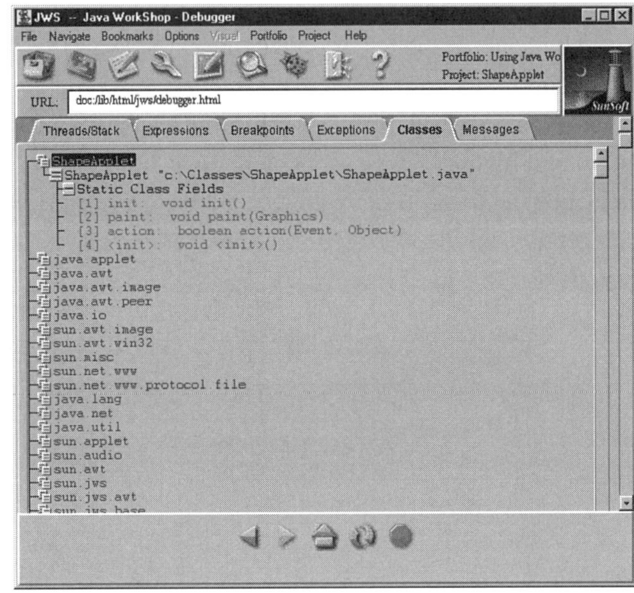

FIG. 17.11
The Classes page enables you to explore the classes that comprise your project.

If you scroll the Classes page upward, you discover controls that you can use to set and clear breakpoints and to bring up the source code for a selected class.

The Messages Page

Debugger's Messages page is the simplest of all the pages. Its task is merely to display status and warning messages from the debugger. Figure 17.12 shows the Messages page during a debugging session with the ShapeApplet applet. As you can see, the upper pane is reserved for application messages, and the lower pane displays debugger messages.

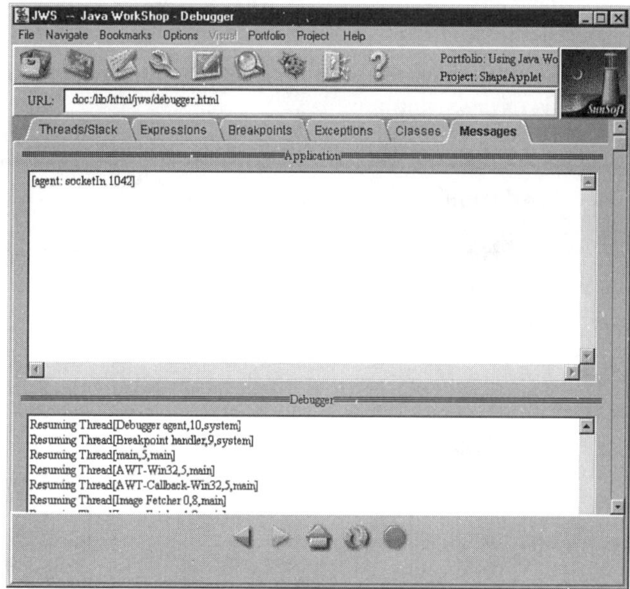

FIG. 17.12
The Messages page displays status and warning messages.

Debugging from Source Editor

You may remember that, when you start a debugging session, Java Workshop brings up three windows: the main debugger window, a browser in which to run the applet being debugged, and Source Editor loaded with the applet's source code. (Source Editor runs automatically only if you've overridden the `init()` method in your applet.) Source Editor itself can be a powerful debugging tool, as figure 17.13 shows. In the figure, each of Source Editor's debugging commands are labeled.

The advantage of debugging from Source Editor is that you can see your program run, both by viewing the source code and by watching the applet in the debugging browser. In Source Editor, the source code displays all breakpoints and highlights the line that will be executed next. The debugging commands on the toolbar perform the following functions:

- *Toggle breakpoint.* Toggles (turns on or off) a breakpoint on the line on which the text cursor is positioned.
- *Restart.* Reloads the program and executes it from the beginning.

- *Resume all.* Resumes program execution.
- *Run to here.* Executes the program up to the source-code line on which the text cursor is positioned.
- *Step over.* Executes the current source-code line. If the line is a method call, it executes the entire method and stops on the line following the method call.
- *Step into.* Executes the current source-code line. If the line is a method call, it steps to the first line of the method and stops.
- *Up a frame.* Moves forward one stack frame.
- *Down a frame.* Moves backward one stack frame.

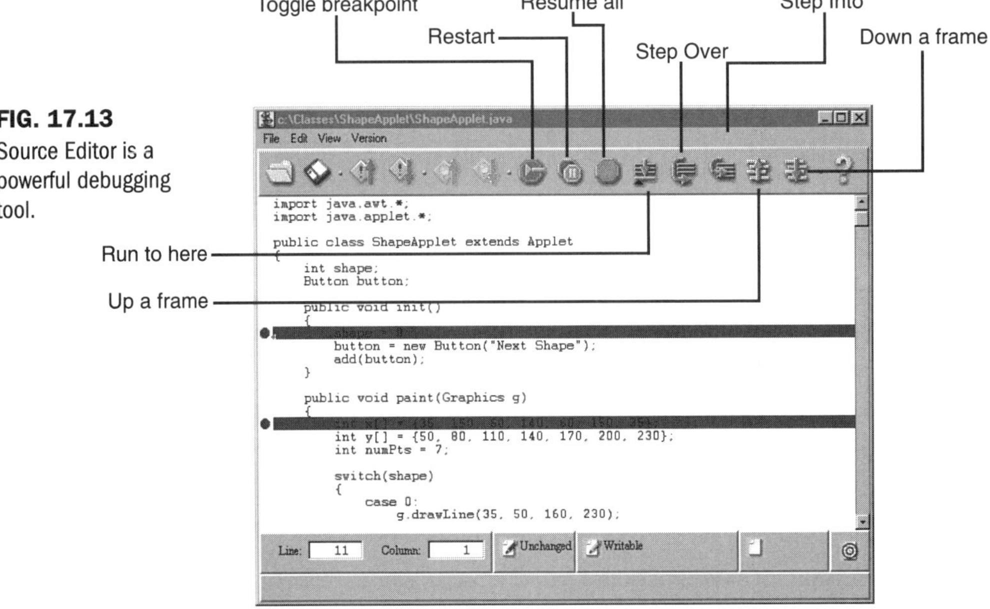

FIG. 17.13 Source Editor is a powerful debugging tool.

From Here...

You can't call a programming job complete until it's been thoroughly debugged. Java Workshop's Debugger tool features a full command set for keeping tabs on program execution and helping you discover where things may be going awry. Using techniques like setting breakpoints, tracing program flow, and watching variables as they are assigned new values enables you to hunt down and exterminate even hard-to-find program errors.

For more information on related topics, please refer to the following chapters:

- Chapter 14, "Portfolio Manager and Project Manager," tells you how to manage and select projects.
- Chapter 15, "Source Editor," describes how to use Java Workshop's editor.
- Chapter 16, "Build Manager and Source Browser," shows how to compile your projects and how to browse through the classes that comprise the project.

CHAPTER 18

Visual Java

- **How to construct a user interface with Visual Java.**

  Using Visual Java, you can create an interface easily by placing components in a grid of cells.

- **Hot to set a component's attributes.**

  Each component you add to Visual Java's grid display has a number of attributes that control how the component looks and acts. By changing attributes, you customize the component to fit your applet's needs.

- **How to resize grid cells and components.**

  You don't have to settle for Visual Java's default component grid. You can add, delete, and change the size of cells, as well as resize the components themselves.

- **How to generate and customize code with Visual Java.**

  Visual Java will generate the Java source code needed to implement the user interface you design, but it's up to you to complete the applet.

Because Visual Java is the newest tool that Sun Microsystems has added to Java Workshop (at least, at the time of this writing), there isn't previous coverage in this book. Even the version of Visual Java that was available for this chapter is preliminary and is liable to undergo many changes before Java Workshop sees its commercial release. Still, you'll probably want to at least get a look at Visual Java before you get to the end of this book, since Visual Java will become one of Java Workshop's most important tools.

Visual Java is an applet construction program that enables you to build your applet's user interface by creating a grid and then placing the various components you need (such as buttons, text boxes, and so on) into the grid. When you've completed creating your interface, Visual Java will generate the code needed to implement the interface, after which you need only add the code needed to make your applet perform as you want it to. ■

Using Visual Java

To use Visual Java effectively, you must perform a number of tasks in the correct order. These tasks are as follows:

1. Create a project for the new applet.
2. Start Visual Java and construct your applet's interface.
3. Instruct Visual Java to generate the code that creates the applet's interface.
4. Add the code needed to make your applet perform the way you want.

The following sections will lead you step-by-step through the above tasks. When you've finished all the steps, you will have created your first Visual Java applet.

Creating a Project for the New Applet

In this chapter, you'll be using Visual Java to create an applet called VisualApplet. The first task in this process is to create a project for the applet. Use the following steps to create the VisualApplet project:

1. In your Classes folder, create a subfolder called VisualApplet.

   The c:\Classes\VisualApplet folder is where Visual Java will store the applet's source code.

2. Choose Project, Create, Applet from Java Workshop's menu bar. Project Manager's Applet display appears in Java Workshop's window. Enter the data shown in figure 18.1 into the Applet display and verify that the Visual Java option button is selected.

   The Visual Java option button instructs Java Workshop to use Visual Java to create the project's basic applet.

3. Click the Apply button to finalize your entries. Java Workshop starts the Visual Java tool, which displays the component toolbox and a separate Panel window, as shown in figure 18.2.

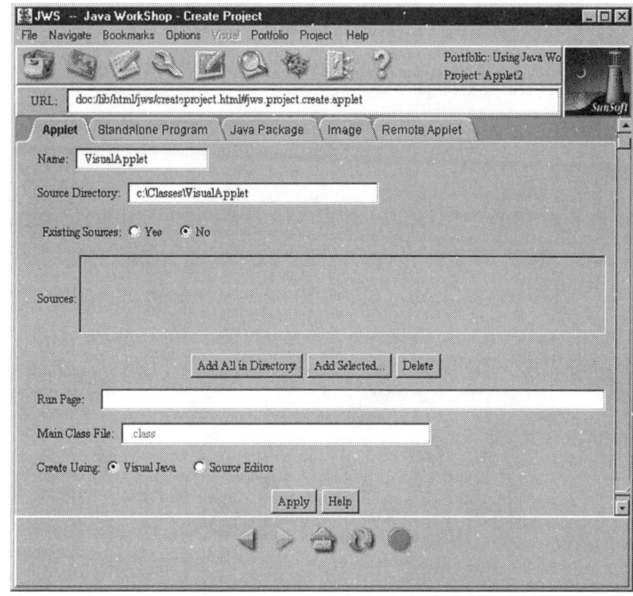

FIG. 18.1
To create a Visual Java project, be sure that the Visual Java option button is selected.

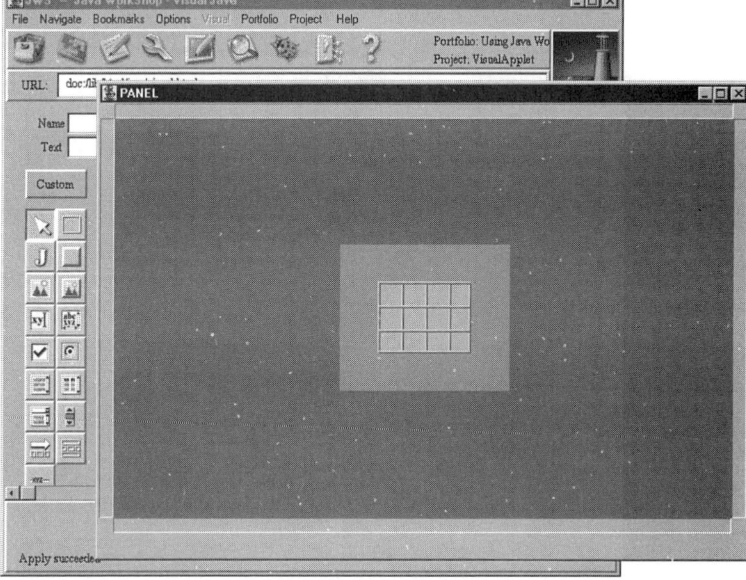

FIG. 18.2
Visual Java includes a component toolbox and a special window for creating a component grid.

Constructing the Applet's Interface

Now that you have the project created and Visual Java up on the screen, you can get to work on your applet's user interface. The following steps will guide you through this process.

1. Click in the component grid's upper-right cell and press your keyboard's Delete key. Visual Java removes cells from the grid, leaving only six. Repeat the process until only a single cell remains, as shown in figure 18.3. (The figure shows the Panel window reduced in size.)

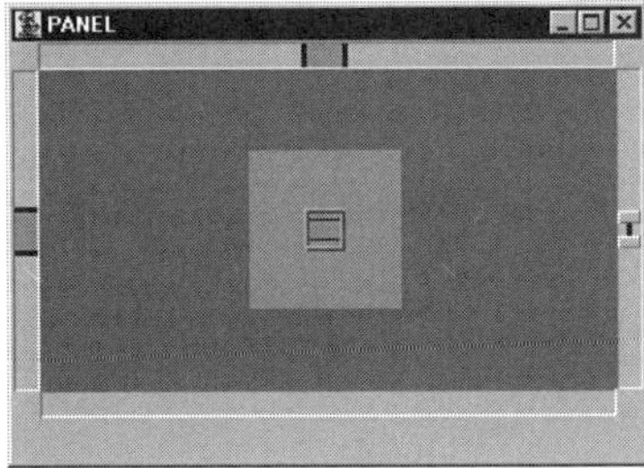

FIG. 18.3
Pressing the Delete key removes cells from the grid.

2. Click on the remaining cell to select it and then press your keyboard's down arrow key. Visual Java adds a cell vertically, as shown in figure 18.4.

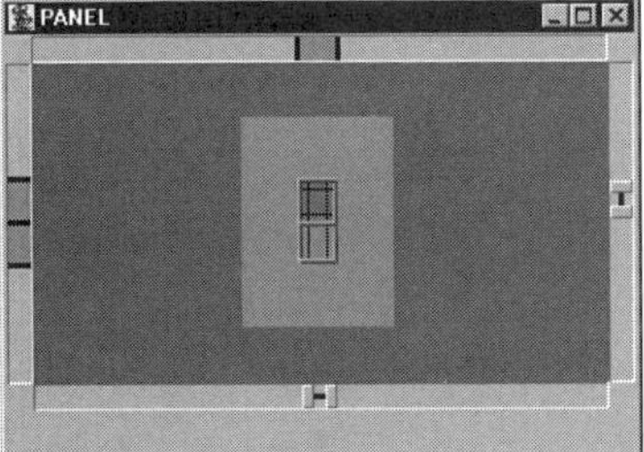

FIG. 18.4
Selecting a cell and pressing your keyboard's arrow keys causes Visual Java to create new cells.

3. On Visual Java's toolbox, select the Text Button tool. Click on the upper cell in the Panel window to place the button in that position (see fig. 18.5).
4. On Visual Java's toolbox, select the Single-line TextField tool and place the text field in the lower cell in the Panel window (see fig. 18.6).

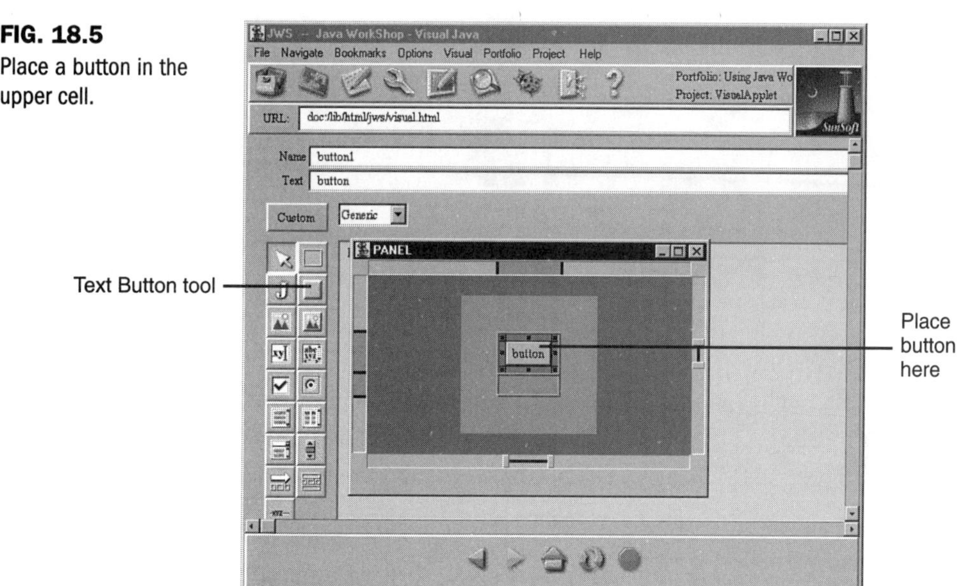

FIG. 18.5
Place a button in the upper cell.

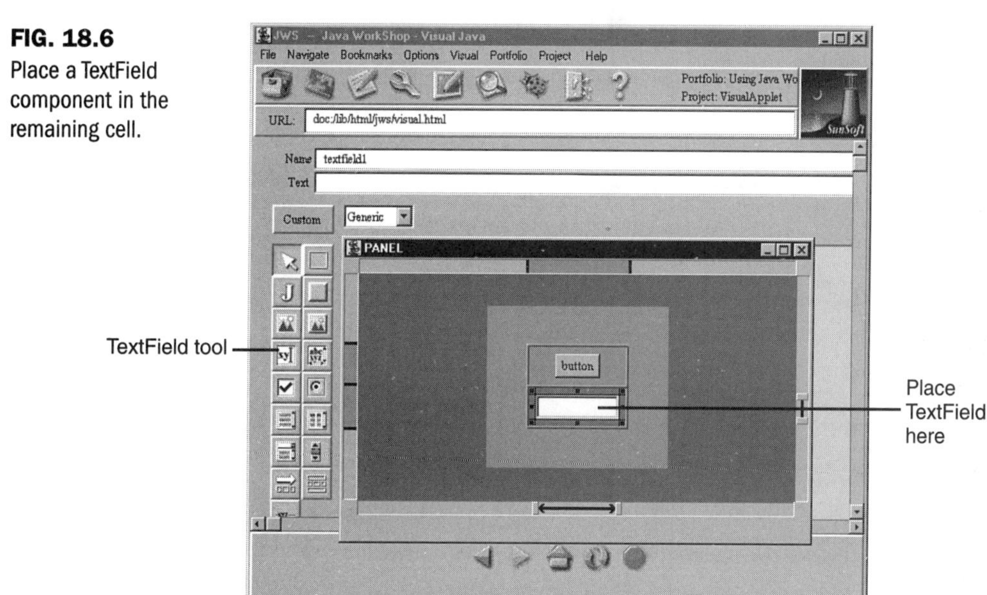

FIG. 18.6
Place a TextField component in the remaining cell.

5. Widen the cells in the grid by using your mouse to drag the arrows below the grid in the Panel window, as shown in figure 18.7.

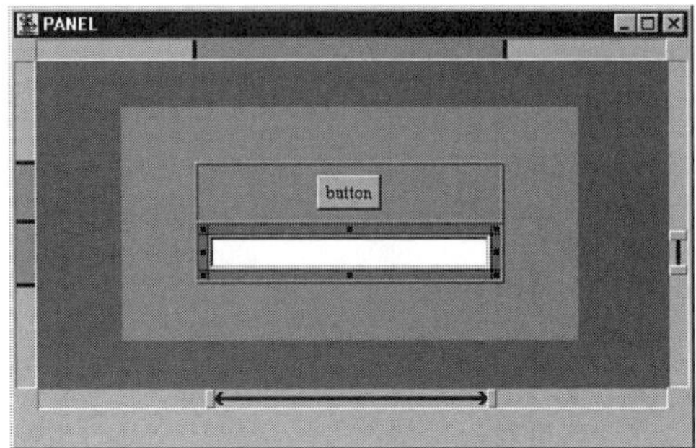

FIG. 18.7
Drag on the arrows to change the size of the grid.

6. Right-click inside the top cell, right below the button to bring up the button's attributes dialog box. Change the Text attribute to Reset Text, as shown in figure 18.8. Click the OK button to change the text label in the button.

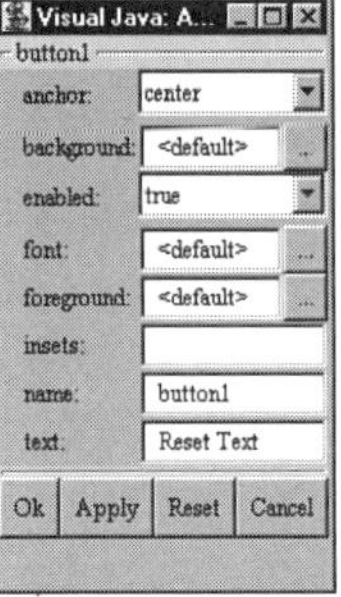

FIG. 18.8
All components have attributes that you can customize.

7. Click inside the text box in the lower cell and then type Default text (see fig. 18.9).

   This text will appear in the text box when the applet is run.

8. To see what your now finished user interface will look like in an applet, click the Preview Mode radio button at the bottom of the Visual Java main window (see fig. 18.10). The small window shown in the figure appears.

9. To save your newly constructed applet interface, choose Visual, File, Save from Java Workshop's menu bar. Visual Java creates the VisualApplet.gui file in your c:\Classes\VisualApplet folder.

   The VisualApplet.gui file contains the information Visual Java needs to reconstruct the interface.

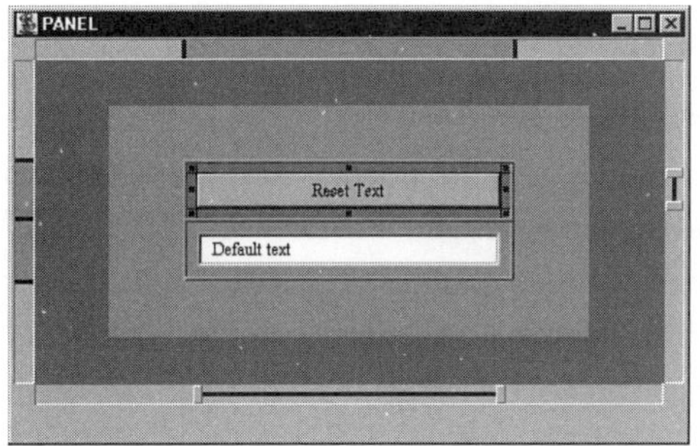

FIG. 18.9
The text you type into a TextField component will appear in the component when the applet is run.

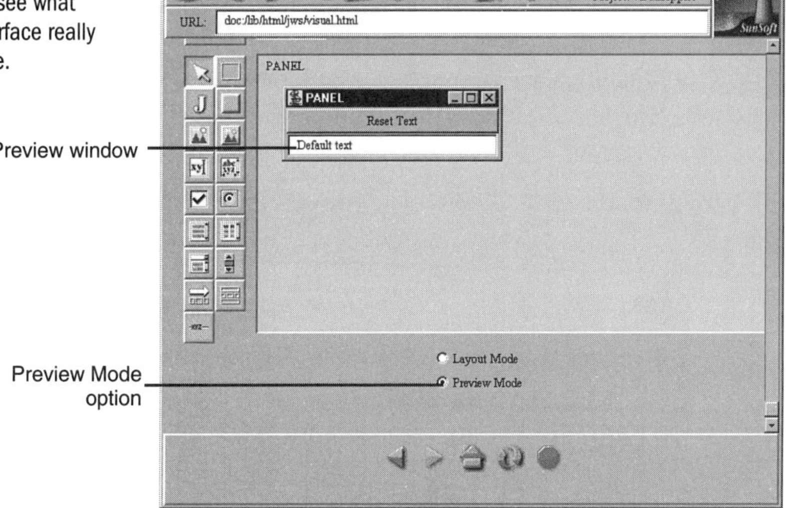

FIG. 18.10
The Preview mode lets you see what your interface really looks like.

NOTE Each component that you can add to an applet's display has its own set of attributes. Many of these attributes are the same from one component to another, while others are specific to one type of component. For example, on most components, the `background` attribute determines the background color, the `enabled` attribute determines whether the user can select the component, the `font` attribute sets the type of text displayed, and the `name` attribute determines the component object's name. An example of component-specific attributes might be `numColumns` and `numRows`, which determine the size of a text area control.

Generating the Code

So far, you have two files in your c:\Classes\VisualApplet directory. The first is VisualApplet.prj, which is the applet's project file. The second is the VisualApplet.gui file, which contains the user interface you constructed in the previous set of steps. Neither of these files, or even both put together, is enough to create your applet. You still need to generate Java source code. Throughout this book, you've been writing your Java source code yourself, but Visual Java can take the .gui file you created when you saved your interface and change it into the source code needed to create an applet that uses the interface. Use the following steps to complete the code-generation task:

1. From Java workshop's menu bar, choose Visual, File, Generate. The Code Generation dialog box appears.
2. Make sure that the Generate GUI and Generate Main option buttons are selected. Also, because this is the first time you've generated code for this project, select the Generate Group checkbox (see fig. 18.11).

   The group source-code file is the file you edit to add your own code to the applet.

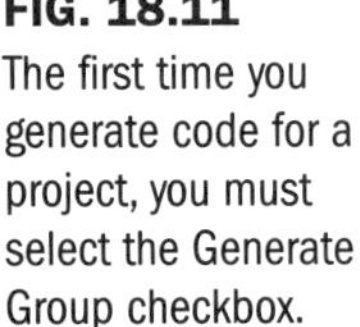

FIG. 18.11
The first time you generate code for a project, you must select the Generate Group checkbox.

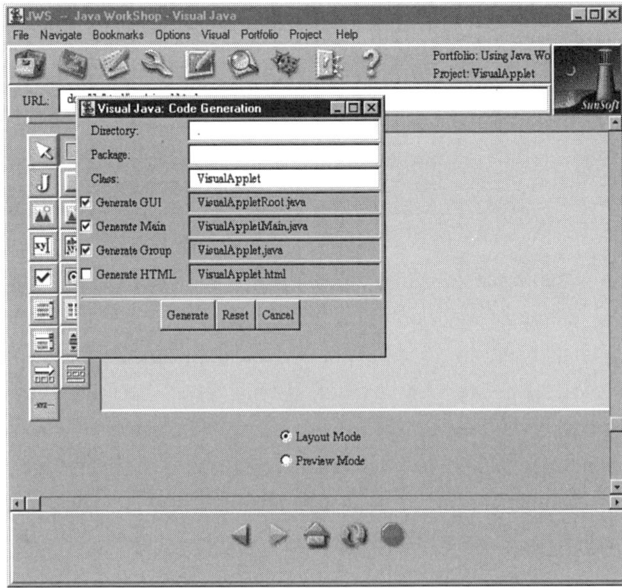

3. Click the Generate button. Visual Java creates the code for an applet that implements the interface described in the VisualApplet.gui file.

After completing the previous steps, you'll have the following five files in your c:\Classes\VisualApplet folder:

- *VisualApplet.prj.* This is the applet's project file.
- *VisualApplet.gui.* This is a description of the applet's user interface.
- *VisualApplet.java.* This is the file you will modify to complete the applet's source code.
- *VisualAppletMain.java.* This is the applet's main class, which you should not modify.
- *VisualAppletRoot.java.* This is the applet's root class, which you should not modify.

At this point, you can build the applet if you want to by clicking Build Manager's button in Java Workshop's toolbar, and then clicking the Build button in Build Manager's toolbar. After the applet has been compiled, you can run it by clicking Project Tester's button in Java Workshop's toolbar.

Adding Code to the Applet

You now have a skeleton program for your applet. This program can be run, but will only create and display the user interface you created. You cannot use the applet to do anything because it doesn't yet respond to events such as a user clicking the button or typing text into the text box. It's up to you to add whatever additional code you need, which is, of course, the toughest part of creating a Visual Java applet. Use the following steps to finish the VisualApplet applet:

1. Click the Source Editor button in Java Workshop's toolbar. Source Editor runs, automatically loading the VisualAppletMain.java source-code file.
2. Use Source Editor's File, Open command to load the VisualApplet.java file (see fig. 18.12), which is the only source-code file you should modify.
3. Add the code in listing 18.1 to the end of the VisualApplet.java file, right before the class's closing brace (see fig. 18.13). As with other applets you've created in this book, the `action( )` method responds to user events.

```
C:\Classes\VisualApplet\VisualApplet.java
File Edit View Version
/**
 * This is a template.  You may modify this file.
 *
 * Runtime vendor: SunSoft, Inc.
 * Runtime version: 0.5
 *
 * Visual vendor: SunSoft, Inc.
 * Visual version: 0.5
 */


import sunsoft.jws.visual.rt.base.AttributeManager;
import sunsoft.jws.visual.rt.base.Group;
import sunsoft.jws.visual.rt.base.Root;
import sunsoft.jws.visual.rt.base.Shadow;
import sunsoft.jws.visual.rt.base.Message;
import sunsoft.jws.visual.rt.base.Registry;
import sunsoft.jws.visual.rt.shadow.java.awt.*;
import java.awt.*;


public class VisualApplet extends Group {
  private VisualAppletRoot gui;

  public VisualApplet() {
Line: 6  Column: 3  Unchanged  Writable
```

FIG. 18.12 You must load the VisualApplet.java file into Source Editor.

Listing 18.1 VisualApplet's *action()* Method

```
public boolean action(Message msg, Event evt, Object obj)
{
  if (msg.target == gui.button1)
  {
    gui.textfield1.set("text", "Default text");
    return true;
  }

  return false;
}
```

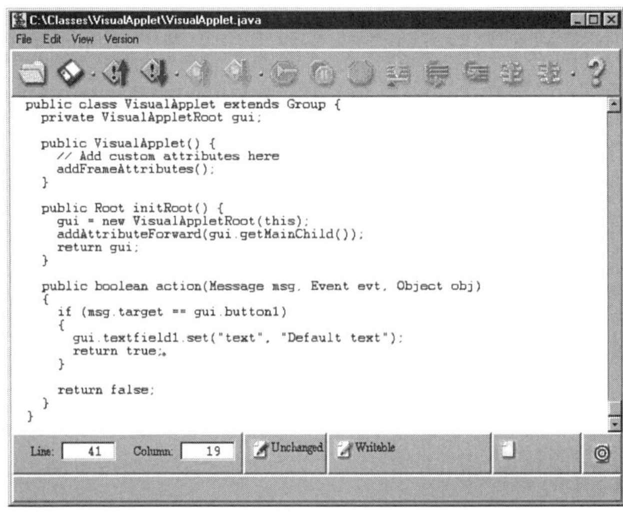

```
C:\Classes\VisualApplet\VisualApplet.java
File Edit View Version
public class VisualApplet extends Group {
  private VisualAppletRoot gui;

  public VisualApplet() {
    // Add custom attributes here
    addFrameAttributes();
  }

  public Root initRoot() {
    gui = new VisualAppletRoot(this);
    addAttributeForward(gui.getMainChild());
    return gui;
  }

  public boolean action(Message msg, Event evt, Object obj)
  {
    if (msg.target == gui.button1)
    {
      gui.textfield1.set("text", "Default text");
      return true;
    }

    return false;
  }
}
Line: 41  Column: 19  Unchanged  Writable
```

FIG. 18.13 Add the `action()` method to the end of the class.

4. Save the newly edited file and close Source Editor.

After completing the previous steps, you can compile the applet with Build Manager and run the applet with Project Tester. When you do, you'll see the window shown in figure 18.14. Click in the text box and enter any new text you like. Then, click the Reset Text button. The applet captures the button event and resets the text to its original state.

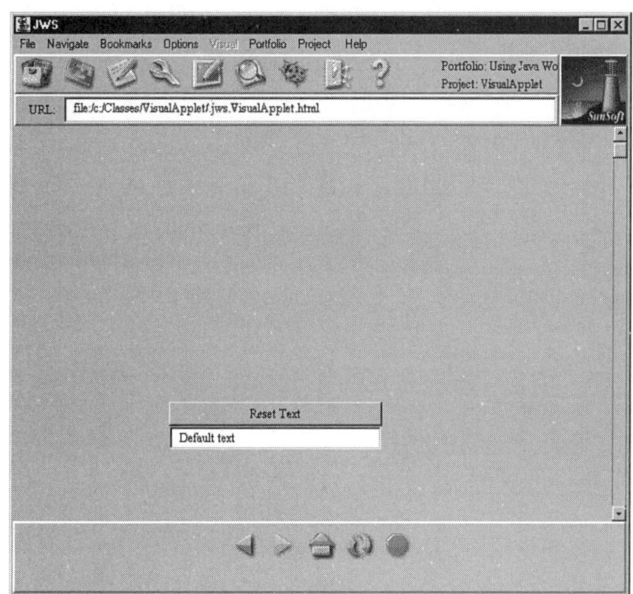

FIG. 18.14 Here's VisualApplet running under Java Workshop.

From Here...

Visual Java relieves you from the trial-and-error programming often required to create the perfect user interface for your applet. Rather than editing, recompiling, and testing source code again and again just to get component placement right, you can simply place components from a toolbox onto a grid of cells. However, keep in mind that, when this chapter was written, Visual Java was brand new and far from complete. By the time you read these words, Visual Java may sport a whole host of new features not mentioned in these pages. (To a lesser degree, the same is true for all of Java Workshop's tools.)

For more information on related topics, please refer to the following chapters:

- Chapter 7, "Java Controls," tells you more about the types of components you can place into Visual Java's grid display.
- Chapter 10, "Events and Configurable Applets," describes how to handle user events in an applet, a skill you need when customizing the Java code generated by Visual Java.
- Chapter 14, "Portfolio Manager and Project Manager," shows how to create and organize Java Workshop projects.
- Chapter 15, "Source Editor," reveals the details of editing source code with Java Workshop's built-in text editor.
- Chapter 16, "Build Manager and Source Browser," describes how to compile and run applets from within Java Workshop.

Index

Symbols

A

D

N

O

P-R

S

W-Z

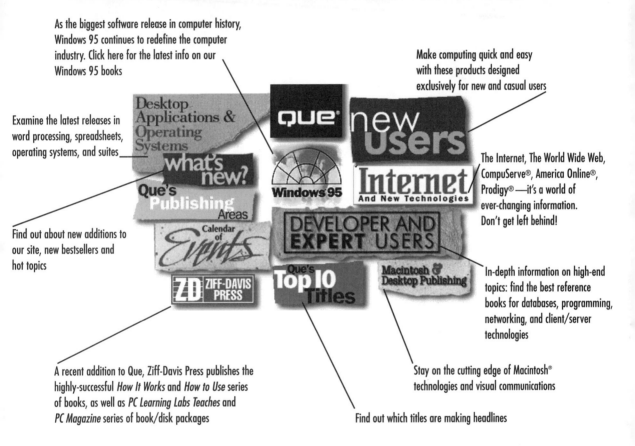

QUE® has the right choice for every computer user

From the new computer user to the advanced programmer, we've got the right computer book for you. Our user-friendly *Using* series offers just the information you need to perform specific tasks quickly and move onto other things. And, for computer users ready to advance to new levels, QUE *Special Edition Using* books, the perfect all-in-one resource—and recognized authority on detailed reference information.

The *Using* series for casual users

Who should use this book?

Everyday users who:

- Work with computers in the office or at home
- Are familiar with computers but not in love with technology
- Just want to "get the job done"
- Don't want to read a lot of material

The user-friendly reference

- The fastest access to the one best way to get things donc
- Bite-sized information for quick and easy reference
- Nontechnical approach in plain English
- Real-world analogies to explain new concepts
- Troubleshooting tips to help solve problems
- Visual elements and screen pictures that reinforce topics
- Expert authors who are experienced in training and instruction

Special Edition Using for accomplished users

Who should use this book?

Proficient computer users who:

- Have a more technical understanding of computers
- Are interested in technological trends
- Want in-depth reference information
- Prefer more detailed explanations and examples

The most complete reference

- Thorough explanations of various ways to perform tasks
- In-depth coverage of all topics
- Technical information cross-referenced for easy access
- Professional tips, tricks, and shortcuts for experienced users
- Advanced troubleshooting information with alternative approaches
- Visual elements and screen pictures that reinforce topics
- Technically qualified authors who are experts in their fields
- "Techniques from the Pros" sections with advice from well-known computer professionals

Complete and Return this Card for a *FREE* Computer Book Catalog

Thank you for purchasing this book! You have purchased a superior computer book written expressly for your needs. To continue to provide the kind of up-to-date, pertinent coverage you've come to expect from us, we need to hear from you. Please take a minute to complete and return this self-addressed, postage-paid form. In return, we'll send you a free catalog of all our computer books on topics ranging from word processing to programming and the internet.

. ☐ Mrs. ☐ Ms. ☐ Dr. ☐

me (first) ☐☐☐☐☐☐☐☐☐☐☐ (M.I.) ☐ (last) ☐☐☐☐☐☐☐☐☐☐☐☐☐☐☐

dress ☐☐☐☐☐☐☐☐☐☐☐☐☐☐☐☐☐☐☐☐☐☐☐☐☐☐☐☐☐☐☐☐☐☐☐
☐☐☐☐☐☐☐☐☐☐☐☐☐☐☐☐☐☐☐☐☐☐☐☐☐☐☐☐☐☐☐☐☐☐☐

y ☐☐☐☐☐☐☐☐☐☐☐☐☐☐☐ State ☐☐ Zip ☐☐☐☐☐ ☐☐☐☐

one ☐☐☐ ☐☐☐ ☐☐☐☐ Fax ☐☐☐ ☐☐☐ ☐☐☐☐

mpany Name ☐☐☐☐☐☐☐☐☐☐☐☐☐☐☐☐☐☐☐☐☐☐☐☐☐☐☐☐☐☐☐☐☐

nail address ☐☐☐☐☐☐☐☐☐☐☐☐☐☐☐☐☐☐☐☐☐☐☐☐☐☐☐☐☐☐☐☐☐

Please check at least (3) influencing factors for purchasing this book.

- ɔnt or back cover information on book ☐
- ecial approach to the content ☐
- mpleteness of content ☐
- thor's reputation ☐
- blisher's reputation ☐
- ok cover design or layout ☐
- lex or table of contents of book ☐
- ce of book ☐
- ecial effects, graphics, illustrations ☐
- her (Please specify): ______________ ☐

How did you first learn about this book?

- w in Macmillan Computer Publishing catalog ☐
- commended by store personnel ☐
- w the book on bookshelf at store ☐
- commended by a friend ☐
- ceived advertisement in the mail ☐
- w an advertisement in: ______________ ☐
- ad book review in: ______________ ☐
- her (Please specify): ______________ ☐

How many computer books have you purchased in the last six months?

- is book only ☐ 3 to 5 books ☐
- ooks ☐ More than 5 ☐

4. Where did you purchase this book?

- Bookstore ☐
- Computer Store ☐
- Consumer Electronics Store ☐
- Department Store ☐
- Office Club ☐
- Warehouse Club ☐
- Mail Order ☐
- Direct from Publisher ☐
- Internet site ☐
- Other (Please specify): ______________ ☐

5. How long have you been using a computer?

- ☐ Less than 6 months ☐ 6 months to a year
- ☐ 1 to 3 years ☐ More than 3 years

6. What is your level of experience with personal computers and with the subject of this book?

	With PCs	With subject of book
New	☐	☐
Casual	☐	☐
Accomplished	☐	☐
Expert	☐	☐

Source Code ISBN: 0-7897-0900-0

7. Which of the following best describes your job title?

- Administrative Assistant ☐
- Coordinator ☐
- Manager/Supervisor ☐
- Director ☐
- Vice President ☐
- President/CEO/COO ☐
- Lawyer/Doctor/Medical Professional ☐
- Teacher/Educator/Trainer ☐
- Engineer/Technician ☐
- Consultant ☐
- Not employed/Student/Retired ☐
- Other (Please specify): ______________ ☐

8. Which of the following best describes the area of the company your job title falls under?

- Accounting ☐
- Engineering ☐
- Manufacturing ☐
- Operations ☐
- Marketing ☐
- Sales ☐
- Other (Please specify): ______________ ☐

9. What is your age?

- Under 20
- 21-29
- 30-39
- 40-49
- 50-59
- 60-over

10. Are you:

- Male
- Female

11. Which computer publications do you read regularly? (Please list)

____

____

____

____

____

____

____

____

***Comments*:** ______________________________

____

____

Fold here and scotch-tape to m

BUSINESS REPLY MAIL

FIRST-CLASS MAIL PERMIT NO. 9918 INDIANAPOLIS IN

POSTAGE WILL BE PAID BY THE ADDRESSEE

ATTN MARKETING
MACMILLAN COMPUTER PUBLISHING
MACMILLAN PUBLISHING USA
201 W 103RD ST
INDIANAPOLIS IN 46290-9042

NO POSTAGE NECESSARY IF MAILED IN THE UNITED STATES